AF745936

WMU Studies in Maritime Affairs

Volume 3

Series Editors

Lawrence P. Hildebrand
Jens-Uwe Schröder-Hinrichs

More information about this series at
http://www.springer.com/series/11556

Momoko Kitada • Erin Williams •
Lisa Loloma Froholdt
Editors

Maritime Women: Global Leadership

Springer

Editors
Momoko Kitada
World Maritime University
Malmö
Sweden

Erin Williams
Brunssum
The Netherlands

Lisa Loloma Froholdt
World Maritime University
Malmö
Sweden

ISSN 2196-8772
ISSN 2196-8780 (electronic)
ISBN 978-3-662-45384-1
ISBN 978-3-662-45385-8 (eBook)
DOI 10.1007/978-3-662-45385-8
Springer Heidelberg New York Dordrecht London

Library of Congress Control Number: 2015931813

© Springer-Verlag Berlin Heidelberg 2015
This work is subject to copyright. All rights are reserved by the Publisher, whether the whole or part of the material is concerned, specifically the rights of translation, reprinting, reuse of illustrations, recitation, broadcasting, reproduction on microfilms or in any other physical way, and transmission or information storage and retrieval, electronic adaptation, computer software, or by similar or dissimilar methodology now known or hereafter developed. Exempted from this legal reservation are brief excerpts in connection with reviews or scholarly analysis or material supplied specifically for the purpose of being entered and executed on a computer system, for exclusive use by the purchaser of the work. Duplication of this publication or parts thereof is permitted only under the provisions of the Copyright Law of the Publisher's location, in its current version, and permission for use must always be obtained from Springer. Permissions for use may be obtained through RightsLink at the Copyright Clearance Center. Violations are liable to prosecution under the respective Copyright Law.
The use of general descriptive names, registered names, trademarks, service marks, etc. in this publication does not imply, even in the absence of a specific statement, that such names are exempt from the relevant protective laws and regulations and therefore free for general use.
While the advice and information in this book are believed to be true and accurate at the date of publication, neither the authors nor the editors nor the publisher can accept any legal responsibility for any errors or omissions that may be made. The publisher makes no warranty, express or implied, with respect to the material contained herein.

Printed on acid-free paper

Springer is part of Springer Science+Business Media (www.springer.com)

Foreword

The World Maritime University: Working Towards Gender Equality

The old maritime world, in which women could be ignored or marginalised, is disappearing, despite the historic dominance of men in seafaring and hence, shore-based jobs. But the maritime sector has changed, and on self-interested grounds. An industry that carries 90 % of the world's goods needs at least 90 % of the best maritime talent, despite being male-dominated by tradition. The industry needs the best lawyers, the best economists, the best scientists, the best logisticians, the best administrators, the best seafarers—and their gender is irrelevant.

Women have moved into top positions across the globe, whether as President of the Republic of Korea or as CEO of the world's top IT-based companies. When measured over a four-year period, research has shown that in the USA, companies in the quartile with the highest proportion of women on their boards outperformed those with the lowest proportion by 26 %.[1] That is not a coincidence, nor is it an accident.

However, the picture globally varies significantly. While we can point to progress at the global level, women make up 35 % of the workforce and only 24 % of the senior management. The proportion of senior female managers varies by region: Asia Pacific leads with 29 % of senior leadership positions held by women, compared to 25 % in the European Union, 23 % in Latin America and 21 % in North America.[2] Action is needed to reach parity—and to make sure that the expertise of women is available for the benefit of all.

The World Maritime University's particular concern is, of course, the maritime sector and building capacity in the developing world. WMU has been playing a key

[1] See also Catalyst document 'Why diversity matters' (2013).

[2] See also Grant Thornton document 'Women in senior management: Setting the stage for growth: Grant Thornton International Business Report 2013' (2013) available at http://www.gti.org/files/ibr2013_wib_report_final.pdf.

role in making sure that there are well-qualified women in the maritime sector. We are also working to reduce institutional and cultural barriers to the advancement of women in the maritime sector, by offering female role models and mentors to both female and male students. With the help of a number of engaged fellowship donors, WMU has made a massive step in increasing the number of female students since 1983, when the university opened, and just two women enrolled in the Malmö MSc program.

WMU was founded in 1983 by the International Maritime Organization (IMO) and offers only postgraduate programs (MSc, PhD and Postgraduate Diplomas). WMU's mandate remains very much the same today as back in 1983:

> postgraduate education in the maritime sector with a mandate to provide capacity building and with particular emphasis towards developing countries.

WMU aims to build knowledge, skill and competences to enhance maritime safety and security and the prevention of marine pollution. Since 1983, the university has grown substantially, offering six specialisations within the Malmö-based Master of Science in Maritime Affairs program, two MSc programs in China, a fast-growing PhD program, an expanding number of postgraduate diploma programs, and a very popular portfolio of executive professional development courses. Since 1983, there have been 3,663 graduates from our academic programs, from 165 different countries.

However, WMU was very conscious that women were under-represented in the student body. With the backing of several fellowship donors, the university set in place an active program to recruit and fund qualified female candidates to the Malmö-based MSc. This program paid dividends: employers were encouraged to put forward their female employees, who had a certain number of fellowships ear-marked for them, and women were assured of a warm welcome at the university. Between 1983 and 1997, the intake of women was in the single digits. However, by 1997, WMU started to observe rapid growth in the numbers. 2010 marked a milestone for WMU, where women comprised more than 30 % of the student population. WMU also pushed for growth in faculty and staff positions. From the 1990s, when there was just one female member of faculty, there are today four, plus six research associates/assistants who work within the university's research programs.

In 2008, WMU hosted its first conference on Empowerment of Women in the Maritime World, which highlighted the problems, challenges and opportunities that professional women faced. It concluded with an invitation to all stakeholders to support and actively encourage the participation of women. This conference was an unqualified success, with more than 300 participants.

Five years later, in March 2014, WMU hosted, in partnership with the International Maritime Organization, a second international conference on Maritime Women: Global Leadership. This conference has been hugely successful, with more than 265 participants from around the world. Furthermore, the conference has had several significant outcomes, including:

1. A declaration that IMO Member States will support the career development and mentoring of women in the maritime sector;
2. Special reports at IMO's Technical Cooperation Committee and at Councils on the conference; and
3. The formation of the WMU Women's Association (WMUWA) to complement and support the global network of Women's Associations developed and encouraged by IMO under their 25-year-old program on the Integration of Women into the maritime sector.

WMU is at the start of a very exciting period of development and change. Its finances are stronger than they have been for many years; we are about to move to our splendid new building in 2015, provided by the generosity of the City of Malmö; and new distance learning courses are coming on line, with a very marked growth in stand-alone Postgraduate Diploma programs. Exciting new collaborations are helping the university to build its reputation, attract new stakeholders and build fruitful partnerships, providing rich knowledge exchange and debates that are truly unique for a small, higher-education institution.

Central to the university's strategic priorities will be to support the role of women in the maritime sector and continue our efforts to strengthen women's participation in our own faculty and the student body. We look forward to hosting a third conference to develop the theme of women in the maritime sector even further.

I invite you to explore our website and get acquainted with the World Maritime University, www.wmu.se.

World Maritime University
Malmö
Sweden

Neil Bellefontaine

Acknowledgements

This volume is a selection of papers from the 2nd International Conference on Maritime Women: Global Leadership, held in Malmö, Sweden, 31 March to 1 April 2014 (MWGL 2014). MWGL 2014 was organized by the World Maritime University (WMU) in cooperation with the International Maritime Organization (IMO). The editors would like to take this opportunity to acknowledge the contribution and assistance of numerous individuals, colleagues, friends, and benefactors, whose efforts led to the successful execution of MWGL and in turn made the publication of this book possible.

We would first like to thank Ms. Pamela Tansey, Senior Deputy Director of the IMO Technical Cooperation Division, for her considerable support throughout the conference with her colleagues, Ms. Helen Buni, Principal Programme Assistant, and Ms. Karine Langlois, New Media Officer. Through the generous sponsorship of IMO, speakers and participants from the IMO's regional support network were able to attend the conference.

Our thanks are extended to the MWGL 2014 keynote speakers, including H.E. Lina Shbeeb, Minister of Transport, Jordan; Dr. Wendy Watson-Wright, Assistant Director General and Executive Secretary of UNESCO-IOC; H.E. Ana Irene Delgado, former Ambassador Extraordinary and Plenipotentiary and General Consul of the Republic of Panama to the United Kingdom of Great Britain and Northern Ireland and Ambassador of the Republic of Panama to the Republic of Iceland; Reverend Ken Peters, Director of Justice and Welfare of Seafarers, Mission to Seafarers; Dr. Judith Melin, Director General of the Swedish Coast Guard; and Rear Admiral Sandra Stosz, Superintendent of the United States Coast Guard Academy.

The editors acknowledge stimulating discussions provided by the speakers from various international organizations, including Ms. Karin Orsel, President of WISTA; Dr. Geraldine Knatz, Board Member of International Association of Ports and Harbours; Dr. Şadan Kaptanoğlu, Vice President of BIMCO; Ms. Katharina Stanzel, Managing Director of INTERTANKO; Ms. Alison McGarry, Coordinator of Women Transport Workers' Department, ITF; and Ms. Julia Lear, Transport & Maritime Specialist of ILO.

Our special appreciation extends to distinguished speakers from public sectors, including Ms. Nancy Karigithu, Director General of Kenya Maritime Authority; Dr. Tanya Tamara Carlucci Sucre, Head of Compliance and Enforcement Department, Merchant Marine Directorate, Panama Maritime Authority; Ms. Claudia Grant, Deputy Director General of Maritime Authority of Jamaica; Ms. Vivette Grant, Deputy Executive Director of Caribbean Maritime Institute; Ms. Mfon Ekong Usoro, Secretary General of MoU on Port State Control for West and Central African Region; Captain Christiana Yustita, Chief of Marine Pollution Prevention and Ship Safety Management, Ministry of Transportation, Indonesia; Ms. Darling E. Rojas Mendoza, Consultation on Gender Equality and Women's Empowerment and Training Programs Maritime Port; Ms. Meenaksi Bhirugnath Bhookhun, WOMESA Chairman and Maritime Officer of the Ministry of Public Infrastructure, National Development Unit, Land Transport & Shipping for the Republic of Mauritius; and Ms. Noelia Mabel López, International Affairs Office of the Argentine Coast Guard.

We further acknowledge valuable speeches offered by the education sector, including Dr. Minghua Zhao, Assistant Director of Greenwich Maritime Institute, University of Greenwich; Dr. Sajid Hussain, Commandant of Bangladesh Marine Academy; Dr. Layla El Saeed, Assistant Academy President of MENA & Africa Arab International Women's Maritime Forum; and Ms. Sohyun Jo, Assistant Professor of Korea Institute of Maritime and Fisheries Technology.

Inspiring speakers from the private sector included Ms. Lena Göthberg, Secretary-General of Institute of Shipping Analysis; Dr. Anne-Marie Warris, Principal of ecoreflect Ltd; Ms. Carla S. Limcaoco, President of Women in Maritime Philippines and Director of PTC Management Corporation; and Captain Anuradha Jha of the Shipping Corporation of India. We extend our gratitude to all the chairs, speakers, and poster presenters who contributed to MWGL 2014. A detailed list of these individuals is provided in the conference programme, that is an Annex in this publication.

Our special thanks are extended to the members of the Scientific Committee who helped review abstracts and papers for the conference, in alphabetical order, Professor Neil Bellefontaine, Dr. Lisa Loloma Froholdt, Dr. Evi Hatziandreou, Dr. Sajid Hussain, Dr. Liping Jiang, Dr. Momoko Kitada, Dr. Joan Mileski, Dr. María Carolina Romero Lares, Ms. Katharina Stanzel, Dr. Tanya Tamara Carlucci Sucre, Dr. Anne-Marie Warris, Ms. Erin Williams, and Dr. Minghua Zhao.

Our genuine appreciation is extended to the MWGL 2014 sponsors, in alphabetical order, A.P. Møller og Hustru Chastine McKinney Møllers Fond til Almene Formaal, IMO, Malmö Högskola, Nippon Foundation, ORIENT foundation, and TORM Foundation. Their generous support greatly enhanced the success of the event.

The editors further appreciate Dr. Björn Kjerfve, former President of WMU, for providing the leadership and vision to support a second women's conference hosted by WMU. Thanks are also extended to Professor Neil Bellefontaine, Acting President of WMU, and Mr. Roger Gregory Jones, former Vice President of WMU and the Chair of the 1st International Conference on "Empowerment of Professional

Women in the Maritime World", for their guidance during the many meetings of the Organizing Committee. The leadership of Dr. María Carolina Romero Lares, Associate Professor of WMU, and the Chair of MWGL 2014, is highly noted.

In terms of WMU Staff, our special appreciation to Ms. Mia Hedin, whose dedication ensured the smooth execution of the conference and that MWGL 2014 was not wanting in expert liaison, secretariat, coordination, logistics, and related practical services. We thank Ms. Maia Brindley Nilsson for her role in the promotion of MWGL 2014, Mr. Saul Isaacson for designing the MWGL logo, program, and posters, Mr. Erik Ponnert for setting up the conference website, Dr. Josefin Madjidian for assisting with the call for papers and the conference sessions, Ms. - Solveig-Karin Erdal, Ms. Alma Koenig, and Mr. Farshad Shamgholi, for helping at the registration desk during the conference, and Mr. Johan Bolmsten, Mr. Jake Hunter, and Mr. Stuart Strange, for streaming the event, as well as recording it for future educational use. Our thanks also extend to the WMU Women's Association (WMUWA) for their assistance with ushering and welcoming participants, and to the students of the WMU MSc Class of 2014 for their support of the event. We would also like to acknowledge the support of Ms. Anna Svan, Conference Services, Malmö University, for the practical and technical arrangement at the conference venue.

The editors express their deepest gratitude to the 265 participants whose valuable input and opinions, although not captured in this publication, contributed to active discussions and helped to make MWGL 2014 a success. We thank them for their contribution as well as the adoption of the MWGL Declaration that is included in this publication.

Last but not least, the editors thank the authors of each paper in this volume for their insight and efforts in bringing critical issues affecting the advancement of maritime women to the forefront of discussion. This publication is a unique collection of research that will serve as a stimulus for further development and study of women in the maritime professions. We would like to thank Ms. Alina Prylipko for her thorough work on references and Ms. Katarina Eriksson for graphical adjustment in this volume. Special thanks are also extended to Dr. Lawrence P. Hildebrand, WMU Professor and co-editor of the WMU book series, and Ms. Aditi Kataria, WMU Research Associate, for their expertise and efforts in finalizing this book. Our special thanks are extended to Dr. Martina Bihn, Dr. Brigitte Reschke, and Ms. Manuela Schwietzer of Springer for their encouragement and support to this publication.

This publication is dedicated to every woman and man who encourages leadership of female professionals in the maritime sector and supports better access to education and employment opportunities for all women. Our collective efforts to advance maritime women will contribute to sustainability in the maritime community, as step by step, we make positive changes together.

In commemoration of the 20th anniversary of the Beijing Declaration,

International Women's Day 2015

Contents

Introduction

Lisa Loloma Froholdt, Erin Williams, and Momoko Kitada

Policies to foster the advancement and empowerment of women have been on the agenda of several international organisations, governmental agencies and non-governmental organisations in the last decades. In particular, the promotion of gender equality has been a goal of the United Nations (UN) and its specialized agencies.

The first programme to promote the advancement of women in the maritime industry was developed by the International Maritime Organization (IMO) in 1988. It was called "Strategy on the Integration of Women in the Maritime Sector" (IWMS) and its main goal was to increase the presence of women in the developing countries' workforce through education, training and knowledge transfer. The role of training in this programme was fulfilled by educational institutions created by IMO at the World Maritime University (WMU) in Sweden and the International Maritime Law Institute (IMLI) in Malta.

The IMO Strategy was accompanied by several initiatives implemented throughout different regions of the world during the 1990s, which were aimed at creating awareness of the situation faced by maritime women in their careers. The number of female alumni graduating from WMU and IMLI began to increase, and consequently these women began to take up positions as managers, administrators, policy advisers and educators in the maritime field worldwide.

In the year 2000, the UN adopted the Millennium Development Goals (MDGs) which are aimed at encouraging development by improving social and economic conditions in the world's poorest countries. Among them, MDG3, "promote gender

L.L. Froholdt (✉) • M. Kitada
World Maritime University, Malmö, Sweden
e-mail: lf@wmu.se; mk@wmu.se

E. Williams
Brunssum, The Netherlands
e-mail: ew@wmu.se

© Springer-Verlag Berlin Heidelberg 2015

M. Kitada et al. (eds.), *Maritime Women: Global Leadership*, WMU Studies in Maritime Affairs 3, DOI 10.1007/978-3-662-45385-8_1

equality and empower women", was adopted, resulting in many specialized agencies of the UN introducing changes within their programmes to comply with this goal. For example, in 2003, the IMO started a process to establish regional support networks for women around the world. As a result, six regional associations for women were created, covering the regions of Africa, Asia, Latin America and the Pacific Islands.

The first phase of IMO's Programme for the IWMS concluded in 2013. But this was not the conclusion of IMO's efforts. Instead, this marked the beginning of a new programme that could be described as a merger between the MDG3 and IMO's response towards strengthening the role of women in the maritime sector. During that same year, IMO released a film entitled "Women at the Helm", thereby showcasing IMO's efforts towards promoting a positive change for women in shipping, while highlighting first-hand experiences of women who have succeeded in the industry. IMO then announced its plan to develop a "Global Strategy for Women Seafarers" in order to continue to improve the diversity of seafarers.

In support of these initiatives and to contribute to the efforts of the maritime stakeholders and the international community, WMU hosted the **2nd International Conference Maritime Women: Global Leadership (MWGL 2014)**, from 31 March to 1 April, 2014 in Malmö, Sweden. The Conference was organized in cooperation with IMO, bringing together key leaders and professionals in the maritime sector to highlight successes of gender diversity in the industry, while discussing future initiatives and opportunities for women. The programme of the Conference is available as an Annex of this book. This second conference built on the success of the first Women's conference that WMU hosted in 2008, entitled "Empowerment of Professional Women in the Maritime World".

MWGL 2014 brought together 265 participants from 174 countries. Representatives from international governmental and non-governmental organisations, governmental officials, executives, practitioners, academics, researchers and students actively participated in the 2-day conference. It was here, where ideas about global leadership, policy, education career opportunities and sustainability were exchanged through discussions on accomplishments so far and follow-up plans required at the international, national and regional levels and from both the public and private sectors in the maritime industry, who have contributed to the advancement and empowerment of women around the world.

The participants shared their views about the development of a Conference Declaration to call on IMO and its Member States, and the shipping industry, as a whole, to make optimal use of women's resources in order to facilitate the achievement of the agreed goals regarding employment, career, education and leadership, which in turn will make sustainable development of the maritime sector a reality. The Maritime Women: Global Leadership Declaration is presented in this book after the conclusion.

1 Conference Theme: "Maritime Women: Global Leadership"

MWGL 2014 aligned itself with the need to develop new strategies to strengthen the role of women in the maritime sector and the idea of sharing the experiences of those who had succeeded in their countries and regions. In particular, MWGL 2014 was a call for strong leadership, mentoring and networking opportunities within the sector. MWGL 2014 aimed at strengthening the leadership role of women, while helping them realize opportunities to succeed in the maritime sector. It showcased the achievements of professional maritime women around the globe and across the entire spectrum of maritime activity. It is expected that this will help in establishing networking opportunities for several associations for professional maritime women, in promoting discussions regarding the value of sustained investment in education and training.

2 Keynote Speakers

The welcoming remarks by Björn Kjerfve, former President of WMU and Conference Chair, María Carolina Romero Lares, Associate Professor of WMU, were followed by the addresses of H.E. Lena Shbeeb, Minister of Transport, Jordan, and Wendy Watson-Wright, Assistant Director General and Executive Secretary, United Nations Educational, Scientific and Cultural Organization (UNESCO)—Intergovernmental Oceanographic Commission (IOC).

These speakers challenged the participants to reflect upon the need to understand womens' perspectives within the maritime sector, to strengthen national competitiveness in the shipping business which can increase employment opportunities for women and men, to remove barriers, preventing women from participating, and to realize that more actions are needed, in order to reach employment gender parity and to ensure that the expertise of women is utilised for the benefit of the maritime world as a whole.

The welcoming remarks were followed by two plenary sessions. Pamela Tansey, Senior Deputy Director of the Technical Co-operation Division of IMO, who chaired the first plenary session, presented the speakers, Rear Admiral Sandra Stosz, Superintendent of the US Coast Guard Academy, and Judith Melin, Director General of the Swedish Coast Guard. Şadan Kaptanoğlu, Vice President of BIMCO, and Managing Director of H.İ. Kaptanoglu Ship Management Company, chaired the second plenary session and presented the speakers, H.E. Ana Irene Delgado, former Ambassador Extraordinary and Plenipotentiary and General Consul of the Republic of Panama to the United Kingdom of Great Britain and Northern Ireland, and Karin Orsel, President of WISTA International, and Vice Chairman of the International Chamber of Shipping (ICS). During these sessions, great emphasis was made on the need to assist developing regions through capacity building in order to contribute towards sustainable development in the maritime field, and on improving levels of competency through focus on education and knowledge-sharing. Maritime peers were encouraged to act as role models and mentors for maritime women, while the importance of the need to build partnerships for optimum benefits was highlighted.

The last plenary session of MWGL 2014 took place on the second day and focused on "Promoting Diversity". This session was chaired by Reverend Ken Peters, Director of Justice and Welfare of Seafarers, Mission to Seafarers. In this session, keynote speakers, Julia Lear from the International Labour Organization (ILO), Alison McGarry, Coordinator of Women Transport Workers' Department at the International Transport Workers' Federation (ITF), and Geraldine Knatz, representing the International Association of Port and Harbours, spoke about the importance of creating women's committees within organisations. Here, stress was put on the fact that while the global maritime community is the most diversified, gender inclusion remains virtually non-existent at sea. The speakers noted that even though there is a strong need in the industry, there is also a lack of women in top-level positions. Women leaders are required to put in the extra time and effort to build the professional relationships and networks inside and outside their work-places that will enable them to break through corporate glass ceilings.

3 Conference Workshops and Poster Presentations

In support of the Conference theme, a series of workshops were organized around five topics—Employment, Policy and Practice; Education for Career Building; Leadership, Mentoring and Networking; Sustainable Development in Shipping; and Regional Perspectives. The first day workshops were dedicated to the first four topics:

- Workshop A: Employment, Policy and Practice;
- Workshop B: Education for Career Building;
- Workshop C: Leadership, Mentoring and Networking; and
- Workshop D: Sustainable Development in Shipping.

The Employment, Policy and Practice Workshop, chaired by Nancy Karigithu, Director General of the Kenya Maritime Authority, focused on the strategic recruitment and empowerment of women, best employment practices, and visibility of women in the workplace. The invited experts addressed policy issues, reporting their research on attitudinal and structural impediments when women work in the maritime industry. From the fishing industry to maritime law firms, many similar issues and concerns were evident across the spectrum, and such challenges need tangible solutions.

In the Education for Career Building Workshop, the chair, Professor Neil Bellefontaine, Acting President of WMU, set the tone for the workshop by highlighting the importance of gaining equal opportunities and access to new knowledge and skills, organisational learning and knowledge transfer. From identifying gaps in how educational programs are marketed, to showcasing the long-term success of women who experienced an international exchange program as a cadet, this workshop hosted a diverse group of presenters with a myriad of experiences.

The Leadership, Mentoring and Networking Workshop was chaired by Lena Göthberg, Secretary General for the Institute of Shipping Analysis. Focusing on the important roles of mentoring and networking when developing a leader, the audience learned about challenges faced by women seafarers in countries where women are severely under-represented, the influence of women who are present on Boards of Directors, and the presence of second-generation bias towards women in the maritime sector is prevalent.

Chaired by Katharina Stanzel, Managing Director at INTERTANKO, the Sustainable Development in Shipping Workshop focused on the contributions of women to sustainable development in the maritime sector, including maritime safety and security, ports, shipping, and marine environmental management. It included presentations on the contribution of women, career opportunities and training needs regarding Port State Control activities in Africa, the issue of challenges on sustainability and Corporate Social Responsibility, and opportunities for women in the areas of ship technology research and vessels inspections. Finally, a presentation discussed how shore-controlled and monitored vessels offer better conditions to female and male crews.

The second day of the Conference included two Regional Perspectives Workshops, hereby drawing on the last topic of the Conference:

- Workshop A: The Americas & Europe; and
- Workshop B: Asia, Arab States & Africa.

To bring together the key themes of the conference, while maintaining a regional focus, the second day of the Conference included the Regional Perspectives Workshops, divided into two regions: The Americas & Europe; and Asia, Arab States & Africa. This allowed presenters to approach the Conference's core topics from the various regional perspectives.

The Regional Perspectives Workshop for The Americas & Europe was chaired by Minghua Zhao, Assistant Director of the Greenwich Maritime Institute. Focusing on the presence of women in managerial positions in the Latin American region and the need for maritime administrations to develop national plans to integrate women from within, participants learned of statistics showing women's limited access to training and to employment in the Latin American region. Furthermore, presenters assessed the effectiveness of the IMO's "Women In Development" programme in the Caribbean region, stressing the need to unite women as a cohesive force for change and development. Additionally, presenters addressed the loss of women at consecutive career stages in marine engineering sciences and technology in the UK and analysed the gender mainstreaming situation in the maritime transport field in Ukraine.

The Regional Perspectives Workshop for Asia, Arab States & Africa was chaired by Carla S. Limcaoco, President of Women in Maritime Philippines, and Director of PTC Management Corporation. The audience learned of challenges faced by female officers and stewards on board Chinese vessels, while addressing the need for Maritime Education and Training (MET) institutions to open enrolment possibilities to female students and identifying the need to give full support to governments for the promotion of gender equality and the empowerment of women seafarers. Finally, presenters shared experiences as members of the Association of Women Managers in the Maritime Sector in East and Southern Africa (WOMESA), with emphasis on regional training workshops, mentorship programmes and networking at local, regional and international levels. Participants learned of the importance and meaning of equality in the sector in terms of equal rights, access and opportunities for women and men, eradication of biases and discrimination, and respect for differences, aspirations, concerns and varied human needs.

The response to the call for papers was incredible. However, it was impossible to accommodate all of the interested speakers who had submitted a research paper to MWGL 2014. The Organising Committee decided therefore, to invite speakers to a special poster session that would be available for conference participants between sessions. The session was visited by most participants and facilitated opportunities for furthering both formal and informal modes of discussion, knowledge-sharing and networking amongst participants. The poster session brought together 22 presenters from 13 countries (United Kingdom, Spain, Portugal, Russia, New Zealand, Turkey, Canada, Poland, Ghana, Ecuador, Latvia, Sweden, and Norway) and was an integral feature of MWGL 2014.

4 This Volume

This book includes five parts that contain a selection of papers presented at MWGL 2014, beginning with a foreword by Acting President of WMU, Professor Neil Bellefontaine, an introduction by the authors; Lisa L. Froholdt, Erin Williams, and Momoko Kitada. These papers were reviewed by an appointed Scientific Committee. The parts are categorised in reference to the MWGL 2014 workshop themes:

- Part I. Maritime Policy and Women's Advancement;
- Part II. Career Development and Gender Issues;
- Part III. Maritime Education and Research: Impact of Women;
- Part IV. Global Leadership for Maritime Women; and
- Part V. Sustainable Issues in Shipping: Women's Contribution.

Part I. Maritime Policy and Women's Advancement Political commitment to combating discrimination and promoting equality in treatment and opportunities at the workplace, is almost universal (ITC-ILO 2009). A number of countries have ratified the ILO conventions such as the Equal Remuneration Convention, 1951 (No. 100), and the Discrimination (Employment and Occupation) Convention, 1958 (No. 111).

Nevertheless, it was not until the 1980s, when statistics of women's marginalisation in careered positions were highlighted and acknowledged (Evetts 1994). The Convention on the Elimination of All Forms of Discrimination against Women (CEDAW) was adopted in 1979 by the UN General Assembly. The Convention defines discrimination against women as "... any distinction, exclusion or restriction made on the basis of sex which has the effect or purpose of impairing or nullifying the recognition, enjoyment or exercise by women, irrespective of their marital status, on a basis of equality of men and women, of human rights and fundamental freedoms in the political, economic, social, cultural, civil or any other field" (UN Women n.d.).

The IMO also developed the Programme for the Integration of Women in the Maritime Sector (IWMS) in 1989, as part of IMO's Integrated Technical Cooperation Programme (ITCP), celebrating its 25th anniversary in 2014. The primary objective of this programme was to encourage the Member States to open the doors of their maritime institutes to women and provide training for women alongside men. The IMO was confident that this would contribute to the high level of competence that the maritime industry demands, at both local and global levels.

The legal provisions to support women to develop their careers were introduced in Europe in the 1970s. The Equal Pay Act 1970 and the Sex Discrimination Act 1975 are well known as such provisions. However, the enforcement mechanism under these Acts is often problematic, as discrimination is not always overt (Shrubsall 1994). The papers in this part highlighted that the shipping industry has been traditionally dominated by men, which accommodates the work culture endorsed by masculine norms and values.

Part I of this book begins with the contribution by Pamela Tansey, who is the Senior Deputy Director, Technical Cooperation Division at the IMO. She lifts the lid on a historic recap of initiatives established and supported by the IMO since 1988, which all seek to strengthen the integration of women in the maritime industry. She rounds off her paper with the inclusion of the MWGL conference at WMU, where, for the first time, participants from all six IMO regional support network for women were present. From workers' perspective, Alison McGarry, who is the Coordinator of the Women Transport Workers' Department, the International Transport Workers' Federation (ITF) describes the ITF Women's Maritime Leadership Programme, and her paper describes how the ITF has supported female transport workers in the maritime sector to develop leadership skills through its own programme, called "Leading change". It provides a structured programme in political and policy contexts, in particular about their unions. Aspasia S. Pastra, Dimitrios N. Koufopoulos, and Ioannis P. Gkliatis inform the analysis of the characteristics of the Board of Directors in their case of the Greek shipping sector. Their paper helps us to understand the current status of the decision-making structures affecting the integration of women in the industry, and rationalise why gender diversity is important for sustainable development in the shipping business. They emphasize that it is the system which matters in the promotion of women in the managerial and leadership positions in the shipping industry. The paper presented by Margarita Dávila Cevallos clearly articulates this problem in the Ecuadorian maritime oil transportation sector. She addresses the mechanism of male-domination, which affects the employment and promotion of women in the industry. Therefore, it is necessary, she emphasises, to change the organisational structure with the help of policy development, to create a mechanism for integrating women in the maritime sector.

Part II. Career Development and Gender Issues The recent study on career mobility and development by the European Community Shipowners' Association (ECSA) and the European Transport Workers' Federation (ETF) (2013), concluded that seafarer career path options are the same today as they were in 2005. The study pointed to a range of barriers for career development, such as lack of information about jobs, lack of funding for further studies, and the argument that shore jobs often demand re-location. This in turn involves a large expense for individual seafarers. Re-locations also entail a string of challenges that are stressful for seafarers, such as difficulties in culture transition to other national cultures (Hofstede 2001) or other corporate cultures (Adler 2002) ashore that are different from those at sea. The study showed that seafarers often experience a lack of recognition from their new colleagues ashore.

Furthermore, the ECSA and ETF study argued that the lack of broadband connections is still a problem in the industry. This not only hinders a seafarer from sustaining relations with family and friends, which can be especially important for mother-child relationships, but also hampers distance learning, which is one way to enhance career mobility and development. More effort and funding is necessary for activities that seek to push career mobility and development towards enabling all maritime professionals, including women. Such activities are gradually taking place and they can enhance the employability of women in the maritime industry at a time when there is a global shortage of seafarers and competence needs[1] have changed (Froholdt 2011).[2] Policies and programmes can also facilitate career development for women, as one of the papers in this part informs.

Chapters from Part II include the paper by Bev Mackenzie, who presents a study of women's participation in STEM (Science, Technology, Engineering and Mathematics). She cites a range of reasons for low participation and those issues that circle the challenges involved in sustaining a career at sea and a family ashore. Claudia Grant and Vivette Grant, provide a Caribbean perspective, based on a study of women who have been promoted to senior leadership positions in the Caribbean and the impact of IMO WID programmes in this development. The paper by Ayşe Aslı Başak presents the role of Turkish women seafarers, whose presence is challenged by cultural barriers. Finally, this part includes the paper by Momoko Kitada, who presents a study of how seafaring mothers have balanced their work life with their family life. She provides cases where the seafarers had to draw on trusted persons to assist in the child upbringing in order to sustain their career at sea.

[1] See Part V. Sustainability issues in shipping.

[2] See also KNOW-ME project under the EU Framework programme 7, http://www.know-me.org/.

Part III. Maritime Education and Research: Impact of Women The European history of women's education dates back to the nineteenth century when middle- and upper-class boys had long been accepted and expected to participate in education as a natural part of preparation for adulthood. Feminists had to fight for securing acceptance of women's right to work and to receive an education and the first Education Act (Forster Act 1870) in Britain, made education compulsory for all children aged between five and ten (Skelton 1993).

The campaign of 'education for all' was the first real step for women to have access to an education, and it has been argued that compulsory education helped working-class girls to be equipped to support a patriarchal system from the domestic sphere. Such an 'ideology of domesticity' contributed to what is understood as the 'good woman', and societal norms of the 'perfect wife and mother'.

When science was first introduced to a curriculum, girls were not allowed to study the subject, although they later were permitted to attend classes. However, the focus was on certain scientific principles applicable for domestic contexts, such as evaporation for drying clothes (Sharpe 1976). Encouraging women to develop their careers in a STEM field is considered to be a key for global leadership today. U.S. President Barack Obama announced the launch of the "Change the Education" initiative on 16 September, 2010.

Maritime Education and Training (MET) is not an exception in this context. It has been overwhelmingly dominated by male pupils, teachers, and practitioners of Maritime Sciences. Maritime Sciences, particularly nautical science and marine engineering, are packaged and presented to appeal to boys, and not to girls. Finally, 'scientific' and 'engineering' thinking seemingly embodies an intrinsically masculine world view.

Part III includes the paper by Chen Qi that reveals the excellent performance of female cadets at the Massachusetts Maritime Academy and how their international exchange programme between United States and China, helped women to widen job opportunities in the maritime labour market. Her paper suggests that a wider opportunity and exposure to an international experience should be encouraged to students, particularly females, for successful career development. Maria Boström Cars and Cecilia Österman analyse the index of gender equality and investigate eight MET institutions in Finland, Norway, Sweden, and the Philippines. Their paper identified the need for a strategic gender awareness approach into MET institutions. Furthermore, the domination of males is noted not only in the field of maritime education, but also within maritime research. Rozane Valente Marins and Juliana Berninger da Costa present their study on women's contribution to the Oceanography Science in Brazil. They evaluate how gender equality in research and education of Oceanography Science has been developed by the social policies in Brazil. The role of education in order to change the status quo for women in the maritime industry, is discussed by Wilson Thoya Baya. His paper further advocates that the global maritime community should work together to support women's integration in the maritime sector.

Part IV. Global Leadership for Maritime Women Today, Brazil, Russia, India and China, the so-called BRIC countries, top the charts with women comprising 26 % of senior managers, with the G7 countries following at 18 % (Thornton 2012).

It is seemingly still difficult to battle global gender-based discrimination in leadership selection. However, the increasing amount of mergers and strategic partnerships, and the global stretch of the maritime sector, continues to bring people together from different organisations and national cultures. Research shows that in general, companies are seeing the benefit of managing diversity, and of how this can enhance potential benefits and costs for an organisation (Kochan et al. 2003; Triandis et al. 1994). In a maritime context, if women are more included as part of a diverse maritime workforce, there is a larger talent pool available for filling leadership and managerial positions, and this is undoubtedly an advantage in today's highly competitive market.

There are tools available that can be installed to empower women; one of which is the use of quotas. Often, for temporary purposes, quotas may increase the number of women to specific senior leadership positions (ILO 2004; Deloitte 2011; Thornton 2012). However, it cannot stand alone. Successful gender integration in managerial positions is the responsibility of a company's Human Resource Department. If not fully anchored in top management and managers throughout the organisation, gender diversity will suffer.

There must be both commitment and tangible action plans from management that aim to create opportunities for women, where they can gain both experience and visibility in positions that actually foster advancement. Another commitment is to provide effective mentoring for women in their career development. Last but not least, is the necessity for management to send a strong message to all employees, that it does not permit gender-stereotype behaviour. These actions will contribute to battle the reasons for the glass ceiling, and this is also discussed in the papers.

The Part IV on Global Leadership for Maritime Women includes papers by Anniek Wouters, Olga Delgado Ortega, Kjell Ivar Øvergård, and Veronica Henden, and Pınar Özdemir and Taner Albayrak. Wouters highlights disparities between women entering the Antwerp law program and the number of women partners in Antwerp, and discusses strategies for women to overcome perceptions and break through the proverbial glass ceiling. Next, Ortega, Øvergård, and Henden compare the self-assessment of leadership skills between men and women, suggesting that women's consistent poor self-promotion and lack of confidence in their own leadership skills, may affect their inclusion in maritime careers. Finally, Özdemir and Albayrak discuss the often over-looked topic of second-generation gender bias and suggest a model based on mentorship and participative leadership to help overcome this.

Part V. Sustainable Issues in Shipping: Women's Contribution Despite the fact that there is only a 2 % increase of women employed on board ships between 2005 and 2010, and predominantly on cruise ships, women are becoming an increasingly larger portion of the shore-side employees in the global maritime cluster (BIMCO and ISF 2010; Theotokas et al. 2014). It is positive that there is an increase, and it is important that this increase can be pushed forward from a holistic point of view as part of the overall task of ensuring sustainable development in the shipping industry.

The importance of ensuring an overall sustainable development of the shipping industry is high on the agenda, partly due to the financial crisis, but also in part due to the economic growth in developing countries. A sustainable industry involves the challenge of ensuring social welfare, environmental protection, economic growth and strengthening the competitiveness of the industry. Being as global an industry as shipping is, special care is needed from policy makers, researchers, educational institutions, and industry, in order to ensure career development and employability for maritime professionals, when seeking to ensure a sustainable maritime industry.

The IMO has worked to ensure a global standard through the STCW 95 Convention and following amendments. However, it is observed that there is 'fast tracking' of MET programmes. Research shows that it is not the lack of seafarers that is behind the fast tracking, but more the quality of the training (Li and Wonham 1999; Leggate 2004). A range of research projects with the European Union (EU) have contributed to strengthen quality training by focusing on maritime competencies and investigating how this can be developed through publically available e-learning courses, and e-portals with information on how career path development can be planned for the individual maritime professionals. Many IMO Member States have also instigated promotion campaign activities in order to attract both the younger generation and professionals from other industries. These projects and activities point out that educational needs have evolved in the industry, which is in line with other studies that point to the global nature and complexity of the industry, that calls for new educational competencies in the areas of logistics, economics and management (Leong et al. 2009; Froholdt 2011). A recent EU project concluded that MET is still predominantly tailored for seafaring, and not aligned to current or future needs, or professionals that come from other industries, seeking employment in the maritime industry.[3] The study also concluded that MET is demarcated from the industry and there are large differences between maritime educational institutions.

A sustainable approach involves activities that include women in maritime clusters; locally, nationally, regionally and globally. It is equally important that women take an active part in developing Human Resource Development Plans for IMO Member States and maritime clusters. This can be achieved through transnational partnerships that can provide potential students complementary and cohesive educational offerings that are aligned to industry needs (Froholdt and Kragesand Hansen 2011).[4]

This part includes a paper by Pengfei Zhang and Minghua Zhao, who have analysed important issues related to the training and recruitment of female seafarers in China. Colin J. Stevenson follows with a paper where he questions the low number of women in the shipping industry at times when there is a critical shortage of seafarers in general. Marlene Calderón, Diana Illing, Ingrid Schipperen, and Pedro Antão, also contribute with a paper on how new technologies, developed through the EU-funded SAFEPEC project on innovative risk-based tools for ship safety inspection, can help increase job opportunities for women in the future.

---

[3] See also KNOW-ME project under the EU Framework programme 7, http://www.know-me.org/.

[4] See also KNOW-ME project under the EU Framework programme 7, http://www.know-me.org/.

In conclusion, the aim of this book is to highlight the value of women's leadership in the maritime sector, and to attract attention to the necessary actions needed in order to enhance gender equality and empower more women. The themes—policy, career, education/research, leadership and sustainability—are just five areas of gender equality issues that were the focus of this book. However, it is the hope that this, together with the Maritime Women: Global Leadership Declaration, can contribute to the work of the IMO and all of those women and men in the sector who continue to strive towards the goals of the UN Conference on Sustainable Development (Rio+20)[5] and the Open Working Group on Sustainable Development Goals,[6] in relation to gender issues. As stated by Roberta Clarke, Regional Director for Asia-Pacific for UN Women, "*gender equality is a societal responsibility and requires the involvement, actions, commitment and will of everyone for it to become a lived reality for all*".[7] As will be evident to the reader, the contributing authors to this volume offer their share of commitment to these goals.

References

Adler, N. J. (2002). *International dimensions of organizational behaviour*. London: International Thomson.

BIMCO, & ISF. (2010). *Manpower 2010 update: The worldwide demand of and supply for seafarers*. Coventry: University of Warwick.

Deloitte. (2011). *Women in the boardroom: A global perspective*. London: Deloitte Global Services Limited.

European Community of Shipowners Association, & European Transport Worker's Federation. (2013). Maritime career path mapping 2013 update. http://www.ecsa.eu/images/files/Rapport_Maritime_Career.pdf. Accesses 1 Apr 2014.

Evetts, J. (1994). Career and gender: The conceptual challenge. In J. Evetts (Ed.), *Women & career: Themes and issues in advanced industrial societies* (pp. 223–233). London: Longman.

Froholdt, L. L. (2011). Facilitating maritime competence development. *Mercator: Maritime Innovation, Research and Education, 12*, 436–439.

Froholdt, L. L., & Kragesand Hansen, E. (2011). Education and competence development in a maritime EU. Resource document. PRESS4TRANSPORT. http://www.press4transport.eu/vpo/temathic_fiches/EducationCompetenceDevelopmentMaritimeEU%20LLF%20FINAL.pdf. Accessed 1 Apr 2014.

Hofstede, G. (2001). *Culture's consequences: International differences in work-related values*. London: Sage Publications.

ILO. (2004). *Breaking through the glass ceiling: Women in management*. Geneva: International Labor Organization.

[5] See also UN Conference on Sustainable Development Rio+20, http://www.uncsd2012.org/.

[6] See also Open Working Group on Sustainable Development Goals, http://sustainabledevelopment.un.org/owg.html.

[7] This statement was delivered by Roberta Clarke, Regional Director for Asia-Pacific for UN Women at the seventh Official Plenary of the Third International conference on SIDS, http://t.ymlp265.net/yjuqaiauhmhwalaeubafawu/click.php.

ITC-ILO. (2009). *Non-discrimination and equality at work: Key concepts.* Turin: Gender Campus – International Training Centre of the International Labour Organisation.
Kochan, T., Bezukova, K., Ely, R., Jackson, S., Joshi, A., & Jehn, K. (2003). The effects of diversity on business performance: Report of the diversity research network. *Human Resource Management, 42*(1), 3–21.
Leggate, H. (2004). The future shortage of seafarers: Will it become a reality? *Maritime Policy and Management, 31*(1), 3–13.
Leong, E. C., Wong, Y. D., & Williams, C. (2009). Conceptual framework for comparing university baccalaureate programmes in shipping management. *WMU Journal of Maritime Affairs, 5*(1), 37–59.
Li, K. X., & Wonham, J. (1999). A method for estimating world maritime employment. *Transportation Research Part E: Logistics and Transportation Review, 35*(3), 183–189.
Sharpe, S. (1976). *Just like a girl: How girls learn to be women.* Harmondsworth: Penguin.
Shrubsall, V. (1994). Equal opportunities at work: EC and UK law. In J. Evetts (Ed.), *Women & career: Themes and issues in advanced industrial societies* (pp. 30–43). London: Longman.
Skelton, C. (1993). Women and education. In D. Richardson & V. Robinson (Eds.), *Introducing women's studies* (pp. 324–349). London: Macmillan Press.
Theotokas, I., Papachristou, A., Stephanidaki, E., & Katradi, A. (2014). Present and future careers in maritime industry. http://www.know-me.org/. Accessed 1 Apr 2014.
Thornton, G. (2012). *Women in senior management: Still not enough.* Washington: Grant Thornton International Ltd.
Triandis, H. C., Kurowski, L. L., & Gefland, M. J. (1994). Workplace diversity. In H. C. Triandis, M. D. Dunnette, & L. M. Hough (Eds.), *Handbook of industrial and organizational psychology* (pp. 770–827). Palo Alto: Consulting Psychologists Press.
UN Women. (n.d.). The convention on the elimination of all forms of discrimination against women (CEDAW): Overview of the convention. http://www.un.org/womenwatch/daw/cedaw/. Accessed 29 June 2014.

Part I
Maritime Policy and Women's Advancement

Women at the Helm: 25 Years of IMO's Gender Programme

Pamela Tansey

Abstract As the United Nation's (UN) specialized agency for the maritime sector, the International Maritime Organization (IMO) supports the integration of women in the maritime sector as part of their capacity building activities through the Technical Cooperation Division. In support of the UN Millennium Development Goals, implementation of IMO's gender equality policies and procedures has been furthered through partnerships with the IMO regional support networks. The six regional associations of women in the maritime sector are effectively increasing recognition and visibility of women in the workplace to support sustainability of the shipping industry.

Keywords UN Millennium Development Goals • Capacity Building • Networking • Visibility • Implementation • Integration of Women in the Maritime Sector • International Maritime Organization

1 "Think maritime – think women"....

...perhaps not the usual slogan that we are used to seeing in our traditionally male-dominated industry. Yet this bold statement was chosen by one of the regional associations for women in the maritime sector, launched in eastern and southern Africa—with the support of the International Maritime Organization (IMO)—to strengthen the channels of communication between women working in managerial and influential maritime posts. And it gives us all food for thought: reversing the well-known mantra "how do we increase the number of women in the industry" so that it becomes far more positive—and indeed realistic: what advantages can the maritime industry derive from the increased participation of women?

The sea has long been a magnet for people with a sense of purpose, of duty; brave in the face of danger and ready to sacrifice their lives for their ship. For centuries it was understood that those seafarers had to be men, primarily because a great deal of physical strength was essential to tend the sailing ships of old. By the end of the twentieth century, the seascape had altered beyond recognition through

P. Tansey (✉)
Technical Cooperation Division, International Maritime Organization, London, UK
e-mail: info@imo.org

© Springer-Verlag Berlin Heidelberg 2015

M. Kitada et al. (eds.), *Maritime Women: Global Leadership*, WMU Studies in Maritime Affairs 3, DOI 10.1007/978-3-662-45385-8_2

the introduction of technologies that require state-of-the-art training rather than brute force. With that change came the recognition that the maritime sector needs "all hands on deck", both male and female, if it is to take on the challenges of carrying the world's goods and fuel in an efficient, safe and clean manner. As we shall see, translating this into action requires bold and forward-thinking administrations—and women prepared to break century-old socio-cultural patterns.

2 IMO and Its Technical Cooperation Objectives

IMO is the United Nations (UN) system's regulatory agency for the maritime sector with the global mandate of "safe, secure, environmentally sound, efficient and sustainable shipping through cooperation". That mandate is translated into reality by adopting international maritime rules and standards that are then implemented and enforced by Governments in the exercise of flag, port and coastal State jurisdiction.

However, not all developing countries are in a position to give full and complete effect to IMO's instruments. For this reason, and as mandated by the Convention that created IMO, the Organization assists countries in building up their human and institutional capacities, through the Integrated Technical Cooperation Programme (ITCP), for uniform and effective compliance with the Organization's regulatory framework. With a relatively limited volume of external donor support for the ITCP, IMO focuses on the transfer of technical maritime knowledge to achieve its aims. This is achieved using the data provided by maritime administrations themselves in their Country Maritime Profile; IMO then identifies the knowledge and skill-gaps for each country, as a basis for designing the training events which characterize the ITCP.

So far, looking at the IMO mandate and the capacity-building focus of its technical cooperation, one can ask: is there anything stated above which would preclude the participation of women?

3 Integration of Women in the Maritime Sector: A Brief History

Back in 1988, IMO was in the vanguard of UN specialized agencies in forging a realistic programme for the Integration of Women in the Maritime Sector (the Programme). The first strategy document was grounded in the vision of equality, enshrined in the United Nations Charter, at a time when few maritime training institutes opened their doors to female students. Then, as now, capacity building is the touchstone of the programme: at the conclusion of the pivotal development phase of the Organization's gender strategy[1] (1988–1996), the programme was marked by a sensitization phase with campaigns across the regions[2] (1997–2004); and thirdly, from 2004 onwards, by the strategic development of regional associations for women maritime professionals.

Under the first phase of programme implementation, an institutional framework was developed to incorporate the gender dimension, formally and systematically, into IMO's policies and procedures. Implementation of the successive phases of development, both of which were shaped by the concurrent developments taking place within the UN system, including the 1995 Beijing Declaration and the subsequent Millennium Development Goals (MDGs), resulted in the following outcomes: formal integration into the IMO governance, through approval by the Technical Cooperation Committee of successive strategies[3] for the advancement of women in the maritime sector,[4] and the adoption of formal resolutions on the topics of access to maritime training, and fostering employment opportunities for women in the maritime sector.

The principles and objectives of IMO's gender strategy were presented at the First International Conference on "Arab Women Managers and Sustainable Development", held in Alexandria in March, 1997. The Conference revealed the practical benefits of regional networking as a mechanism for supporting individual women in professions where women represented a minority percentage of the managers and decision-makers. The women employed in the maritime sector faced similar organizational constraints which stemmed from the lack of a nucleus or core-group: the isolation of women in their respective professional forums was a proven disadvantage in terms of receiving practical support on operational issues which were compounded by long-term consequences relating to promotion opportunities.

The Programme objectives are practical and direct:

1. to integrate women into mainstream maritime activities;
2. to improve access for women to maritime training and technology; and
3. to encourage the appointment and promotion of women to senior managerial posts within the maritime sector.

Ultimately, IMO also seeks to make women more "visible" as resources for the maritime sector.

In celebration of the 25th Anniversary of IMO's capacity-building and gender programme for women in the maritime sector, a video entitled "Women at the Helm" was produced using material and interviews sourced during the Women in Shipping and Trade Association (WISTA) Annual Conference (Paris 2012), and the

---

[1] Phase 1: Establishment of formal institutional structures and awareness-building (1988–1996).

[2] Phase 2: Supporting capacity-building and fostering regional co-operation (1997–2004).

[3] TC 37 (June 1992): approval of Medium-term Plan for the Integration of Women in the Maritime Sector (1992–1996).

[4] TC 44 (June 1997): approval of Action Programme for Equal Opportunities and Advancement of Women in the Maritime Sector (1997–2001).

annual WOMESA meeting (Namibia 2012), which includes interviews with female welders and carpenters employed by the Port of Walvis Bay. The video was screened for the first time at the Regional Conference on the Development of a Global Strategy for Women Seafarers,[5] held in Busan, Republic of Korea, in April 2013.

4 Capacity Building: The Cornerstone of Development

Two fundamental aspects determine the promotion of women as an integral resource for the maritime sector: first, facilitating their acquisition of the necessary education and skills to participate in the workforce; and, second, promoting their entry and progressive career advancement in actual employment.

Consequently, support from IMO through training and fellowships has been a constant element of the gender strategy since its inception. "Why do we need gender-specific fellowships?" is a frequently asked question—well, the aim of such gender-specific fellowships is twofold: to improve national maritime capacities and to facilitate the integration of women into the mainstream sectoral development of the maritime industry by overcoming attitudinal and structural constraints. The Programme provides the initial impetus to overcome some of the barriers of accession to the highest level maritime posts, by circumventing situations where male candidates may traditionally be given preference, particularly when funding is scarce.

5 "Networking": Developing Regional Partnerships

The isolation of women at the professional level has long been a proven disadvantage in terms of those women receiving practical support on operational issues, compounded by long-term consequences relating to promotion opportunities. Yet, in the maritime and shipping industry, considerable benefit can be derived from a regionally cohesive approach to the harmonized implementation of IMO instruments; and key to that strategy is the work undertaken by formal associations, hitherto mostly organized by male officials whose networks provide practical operational tools for improved communication. Consequently, building on that concept, the Programme facilitated the launch of regional associations for women managers in the maritime and port sectors, with vigour and enthusiasm coming from the women. To-date, the following networks have been established:

[5] The Conference was concluded with the Busan Declaration: http://www.imo.org/MediaCentre/HotTopics/women/Documents/BUSAN%20DECLARATION(Revised1)%20(3).pdf.

- Pacific Women in Maritime Association (PacWIMA)—established February 2004;
- Network for Professional Women in the Maritime and Port Sectors of the West and Central Africa region—established February 2007;
- Arab International Women's Maritime Forum for MENA[6] and Africa—established July 2007;
- Association for Women Managers in the maritime sector of the Eastern and Southern Africa (WOMESA)—established December 2007;
- Association for Women Managers in the Maritime Sector, Asia (WIMA-Asia)—established in January 2010; and
- Forum for Women Managers in the Maritime Sector, Latin America—established March 2012.

In a nutshell, how do women managers benefit from these networks?

- Greater training opportunities;
- Greater visibility in the work-place;
- Increased recognition from colleagues and employers;
- Practical forum for the exchange of information on the effective implementation of international instruments; and
- Increased awareness, by national administrations, of the role of women as a valuable professional resource.

Back to the innovative slogan "think maritime – think women": it belongs to WOMESA, a network which represents the "best-practice" for replacing the isolation of women with specific and above all, practical channels of communication: between ports, maritime authorities, shipping agents, and indeed all maritime stakeholders in the subregion. Constructive use of the formal framework started with the linch-pin which is the third MDG "Promoting gender equality and empowering women"; WOMESA also hitches its goals to the Abuja Maritime Transport Declaration on "The role of maritime transport in the development of Africa", and to the Plan of Action adopted in 2007 which specifies the need to "enhance the capacities and promote integration of women in the maritime sector".

6 Supporting the "Maritime Women: Global Leadership"

Amongst the plethora of milestones reached at the Maritime Women: Global Leadership Conference, one of the most significant was the gathering, for the first time, of participants from all six regional associations for maritime women—truly a global example of the wealth of skills and knowledge already available to the maritime sector.

[6] MENA: Middle East and North Africa.

Marking the outcome of the Leadership Conference, this book is testament to the dedication of those women who, at a time when the industry was staunchly male-dominated, had the vision to appreciate the value of seafaring and shipping as a fulfilling career. In addition, the articles bear witness to the foresight of the administrations that forged the way for those women by facilitating their access to training at their national maritime academies and thereafter to employment on national vessels and in administrations. By peeling back the layers of progression of the pivotal phases in maritime history, the articles disclose to the reader the rich testimonials of individual women who served in shipping and whose personal experiences as "ice-breakers" give the true flavour of "maritime life" for a woman.

By publicizing past achievements, the book will serve to encourage many new female and male recruits to the maritime industry in all its forms.

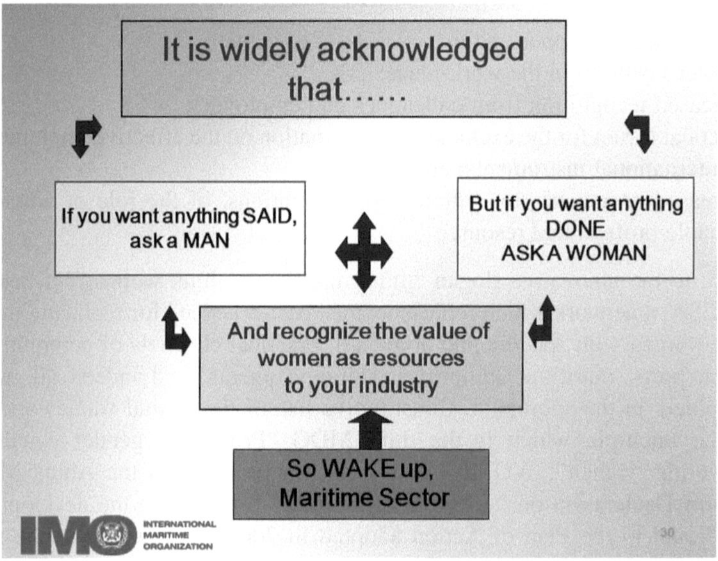

Leading Change: The ITF Women's Maritime Leadership Programme

Alison McGarry

Abstract Women activists in the International Transport Workers' Federation (ITF), face significant challenges in providing leadership for working men and women in maritime industries. But a leadership programme developed specifically for women members, can do more than provide them with the skills and tools necessary to lead within the affiliate unions of the ITF. Building women's leadership is crucial for the strength of global unions. Union density is falling, which demands that leaders find new methods to organise and bargain to build workers' power. The strongest unions will have women involved at all levels of their organisations. The ITF women's leadership programme—Leading Change—prepares women activists to meet the challenge of dynamic leadership within their unions and global society. Elected and emerging women leaders have the opportunity to develop their leadership strengths and identify ways to make their unions stronger. Leading Change, developed in concert with the Harvard Trade Union Program, seeks to enable participants to plan strategic change to lead ITF affiliates, to strengthen the international trade union movement and to advance the cause of women workers across the globe.

Keywords Leadership • Organising • Transport • Unions • Women

1 Background: The ITF and Global Union Federations (GUFs)

The ITF is a global union organisation with member unions in 148 countries worldwide. Any independent trade union with members in the transport industry is eligible for membership in the ITF. Approximately 700 unions, representing over 4.5 million workers in all modes of transport, are members of the ITF. It is one of several Global Union Federations, or GUFs, allied with the International Trade Union Confederation (ITUC). Although the ITF is involved in a range of activities

A. McGarry (✉)
International Transport Workers' Federation, Women Transport Workers' Coordinator, London, UK
e-mail: Mcgarry_Alison@itf.org.uk

© Springer-Verlag Berlin Heidelberg 2015
M. Kitada et al. (eds.), *Maritime Women: Global Leadership*, WMU Studies in Maritime Affairs 3, DOI 10.1007/978-3-662-45385-8_3

with respect to its affiliate unions, most of these fall under one of four key headings: (1) representation—helping affiliate unions defend the interests of their unions; (2) information—providing research and information services to affiliate unions about developments within the international transport industry; (3) practical solidarity—organising international solidarity when transport unions in one country are in conflict with employers or government and need direct help from unions in other countries (the ITF's worldwide campaign in the maritime industry against the use by ship owners of so-called Flags of Convenience to skirt national laws and worker protections, is one recent example); and (4) organising—assisting affiliates to organise new members into their ranks.

The ITF and its member unions, face enormous challenges in today's fast-growing—and quickly changing—globalised transport industry. The global downturn, combined with privatisation, deregulation and commercialisation, have resulted in significant job losses and reduced union membership. At the same time, however, the transport industry is growing, creating new areas of employment that are often casual, precarious and unregulated.

2 The ITF and Women Transport Workers

Women transport workers are entering transport-related industries in growing numbers. According to ITF data, more than a quarter of a million women belong to the ITF, comprising between 13 and 17 % of the membership. The biggest proportion of ITF's women members can be found in the passenger air transport sector, while the highest proportion of women working within the transport sector overall, is in tourism-related transport. Despite occupational segregation, more women are working in operational transport jobs that were previously the preserve of their male colleagues (Turnbull et al. 2009). A growing number of women work in ports as crane operators and stevedores, train and truck drivers, ship's officers and airline pilots. Women transport workers can be found in Argentina's merchant fleet, driving trains in Morocco and operating cranes in India. These women tend to join trade unions, as they are a recognised part of the traditional transport workforce.

But women's involvement in this sector goes beyond operational transport jobs. Women's employment in the transport industry has changed along with the industry itself. Globalisation demands effective supply-chain management and depends on distribution centres to store and assemble goods, on transnational company alliances to deliver cheap goods and passenger services, on call centres to take bookings, and on express delivery services to get goods to consumers. Many of the new workers in these areas are women, who work in large numbers in service, information and administration jobs related to transport. Such jobs include security guard positions created in ports in response to new security measures, as well as logistical, technical and administrative positions. Huge new warehouses that serve the international transport industry and function as logistical hubs in locations such as Hong Kong, also employ significant numbers of women. Significantly, women working in the transport-related jobs described above, are much less likely to be organised. The outsourcing and offshoring of ticketing and business processes in rail and aviation, has meant an increase in transport-related call-centre staff in India and the Philippines, for example, most of whom do not belong to a union (Holman et al. 2007).

3 Why Organise Women Workers

In most countries, less than 40 % of the employed population belongs to unions, and women tend to join in lower numbers than men.[1] Yet trade unions are unquestionably beneficial for working women (ILO 2007). According to the ITUC, the gender pay gap, estimated at approximately 22 % globally, is generally lower for women who are members of trade unions. Meanwhile, the impacts of globalisation and global recession have been borne disproportionately by women workers. Women were more likely to lose their jobs first, and lost more jobs than men during the global economic crisis (Stavrapoulou and Jones 2013). They are more likely to hold part-time or non-permanent jobs, or to work in the informal economy where work is insecure, wages are low, working conditions are poor, and workers are least likely to be protected by conventional social insurance programmes. Organising such workers into effective unions, can provide a meaningful opportunity to improve their workplaces, their standards of living and their status in society.

Unions can also play a key role in responding to big social issues that disproportionately impact women. The ITF has been at the forefront of pioneering work on HIV/AIDS, public transport provision and other transformative community initiatives. In addition to organising and collective bargaining in order to win concrete financial and workplace benefits for women members, the ITF also sees itself as having an important social role to play in responding to climate change—and its particular impact on women—violence and global pandemics. In turn, broadening the vision of unions to incorporate issues far beyond traditional workplace concerns, has the added benefit of attracting women to unions. Women workers want their unions to address, not just workplace issues, but conditions that affect their families, their health and their social status (Kirton and Healy 2013).

As women represent a growing portion of global transport workers, ITF and other unions in this sector must be able organize and represent women workers more effectively, if the unions are to survive and thrive. There are some positive signs on this front. A recent gender audit of membership, carried out by the ITF of maritime members, indicated that by far the strongest growth of membership is amongst women members (ITF 2014). But organizing is only part of this equation. Women members must also be able to participate in all areas of union life, including leadership. For traditionally male-dominated unions like the ITF, such a transition requires a multi-pronged effort that entails changing the culture of the union, creating separate structures for women leaders and providing training and

[1] UNIFEM, World Value survey database 1999–2004.

leadership development opportunities in order that women members can lead change in the ITF and in their own communities.

4 History of Women in the ITF: Barriers to Involvement

Historically, women in the ITF have faced significant barriers, both to leadership and to full participation in the lives of their affiliates. The low density of women in the affiliate unions, particularly in the maritime industries, has meant that women members have often been relatively marginalized in their unions (Turnbull et al. 2009). Significantly, this has left women unable to exert influence upon a traditionally male-oriented collective bargaining agenda, meaning that the concerns of women members have been largely excluded in that agenda.

Despite the increasing numbers with which women are entering the transport industry, both the industry and its unions remain male-dominated. This gender imbalance serves to effectively shape the culture of trade unions in a way that tacitly discourages, or actively prevents, the full participation by women members. In surveys of women unionists, they consistently identify the following as limits to greater involvement in their unions (ITF 2013):

1) Practical barriers, including a lack of time for participation due to family activities;
2) Cultural barriers, including meetings that are confrontational and aggressive, and in which women members struggle to make their voices heard; and
3) Stereotyped expectations, in which leadership traits are defined as masculine.

5 Separate Union Structures for Women Unionists

Structures specific to women members originated within labor unions as a counter to the exclusion of women from male-controlled unions. As the workforce participation of women increased dramatically after World War II, women union members began to press for more participation and representation. Unions have approached the representation of their women members through a variety of mechanisms, ranging from formal structures such as women's committees, to representation on union policy-making bodies or the establishment of women's schools, as well as less formal arrangements, such as networks and women's committees.

The introduction of such structures has not always been received positively. Male unionists have often regarded women's committees and the like as "divisive of labor unity" and a drain on resources that should go to all members, regardless of gender. Women unionists, meanwhile, have argued that the creation of separate structures marginalizes them within their organizations (Kirton and Healy 2013). A significant body of scholarly research, however, indicates that separate structures for women members are both necessary and effective in developing the participation, representation and leadership of women. Union structural changes to develop women leaders require:

- Independent space which is key to allowing women to establish their own culture where they can identify issues of importance to them and strategize how to engage and change the dominant culture (Needleman 1996);
- Women-only groups, to enable women unionists to support one another, share ideas and to benefit from the experience of more senior women who can "mentor the less experienced without the opportunity for men to take center stage, as is so frequently the case in the union environment" (Kirton and Healy 2013); and
- Women's committees, which play a role in politicizing women unionists, enabling them to become a more effective constituency within their organisations (Kirton and Healy 2013).

6 Formation of the ITF Women Transport Workers Committee

In recent years, the ITF has made a concerted effort to build the democratic and active involvement of women members at all levels of trade union life. The ITF supports a two-staged approach to bringing about change within the union and its affiliates: building women's or equality structures, leading to eventual gender mainstreaming. Key to this process of strengthening women's involvement, was the creation of a women's committee to ensure that women's voices were heard throughout the federation and its affiliate unions.

Delegates to the ITF's 39th congress in New Delhi in 1994, voted to create the ITF Women Transport Workers Committee, to consist of elected representatives by geographic region and industry section. The goals of the new committee were set forth as: (1) collecting information, including member surveys; (2) assisting with collective bargaining; (3) supporting organising activity; (4) developing and strengthening a network of women within the ITF; (5) monitoring women's involvement within the ITF and identifying areas where participation targets needed to be set; (6) focusing on women's education, including ITF-run training courses; and (7) ensuring a gender dimension to all ITF activities.

The ITF Women Transport Workers' Committee currently consists of 37 members, representing over 27 different countries, and includes a chair, along with sectional and regional representatives. The ITF vice-president and four women ITF executive board members, have reserved seats on the committee. Members of the ITF Women Transport Workers Committee are elected at Congress, the ITF's top decision-making body. The committee, which meets twice yearly, oversees the work of the women's policy and work programme within the ITF.

In the two decades since it was formed, the ITF Women Transport Workers Committee has had a particular focus on developing women trade union leaders, to lead both workplace campaigns and build union/community alliances. The development of women leaders helps the ITF both to move towards achieving gender equity within the union, and building the union capacity necessary to undertake campaigns on big social issues that impact women, including climate change, HIV and the lack of accessible public transport. Creating networks, both formal and informal, among women members from different sectors and regions, has been another priority. Such networks, now operating in Africa, the Middle East and the West, enable women transport trade unionists to link up with each other to exchange experiences, materials and information.

Diana Holland, the Chair of the ITF Women's Committee from its creation commented, "The ITF Women Transport Workers' Committee, which I have the great honor to chair, ensures action at the workplace and in the wider community for women transport workers: on violence against women, sexual harassment, on pregnancy discrimination, maternity and family rights, on equal pay, women's health and appropriate protective clothing and uniforms; and the ITF also supports positive action and union education to tackle under-representation of women in the transport workplace and in union leadership roles. Women transport workers make transport unions stronger!"[2]

7 ITF's Women's Leadership Programme

Following a recommendation from the ITF Maritime Section Women's Committee representatives, the ITF women's conference held in 2010, mandated the ITF Women's Department to introduce a leadership development programme for women activists, to be rolled out to affiliated unions through ITF regions and sections. The programme, called *Leading Change*, was created with the aim of preparing women activists to meet the challenge of dynamic leadership within their unions and global society. But it also had a more practical focus. As the ranks of women members within the ITF swelled, there was also an increase in the number of women holding elected office within ITF affiliates—and yet they often lacked the knowledge or experience to function effectively. Jacqueline Smith, the President of the Norwegian Seafarer's International Union, and a member of the ITF Women Transport Workers' Committee, explains the need for a leadership development programme this way:

> We're having a lot of women elected within the ITF but they need to be developed as leaders. We need a serious programme in order to help the sisters understand the work. Our women members need an analysis and understanding. They need to be able to stand up and speak, utilizing their own experience in a constructive and useful way so that they can inspire others to take action.[3]

---

[2] Interview with Diana Holland, March 20, 2014.

[3] Interview with Jacqueline Smith, January 23, 2014.

Smith and other leaders of the ITF Women Transport Workers' Committee, stressed the need for a serious, structured programme that would educate women members about unions and the political and policy context in which they operate. But most importantly, the leadership programme, to be planned, developed and delivered by the ITF Women's Department, would introduce ITF leaders-in-training to the concept of strategic planning. Such training, Smith and others argued, would develop the leadership strengths of emerging women leaders, as well as helping them to identify opportunities to strengthen their unions. Members of the ITF Women Transport Workers' Committee, also saw the leadership programme as essential to realizing their larger goal of gender equality, in the ITF and beyond. In short, a successful leadership development programme would enable participants to plan the strategic change to lead ITF affiliates, strengthen women's involvement in the ITF and other trade unions, and progress the women's agenda.

8 Partnership with the Harvard Trade Union Programme

From its inception, the programme reflected collaboration between the Women Transport Workers Coordinator at the ITF and the Harvard Trade Union Programme (HTUP), directed by Dr. Elaine Bernard. Begun in 1942, the HTUP prepares union activists to meet the challenge of dynamic leadership within their unions and society (Trumpbour 2008). Through an intensive 6-week executive training programme, based at the Harvard University Law School in Cambridge, MA, the HTUP helps union leaders develop keener analytical, managerial and problem-solving skills, as well as discover ways to deepen public understanding of the value and importance of labor unions. The programme has an explicit focus on helping union leaders to respond to the unprecedented change and profound challenges within today's labor movement, including dramatic changes in the world economy and the nature, size and composition, all of which demand new approaches to organizing, bargaining and union administration.

Working with Dr. Bernard, the ITF Women's Department, along with leaders of the ITF Women Transport Workers' Committee, set out to create a leadership development programme modeled upon the HTUP.[4] While necessarily more limited in scope and focus than the HTUP, the ITF women's leadership programme drew upon key components of the Harvard training, including strategic planning and SWOT analysis, in which members analyze strengths, weaknesses, opportunities, and threats in a project or campaign. Explains Bernard: "The thinking behind this kind of analytic training, is that members learn the skills they need to first assess the context in which their unions operate, and then they can actually drive change from within their unions".[5]

---

[4] Graduates of the Leading Change programme receive a joint certificate issued by the ITF and Harvard University.

[5] Interview with Elaine Bernard, February 15, 2014.

9 Inaugural Session of Leading Change

An invitation to potential women leaders within the ITF went out the affiliate unions within the maritime sections in May of 2011. Women activists were invited to attend a weeklong conference that would:

- Support women activists to develop their leadership strengths; and
- Identify opportunities for the ITF and its affiliates to build strong unions to enable the women participants to plan strategic change to lead ITF affiliates to take advantage of the integrated global transport supply chain.

Due to space and budget constraints, participation was limited to women leaders who held elected positions within the ITF and/or the national union level. Affiliates were also encouraged to recommend women activists who held leadership positions within the company or workplace level. Furthermore, only participants directly involved in union organizing, collective bargaining and/or organizational change, were eligible to attend.

Forty-three leaders from ITF maritime unions across the globe attended the first conference of the women's leadership programme, entitled Leadership, Strategy and Organizing. The initial training was held at the Paul Hall Center for Maritime Training and Education, of the Seafarers International Union (SIU), thanks to the support of Dave Heindal, chair of the ITF Seafarers' Section. Heindal supported the programme from its inception and provided the SIU training facility at no charge. The 6-day conference dove deep into leadership, including analyses of what leaders do and how they do it. Subsequent sessions focused on strategic planning, in which activists were taught how to assess their unions, as well as the contexts in which their organizations operate. And because the women activists all came from the maritime sector, the focus of the teaching was specifically targeted to address issues in that sector. Participants reviewed the 1998 Maritime Union of Australia dispute from a strategic change perspective, then used their new knowledge to analyze ITF campaigns within the maritime sector.

The final sessions of the conference were devoted to action planning for the women activists to take back to their unions and workplaces. As Bernard explains, the action plans required the leaders to incorporate what they'd learned about strategic planning into a vision for change to be implemented once they returned to their unions and workplaces. "It's a very action-oriented approach. The participants leave, not just with an understanding of their industry, their union and the larger trade-union movement, but with the skills to be able to lead real change as women union members".[6]

Most importantly, says Mich-Elle Myers, the National Officer, Growth and Campaigns Team for the Maritime Union of Australia, the leadership programme was both targeted to and delivered by women.[7]

[6] Interview with Elaine Bernard, February 15, 2014.

[7] Interview with Mich-Elle Myers, ITF Women's Committee meeting, May 13, 2014.

> The leadership programme is effective, as it is targeted to women and delivered by women. The course content is tailored to assisting women become leaders in their own right. Provide women with the essential tools of organizing, combine that with leadership techniques and analyses of your own personality and you have a whole package for the leader of tomorrow.

ITF staff and leaders of the ITF Women Transport Workers' Committee, viewed the inaugural women's leadership programme as an unqualified success. Not only had they successfully pulled off an intense conference that took the HTUP's focus on strategic planning and introduced it to emerging women leaders, but the programme participants gave the training rave reviews—and pushed for follow-on events that their colleagues could attend. But the organizers also recognized that the first programme was essentially a pilot project, limited to women members within a single ITF sector. While the benefits of sector-specific training were obvious, and easily replicable, it remained to be seen whether organizers could bring together women from various sectors within the ITF, while still maintaining the same structured focus. Organizers also began to think about offering regionally-specific training to women members based in India, Africa the Caribbean and beyond.

10 Leading Change, Phase II: Expanding Regional Reach

The second session of Leading Change was held in London in 2012, and was offered to aspiring women leaders in ITF affiliate unions across industry sectors, including road, rail, maritime and civil aviation. Forty-five women activists participated, including several members of the ITF Women Transport Workers' Committee, who had enrolled in the inaugural session. While the training once again emphasized strategic planning and analysis, the perspective was broader this time, centered on the global transport industry as a whole and the forces of globalization and privatization that are rapidly transforming it. For the organizers, the success of the session offered proof that the training could be just as effective when offered to women members across sectors. But the London programme also made clear the challenges of scaling up the training to any significant degree. While the inaugural session had been offered with the financial assistance of another union, most of the expense of the London training was borne by the ITF.[8] And the costs of bringing members of a global union to a central location, can be prohibitive.

Organizers also launched an ambitious effort to offer the training programme to women leaders in different regions, including India, Africa, Europe and the Caribbean. In India, for example, emerging leaders received training on how to lead and

[8] The ITF pays two thirds of the cost of the training, including transport, visas and accommodations for supported participants. The remaining third of the participant's costs is picked up by the members' affiliate unions.

organize within the fast-growing, and often female-dominated, global transport-related sector. Seema Mohan, an organizer for the transport and dock workers' union in India, says that the leadership training enabled her to reflect upon her leadership from a different angle: "There are many qualities that I can develop so that I can work towards organizing at my workplace," says Mohan.[9]

Twenty-five women from all over Africa attended a leadership programme in Addis Ababa, Ethiopia. The training explicitly combined the development of strategic planning skills with a deepened understanding and analysis of the social forces and pressures upon women trade unionists in Africa. Betty Makena Mutugi, a leader of the Dockworkers' Union of Kenya, says that the training she received as the first female ITF inspector in Africa, has enabled her to challenge the gender dynamics within African trade unions more broadly.[10]

> The training was excellent, and it really helped me become a stronger trade union leader. Before the training, I thought only men could be ITF inspectors. I also learned how to do the job well, including how to handle the captain. The training also taught me that leadership is not only for men. African trade unions are dominated by men, and it's not easy to become a leader because you have to challenge the men. When I become an ITF inspector, my male colleagues thought I couldn't do it. They were looking at me as a woman, forgetting that I am also a trade union leader. But because I had such good training on leadership at the ITF, I was able to prove to them that I can do it. Now the men think of me as a role model and want me to talk to women in their unions about taking leadership positions.

A training course for women members in the Caribbean, held in Barbados in 2013, shed light on another challenge of offering the programme in specific regions where the ITF and its affiliates have a relatively weak presence. The global economic crisis battered the Barbados Workers' Union (BWU), an ITF affiliate that represents 25,000 Barbadians, including transport workers in air, sea and road.[11] The 5-day programme, which was jointly presented by Dr. Bernard of the HTUP, combined an emphasis on strategic planning and leadership development for women trade unionists, with a more practical "nuts-and-bolts" focus on rebuilding unions in a time of retrenchment. The goal: to develop stronger individual women union leaders, who can then work together across the Caribbean to leverage their collective strength in order to address common challenges. "The effect of the global economic crisis has hit Caribbean transport unions and our membership hard," said Wilma Clement, assistant general secretary at the BWU. "Finding membership dues for organizations like ITF are more and more difficult, so it's been helpful to share experiences with other transport workers in the region".[12]

---

[9] Interview with Seema Mohan, September 20, 2012.

[10] Interview with Betty Makena Mutugi, March 14, 2014.

[11] Wilma Clement, ITF Women's Committee report, October 2013.

[12] Wilma Clement, ITF Women's Committee report, October 2013.

11 Leading Change, Phase III: Building Sector Leaders

The third phase of the ITF's leadership development programme, has continued to build on the sector and regional foci of the initial sessions, but with a more targeted emphasis on equipping women unionists to become sector leaders. In April of 2013, the ITF brought Leading Change to Vigo, Spain for a week-long course offered to women ITF inspectors, port leaders who work directly with seafarers in a field that is both male-dominated, and, in an age of heightened security concerns, increasingly complex. 12 of the ITF's 136 inspectors are women, from countries including Germany, Kenya, Korea, Spain, Sweden, Ukraine and the US.

The week-long training sought to provide the women inspectors with leadership and strategic organisational skills, helping the participants identify ways to work better together, as well as to develop a greater presence of women in the sector. The programme also focused on a specific ITF campaign: the Flags of Convenience Campaign, an effort to enforce minimal acceptable standards applicable to seafarers serving on FOC vessels, and in which ITF inspectors play a key role. While the inspectors represent a single occupation in a single sector, the approaches of their different nations to port enforcement vary widely. The course enabled the women to use practical examples from their own work, in order to compare and contrast the approaches of other nationalities to enforcing labor regulations in the maritime sector.

12 Leading Change: Next Steps

Now entering its third year, the ITF women's maritime leadership programme has succeeded in accomplishing the goals set by the ITF Women Transport Workers' Committee and the women's policy and work program staff. *Leading change* is a serious, structured introduction to strategic planning and leadership development, that is giving women in the ITF the tools to lead within their workplaces and their unions. Yet important work remains to be done. While participants are surveyed at the conclusion of each session, no formal evaluation has yet been carried out to measure the programme's effectiveness and its impact on the leadership abilities of women trade unionists. A training course offered at the Seafarers International Union (SIU) training facility in Maryland in November of 2014, will reconvene participants in earlier sessions, in an effort to begin to quantify the impact of the training in helping to develop women union leaders. The course will also give participants the opportunity to build on the leadership skills they developed during earlier training.

Ironically, the anecdotal success of the programme has led to calls to expand its reach beyond women, to include aspiring trade union leaders of both sexes. As participants return home to their workplaces and union and report their experiences in the leadership programme, their male colleagues have begun to express a strong interest in developing their own leadership skills. At the ITF Seafarers Conference in Chicago in 2013, leaders praised *Leading Change* and suggested it be developed for male trade union leaders.

Stephen Cotton, ITF General Secretary Elect, commented, "The Leading Change programme has raised the bar for leadership development in the ITF; now we need to look at how we can extend the programme to all ITF union leaders".[13]

References

Holman, D., Batt, R., & Holtgrewe, U. (2007). The Global Call Center report: International perspectives on management and employment. Resource document. The Global Call Center Project. http://www.ilr.cornell.edu/globalcallcenter/upload/gcc-intl-rept-us-version.pdf. Accessed 1 Apr 2014.

ILO. (2007). *Equality at work: Tackling the challenges. Global report under the follow-up to the ILO declaration on fundamental principles and rights at work report of the director-general.* Geneva: International Labour Office.

ITF. (2013). Winning a better deal for women: Maritime women's best practice guide. http://www.itfseafarers.org/files/publications/39317/Maritime_Womens_BPG.pdf. Accessed 1 Apr 2014.

ITF. (2014). ITF Women's Conference 2014 – From global crisis to global justice: Women transport workers fight back. http://www.itfwomen2014.org/ITFWomensConference/about. Accessed 1 Apr 2014.

Kirton, G., & Healy, G. (2013). *Gender and leadership in unions*. London: Routledge.

Needleman, R. (1996). Space and opportunities: Developing new leaders to meet labor's future. *Labor Research Review, 1*(20), 5–20.

Stavrapoulou, M., & Jones, N. (2013). Off the balance sheet: The impact of the economic crisis on girls and young women. Resource document. Plan International. http://plan-international.org/files/global/publications/economics/off-the-balance-sheet-english.pdf. Accessed 1 Apr 2014.

Trumpbour, J. (2008). A short history of the Harvard Trade Union Program: 1942–2007. Resource document. Harvard Law School. http://www.law.harvard.edu/programs/lwp/htup/htup08/2008HTUPArticle.pdf. Accessed 12 Mar 2014.

Turnbull, P., Fairbrother, P., Heery, E., Martínez Lucio, M., & Stroud, D. (2009). *Report for the ITF/ETF: Women in ports*. Cardiff: Centre for Global Labour Research, Cardiff University.

[13] Commented on March 2014.

Board Characteristics and the Presence of Women on the Board of Directors: The Case of the Greek Shipping Sector

Aspasia S. Pastra, Dimitrios N. Koufopoulos, and Ioannis P. Gkliatis

Abstract Shipping is a vital sector of the Greek economy. According to the Foundation for Economic & Industrial Research (2013), more than 52 % of the shipping companies listed in the New York Stock Exchange (NYSE) and the NASDAQ Stock Market (NASDAQ) are owned by Greek nationals. Current demands for transparency in the decision making of the shipping firms, led boards to take various initiatives so as to comply with international regulations. This article attempts to discuss the findings of the Hellenic Observatory of Corporate Governance (HOCG) about the Board Characteristics (CEO duality, Board size, Independent Directors, cross directorships, tenure, age and gender) of the Greek-owned public shipping companies which are listed in foreign Stock Exchanges for the period 2001–2012. Special emphasis is given on the presence of Women on the Board of Directors. Possible reasons why women's access to board seats has been limited are discussed, and some practical suggestions to the Shipping owners to consider adding qualified women to the board are presented.

Keywords Board characteristics • Greece • Listed companies • Shipping sector • Women

1 Introduction

Some of the highly-publicized frauds that shocked public confidence and investors, include those of Enron, Tyco International, World Com and Adelphia. These scandals have cost investors billions of dollars, as the share price of these companies collapsed. One of the immediate steps that were taken for proper corporate governance practices, was the federal law called the Sarbanes-Oxley Act (SOX) enacted July 30, 2002. The Act affects all companies that are registered on US

A.S. Pastra (✉)
Gnosis Management Consultants, London, UK
e-mail: aspasia@gnosisconsultants.com

D.N. Koufopoulos • I.P. Gkliatis
Brunel University, Brunel Business School, Uxbridge, UK

© Springer-Verlag Berlin Heidelberg 2015
M. Kitada et al. (eds.), *Maritime Women: Global Leadership*, WMU Studies in Maritime Affairs 3, DOI 10.1007/978-3-662-45385-8_4

Equity Markets and which are required to file financial reports with the Securities & Exchange Commission (SEC). The recent surge of interest in corporate governance is a result of these corporate accounting and fraud scandals.

One of the most widely used definitions of corporate governance is "the system by which companies are directed and controlled" (Cadbury 1992). This system, through various mechanisms and controls, oversees top management and protects the interests of the various stakeholders. The Board of Directors (BoD) play an important monitoring role in the governance structure of the organization and a large volume of literature has been focused on the board composition. Unfortunately, research in corporate governance and Board of Directors in shipping companies is still weak. Koufopoulos et al. (2010) affirm that Greek shipping firms are an interesting field of study, due to several structural traits that these firms have. These companies operate in international freight markets and struggle to comply with standards of their financiers and with global regulations on safety, marine pollution and quality excellence. In the last 12 years, a number of Greek shipping firms have gone public and altered the way they are organized and managed. According to The Foundation for Economic & Industrial Research, IOBE (Foundation for Economic & Industrial Research 2013), more than 52 % of the shipping companies listed in NYSE and NASDAQ are owned by Greek nationals.

For 5 years, the annual maritime studies of the Hellenic Observatory of Corporate Governance (HOCG) have been dedicated to the study of corporate governance principles in the Greek Business environment. This article discusses the findings of the HOCG about the Board Characteristics (CEO duality, board size, external independent directors, cross directorships, tenure, age and gender) of the Greek-owned public shipping companies which are listed in foreign Stock Exchanges for the period 2001–2012. The study aims to increase our knowledge of board characteristic in Shipping Companies, while providing evidence on women's underrepresentation on the Board of Directors.

2 Theoretical Framework

2.1 Board Composition

With the term Board Characteristics, we refer to the Board Composition as well as to the demographic characteristics of the Board. One important issue of discussion under agency theory is the Board composition, as it is considered a crucial element to the board's ability to achieve the organization's goals, by protecting the interests of the shareholders. A Board's composition is of paramount importance for achieving the organization's aims, but there is not a unanimous description of which characteristics could lead to a successful board. For the purposes of this research, we will discuss the major dimensions of board composition, which are CEO duality, Board size, independent directors, cross directorships as well as the Demographic Characteristics which include tenure, age and gender.

2.1.1 CEO Duality

"CEO duality" occurs when the same individual holds both the CEO and Chairperson's positions in a corporation (Rechner and Dalton 1991). Should the CEO also serve as the Chairman of its board of directors? This is a critical question in board governance, but a definite answer has not been given yet, since a number of factors, such as size of the organization, the industry and the external environment, have to be taken into consideration. Various arguments, fortified by the Agency theory, have been raised about the separation of the two roles. Two of the basic arguments for the separation of the Chairman and CEO role are based on the improvement of the financial performance and the enhancement of the BOD's monitoring role over a powerful CEO. A dominant CEO could affect negatively the interests of the shareholders, since he/she has the power to focus mainly on his/her personal interests. The paradox of CEO duality for agency theorists, is that the CEO cannot be the leader of the team that has been created to evaluate his/her own performance. The CEO chair is a demanding role, that requires setting the strategy for monitoring the daily operations of the organisation. Syriopoulos and Tsatsaronis (2012), in their study of 43 listed shipping firms, found that CEO separation has a positive impact on the financial performance of shipping firms (as Return on Equity and Return on Assets), in support of agency theory.

On the other hand, supporters of stewardship theory (Donaldson and Davis 1991) put forward arguments about CEO duality, since in this way, a uniform command chain can be achieved (Peng et al. 2007). Under stewardship theory, the CEO does not act opportunistically, but serves as a steward of the organization. Duality has also been associated with increased corporate performance (Donaldson and Davis 1991; Davis et al. 1997) and corporate reputation (Musteen et al. 2010).

2.1.2 Board Size

Board Size is an indicator of the heterogeneity found on the board. Determining the optimal size of a board of directors, one that maximizes corporate performance, remains an ongoing challenge for management scholars. Some researchers have suggested a 'sweet spot' of 8–10 members (Lipton and Lorsch 1992) while others suggest that boards should be sufficiently large, but not larger than 7 or 8 members (Jensen 1993). Larger boards prevent the CEO from taking actions against shareholders' interests (Singh and Harianto 1989) and blend together a broad set of experiences. Upadhyay and Sriram (2011) proposed that for companies who encounter an information gap between managers and outside investors, larger boards bring significant advantages, by creating a better information environment, than smaller boards. Dalton et al. (1999) in their meta-analysis of 131 samples, provided evidence that larger boards could improve performance, as a consequence of the ability of the firm to form environmental links and secure critical resources.

However, a smaller group allows for increased participation and social cohesion (Muth and Donaldson 1998) and due to that, it increases board's performance (Koufopoulos et al. 2008). A growing body of research has examined the relationship of board size on the performance of the firm. Eisenberg et al. (1998), consistent with the findings of Yermack (1996), revealed a negative correlation between a firm's profitability and board size in small firms.

2.1.3 External Independent Directors

A high proportion of outsiders on the board has been considered a sign of good corporate practice. In the literature, it is strongly argued that high participation of independent directors can bring different attributes to the boardroom, and objectivity in strategic decision making (Fama and Jensen 1983). Independent directors are in line with the agency theory, since they boost the monitoring function of the Board. In addition to the agency theory, the appointment of external directors in a board can also be useful in terms of provision of critical resources (Hillman et al. 2009). Different sizes and types of organizations may require different quotas of external directors. For example, García-Ramos and Olalla (2012), who examined firms with family ownership structure, found that there is an ideal level of independent directors in those firms run by the second or later generations, and excessive monitoring by independent directors could prove detrimental to company performance over generations.

2.1.4 Cross Directorships

Cross directorships is used in this paper to describe the phenomenon that is widely discussed as interlocking directorate in the literature (Bazerman and Schoorman 1983; Davis 1991; Shipilov et al. 2010). An interlocking directorate occurs when a person affiliated with one organization sits on the board of directors of another organization (Mizruchi 1996). Schoorman et al. (1981) support that interlockings reduce uncertainty in the market environment of the firm via the following ways: (a) establishment of horizontal coordination between competitors; (b) establishment of vertical coordination; (c) knowledge and expertise of the Director; and (d) increased reputation. It has also been pointed out in the literature, that directors who serve on multiple boards, have an increased workload and cannot spend enough time on their monitoring role (Core et al. 1999).

2.2 Demographic Characteristics

2.2.1 Tenure

Long-tenured executives could bring significant advantages to the organization and perform their duties with greater skills and knowledge. "Longer tenure of top executives is accompanied by greater identification with the organization, and leads to the development of firm-specific sets by senior executives" (Singh and Harianto 1989). Longer-term tenure improves both social integration and ease of communication (Smith et al. 1994). Nevertheless, different findings have also been presented, demonstrating that longer tenure could benefit management at the expense of shareholders (Vafeas 2003). Executives with longer tenures used to reap many direct and indirect benefits, and their appointment was usually a source of pride. But, in recent years, interesting discussions have been made about executive's tenure and whether there should be limits on the length of service, to protect shareholder's value and avoid entrenchment.

2.2.2 Age

Older directors have great experience and knowledge in the field under consideration. On the other hand, there is evidence of risk aversion for new ventures, since there are times that their career security is their main priority. It has been supported that younger generations of directors have more environmental and ethical concerns (Hafsi and Turgut 2013). There seems to exist a positive relationship between managerial youth and corporate growth (Child 1974). Wiersema and Bantel (1992) found that the firms most likely to undergo changes in corporate strategy, had top management teams characterized by lower average age, and Golden and Zajac (2001) found that board member age is positively related to strategic change. The age of the CEO has also been discussed in the literature. For example, Platt and Platt (2012) found that CEOs of not-bankrupt companies, are on average 55 years old, and CEOs of bankrupt companies are just 52.8 years old; confirming that firms with younger CEOs are prone to bankruptcy.

Despite the age caps and limits on length of service that have been proposed, the Spencer Stuart U.S. Board Index (Spencer Stuart 2013) reveals that there is an increased number of boards that raised their mandatory retirement age to 75, or older. Another finding of this Index also reveals that 44 % of S&P 500 boards have an average age of 64 years or older.

2.2.3 Gender

Various studies have presented the significant effects in firm value and financial performance, that stem from female representation in the boards. Carter et al. (2003) examined the association between board diversity and firm value in the context of agency theory, and noted a significant positive relationship between the fraction of women on the board and firm value, as measured by Tobin's Q. Cambell and Mínguez-Vera (2008) presented the peculiarities of the environment of Spanish companies and examined, using panel data analysis, the link between gender diversity and firm value. Their findings revealed that the presence of women on the board of directors does not, in itself, affect firm value. What affects firm value, is the diversity of the board, namely the ratio between women and men.

Erhardt et al. (2003), examining the effects of the executive board of director diversity, found a positive relationship between the percentage of women on the boards of large U.S. firms and return on assets, as well as return on investment. Catalyst (2004) tested 353 *Fortune 500* companies and confirmed that companies with the highest representation of women on their top management teams, had significantly higher Returns on Equity and Total Shareholder Returns, compared to the companies with the lowest female representation. Gul et al. (2013) examined the link between gender diversity and analysts' earnings forecast accuracy, and they concluded that their proxies for properties of analyst earnings forecasts, are significantly correlated with the presence of women on boards.

However, Rose (2007), examining the link between performance and female board representation, found no significant association between them. Haslam et al. (2010), in their study of FTSE 100 companies for the period 2001–2005, consistent with work by Adams et al. (2009), found no relationship between women's presence on boards and the profitability of the company, expressed by the return on assets and return on equity. The interesting aspect in the research, was the negative link between women's presence on boards and 'subjective' stock-based measures of performance.

3 Methodology

3.1 Population/Sample

Data was collected both from the annual reports found in the corporate websites of the Greek maritime companies and from the websites of the stock exchanges in which the company was listed. As such, the Securities & Exchange Commission (SEC),[1] the New York Stock Exchange,[2] the London Stock Exchange,[3] the Nasdaq Stock Market[4] and the Singapore Stock Exchange[5] were consulted. The data

[1] www.sec.gov.

[2] www.nyse.com.

[3] www.londonstockexchange.com.

[4] www.nasdaq.com.

[5] www.sgx.com.

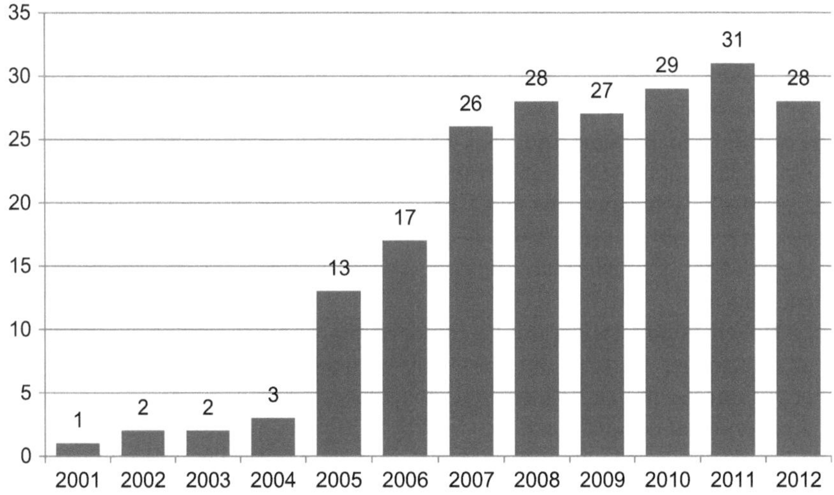

Fig. 1 Number of Greek Maritime Listed Companies (2001–2012)

collection process took place during the summer of 2013, while the analysis was based on 34 maritime companies.

In Fig. 1, we can see the number of Greek-Owned, Abroad-listed Maritime companies operating during the years 2001–2012.

3.2 *Variables Analyzed*

The study examined the following variables for the period 2001–2012:

CEO Duality, as of December 31st of each year, was captured by examining whether the CEO was also the Chairperson, or whether the two positions were separate.

Board Size was measured by capturing the number of serving directors of each company, as of December 31st of each year.

Average Board Size was measured by calculating the average of each company's board size, throughout the years.

External Independent Directors was measured by calculating the sum of all Independent Directors that served on the Boards of the Companies.

Average Tenure of the Board members was measured by calculating the sum of the serving period (in months) of all directors (including Chairman and CEO), divided by their total number for each company.

Average Tenure of Board Members (in months) was measured as the "Average Tenure of the Board", but excluding the Chairperson(s) and the CEO(s).

Average Tenure of Chairpersons and **Average Tenure of CEOs** was measured by calculating the sum of the serving period (in months) for the Chairpersons or

CEOs of each company, divided by the total number of Chairpersons or CEOs that served in each of the companies throughout the years.

Board Member age was captured by recording the date of birth of directors and calculating their age for December 31st 2012.

Age of the Chairpersons and the CEOs was captured by recording their date of birth and calculating their age by the end of each year, for the period 2001–2012.

The gender of Chairpersons and CEOs was identified by their full names.

Cross Directorships were identified by the directors that were serving in more than one board simultaneously, and recorded along with the corresponding companies.

Total Board Memberships was captured **for the whole sample**, by the number of all directorships through the years. This particular variable captures the number of positions/seats that Boards have, rather than the number of persons (individual directors) that occupy them.

Total Male Board Memberships (for the whole population and all years) was captured by the absolute number of male directorships that existed within the Boards through the years. The exact number was ascertained by examining both their names and surnames. Further, we calculated the **total male board members**, by excluding any cross directorships and/or mobility.

Total Female Board Memberships (for the whole population and all years) was captured by the absolute number of female directorships that existed within the Boards through the years. The exact number was ascertained by examining their names and surnames. Additionally, we calculated the **total female board members** by excluding any cross directorships or/and mobility.

Total Board Members was calculated by excluding any mobility and/or cross directorships from the total board memberships. This variable captures the absolute number of directors that serve as board members in one or more companies.

The number of Chairpersons and CEOs was calculated by counting the absolute number of Chairpersons and CEOs respectively, for each company through the years.

3.3 Greek Shipping Context

Greece is a global leader in the maritime industry and the Greek ship-owners are well known for their entrepreneurial skills. Boston Consulting Group (2013) revealed that Greek-owned fleets rank first in the world in total capacity, and Greek owners control more than 4,000 ships, whereas Petrofin Research (2013) found that there were 690 Greek-based ship management companies in 2013.

Greek ship-owners' foresight is particularly evident when shipping is getting drowned by bursting credit and commodity bubbles. There are shipping families that count up to seven generations of maritime expertise, and have been considered as the most dominant shipping dynasties of the world. Strong family ties in ownership, informal networks and clustering, are an important uniqueness of the sector. In the last 9 years, a number of Greek shipping firms have gone public, and altered their way of being organized and managed; it is very interesting to depict what a board in this sector looks like. According to the Foundation for Economic & Industrial Research (2013), more than 52 % of the shipping companies listed in NYSE and NASDAQ by the end of 2012, were owned by Greek nationals.

4 Findings

4.1 Board Demographics

4.1.1 CEO Duality

In our study, the CEO duality/separation was examined at the end of December for the period 2001–2012. Figure 2 illustrates that across the years, there is a tendency for many companies towards a more concentrating structure of governance, where the Chair and the CEO is the same individual. In 15 (53.6 %) out of the 28 companies listed in Stock Exchanges for the end of 2012, CEO and Chairperson positions were in control of one person.

4.1.2 Board Size

For the period 2001–2012, the average board size was 6.61, noting that most companies prefer a board between 6 and 7 members, as depicted in Fig. 3. A board of 7 members seems to be the preferred size for a large majority of companies (44.1 %), followed by a board of 6 members (17.6 %). The smallest board comprised 4 members, and the largest 10. If we look solely at the companies that were listed in the stock exchanges for 2012, we note that for these 28 companies, the findings are similar to the 34 companies examined in the period 2001–2012, since these companies prefer a BOD between 6 and 7 members.

We should also note that the average board size, as of December 31st each year, fluctuated from 6 to 9 members in the years 2001–2012 (Fig. 4).

4.1.3 External Independent Directors

For the 305 BOD positions that were created in these 12 years, 174 seats were occupied by Independent Directors (Fig. 5). If we focus solely on the 259 BOD persons (and not positions) that served in the boards all these years, we deduce that 57.52 % of the Directors are Independent. It is interesting to note that out of the 32 Chairperson positions that were created in these years, there were 9 Independent

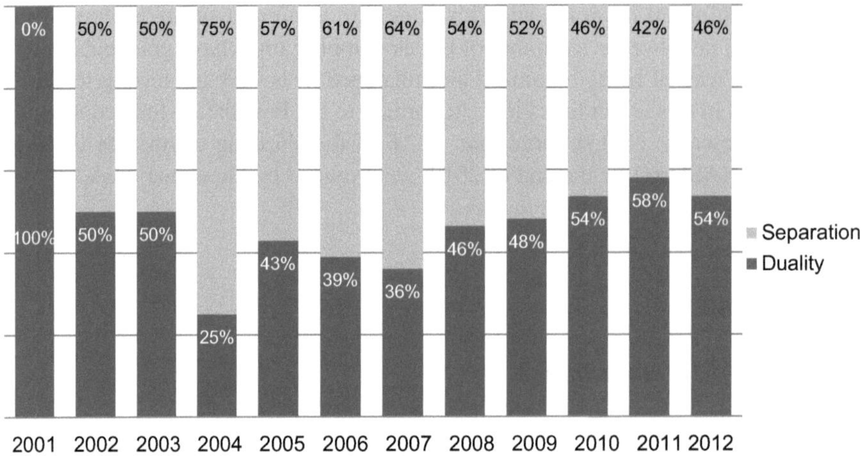

Fig. 2 CEO duality vs separation for the period (2001–2012)

Chairpersons (28.1 %). However, for the 42 CEO positions, there were no Independent CEOs.

4.1.4 Cross Directorships

For the period 2001–2012, we found 305 directorships, of which 84 were held by 38 directors who possessed simultaneous positions in two or more different listed companies' Boards during their tenure. Out of these 38 directors, there were 30 (78.9 %) who held positions in 2 different boards, while 8 (21.1 %) directors served in three companies.

The total number of directorships by chairpersons for these twelve (12) years was 41, while the exact number of Chairpersons was 32, due to cross directorships. It is notable, that in 29 out of the 34 companies (85.3 %), there was no change of the Chairperson during the examined period. For the rest of the companies, it was found that 4 companies had changed their Chairperson once and 1 company twice. The total number of CEO positions was 42, while the exact number of CEOs was 33, due to cross directorships. There were 27 companies (79.4 %) that did not change their CEO at all, 4 changed only once, and 3 that replaced the person twice.

4.2 Demographics

4.2.1 Board Tenure

For the year 2012, we found 14 departures of BOD Members. Four new BOD members were appointed in the respective companies, and if we incorporate the

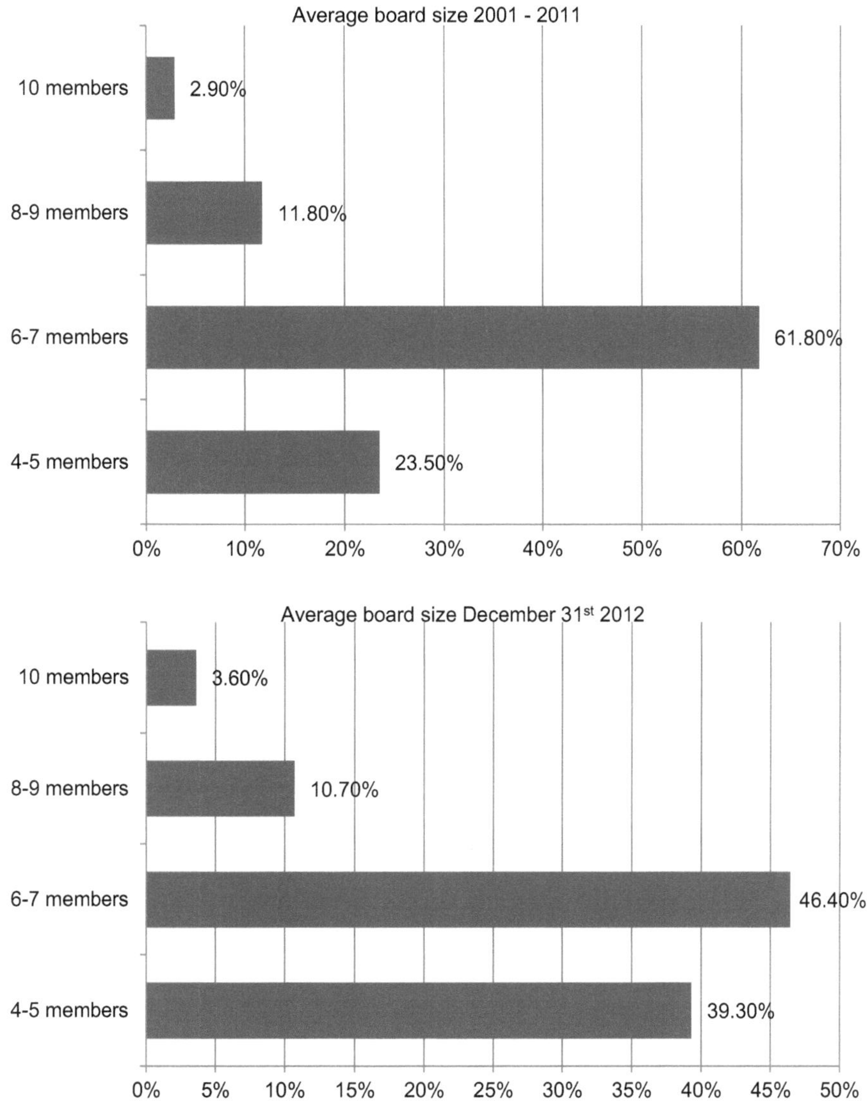

Fig. 3 Average board size for the period 2001–2012 and for the year ended December 31st 2012

BOD members of the newly formed company GAS LOG, we find 13 new appointments of Directors. For the top positions in the Board, we noticed only 2 CEO appointments and only 1 departure. No change took place in any Chairman's position.

The average tenure of the board members varies significantly from company to company, and this could be explained by the diversity that exists on the year that each company listed in a Stock Exchange. The average Tenure of the whole Board

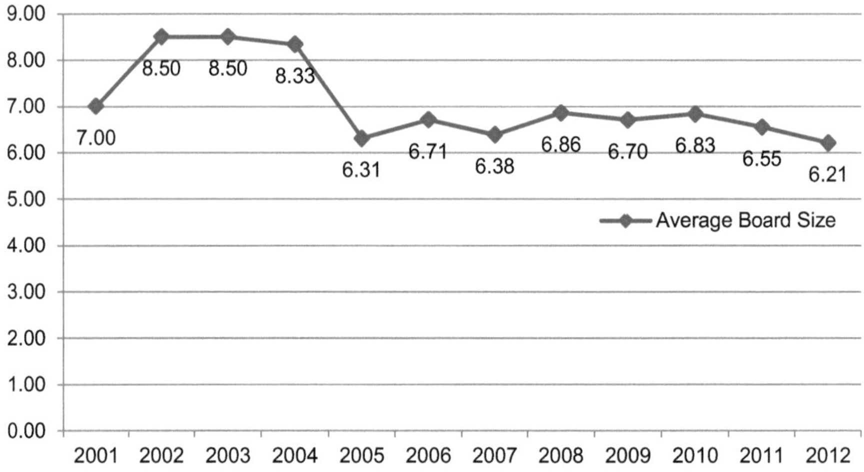

Fig. 4 Yearly average board size as of December 31st

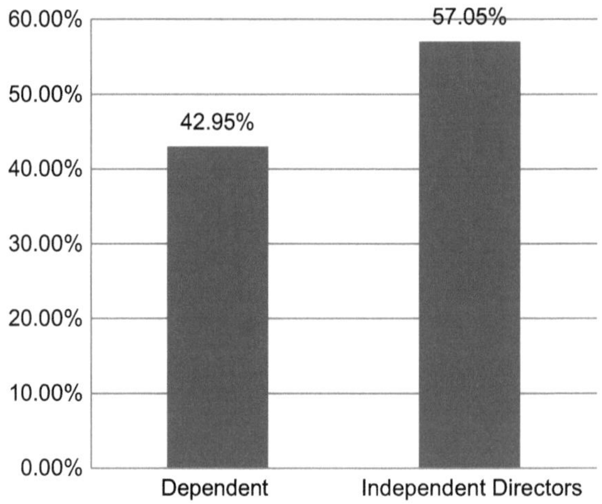

Fig. 5 Dependent vs independent directorships

is 48.33 months, with a standard deviation of 22.2. An equal percentage of 35.3 % has average tenure from 2 to 4 years and from 4 to 6 years (Fig. 6).

The average Tenure of Directors, after excluding the tenure of the Chairman and CEO, was 58.58 months, with a very high standard deviation of 74.93.

Interestingly, the average Tenure of CEO (Fig. 7) was 57.32 months, with a standard deviation of 32.67 months. More than half of these companies (58.8 %) have CEOs with high tenure, since they served in this position more than 4 years. In some companies (8.8 %), the CEO has served the company for approximately 10 years.

As for the average Tenure of the Chairperson (Fig. 8), we note that it had an average of 59.34, with a standard deviation of 30.70 months. Listed shipping

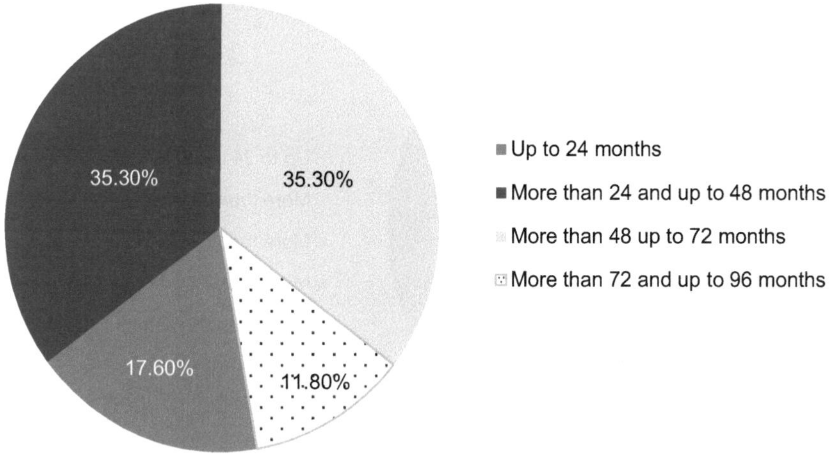

Fig. 6 Average tenure of the whole board (n = 34)

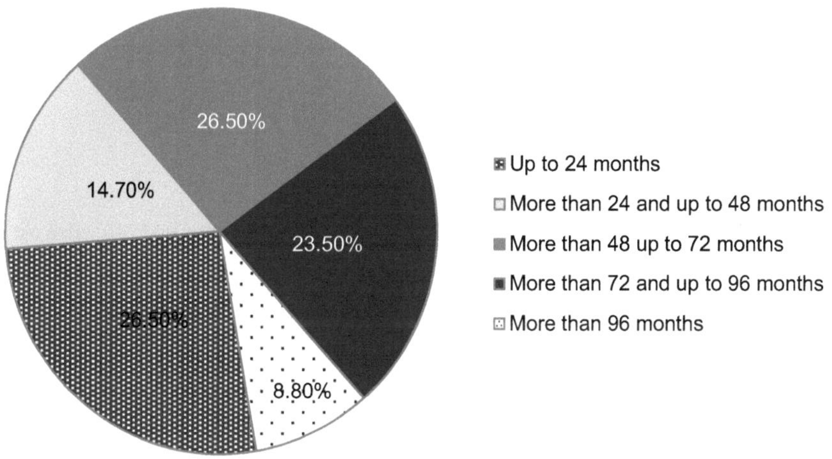

Fig. 7 Average tenure of the CEO (n = 34)

companies have Chairpersons with a high tenure, and we note that 67.6 % of these companies have Chairpersons who serve for more than 4 years in the Board. In one company, the Chairperson served for approximately 10 years, and in another one, the Chairperson had tenure of approximately 11 years.

4.2.2 Age

Figure 9 presents the distribution of age of all directors on a board of the 28 companies which were listed in the Stock Exchanges on December 31st 2012. Our findings showcase that the average age of directors who hold positions in the Board

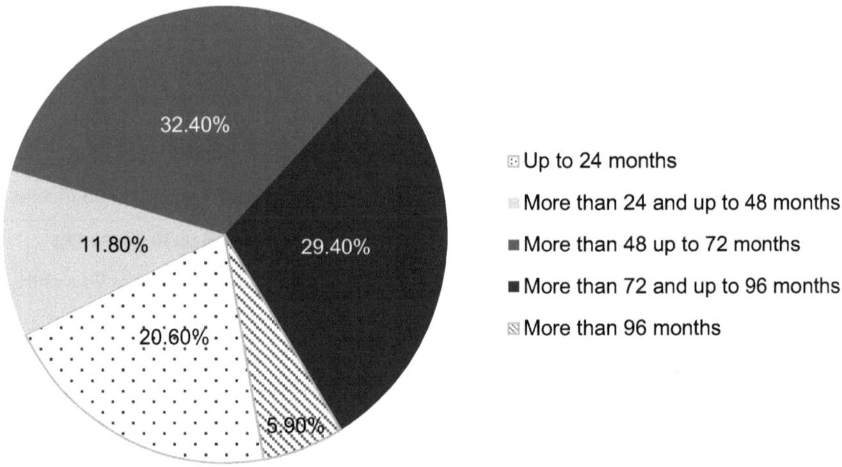

Fig. 8 Average tenure of the chairperson (n = 34)

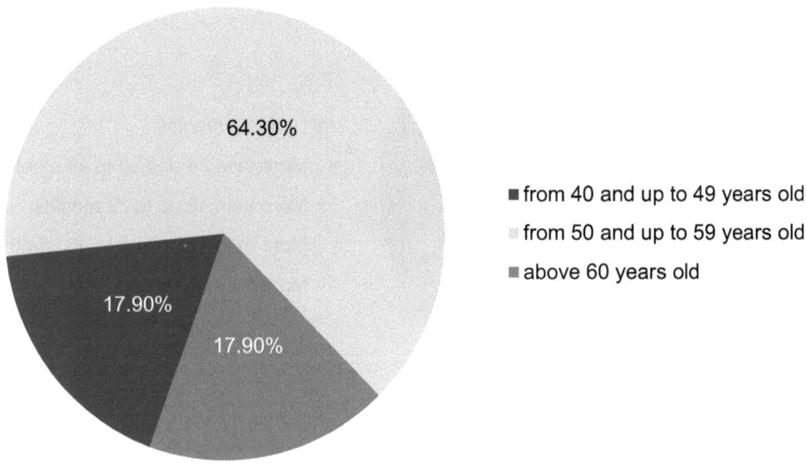

Fig. 9 Average age of directors in Greek Maritime Companies (n = 28, mean = 55.5 and SD = 5.6)

as of December 31st 2012, was 55.5 years old. The majority (64.3 %) of the companies had directors between 50 and 59 years old.

At the end of 2012, the average Chairperson's age is 50 years old, while the CEO's is 56 years old. The two youngest CEOs were 35 years old and the oldest CEO was 71 years old. Besides, the younger Chairperson was 42 and the oldest, 80 years old.

Table 1 Total memberships, men and women served on boards (n = 34)

	Total directorships	Male directorships	Female directorships
Mean	8.97	8.58	0.38
Standard deviation	3.23	3.33	0.81
Min	4.00	3.00	0.00
Max	19.00	18.00	3.00
Sum	305	292	13

4.2.3 Gender

For the 34 companies examined in the period 2001–2012, 292 out of 305 directorships (BOD positions) were held by men, with an average of 8.6 per company. Respectively, there were only 13 directorships held by women, with an average of 0.4. The sharp discrepancy that exists between men and women in the board composition is depicted in Table 1.

The total number of directors was 259, after excluding mobility (6 directors) and cross directorships. Out of these, 249 (96 %) were men; while there were only 10 female directors (4 %). Only one woman was simultaneously the Chairperson and the CEO of three different maritime companies (Navios Maritime Holdings, Navios Maritime Partners and Navios Acquisition), which preferred the duality structure for their governance. Besides, one woman was the CEO of the company.

5 Discussion: Why Gender Diversity on the Boards Should Be Considered by Ship-Owners

There is a demanding need for companies to consider the diversity in their board and blend talents, knowledge and experiences from the overall labor market. The benefits of a diverse board, in terms of attributes and demographics on the performance of the organization, have been underlined in the literature (Dalton et al. 1998; Hillman and Dalziel 2003). For the aim of the Maritime Women: Global Leadership conference in 2014, we would like to underline the importance of gender diversity on BODs.

Board appointments have been considered in the literature as a "black box", which needs much more research to reveal the appointment process. Although countries such as Norway, Belgium, Iceland and France have passed legislation for a minimum percentage of women in BODs, BOD positions are still a man's world. For example, the executive search consulting firm, Spencer Stuart (2013) informs us that 35 S&P 500 boards, or 7 % of the total, have no female directors, a slight decline from 2012, when 9 % of boards did not have a woman. According to the study, companies operating in IT, energy and industrial sectors, usually have no females in their Boards.

However, studies examining the link between women in the board and performance of the organization, have found a positive relationship (Carter et al. 2003; Erhardt et al. 2003). More specifically, Catalyst (2004), which reported on 353 Fortune Companies for 4 years of data, found that companies with higher percentages of women board directors, outperformed those with less by 35.1 %, in terms of Return on Equity (ROE), and by 34 % in terms of Total Returns to Shareholders (TRS).

Apart from the economic benefits that women may bring into the organization, they also bring different experiences and qualities. Their greater risk aversion, that has been supported by various researchers (Vandegrift and Brown 2005; Wei 2007), allows them to spend more time on their monitoring role. Through their stringent monitoring of the processes of the organisation, they could also bring significant advantages to the financial reporting function.

Why do some organizations have women on their BODs, and others don't? This question has been investigated by Hillman et al. (2007) and by using resource dependence theory, and a sample of 1,000 U.S. listed firms with large volume of sales, they found that parameters such as size of the firm, industry type, firm diversification strategy, and networks, impact the likelihood of female representation on boards of directors. Larger organizations are more likely to comply with societal pressures for greater gender diversity in their corporate boardrooms.

Dunn (2012) confirmed that when women are appointed into male-dominated groups, they bring with them specialized knowledge skills. From these findings, we conclude that women could break the barriers and contribute in specific areas of the shipping companies, where specialized knowledge is needed. For example, they could bring valuable knowledge in areas such as economics, finance and maritime law.

There are also ethical concerns from the underrepresentation of women in Boards. However, moving a step forward for women representation on boards it is not only about equal opportunities; it is mainly an issue of good corporate practice.

Another point for discussion, is the optimal number of women on a board. Elstad and Ladegard (2012) found the increasing ratio of women directors is associated with decision-making dynamics and a high level of influence on the decisions of the board. Recent research supports the magic number of "3" women on boards (Torchia et al. 2011; Konrad and Kramer 2006), since only one female in the board cannot boost the performance of the organization.

The recent report of McKinsey *Women Matter 2013* (Devillard et al. 2013), presents that companies with more female executives achieve higher performance than those with no women. The most basic reason for this outperformance, lies in specific attributes of their leadership behaviour, which are concentrated on (a) people development; (b) expectations and rewards; and (c) role model. Overall, we notice in the literature that female board members are more likely to set challenging questions and increase the collaboration capacity of the board.

6 Conclusion

The fifth annual study of the Hellenic Observatory of Corporate Governance, captured the status quo on the Board's characteristics of Greek-owned Maritime Shipping Companies which are listed in foreign Stock Exchanges.

In our study, we noticed a concentrated structure of governance, where the position of the Chairman and the CEO is held by the same person. In 15 out of the 28 companies operating in 2012 (53.6 %) we found a dominant CEO who holds both positions. Regarding the Board Size, we found that most of these maritime companies (44.1 %) prefer the size of the Board to be between 6 and 7 members.

Our study attempted also to record the presence of External Independent Directors, and from the 305 BOD positions that were created in the sector, 174 were occupied by Independent Directors. We should underline that the real number of Directors (not BOD positions) for the whole period was 259, and a remarkably high percentage (57.2 %) has been appointed as Independent Directors.

For the period 2001–2012, out of the 305 directorships that were created in the industry, 84 were held by 38 directors, who possessed simultaneous positions in two or more listed companies' Boards during their tenure.

Directors stay in office for 48.33 months on average, while there is even more stability with the Chairperson's and CEO's position, with an average 59.34 and 57.32 months, respectively. Notably, for the period 2001–2012, 85.3 % of these companies retained the same Chairperson and 79.4 % of them didn't change their CEO. As for the board's age, a remarkably high percentage of board members (64.3 %) as of December 31st 2012, was the age of 55.5 on average.

For the whole period of these 12 years, only 13 out of 305 directorships were held by women. More specifically there were only 10 women directors, compared to 249 men. Besides, 29 out of the 34 companies have never appointed a woman on the Board. From our study, it is evident that there is plenty of room for public-listed maritime companies to consider an increase in the number of women on their boards, as the percentages are extremely low.

Concluding our research, we should mention that Greek shipping companies contribute significantly to the Greek economy in a number of ways. Despite the recent financial crisis, Greek shipping companies have remained competitive and have attracted global recognition. Corporate governance may not be in the high priorities' list of Greek maritime companies, but, nowadays, it is a key factor towards gaining access to the international equities' markets. Ship-owners should keep in mind, that a proper balance of power in the upper echelons of an organization, requires for a good diversity in management.

References

Adams, S. M., Gupta, A., & Leeth, J. D. (2009). Are female executives over-represented in precarious leadership positions? *British Journal of Management, 20*(1), 1–12.

Bazerman, M. H., & Schoorman, F. D. (1983). A limited rationality model of interlocking directorates. *Academy of Management Review, 8*(2), 206–217.

Boston Consulting Group. (2013). Impact assessment of the shipping cluster on the Greek economy & society. http://www.bcg.gr/documents/file135208.pdf. Accessed 20 Oct 2013.

Cadbury, A. (1992). *Report of the committee on the financial aspect of corporate governance.* London: Gee & Co. Limited.

Cambell, K., & Mínguez-Vera, A. (2008). Gender diversity in the boardroom and firm financial performance. *Journal of Business Ethics, 83*(3), 435–451.

Carter, D. A., Simkins, B. J., & Simpson, W. G. (2003). Corporate governance, board diversity, and firm value. *Financial Review, 38*(1), 33–53.

Catalyst. (2004). The Bottom line: Connecting corporate performance and gender diversity. http://www.catalyst.org/knowledge/bottom-line-connecting-corporate-performance-and-gender-diversity. Accessed 20 Jan 2013.

Child, J. (1974). Managerial and organizational factors associated with company performance. *Journal of Management Studies, 11*(3), 13–27.

Core, J., Holthausen, R. W., & Larcker, D. F. (1999). Corporate governance, chief executive officer compensation and firm performance. *Journal of Financial Economics, 51*(3), 371–406.

Dalton, D., Daily, C., Ellstrand, A., & Johnson, J. (1998). Meta-analytic review of board composition, leadership structure and financial performance. *Strategic Management Journal, 19*(3), 269–290.

Dalton, D., Daily, C., Ellstrand, A., & Johnson, J. (1999). Number of directors and financial performance, a meta-analysis. *Academy of Management Journal, 42*(6), 674–686.

Davis, G. (1991). Agents without principles? The spread of the poison pill through intercorporate network. *Administrative Science Quarterly, 36*(4), 583–613.

Davis, J., Schoorman, D., & Donaldson, L. (1997). Toward a stewardship: Theory of management. *Academy of Management Review, 22*(1), 20–47.

Devillard, S., Sancier, S., Werner, C., Maller, I., & Kossoff, C. (2013). *Women matter 2013. Gender diversity in top management: Moving corporate culture, moving boundaries.* Paris: McKinsey & Company.

Donaldson, L., & Davis, J. (1991). Stewardship theory or agency theory: CEO governance and shareholder returns. *Australian Journal of Management, 16*(1), 49–64.

Dunn, P. (2012). Breaking the boardroom gender barrier the human capital of female corporate directors. *Journal of Management & Governance, 16*(4), 557–570.

Eisenberg, T., Sundgren, S., & Wells, M. T. (1998). Larger board size and decreasing firm value in small firms. *Journal of Financial Economics, 48*(1), 35–54.

Elstad, B., & Ladegard, G. (2012). Women on corporate boards: Key influencers or tokens? *Journal of Management and Governance, 16*(4), 595–615.

Erhardt, N., Werbel, J., & Shrader, S. (2003). Board of director diversity and firm financial performance. *Corporate Governance, 11*, 102–111.

Fama, E. F., & Jensen, M. C. (1983). Separation of ownership and control. *Journal of Law and Economics, 26*(2), 301–325.

Foundation for Economic & Industrial Research. (2013). The contribution of ocean-going shipping to the Greek economy: Performance and outlook. http://www.iobe.gr/docs/research/en/RES_05_F_07012913REP_ENG.pdf. Accessed 20 Jan 2014.

García-Ramos, R., & Olalla, M. G. (2012). Independent directors, family ownership structure and firm financial performance. *International Research Journal of Finance and Economics, 90*, 6–24.

Golden, B., & Zajac, E. (2001). When will boards influence strategy? Inclination x power = strategic change. *Strategic Management Journal, 22*(12), 1087–1111.

Gul, F. A., Hutchinson, M., & Lai, K. M. Y. (2013). Gender-diverse boards and properties of analyst earnings forecasts. *Accounting Horizons, 27*(3), 511–538.

Hafsi, T., & Turgut, G. (2013). Boardroom diversity and its effect on social performance: Conceptualization and empirical evidence. *Journal of Business Ethics, 112*(3), 463–479.

Haslam, S. A., Ryan, M. K., Kulich, C., Trojanowski, G., & Atkins, C. (2010). Investing with prejudice: The relationship between women's presence on company boards and objective and subjective measures of company performance. *British Journal of Management, 21*(2), 484–497.

Hillman, A., & Dalziel, T. (2003). Boards of directors and firm performance: Integrating agency and resource dependence perspectives. *Academy of Management Review, 28*(3), 383–396.

Hillman, A. J., Shropshire, C., & Cannella, A. A. (2007). Organizational predictors of women on corporate boards. *Academy of Management Journal, 50*(4), 941–952.

Hillman, A. J., Withers, M. C., & Collins, B. J. (2009). Resource dependence theory: A review. *Journal of Management, 35*(6), 1404–1427.

Jensen, M. C. (1993). The modern industrial revolution, exit and the failure of internal control systems. *Journal of Finance, 48*(3), 831–880.

Konrad, A. M., & Kramer, V. (2006). How many women do boards need? *Harvard Business Review, 84*(12), 22.

Koufopoulos, D. N., Georgakakis, D. G., & Gkliatis, I. P. (2008). Boards and organisational performance in non-profit, public healthcare organisations: The Greek perspective. *International Journal of Business Governance and Ethics, 4*(4), 330–348.

Koufopoulos, D. N., Lagoudis, I., Theotokas, I., & Syriopoulos, T. (2010). Corporate governance and board practices by Greek shipping management companies. *Corporate Governance, 10*(3), 261–278.

Lipton, M., & Lorsch, J. (1992). A modest proposal for improved corporate governance. *Business Lawyer, 48*(1), 59–67.

Mizruchi, M. S. (1996). What do interlocks do? An analysis, critique, and assessment of research on interlocking directorates. *Annual Review of Sociology, 22*, 271–298.

Musteen, M., Datta, D., & Kemmerer, B. (2010). Corporate reputation: Do board characteristics matter? *British Journal of Management, 21*(2), 498–510.

Muth, M., & Donaldson, L. (1998). Stewardship theory and board structure: A contingency approach. *Corporate Governance: An International Review, 6*(1), 5–28.

Peng, W., Zhang, S., & Li, X. (2007). CEO duality and firm performance during China's institutional transitions. *Management and Organization Review, 3*(2), 205–225.

Petrofin Research. (2013). 2013 Greek fleet statistics. http://www.petrofin.gr/Upload/2ndPart-2013-Petrofin_Researcht-GreekFleetStatistics.pdf. Accessed 1 Nov 2013.

Platt, H., & Platt, M. (2012). Corporate board attributes and bankruptcy. *Journal of Business Research, 65*(8), 1139–1143.

Rechner, P. L., & Dalton, D. R. (1991). CEO duality and organisational performance: A longitudinal analysis. *Strategic Management Journal, 12*(2), 155–160.

Rose, C. (2007). Does female board representation influence firm performance? The Danish evidence. *Corporate Governance: An International Review, 15*(2), 404–413.

Sarbanes-Oxley Act (2002). Public Law 107-204, July 30, 2002.

Schoorman, F. D., Max, H. B., & Atkin, S. R. (1981). Interlocking directorates: A Strategy for reducing environmental uncertainty. *The Academy of Management Review, 6*(2), 243–251.

Shipilov, A. V., Greve, H. R., & Rowley, T. J. (2010). When do interlocks matter? Institutional logics and the diffusion of multiple corporate governance practices. *Academy of Management Journal, 53*(4), 846–864.

Singh, H., & Harianto, F. (1989). Top management tenure, corporate ownership structure and the magnitude of golden parachutes. *Strategic Management Journal, 10*(1), 143–156.

Smith, K. G., Smith, K. A., Olian, J. D., Sims, H. P., O'Bannon, D. P., & Scully, J. A. (1994). Top management team demography and process: The role of social integration and communication. *Administrative Science Quarterly, 39*(3), 412–438.

Spencer Stuart. (2013). Spenser Stuart U.S. Board Index https://www.spencerstuart.com/~/media/PDF%20Files/Research%20and%20Insight%20PDFs/SSBI-2013. Accessed 20 Oct 2013.
Syriopoulos, T., & Tsatsaronis, M. (2012). Corporate governance mechanisms and financial performance: CEO duality in shipping firms. *Eurasian Business Review, 2*(1), 1–30.
Torchia, M., Calabro, A., & Huse, M. (2011). Women directors on corporate boards: From tokenism to critical mass. *Journal of Business Ethics, 102*(2), 299–317.
Upadhyay, A., & Sriram, R. (2011). Board size, corporate information environment and cost of capital. *Journal of Business Finance & Accounting, 38*(9–10), 1238–1261.
Vafeas, N. (2003). Length of board tenure and outside director independence. *Journal of Business Finance & Accounting, 30*(7–8), 1043–1064.
Vandegrift, D., & Brown, P. (2005). Gender differences in the use of high-variance strategies in tournament competition. *The Journal of Socio-Economics, 34*(6), 834–849.
Wei, X. (2007). Wage compensation for job-related illness: Evidence from a matched employer and employee survey in the UK. *Journal of Risk and Uncertainty, 34*(1), 85–99.
Wiersema, M. F., & Bantel, K. A. (1992). Top management team demography and corporate strategic change. *Academy of Management Journal, 35*(1), 91–121.
Yermack, D. (1996). Higher market valuation of companies with a small board of directors. *Journal of Financial Economics, 40*(2), 185–211.

Participation of Ecuadorian Women in the Maritime Oil Transportation Sector

Margarita Dávila Cevallos

Abstract It has been commonly observed that women in Latin America, including Ecuadorian women, tend to prioritize the responsibility of domestic work such as childrearing, while studying at university to get qualified for and gain access to the professional positions at work. In the Ecuadorian oil transportation sector, for example, all clerical and administrative positions are traditionally assigned to women and with very few exceptions; women do not occupy high-ranking positions in chartering, planning and financial areas. The oil transportation business in Ecuador has been dominated by a single company owned by the Ecuadorian Navy, EP Flota Petrolera Ecuatoriana (FLOPEC), where all key positions are reserved for male retired navy officers who are appointed by the Board of Directors, chaired by the Commander-in-Chief of the Navy. This reality, and the fact that the only company dedicated to the oil transportation business belongs to the navy, which has been always led by men, has made an impact on the ways of professional growth. As a result, it is possible to argue that limited opportunities were given to women to pursue a management career inside FLOPEC. The company, by law, is forced to deal with a domestic monopolist market. Hence, the lack of competitiveness has led to limitation in terms of the development and growth of the company itself, as well as the timely training and professionalization of human resources. This paper aims to analyze the role of women in the Maritime Oil Transport Sector in Ecuador and offer some practical suggestions for the integration of women in this sector in the future.

Keywords Ecuador • Limited opportunities • Monopolistic market • Oil shipping industry • Women

M. Dávila Cevallos (✉)
Oil Trading & Shipping Consultant, Quito, Ecuador
e-mail: margarita.davila@andinanet.net

© Springer-Verlag Berlin Heidelberg 2015

M. Kitada et al. (eds.), *Maritime Women: Global Leadership*, WMU Studies in Maritime Affairs 3, DOI 10.1007/978-3-662-45385-8_5

1 Introduction

Women in Latin America, including Ecuador, tend to prioritize the responsibility of domestic work such as childrearing, while studying at university to get qualified for and gain access to the professional positions at work. Ecuador is the first country in Latin America which has introduced women's voting rights in their Constitution, since 1929. According to the Global Gender Gap Index (World Economic Forum 2013), which provides comparative data on national gender gaps on economic, political, education- and health-based criteria, Ecuador was rated at 0.7035, placing the country 45th out of the total of 135 countries. In the report (World Economic Forum 2013), Ecuador was considered to improve in narrowing gaps in the areas of labour force participation, wage equality for similar work, professional and technical workers and parliamentary positions.

However, inequality still persists. In this regard, the Ecuadorian oil transportation sector is not an exception. All clerical and administrative positions are traditionally assigned to women, with very few cases of them occupying high-ranking positions in chartering, planning and financial areas. There is a systemic problem behind this glass-ceiling phenomenon. The oil-transportation business in Ecuador has been monopolized by a single company owned by the Ecuadorian Navy, EP Flota Petrolera Ecuatoriana (FLOPEC), where all key positions are reserved for male retired navy officers who are appointed by the Board of Directors, chaired by the Commander-in-Chief of the Navy. Hence, it is arguable that the lack of competitiveness would lead to limitations in terms of the development and growth of the company itself, as well as the timely training and professionalization of human resources. This paper presents an analysis on the role of women in the Maritime Oil Transportation Sector in Ecuador and offers some practical suggestions for the integration of women in this sector in the future.

2 Ecuador's Economy Brief

Ecuador is a democratic Republic and its economy is mainly based on the export of primary products such as shrimp, flowers and especially oil. During the last few years, the Ecuadorian economy has experienced a sustained growth as a result of the introduction of the U.S. Dollar as its national currency in 1999. This controversial measure did contribute to the country's monetary system stability, but failed to change its internal production structure, which has not diversified enough in industrial production. Therefore, the economy continues to depend on oil exports as the main source of wealth.

Ecuador has been growing consistently: 8 % in 2011, 5.1 % in 2012 and 3.7 % in 2013. Its GDP reached US$89,834 million and its per capita income of US$9,191 is the twelfth in Central and South America. The year of 2013 closed with an inflation rate of 2.7 % (Ecuadorian Central Bank 2013).

Ecuador is making great efforts to move from an extractive to a value-added economy. This is why the Government is strengthening the education sector.

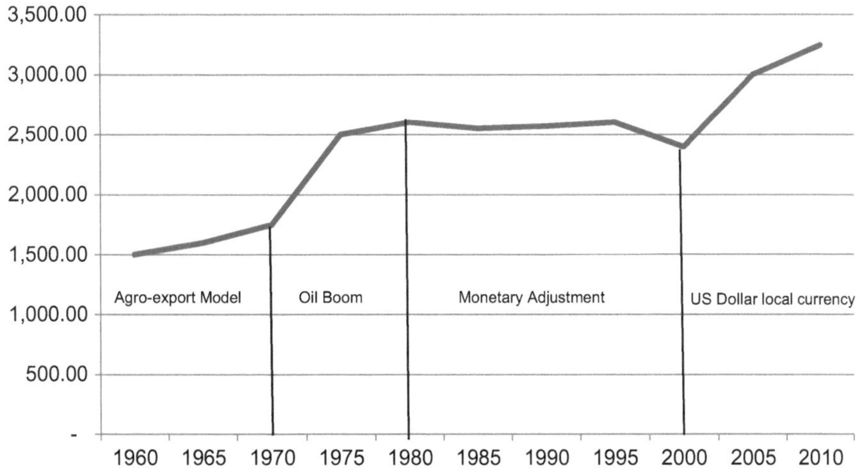

Fig. 1 Per capita GDP evolution in Ecuador between 1960 and 2010

The 2014 education budget increased by 5 % from 2013 and represents 11 % of the national budget. New regulations have been put in place and, in order to improve the academic level of the local universities, the government is offering scholarship options to attend prestigious universities abroad, to students qualifying to do so.

Importance of Oil in the Ecuadorian Economy Ecuador started its oil production in 1972. Exports of the first years brought a boom to the Ecuadorian economy. Between 1972 and 1981, the per capita GDP grew at an average rate of 4.05 % per annum. The first decade of Ecuadorian oil export is known as the oil-boom period, dominated by high international oil prices. Later, in the period 1982–2000, the economy suffered a severe stagnation as a consequence of an aggressive external indebtedness policy and low oil prices. In these years, the average per capita GDP grew at a negative rate of −0.14 % per annum.

For almost two decades, the Ecuadorian economy was immobilized due to the lack of investment, public and private, constant devaluation of the currency and a permanent growing inflation rate, which led to a deep financial crisis that pushed the authorities to adopt the dollar, as its national currency, in 2000. Between 2001 and 2013, the economy grew at a rate of 2.80 % per year, mostly supported by high oil prices (Fig. 1).

Clearly, the Ecuadorian economy's growth has been based on the exploitation and export of oil. However, the volatility of international oil prices has had an impact on the economy, making the process of economic growth dependent on external variables such as the probability of finding larger oil reserves, or the expectation of oil prices to rise, rather than relying on a change of its development model, one more focused on increasing local production, the substitution of some imported commodities and procuring to provide people with a decent income to strengthen the domestic markets.

Currently, Ecuador is the largest exporter of crude oil in the American Pacific Rim. It has a production of around 550,000 barrels per day, of which about 400,000 are exported; representing 46 % of total exports. Coffee followed with 24 %, bananas with 14 % and the rest is flowers and tuna, among the main products (Ecuadorian Central Bank 2013). Ecuador's National Oil Company owns and operates three oil refineries to process crude oil; however, given the low complexity of them, domestic production of derivatives is not enough to cope with domestic demand, so it is necessary to import products.

In 2013, Ecuador exported 130 million barrels of oil. Sixty-eight percent of this volume went to the United States, while 32 % went to Peru, Chile and Asia. Transportation of crude oil and petroleum products is performed in oil tankers of different sizes, ranging from 40,000 up to 200,000 tons.

Transportation of Oil Exports and the National Ecuadorian Oil Fleet, EP FLOPEC Oil transportation, according to Ecuadorian law, is totally reserved for companies in which the Ecuadorian state controls at least 51 % of the stock. Currently, only one company meets this requirement, FLOPEC, a shipping company established in 1973, owned and run by the Ecuadorian Navy, that enjoys the unique position to operate in a monopolistic market allowing it to determine, regulate and control freights.

FLOPEC is a state-owned company whose organizational structure is hierarchical, led by a general manager, area managers and department heads. This hierarchical structure slows the process of decision making. However, given that structure and the characteristics of the market in which it operates, it needs the flexibility of a private company. The oil transport market is highly competitive, where the law of supply and demand determines the market dynamics.

FLOPEC has a monopoly on the transportation of oil exported from Ecuador; however it not only operates in the Ecuadorian market, but also does so in the international market, where it must necessarily compete in order to maintain a solid position and a market share. Approximately 50 % of FLOPEC's operational income comes from freights not involving Ecuadorian ports. FLOPEC has been successfully competing with others because of its unique position in the Ecuadorian market and due to the fact that Ecuador is the only south Pacific country that produces oil and has its own tanker fleet.

In the early 1970s, waterborne crude oil transportation was a brand new activity in Ecuador and, at that time, there were no trained people to deal with commercial, technical and financial aspects necessary to run a shipping company. Therefore, at the beginning of the existence of the company, personnel provided by FLOPEC's partners, Kawasaki of Japan, were the pioneers in this activity (all men) occupying key positions (chartering, technical maintenance, etc.) and hired young Ecuadorian personnel, with incipient academic background, especially women, to perform secretarial tasks and fulfill clerical functions.

FLOPEC has been managed by a Board of Directors composed of active navy officers, headed by the Commander-in-Chief of the Navy who appoints the General Manager as well as the rest of Officers—all of them retired navy officers—without following a selection process based on profiles or academic credentials, in which case, none of them would have been in a position to fulfil them.

This critical issue will be discussed in Sect. 4, in relation to women's participation in the Maritime Oil Transportation Sector in Ecuador. The next Sect. 3, attempts to conduct a secondary data analysis, to understand the general status of Ecuadorian women in education and labour market.

3 Ecuadorian Women in Education and Labour Market

Until recently, women in Ecuador were relegated to occupy a secondary role as homemakers. In the last decades, however, this situation has changed and the new generations of women are more actively participating in the academic and labor markets. The new Constitution,[1] recently approved in Ecuador, ensures an equal participation of women in society. Important developments have been achieved in recent years, regarding women's access to education in Ecuador and gender equality balancing. By 2010, 16 % of all graduated students from college attended an institution of higher education.

While progress regarding women's access to higher education and gender equality treatment has been positive, discrimination persists. In accordance with "*New Century, Old Disparities: income gaps by gender and ethnicity in Latin America*" (Ñopo 2012), a research study published in 2012 by the Inter-American Development Bank (BID), Latin-American men and women of the same age and the same educational level, shows us that men's salary is 17 % higher than women's. Women hold only 33 % of the highest paid professions in the region, such as architecture, law or engineering. In these occupations, the wage gap between men and women is much more pronounced, reaching an average of 58 %. According to Ñopo (2012) in Ecuador, regardless of the nature of the activity or sector that women work for, women's salaries are 27 % lower than men's. This situation is caused, among other factors, by gender discrimination, which still persists, despite a very small education and training gap between men and women.

According to an analysis by Becker (2011), there are two main factors for this differentiation: discrimination against women and the perception that men have more experience and work longer hours. Becker argues that the traditional division of labour in the family disadvantages women in the labour market, as women devote substantially more time and effort to housework and have less time and effort available for performing market work. Moreover, the OECD (2002) found that women work fewer hours because in the present circumstances, the "responsibilities for child-rearing and other unpaid household work are still unequally shared among partners." Such discrimination is also evident in the unemployment rate, which, according to statistical information provided by the National Institute of Statistics and Census of Ecuador (2013), measured women's unemployment rate was 6.1 %, while men's was 4.0 % in 2013. Many economists argue that a large number of rational and freely adopted decisions by women explain their secondary position in the labor market. In this sense, their desire to combine family life and

[1] Constitución Política de la Republica de Ecuador, 2008.

Table 1 Percentage of female graduates in different careers as a percentage of the total

Country	Education	Welfare	Law	Human arts	Social services	Science	Engineering and construction
Argentina	81	73	64	74	53	51	34
Brasil	78	74	55	58	65	37	29
Chile	78	76	56	57	46	28	20
Colombia	57	60	47	39	n.a.	39	26
Ecuador	**70**	**69**	**60**	**58**	**66**	**41**	**25**
Uruguay	74	75	65	65	30	48	47
Latin America	73	71	57	57	50	40	29

Source: Originally published by Ñopo (2012); published with kind permission of © Ñopo. All rights reserved

professional development restrict their field in the labor market. Women in a way, feel certain "pressure" that society expects them to play in their roles as wives and mothers. This would result in:

a) Higher dropout rates and intermittency in the workplace than men;
b) Preference for occupations with part-time work or flexible schedules, rejecting those that entail greater responsibilities and requirements;
c) Less investment in women than men in terms of human capital development, as a result of providing less professional dedication to, as well as spending less time and money on, women's education; and
d) A job characterized by a smaller geographical and occupational mobility than men, which also means fewer job opportunities.

Despite the increasing number of women enrolling in professions, related to numbers, they tend to focus on careers such as psychology, teaching or nursing, where the developments of quantitative skills are not required. This situation is mainly due to the fact that Latin-American women give priority to care for their children, rather than their profession. The statistics regarding women pursuing careers imply the situations where women are under pressure of dedication and commitment, allowing very little time to devote to home.

On average, more women than men graduate from university in Latin America. However, most specialize in programs that do not develop quantitative skills, those that are best paid in the labor market (Table 1).

In spite of this inequality, current figures of women's access to education are promising. Even though males still represent a higher school enrolment percentage, females' rate of attendance, compared with males', has been higher during the last 10 years. This situation has helped women to improve the quality of their education. Nevertheless, as for post-secondary education, women still sign up for professions matching the roles traditionally assigned to them, such as nursing and teaching, which are poorly paid and not appreciated. According to statistical information supplied by the Ecuadorian Professional Training Service (2012), the majority of women sign on for courses in administration, garment manufacturing and handcrafts.

4 Women's Participation in FLOPEC

As discussed earlier, FLOPEC is a state-owned company which monopolizes the oil export transportation business in Ecuador, managed by a Board of Directors composed of active navy officers, predominantly men. Even with this reality, they have been successfully managing the company thanks to the company's staff, mostly women, who have worked for many years in the business and have been able to specialize without proper academic preparation in most of the cases. Only two women, who already left the company, had top-level professional titles.

During FLOPEC's history, only four women reached leadership positions in the company. Those women worked in the chartering, finance and strategic planning areas. Except for the person heading the Strategic Planning Department, the other three executives began their careers from the very bottom of the organization, being secretaries, assistants (one of them with university studies), until they occupied executive positions as a result of their experience accumulated over the years. These women had to face several challenges in order to achieve executive positions within the organization. The main challenges were to specialize in such a competitive business without neglecting their responsibilities as mothers, and the fact of being surrounded by men who played key executive positions in the company in the decision-making process. The main motivation for access to executive positions was their desire for self-improvement and dedication to work.

At the end of 2012, 80 people worked in the administrative offices of FLOPEC; 34 were men and 46 women. Of the 46 women, only 17 are professionals and had the opportunity to attain university education, and only two of them earned Master in Science degrees.

The fact that Management positions are solely occupied by Ecuadorian retired navy officers, has limited the professional growth of women in FLOPEC, despite their long experience and knowledge of the industry and, in some cases, a solid university education, including graduate-level training in Shipping Management. They never had the opportunity to occupy top management positions because of their condition of being female. The fact that historically, the company has been run by retired officers of the Ecuadorian Navy, has definitely been the main factor that has limited the access of these women to manager-level positions.

Most of the staff has worked in the company for many years, which has allowed them to specialize in shipping; however, such specialization is not precisely a result of appropriate company training, even though FLOPEC has enjoyed a privileged economic situation. In fact, in the last 6 years, the company only dedicated 3.1 % of their operating income to train their personnel.

Economic Growth Without Competition and the Future Risk The reason why FLOPEC has reached a sustained growth over time, is the operation of its fleet under a monopolistic market in Ecuador, a fact that has enabled the company to control the Pacific market and generate higher rates in comparison to other market rates in the region, such as the Caribbean.

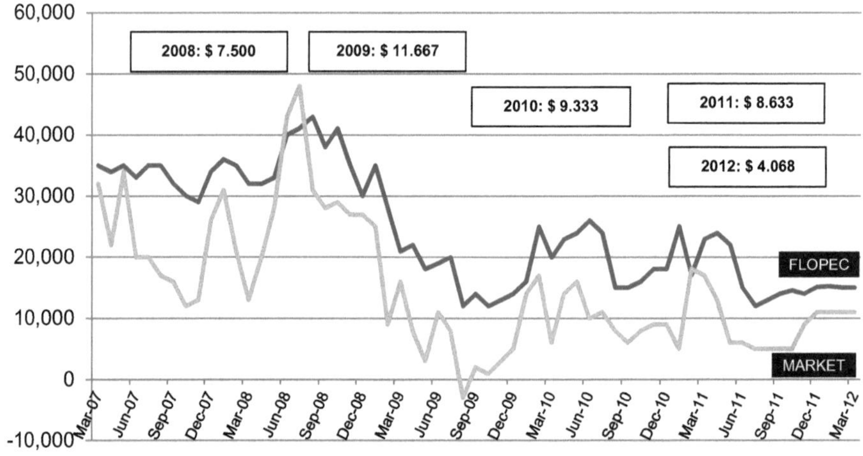

Fig. 2 Time charter equivalent of FLOPEC and the Caribbean market (US Dollars per day) (according to financial statements provided by EP Flota Petrolera Ecuatoriana). *Source*: Originally published by EP Flota Petrolera Ecuatoriana (2007–2012); published with kind permission of © EP Flota Petrolera Ecuatoriana. All rights reserved

The participation of women in the maritime transport of oil has been very important to FLOPEC. As mentioned above, the company operates in a monopoly market only in Ecuador; its operation in the international market has forced it to maintain international standards in order to successfully compete with other owners with more experience, more capital investments and larger fleets.

On average, over the last 5 years, the freight rates realized by FLOPEC, in the Ecuadorian market, have been approximately US$10,000 per day higher than in the Caribbean market, which operates under an open market, where supply and demand set the rates. Figure 2 illustrates this situation.

This excellent situation has allowed FLOPEC to maintain its equity, steadily growing at a rate of 19 % per annum, regardless of the difficult situation the international shipping market has been experiencing lately (Fig. 3).

Even with the positive net result of the company, FLOPEC's tonnage has not grown in a similar proportion to its equity, in spite of it being the only company enabled, by law, to perform the maritime transportation of the total crude oil exports and product imports.

The explanation of this lack of growth is the absence of competitiveness in the Ecuadorian market which, at the same time, creates a lack of challenges and incentives for becoming more efficient and discouraging the personnel to pursue growth. After operating for 43 years, enjoying a monopolistic position, FLOPEC should have grown in tonnage and should operate a larger number of tanker vessels, of various sizes, to cover the totality of the Ecuadorian market and a percentage of the regional market.

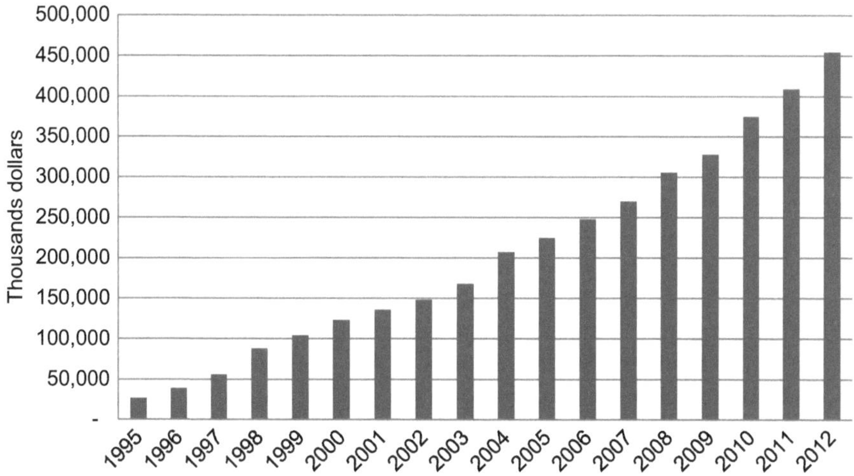

Fig. 3 FLOPEC's equity evolution (1995–2012) (according to financial statements provided by EP Flota Petrolera Ecuatoriana). *Source*: Balance sheets, originally published by EP Flota Petrolera Ecuatoriana (1995–2012); published with kind permission of © EP Flota Petrolera Ecuatoriana. All rights reserved

5 Suggestions for Active Participation of Ecuadorian Women in the Maritime Oil Transportation Sector

The current Constitution of Ecuador is the basis for promoting labor equality for both men and women. The Constitution recognizes several women's demands, such as the institutional framework for gender equality, non-discrimination and their universal right to education, among others.

There are several actions that can be performed in FLOPEC for the promotion of women to senior positions, given their experience and business knowledge. One is to improve fluency in English, which is the language widely used in this activity, as well as an adequate academic preparation in issues related to oil transportation and financial skills associated with the business. FLOPEC's management should honestly be ready to offer both genders, with similar skills and equal opportunities, to climb up in the organization.

Ecuador, as a signatory member of the International Maritime Organization (IMO), should participate more actively in the committees responsible for the evaluation of women's participation in the shipping business. Initiatives such as "The Global Programme on the Integration of Women in the Maritime Sector", conducted by IMO, shows the interest that women have in participating actively in shipping. Therefore, the Ecuadorian Government, through its representative at IMO, must promote, not only in Ecuadorian maritime schools, but also in local universities, the participation of more women, in order to contribute to their full engagement in this sector through educational programs and proper training according to the demands of the sector.

Another initiative that the delegate of Ecuador should develop, is the dissemination of women's worldwide associations networking in the shipping industry, in order to enable an active participation of Ecuadorian women by exchanging information and being part of an international network that helps in designing a strategy to strengthen ties with organizations of this international activity.

There are a number of seminars and conferences organized by these associations, such as Maritime Authorities of the Americas (ROCRAM), Operative Network and the Regional Cooperation on Maritime Matters, in which Ecuadorian women should be involved, with the idea of identifying training needs and helping to develop a country strategy that may lead to the formulation of state policy for the active participation of women in the maritime transportation sector.

The Ecuadorian delegate to IMO should play a leading role in promoting the inclusion of women in the Ecuadorian shipping industry through the dissemination, in various branches of government, the opportunities that exist for women in the sector. The Ecuadorian representative to IMO is the naval attaché in the United Kingdom, whose main function is to represent the country in protocolary and state issues, leaving him little time for an active participation in IMO meetings.

Moreover, Ecuador, as a member of the International Labour Organization, which recommends the incorporation of local women labour, should regulate not only the hiring of women in both private and state-owned oil companies operating in Ecuador, but also in the maritime transportation sector, assigned historically mostly to men.

Regulations, as referred above, will demand the training of women in the area of oil transportation that constantly demands tonnage to transport growing volumes of crude and crude products, in which case the state must allocate the necessary funds for the development of centres of study that should include maritime transport of oil as a career, and encourage the participation of women in this field through scholarships and exchanges with specialized universities.

In the mid-term, Ecuador will have a new refinery that will allow the country to export refined products, increasing the demand for shipping and therefore of tankers, prompting the need for academic training of captains, officers and crew. The Merchant Marine Academy in Ecuador, as part of the Ecuadorian Navy, should support and encourage the enrolment of female personnel, in anticipation of the future demand of qualified crew members.

6 Conclusion

During the last decade, important steps have been taken by the Ecuadorian Government to promote women's university education. Nevertheless, as in the rest of Latin-American countries, most of the jobs that demand a qualified workforce, are covered by men, especially in those careers that are not considered traditional. Most of the women choose careers such as nursing and education, which are not well paid.

There is a gap of 33 % between the wages received by men and women, meaning that the gender inequality has not been eradicated yet, despite the steps taken. The main problems can be summarized as:

- In FLOPEC, there has not been a selection process for top executive position appointments based on their academic preparation; these positions have been assigned solely to former Navy officers;
- In FLOPEC, there are a few women who had access to university education and even higher education levels and gained great experience during the years they worked for the company. They had sufficient credentials to allow them to occupy top management positions, but never did, because these positions were reserved for former Navy officers; and
- The lack of competitiveness, instead of positioning the company as a market leader in the transportation of hydrocarbons in the region, prevented the company from increasing its tonnage and to train and prepare their personal, especially women, to achieve growth.

The Ecuadorian representative to the IMO has not been providing timely information regarding developments, programs, seminars, courses or trainings, depriving people of that valuable information and reducing business and working opportunities for both men and women. The big challenge for Ecuadorian women involved in the maritime transportation sector, is to overcome stereotypes and change the limited vision of women's role in society.

References

Becker, G. (2011). *Human capital, effort, and the sexual division of labor*. New York: New York Times.

Ecuadorian Central Bank. (2013). Macroeconomic synthesis. http://www.bce.fin.ec/index.php/indicadores-economicos. Accessed 1 Apr 2014.

Ecuadorian Professional Training Service. (2012). SECAP – Servicio Ecuatoriano de Capacitación. http://www.educaedu.com.ec/centros/secap--servicio-ecuatoriano-de-capacitacion-profesional-uni2011. Accessed 1 Apr 2014.

National Institute of Statistics and Census of Ecuador. (2013). Social statistics. http://www.ecuadorencifras.gob.ec/empleo-encuesta-nacional-de-empleo-desempleo-y-subempleo-enemdu/. Accessed 1 Apr 2014.

Ñopo, H. (2012). New century, old disparities: Income gaps by gender and ethnicity in Latin America. Resource document. Inter-American Development Bank and World Bank. http://www10.iadb.org/intal/intalcdi/PE/2012/10588.pdf. Accessed 1 Apr 2014.

OECD. (2002). *Employment outlook, 2002*. Paris: Author.

World Economic Forum. (2013). The global gender gap report 2013. http://www.weforum.org/reports/global-gender-gap-report-2013. Accessed 1 Apr 2014.

Part II
Career Development and Gender Issues

The "Leaky Pipeline": Examining and Addressing the Loss of Women at Consecutive Career Stages in Marine Engineering, Science and Technology

Bev Mackenzie

Abstract In mid-2013, the House of Commons Select Committee on Science and Technology, of the UK Parliament, held an inquiry into Women in STEM (Science, Technology, Engineering and Maths). The inquiry sought to address the "leaky pipeline"—the continuous loss of women at consecutive career stages within STEM, where these gradual losses reduce the numbers of women retained in STEM further education and work. The Institute of Marine Engineering, Science and Technology (IMarEST) consulted its 15,000 members (of which only 3 % are female) to determine whether the problems facing women were exacerbated by the additional challenges of working within the marine sector and to examine how it could develop proactive solutions for addressing the issue. This paper delves into some of the results from the consultation, both anecdotal and evidence-based, and debates the issues. These include:

(1) That the "leaky pipeline" is not the result of women choosing not to progress their careers and those who wish to succeed will do so. However, supportive employers who demonstrate willingness to offer women opportunities to progress, are a must.
(2) That many of the issues apply to women across all careers and are related to work-life balance and the consequences of having a family. However, there are specificities in a career in marine STEM that make it harder for women to succeed compared to other careers and, in particular, STEM careers. These include disproportionately low numbers of women in all roles and the additional challenges of working offshore or on board ships.
(3) Female role models in STEM are vital, but these role models must be carefully selected.

There is a perception that many of the role models in marine STEM have got to high level positions by compromising; by not having a family or by becoming "one of the boys", having the opposite of the desired effect.

B. Mackenzie (✉)
IMarEST, London, UK
e-mail: bev.mackenzie@imarest.org

© Springer-Verlag Berlin Heidelberg 2015

M. Kitada et al. (eds.), *Maritime Women: Global Leadership*, WMU Studies in Maritime Affairs 3, DOI 10.1007/978-3-662-45385-8_6

Keywords Careers • Leaky pipeline • Marine engineering • Marine science • Marine technology • STEM

1 Introduction

The report on women in scientific careers (House of Commons Science and Technology Committee 2013) highlighted the issue of a skills shortage within the UK in the areas of Science, Technology and Engineering. The report estimated that around 820,000 science, engineering and technology professionals will be required by 2020, to address the skills gap (House of Commons Science and Technology Committee 2013). For an island nation, it can therefore be assumed that it is particularly relevant for the marine and maritime sector, where many of the jobs require some level of basic training in science, technology, engineering or maths (herewith called 'STEM'). The UK economy quite simply needs more skilled scientists and engineers, with the obvious solution being to recruit and retain talented women into the sector. Not only will actions to attract and keep women in science and engineering jobs help maintain and grow the UK economy and competence, it can be argued that having a diverse workforce (in terms of both gender, race and disability) brings a wealth of benefits to a company or organisation (Royal Academy of Engineering 2009). These include 'cost benefits' and 'retaining intellectual capital'.

Cost Benefits Better retention of staff results in a better return on the financial investments into recruitment and training. The Society of Biology, in its comments to the UK Government, state that increasing women's participation in the UK labour market could be worth between £15 billion and £23 billion [1.3–2.0 % of GDP], with STEM accounting for at least £2 billion of this (House of Commons Science and Technology Committee 2013). In Scotland, it has been estimated that a doubling of women's high-level skill contribution to the economy would be worth as much as £170 million per annum to the national income (Royal Society of Edinburgh 2012).

Retaining Intellectual Capital When staff members leave a company, the knowledge base is eroded. This is particularly relevant for women returning from maternity leave into lower level roles in terms of the followings:

- Innovation: a diverse mix of employees will create a better environment for creativity and innovation—different ideas and ways of thinking to the company.
- Better access to markets: to maintain a competitive edge, companies must have an understanding of all potential customers and markets.
- A motivated, productive workforce: where individuals feel valued by their employer and see other individuals feeling valued, they are generally more motivated and committed.
- Wider benefits for STEM: maximising diversity will lead to new priorities, questions and perspectives in STEM, and ultimately affect the directions of STEM.

However, some caution does need to be applied regarding cost-benefit, with "The Business Case for Equality and Diversity" (UK Government 2013) arguing that although studies appear to have found evidence that firms have reaped business benefits from equality and diversity, not all firms benefit in all contexts at all times. Indeed, the review found that if diversity management is applied poorly, then it can increase costs for a business.

2 Background Information

It has been reported that currently, across engineering in the UK, approximately 8.7 % of professional engineers are women—one of the lowest figures in Europe (IMarEST 2013). Similarly, the US, in its 2001 Current Population Survey (US Department of Labor 2002a), identified that 10 % of employed engineers were women, rising to 20 % for engineering technologists and technicians. Among engineering specialties, industrial, chemical, and metallurgical/materials engineers were the only occupations in which women were more highly represented than the overall percent of total women engineers, where women made up 17 % of all industrial engineers, 12 % of metallurgical/metal engineers, and 11.5 % of chemical engineers. Among all other engineering specialties (e.g., aerospace, mining, petroleum, nuclear, agricultural, civil, electrical/electronic, mechanical), women represented fewer than 11 % and it is in this category where marine engineers or naval architects fall, indicating potentially low numbers (US Department of Labor 2002b).

Among natural scientists, the statistics are somewhat more comforting. In 2001, women represented 51.6 % of medical scientists and 44.4 % of biological and life scientists (which would include marine biologists), but again accounted for a smaller portion of geologists and geodesists (24.0 %), physicists and astronomers (7.7 %) (the category which would include oceanographers, meteorologists and marine geologists). In order to address the low numbers, it is first imperative to try and understand why the numbers are so low, and at what stage in a career path that problems are likely to occur, and why.

Whilst at school, females regularly outperform their male peers in STEM subjects (House of Commons Science and Technology Committee 2014) so the imbalance appears to occur as females move higher up the academic ladder. For example, in 2012 only 22 % of "A" level physics students in the UK were female. The numbers then reduce at university undergraduate level, with approximately 12 % of females making up engineering degrees, although this is somewhat higher across Engineering and Technology in Scotland. Comparison can also be made at this stage with the employment figures from the US, where the percentages of females on undergraduate courses rise to about 45 % in mathematics and to around 60 % in subjects associated with the life sciences, such as medicine, dentistry, biology and biological sciences. There are of course, other pathways to becoming a scientist, engineer or technologist, such as via an apprenticeship. However, a recent WISE (Women in Science and Engineering) survey (Botcherby and Buckner 2012) confirmed that in 2011, only 430 females completed an engineering apprenticeship, compared to 10,800 males—staggeringly low 4 %.

As well as overall numbers of females studying STEM subjects, the conversion from academic learning to moving into suitable employment, is low. As recently as 2009, only 27 % of women graduating in STEM in Scotland were employed in STEM professions, compared with 53 % of their male counterparts (House of Commons Science and Technology Committee 2014). In the universities themselves, the proportion of women in STEM departments falls with each step up the academic ladder. Across the board in STEM (engineering, life sciences, and health sciences), more than half of STEM students are women, but once at the level of full professor, the proportion of women has fallen to about 10 % (House of Commons Science and Technology Committee 2014).

Quite clearly, problems occur at all stages of the career path, from choosing education options at "A" level (typically at around age 15), to choice of university or apprenticeship, through to choosing a field of practice and then progressing within that field.

3 General Issues Facing Retention of Women in STEM

Assuming a woman chooses to pursue a career in STEM, what are the key factors that influence whether she will remain in that career and progress along the career ladder? Motherhood has often been listed as the most important factor that results in women leaving a scientific career (Adamo 2013; Ceci and Williams 2012; Goulden et al. 2011). In the US, women with children are more likely to leave science than are single women or men [where having children appears to have no negative impact on male retention in science (Goulden et al. 2011)]. Academic careers seem to be particularly affected by this—where the most intense period of competition (for funding, for promotion, for lecturing positions) occurs during the period where many women have partners or children. In addition, women with partners are less geographically mobile, which constrains their ability to apply for and accept rare faculty positions (Goulden et al. 2011). Additionally, once a woman has children, short-term postdoctoral positions are less likely to be suitable due to the financial insecurity. Although men are parents too, and are also affected by these issues, studies have repeatedly shown that women invest more time in childcare and household duties than do men. Goulden et al. (2011) reported that marriage and children do not have a negative impact on a man's scientific career. Work undertaken by the IMarEST also raised the issue of dual-career couples, where in most instances, highly educated, well trained women tend to have highly educated, well trained partners. For a heterosexual couple, it is generally accepted that the male in the relationship will have a higher salary (greater by between 9 and 10 %) (Office of National Statistics 2012).

Adamo (2013) also notes that workload, high stress levels, and motherhood do not appear to be barriers to the recruitment and retention of women in careers such as medicine. As such, it can be implied that they are also unlikely to be the main drivers of female attrition in STEM. Many consider that the under representation of women in some fields is caused quite simply by sex discrimination (by funding bodies, journal reviewers, interview panels, for example) but women often fare as well as men in hiring, funding, and publishing if the resources are available and the playing field is level. As such, the primary reason for under representation is due primarily to factors surrounding family formation and childrearing, gendered expectations, lifestyle choices, and career preferences—some originating before or during adolescence.

However, Bell-Burnell (2012) argued that women simply do not receive the same career opportunities and encouragement as men. She argues that both men and women hold implicit biases and both judge women more harshly. This was backed up by comments received during the IMarEST study, where young female PhD students reported that female supervisors are less supportive than men, with a sense of rivalry rather than camaraderie ensuing. In many cases, men were seen as better role models within academia. However, women typically receive less mentoring than men, both formally and informally. This may be because there is some stigma against senior men associating with junior women (either real or perceived) (IMarEST 2013). Bell-Burnell (2012) also raises the point that recruitment panels are frequently dominated by men, and their membership is most comfortable recruiting somebody like themselves. In addition, there are more subtle institutionalised instances of sexism, such as application forms that request the sex or gender of applicants, always offering the male option first. These seemingly small things send out messages that discourage female participation, drip, by drip, by drip.

In conclusion, it should be noted that the issues facing women in STEM careers are not necessarily specific to STEM. Many of the issues apply to women across all careers and are related to work-life balance and the consequences of having a family. However, the under-representation of women in itself is a barrier to progression, and this under-representation is less evident in other sectors.

4 An Overview of the Marine and Maritime Sector in the UK

The Crown Estate (2008) estimates that the wider maritime-related economy generates around £46 billion of UK GDP and provides 890,000 jobs, defined by any position on or related to the sea. This £46 billion accounts for approximately 3 % of the global maritime-related market of £2 trillion. In addition, the majority of UK trade is dictated by the sea, with over 90 % of the UK's goods, and half of its energy resources, shipped in to the UK from around the world. Shipping remains the cornerstone of the UK economy, generating more than £1 million every hour of every day, making a £6.1 billion value-added contribution to UK GDP. The shipping industry alone directly supports 537,500 jobs and provides £8.5 billion in tax receipts to the UK exchequer (Department for Business Innovation and Skills 2012; Oxford Economics 2012).

Since 2000, the UK-owned fleet of vessels has increased by 200 % (UK Chamber of Shipping 2012), creating on the one hand, great opportunities for growth, and on the other, a skills shortage, as demand outstrips supply. Again, it should be noted it is not simply about new entrants and graduates. A review conducted by UK NEST concluded the maritime sector in general has a disproportionate number of retirees and a distinct lack of engineers in the '35–45' age range (UK NEST 2013). The age profile of the IMarEST membership provides further evidence of this, where the average age of an IMarEST member in October 2013 was 55 years. Without transferring knowledge and bolstering the mid-career talent pool, a huge amount of experience will be lost to the industry within the next 5–10 years.

An IMarEST study conducted in association with recruitment specialist MatchTech, examined the skills gap across the UK Marine and Maritime industry and examined the issue of gender diversity (IMarEST and MatchTech 2014). Forty-two percent of organisations involved in the study stated that over the past 5 years, there had been some positive improvements in diversity, with 54 % of respondents reporting no change at all. However, despite a number of incentives and initiatives to increase the number of female engineers over recent years, it would appear that organisations within this industry are not reaping the benefits, with a staggering 67 % of respondents confirming that their workforce is currently made up of less than 5 % of females. This is 3 % lower than the very poor statistic of 8.7 % of female professional engineers in the UK (IMarEST and MatchTech 2014). Even more concerning, was that for 36 % of organisations, their workforce was less than 1 % female. The potential untapped talent of women in engineering may go some way to bridge the future skills gap within the industry, but of course, requires industry to engage and educate young women on the opportunities available. Clearly, with only 12 % of students with engineering degrees being female (House of Commons Science and Technology Committee 2014), without positive intervention, it will take many years for diversity to show in employment figures.

Although the IMarEST study gives some indication of the proportion of women employed across UK marine STEM, there are no published figures available on the total numbers of women working in the UK in marine STEM. However, the numbers are assumed to be low (particularly at middle to senior management levels) given global trends. According to the International Transport Workers' Federation (ITF 2014), women make up only an estimated 2 % (23,000 individuals) of the world's seafaring workforce.

The IMarEST membership figures can also be used to provide some indication of employment levels. The IMarEST, in October 2013, had 427 female members, comprising just over 3 % of the total membership. However, only 1.5 % of IMarEST members who are registered as Chartered Engineer (CEng) (the highest recognition of professional competence) are women, in comparison to 35 % of female IMarEST members who are registered as Chartered Scientist (CSci). This figure of 35 % is consistent with other Science Council-licenced bodies who also cover health and life sciences- sectors where previous discussion has shown much higher proportions of women. This implies that the issues facing women in marine engineering are much more pronounced than those in marine science and technology.

One further example from the marine science sector in the UK, is the employment figures from one of the leading research centres, the Plymouth Marine Laboratory (PML), as reported to the House of Commons Science and Technology Committee (2014). Of the current scientific staff employed at PML, 44 % are female and of the current PhD students, 47 % are female (House of Commons Science and Technology Committee 2014). These percentages have remained fairly constant over the last 3 years. Whilst the percentage of female/male scientific staff is broadly equivalent, there are significant differences at both ends of the grade structure. Female employees make up 100 % of the lowest technician grade and 75 % of the junior scientist level, whereas at the two highest grades, they represent one third and one quarter, respectively, of the community (House of Commons Science and Technology Committee 2014).

It is also interesting to place this in an international context. The Intergovernmental Oceanographic Commission of UNESCO (IOC of UNESCO) reported (Santoro, personal communication, 2013) that around 25 % of representatives (comprised of senior figures in Ocean Sciences in the UN member states) at its 2013 General Assembly, were women. The commission itself has a female Executive Secretary and a secretariat of 30 % female staff. However, this number drops to 9 %, if only the technical secretariat staff are considered (i.e., those actively working in STEM roles).

At the recent meeting of the International Maritime Organization's (IMO) Pollution Preparedness and Response (PPR1) sub-committee, held at their Headquarters in London from 3rd to 7th February 2014, an analysis of the names on the registration list (not publically available) inferred that approximately one in five of those registered as either representatives or advisors to member states, were women (20 %). However, looking more closely at the figures, it was seen that the women tend to represent a handful of member states—primarily those within Europe, the US and Canada. The United Kingdom, like many other member states, had no female members within its delegation. Amongst Non-Governmental Organizations in attendance, the ratio is lower, with only one in ten (10 %) registered attendees being female. This could be attributed primarily to the smaller size of NGO delegations, but it would be an interesting further piece of work to discover the gender diversity within either the executive staff or the membership (if appropriate) of the NGOs represented at the meeting. The IMO secretariat, however, fares much better, with around 50 % of secretariat staff supporting the meeting being female. It is assumed, due to the nature of the meeting largely covering environmental issues, that there would be a higher proportion of women at this meeting than in others, such as those related to safety, for example. However, again, further research would need to be conducted.

5 Issues Facing Women Working in the Marine and Maritime Sector

The issues facing women working in STEM in the marine and maritime sector in the UK are, as discussed, similar to those working in other STEM jobs and indeed in other careers. However, the nature of the industry can create additional challenges. The survey of female IMarEST members conducted in 2013, raised the following issues as key:

Lack of "Strength in Numbers" According to the ITF, women seafarers work mainly in the cruise and ferries sector, often for Flags of Convenience (FOC) vessels, which means they are subject to the labour laws (or lack thereof) of the country to which the ship is registered. The ITF report that these are among the worst paid and least protected of all jobs at sea. In addition, women also tend to be younger, and fewer are officers than their male crew mates. The ITF report that the low number of women employed means that it is inevitable that discrimination and harassment will occur (ITF 2014).

The Nature of a "Mobile Career" Being less able to travel for work because of family commitments, was recognised as seriously hampering career progression. This was reported as being particularly relevant in marine science, when scientific research cruises may be days, weeks or even months in duration, and this of course is also relevant for women seafarers. In addition, presenting at conferences (normally overseas) and working in collaborative projects, are nearly impossible for women with young children and opportunities for informal networking with peers are missed. Senior academics and managers want to be able to send their staff to events to raise their organisation's profile and will potentially be reluctant to employ women who can't travel for extended periods. Although it was noted that shipping companies and offshore companies cannot do much about the mobile nature of their work, they should offer other opportunities within the company so that while a woman raises her family, she may be able to work in a shore-based role, and should be given every opportunity to do so, such as relocation, etc.—which is not uncommon in other shore-based industries.

Legacy Some of the more senior members who responded to the consultation, commented that between 20 and 30 years ago, there was a lot more discrimination. Although positive steps have been made, there is a legacy that far fewer women in their 50s have spent the past 30 years working their way up the career ladder as men, so there are not many available in senior positions. Although there may be many more young women around now at lower levels, they do not tend to have any women in the chain of command above them. When they look upwards, what do they see—an all-male line. Many have no female role models in their company. They get discouraged, and leave to join a company with a better track record for promoting women. This is particularly prevalent in the maritime sector, where there are very few females in the senior positions, both on-board ship and ashore. It was noted that one of the better shipping companies, who offer opportunities to young female cadets, still only has “one” female chief engineer on their fleet of ships and no female captains. Ashore, there are very few female Superintendents and women appear mostly in personnel and human resources roles.

Perceived Excuses for Discrimination A number of those who responded to the consultation raised the issue of facilities for those women working offshore or at sea. For example, on offshore platforms, it was commented that there are often no female toilets and often only communal showers. There was a perception that men regard offshore platforms as a male preserve, where they can carry out activities that are not acceptable in mixed gender employment. In addition, many offshore platforms do not have single rooms. Accommodation is very tight and beds cannot afford to be left empty. Some companies get around it by only employing women in even numbers. There are often female catering and cleaning staff, which the female engineers can be paired with. Others pair a woman with a man who is on a different shift, so that they are never in the cabin at the same time. However, others use it as an excuse not to take women at all.

6 Steps Required to Make Change

6.1 STEM Education

There are numerous and well documented initiatives to engage women within the marine sector. This includes targeted initiatives to encourage girls to follow a science career and to try to overturn stereotypes. The report of the House of Commons Science and Technology Committee (2014) states that, for example, “70 % of people around the world associate being a scientist with being a man”; that there is a strong popular perception among students and parents that particular STEM careers, particularly those in the physical sciences, are masculine; and that there is a lack of knowledge about STEM careers, often coupled with a lack of female role models. In addition, both girls and boys are more likely to aspire to STEM when their families “possess substantial ‘science capital’, i.e., science-related qualifications, ‘know how’ and contacts”.

However, it needs to be considered that increasing activities to encourage girls to follow marine careers, is not meant to dissuade girls from aspiring to be doctors, veterinarians, and biologists [fields in which women are becoming a majority (National Science Foundation 2013)] but rather to ensure they do not opt out of the marine sector due to misinformation, the lack of role models, or because of stereotype.

In addition, it must always been considered, that if the focus is on investment in STEM education, then there still needs to be focus on the loss, through attrition, where girls need to be able to see where their career path will lead them.

6.2 Importance of Role Models

The IMarEST research highlighted that role models cannot simply be women in senior positions; "role models need to include women who are juggling a career in STEM with some form of work-life balance and/or having a family". There is a perception "that to succeed in a STEM career, women have to be 'super-human' or to sacrifice having a family to succeed". In addition, highlighting male scientists and engineers who have combined career with childcare and family responsibilities, could help to counter perceptions that these are women's issues rather than matters that concern all parents. However, it was also noted that women who really wish to succeed in their field, will do so against the odds and will overcome whatever is thrown their way.

6.3 Mentoring and Networking

There is strong support for mentoring schemes and evidence that it encourages women to apply for promotions and other opportunities. In addition, networking is seen as extremely important. BP is one company who have implemented a networking scheme with several internal networks that provide mentoring and encouragement for women, such as BPWIN (our global women's network) and WISE (Women in Science and Engineering).

6.4 Training

BP again, can be used as an example, where they have a number of required training programmes, including one that teaches employees how to transcend issues arising from differences in gender or culture. The company also has various training programmes covering how to deal with a difficult employee, how to conduct a performance discussion and how to go through a review process, to name just a few examples. However, the University of Manchester, in its comments to the House of Commons Science and Technology Committee (2014), cautioned that while many institutions are starting to deliver training, there could also be a lack of take-up of this training, by those who need it most.

7 The Role of Professional Bodies

The IMarEST and other professional bodies have an important role to play to try and address the "leaky pipeline". They have strength in numbers, often having large numbers of like-minded professionals, they have proven track records in training, provide support for education initiatives from school-aged children onwards, and have focused goal-based career pathways and regional and local support structures and existing networks.

The gender diversity situation within the professional body sector is quite different from, for example, the FTSE companies (i.e., the 100 companies listed on the London Stock Exchange with the highest market capitalization), with an average of one in three CEOs and members of the governing body being female. According to a 2013 study by Cranfield University (2013), 17 % of FTSE 100 directors were women, whilst only 6 % of executive directors were female and only 3 % of organisations had female CEOs. By comparison, the proportion of women in senior positions within the professional body sector is very high. On average, 32 % of those serving on governing bodies in the UK were women, according to the Professional Associations Research Network's 2012/2013 International Benchmarking Survey (Professional Associations Research Network's 2013). Even more striking is the fact that 36 % of CEOs of professional bodies in the UK are female. This is more than ten times higher than the proportion of CEOs in FTSE 100 or 250 companies. However, it should again be noted that professional bodies, in the Health sector had a particularly high proportion of women CEOs and on governing bodies with almost half (49 %) of the organisations reporting senior roles for women. In contrast, engineering professional bodies came out with the lowest incidence, with 26 % female CEOs and 21 % women on governing bodies.

Although leadership does not seem to be an issue in professional bodies, the membership profiles are still cause for concern, and action does need to be taken. Learned and professional bodies should agree and publicise a statement welcoming and encouraging the full participation of women in that body and its academic discipline. They should make the qualities expected of successful candidates publicly available, ensuring language is gender-neutral (Royal Society of Edinburgh 2012).

8 Conclusion

Although the numbers of women working in STEM in the UK, in particular in marine and maritime STEM, are low, this has been recognised and steps are being taken across the industry and at government level and by organizations such as the IMarEST. The barriers to progression of women in STEM in general can be applied to marine and maritime STEM, but are often exacerbated by the additional challenges faced by a mobile career, where much time can be spent offshore or at sea.

The UK has a series of laws designed to protect women at work such as the Equality Act 2010 and to support them if they chose to have a career break to raise a family, including statutory maternity leave allowance and pay. With this in mind, the foundations, and certainly the desire, exist to improve the recruitment and retention of women into the marine and maritime sector in the UK across STEM. The UK has the opportunity to set a strong example to other nations in this area and should do so.

References

Adamo, S. A. (2013). Attrition of women in the biological sciences: Workload, motherhood, and other explanations revisited. *BioScience, 63*(1), 43–48.

Bell-Burnell, J. (2012). Still more to be achieved. *The Journal of the Foundation for Science and Technology, 20*(8), 19–20.

Botcherby, S., & Buckner, L. (2012). Women in science, technology, engineering and mathematics: From classroom to boardroom: UK Statistics 2012. Resource document. WISE. http://www.wisecampaign.org.uk/files/useruploads/files/wise_stats_document_final.pdf. Accessed 16 Feb 2014.

Ceci, S. J., & Williams, W. M. (2012). Understanding current causes of women's underrepresentation in science. *Proceedings of the National Academy of Science, 108*(8), 3157–3162.

Cranfield University. (2013). The FTSE female index. http://www.som.cranfield.ac.uk/som/ftse. Accessed 16 Feb 2014.

Department for Business Innovation and Skills. (2012). UK marine industries strategic framework. http://www.bis.gov.uk/assets/biscore/business-sectors/docs/10-647-marine-industries-strategic-framework. Accessed 16 Feb 2014.

Goulden, M., Mason, M. A., & Frasch, K. (2011). Keeping women in the science pipeline. *Annals of the American Academy of Political and Social Science, 638*, 141–162.

House of Commons Science and Technology Committee. (2013). Educating tomorrow's engineers: The impact of Government reforms on 14–19 education: Seventh report of Session 2012–13. http://www.publications.parliament.uk/pa/cm201213/cmselect/cmsctech/665/665.pdf. Accessed 16 Feb 2014.

House of Commons Science and Technology Committee. (2014). Women in scientific careers: Sixth report. http://www.publications.parliament.uk/pa/cm201314/cmselect/cmsctech/701/70102.htm. Accessed 16 Feb 2014.

IMarEST. (2013). Written evidence submitted to the UK House of Commons Science and Technology Committee on women in STEM. http://data.parliament.uk/writtenevidence/committeeevidence.svc/evidencedocument/science-and-technology-committee/women-in-stem-careers/written/1768.html. Accessed 1 Jun 2014.

IMarEST, & MatchTech. (2014). Mitigating the skills gap in the maritime and offshore oil & gas market. http://www.imarest.org/policy-news/representing-members/skills-gap/375-mitigating-the-skills-gap-in-the-maritime-and-offshore-oil-a-gas-market/file. Accessed 1 Jun 2014.

ITF. (2014). Woman seafarers. http://www.itfseafarers.org/ITI-women-seafarers.cfm. Accessed 1 Jun 2014.

National Science Foundation. (2013). Women, minorities, and persons with disabilities in science and engineering. http://www.nsf.gov/statistics/wmpd/2013/digest/. Accessed 1 Jun 2014.

Office of National Statistics. (2012). Annual survey of hours and earnings, 2012 provisional results. http://www.ons.gov.uk/ons/rel/ashe/annual-survey-of-hours-and-earnings/2012-provisional-results/stb-ashe-statistical-bulletin-2012.html. Accessed 16 Feb 2014.

Oxford Economics. (2012). The economic impact of the UK shipping industry. http://www.ukchamberofshipping.com/media/filer/2013/11/27/economic_impact_of_uk_ports_sector_-_feb_2013_including_regional.pdf. Accessed 16 Feb 2014.
Professional Associations Research Network's. (2013). A third of professional bodies' leaders are women. http://www.parnglobal.com/a-third-of-professional-bodies-leaders-are-women. Accessed 16 Feb 2014.
Royal Academy of Engineering. (2009). Inspiring women engineers. http://www.raeng.org.uk/news/publications/list/reports/Inspiring_Women_Engineers.pdf. Accessed 16 Feb 2014.
Royal Society of Edinburgh. (2012). Tapping all our talents: Women in science, technology, engineering and mathematics: A strategy for Scotland. http://www.royalsoced.org.uk/cms/files/advice-papers/inquiry/women_in_stem/tapping_talents.pdf. Accessed 16 Feb 2014.
The Crown Estate. (2008). Socio-economic indicators of marine-related activities in the UK economy. http://www.thecrownestate.co.uk/media/5774/socio_economic_uk_marine.pdf. Accessed 18 Aug 2014.
UK Chamber of Shipping. (2012). Annual review. http://www.ukchamberofshipping.com/information/publications-and-briefings/annual-review/. Accessed 16 Feb 2014.
UK Government. (2013). The business case for equality and diversity – A survey of the academic literature. https://www.gov.uk/government/publications/the-business-case-for-equality-and-diversity-a-survey-of-the-academic-literature. Accessed 16 Feb 2014.
UK NEST. (2013). The naval engineering workforce: A UK NEST review. https://www.uknest.org/node/379. Accessed 16 Feb 2014.
US Department of Labor. (2002a). Highlights of women's earnings in 2001. http://www.bls.gov/cps/cpswom2001.pdf. Accessed 1 Jun 2014.
US Department of Labor. (2002b). Women in high-tech jobs. http://www.dol.gov/wb/factsheets/hitech02.htm. Accessed 1 Apr 2014.

Women in the Maritime Sector: Surviving and Thriving in a Man's World—A Caribbean Perspective

Claudia Grant and Vivette Grant

Abstract Caribbean governments have recognized the importance of the empowerment of women as an essential poverty-reduction strategy, with the primary vehicle being their access to education and training. The International Maritime Organization's (IMO) Women in Development (WID) Programme, since its inception, has provided this access for many Caribbean women, to equip them to enter and contribute in what is undoubtedly a very specialised and male-dominated industry. The milestone of 25 years of IMO WID, is an important juncture to assess the extent to which the maritime sector of Caribbean countries has been impacted by the contribution of women. This study attempted such an assessment, utilizing a survey/questionnaire administered to women who have risen to senior leadership positions in various sectors of the maritime industry in the Caribbean. It evaluated the extent of the role of the IMO WID Programme in supporting their professional advancement and assessed the contribution of these women on the sustainable development of the sector. This study also identified the challenges faced and strategies employed, in order to gain insight which could be used to support the formulation of strategies to further inform the agenda to attract and promote the advancement of women in the maritime sector. It suggests the need for more in-depth research to inform future programmes to empower women in the maritime sector of the Caribbean.

Keywords Caribbean • Development • Maritime • Poverty • Training • Women

C. Grant (✉)
Maritime Authority of Jamaica, Kingston, Jamaica
e-mail: cgrant@jamaicaships.com

V. Grant
Caribbean Maritime Institute, Kingston, Jamaica

© Springer-Verlag Berlin Heidelberg 2015

M. Kitada et al. (eds.), *Maritime Women: Global Leadership*, WMU Studies in Maritime Affairs 3, DOI 10.1007/978-3-662-45385-8_7

1 Introduction

The structure of Caribbean economies has been changing in recent decades, with the main income earners shifting from agricultural production to tourism and other services. This has created its own economic vulnerabilities. Growth in the Caribbean has largely stagnated in the last two decades, and today many of these economies face high and rising public debt-to-Gross Domestic Product (GDP) ratios and high unemployment (Parsan 2012).[1] This jeopardizes prospects for medium-term debt sustainability, growth and poverty reduction. Faced with the twin objectives of stimulating economic growth and poverty reduction, the governments have included among the strategies, the development of their maritime sectors and the empowerment of women.

Being predominantly island States, maritime transport is the lifeline of Caribbean economies. Over 90 % of the trade of these countries is by sea, yet historically, the maritime sector has largely remained invisible. Investment in the sector had been limited to port development and employment and income revolved around port activities. Over the years, interest in the sector has grown and today, several governments have targeted the maritime sector as an engine of growth for their economies and are seeking to attract and develop a more diversified array of maritime activities, in response to the imperatives to develop economic alternatives.

Women represent more than 70 % of the poor in both developed and developing countries (OECD 2008). They tend to be employed in low-earning jobs, concentrated in informal employment, where pay and conditions of work are worse than in formal or public jobs. Notwithstanding, there is a high dependence on female income for the sustaining of many households, particularly in the Caribbean, where the incidence of female-headed households is as high as 50 % (Economic Commission for Latin America and the Caribbean 2010). Governments have recognised that because of their essential contributions to household welfare, women are the key to poverty reduction and that sustainable economic growth depends on their access to education and training and decent, appropriately remunerative work, where full use can be made of their skills and qualifications. They have therefore pursued policies and programmes for the empowerment of women. However, little convergence is evident between the commitments made to empower women and the strategies being employed to develop the maritime sector in pursuit of economic growth and development.

As the United Nations specialized agency with responsibility for shipping, the International Maritime Organization (IMO) has, since 1989, spearheaded the drive to empower women to participate in the maritime sector through its Women in Development (WID) programme, which seeks to integrate women into mainstream maritime activities by improving their access to all levels of training and employment in

[1] See also "The Caribbean marketplace; succeeding in a globalizing world" by E. Tromp available at www.centralbankan/indexphp?eid=1734; "The Caribbean Subregional Review and Appraisal Report on the Implementation of the Beijing Platform for Action" by Economic Commission for Latin America and the Caribbean available at http://www.eclac.org/publicaciones/xml/1/9871/carg0583.pdf.

the maritime sector. Scores of women in the Caribbean have been the recipients of training under the IMO WID.

This paper assesses the extent to which the beneficiaries of the IMO WID Programme have been empowered to contribute meaningfully in the maritime sectors of their countries, and the stated goals of the IMO WID are being achieved. By so doing, it makes the case for gender mainstreaming in the maritime development strategies of the countries of the Caribbean. It also points to the continued role of the IMO WID in the empowerment of the women of the Region to take part in these planned developments.

2 Overview of Socio-Economic Status and Imperatives of Caribbean Countries

The governments of Caribbean countries[2] are challenged to find strategies to arrest the continuous decline in their economies and the concomitant rise in the social ills of poverty and crime. The majority of these countries are small-island states with a limited resource base. They have small open economies, which are vulnerable to international developments and external shocks.

Growth in the Caribbean has largely stagnated in the last two decades and today, many of these economies face high and rising debt-to-Gross Domestic Product (GDP) ratios, which jeopardize prospects for medium-term debt sustainability and growth. It will be noted from Table 1, which presents data on public debt and GDP for Caribbean countries, that in 2012, overall public sector debt was estimated at an average of 70 % of regional GDP and for two countries, it was more than double this amount (International Monetary Fund 2013).[3]

The global financial crises, coupled with structural adjustment programmes, whether internally or externally driven, have threatened and may have even reversed the attainment of the critical Millennium Development Goal of halving poverty. Despite their best efforts, governments face considerable challenges in seeking to generate sustained economic growth rates that exceed the rates of unemployment, and poverty. The forecast is for unemployment rates to remain elevated for sometime, within the range of 11–21 %. (Economic Commission for Latin America and the Caribbean 2013).[4] The negative fallout is a decline in real

[2] For the purposes of this paper, Caribbean countries are defined as the English speaking countries of the Caribbean that are members of the Caribbean Community (CARICOM) integration movement, as shown in Table 1.

[3] See also "The Caribbean Subregional Review and Appraisal Report on the Implementation of the Beijing Platform for Action" by Economic Commission for Latin America and the Caribbean available at http://www.eclac.org/publicaciones/xml/1/9871/carg0583.pdf.

[4] See also "Building growth into the Caribbean sustainability agenda: A concerted approach" by W. Smith available at http://www.caribank.org/uploads/2012/05/Opening-Remarks-by-President-Bahamas-September-19-2013-FINAL.pdf.

Table 1 Selected indicators for CARICOM states, 2012

	GDP (US$, billion)	Population (million)	GDP per capita (US$)	Real GDP growth (%)	Gross public debt % of GDP
The Bahamas	8.2	0.4	23,417	2.5	52.6
Barbados	4.5	0.3	16,309	0.7	70.4
Belize	1.5	0.3	4,386	2.3	81.0
Guyana	2.8	0.8	3,596	3.7	60.4
Jamaica	15.3	2.8	5,526	0.9	143.3
Suriname	5.1	0.5	9,339	4.0	18.6
Trinidad and Tobago	23.8	1.3	17,935	0.7	35.7
Anguilla	0.3	0.0	17,307	0.5	21.2
Antigua and Barbuda	1.2	0.1	13,401	1.0	97.8
Dominica	0.5	0.1	7,022	0.4	72.3
Grenada	0.9	0.1	8,133	0.5	105.4
Montserrat	0.1	0.0	12,825	2.0	4.3
St. Kitts and Nevis	0.7	0.1	12,869	0.0	144.9
St. Lucia	1.3	0.2	7,509	0.7	78.7
St. Vincent and the Grenadines	0.7	0.1	6,537	1.2	68.3
Caribbean	66.9	7.0	9,544	1.4	70.3

Source: Originally published by Acevedo et al. (2013); published with kind permission of © IMF. All rights reserved

Table 2 Unemployment rates 2006–2012 (percentages)

	2006	2007	2008	2009	2010	2011[a]	2012[a]
The Bahamas	7.6	7.9	8.7	14.2	–	15.9	14.7
Barbados	8.7	7.4	8.1	10.0	10.7	11.3	11.6
Belize	9.4	8.5	8.2	13.1	–	–	14.4
Jamaica	9.6	9.4	10.6	11.4	12.0	12.6	13.7
Suriname	12.1	12.0	11.1	10.0	9.2	9.0	7.5
Saint Lucia	16.6	13.9	15.6	18.1	20.6	21.2	20.6[b]
Trinidad and Tobago	6.2	5.5	4.6	5.3	5.9	5.1	4.9[c]
Caribbean	10.0	9.2	9.6	11.7	11.4	12.5	12.5

Source: Originally produced by Gomes and Chase (in preparation); published with kind permission of © ECLAC Subregional Headquarters for the Caribbean. All rights reserved

[a]Preliminary data excluding Barbados in 2011

[b]Third quarter data

[c]Second quarter data

wages and an increase in the number of vulnerable persons and communities, with a resultant increase in poverty.

Table 2 presents unemployment rates for some Caribbean countries for the 2006–2012 period. An increasing trend in unemployment is evident among the States since 2008, with the exceptions of Suriname and Trinidad and Tobago.

3 Status of Women in Economic Development

Women represent more than 70 % of the poor in both developed and developing countries (OECD 2008). Studies have shown that this is a factor both of their socio-economic status in the home, as well as the labour market. Women tend to be employed in low-earning jobs (Maniam et al. 2010), concentrated in informal employment, where pay and conditions of work are worse than in formal or public jobs.

Another factor is the high dependence on female income for the sustaining of many households. One fourth of all households worldwide are reportedly headed by women and many others are dependent on female income, even where men are present (UN 1995). In the Caribbean, the incidence of female-headed households is said to be as high as 50 % (Economic Commission for Latin America and the Caribbean 2010).

Female-headed households are very often among the poorest, because of wage discrimination, occupational segregation patterns in the labour market, and other gender-based barriers (Wilson 2011; The Jamaica Gleaner 2012). Gender differences are also apparent in unemployment, with women more likely than men to be unemployed. In the Caribbean, women's unemployment rates are almost double those of men.

A UN report indicates that despite the low pay that women receive, their income has important welfare consequences for children and families. This is because women are more likely to spend their income on food, education, and healthcare that embrace the welfare of their children as well as their own (UN 2005). Because of their essential contributions to household welfare, women are the key to poverty reduction in developing countries.

The governments of the Caribbean Community (CARICOM) have realised the importance of the empowerment of women in the quest for economic development and poverty alleviation. This is evident by their decision to entrench, in the Revised Treaty of Chaguaramas which establishes CARICOM (adopted in 1992), with the mandate to: "establish policies and programmes to promote the development of youth and women in the Community with a view to encouraging their participation in social, cultural, political and economic activities" (CARICOM Secretariat 2000).

The last two decades or so have seen steady progress by the Region in implementing legal reform and institutional structures and programmes to promote the empowerment of women in areas such as property and inheritance, maternity leave, minimum wage, domestic violence, sexual offences, provision of equal access to all levels of education, and the development of training programmes to facilitate the acquisition of skills by women in efforts to expand their employment and income (Bureau of Women's Affairs 2011; Economic Commission for Latin America and the Caribbean 2010).

Despite this, as indicated previously, the Region still faces high unemployment and underemployment among its female population, in comparison to males. While advancements have been made relative to increased participation in the labour force, this continues to be in lower-paying professions—a reflection of the gender bias in the educational system. Even where women are qualified in the more technical professions, there is evidence of discriminatory hiring practices in favour of men and the persistence of an appreciable wage gap. While the wage gap between males and females has narrowed, it is still significant, with men earning an average of 12–25 % above the average income of women, according to a study by the Inter-American Development Bank, based on evidence from Jamaica and Barbados (Bellony et al. 2010).

Undoubtedly, much remain to be accomplished in the quest for gender equality and empowerment. One of the constraints facing the governments of the Region in making further progress in dismantling the socio-cultural and economic barriers which have restricted the ability of women to make a greater contribution to economic development, is the limited growth of the economies themselves. Caribbean economies face the twin challenges to increase growth and productivity and to provide greater numbers of high-quality jobs.

The profile of Caribbean economies presented earlier, has forced governments to identify new sectors which can provide for sustained growth of their economies and deliver the level of income at the individual and national level, which will raise the standard of living and provide fiscal space to maintain and strengthen social systems which will further alleviate poverty. Increasingly, they have been turning to the maritime sector as a pivotal engine of growth for their economies, because of its demonstrated ability to generate foreign exchange and employment.

4 Strategic Importance of the Maritime Sector of the Caribbean

By virtue of being predominantly island States, maritime transport is the lifeline of Caribbean economies. Over 90 % of the trade of these countries is by sea, yet historically, the maritime sector has largely remained invisible. Investment in the sector had been limited to port development and employment and income revolved around port activities. During the containerization era, several countries sought to expand the economic contribution of their ports by investing in infrastructure to attract container transhipment, thereby increasing port activity and income.

Over the years, interest in the sector has evolved in seeking to attract and develop a more diversified array of maritime activities, fuelled in part by increased pressure to find economic alternatives, and the growing awareness of a number of developed and developing countries whose maritime sectors have contributed significantly to their sustained economic development (Commonwealth Secretariat 2012).[5] Another factor has also been the training of nationals in maritime-specific skills, which has equipped them with the required skills and knowledge to be credible messengers of the potential of the sector.

Today, these States are deriving significant income and employment from such non-traditional areas as ship repair and marine construction, bunkering and international ship registration. Some have included the maritime sector in their national development plans, with strategies to grow their maritime cluster, with the intent of being established as regional and global shipping and logistics hubs. But in the words of a former UN Secretary General "...there is no effective development strategy in which women do not play a central role. When women are fully involved, the benefits can be seen immediately: families are healthier, and better fed; and their income, savings and reinvestment go up. And what is true of families is also true of communities, and in the long run, of whole countries" (Economic Commission for Latin America and the Caribbean 2005).

Yet there are no conscious policies or expressed intent which could be identified by the authors of this paper, which indicated that a gendered approach will be taken to the targeted promotion of development in the maritime sectors of these countries. Without the inclusion of issues related to gender equality and empowerment in the development of its maritime plans and policies, the contribution of the maritime sector to the reduction of poverty will be severely limited.

The lack of explicit policies at the national level to integrate women in the plans to develop the sector may well stem from the traditional and male-dominated nature of the maritime sector itself. However, the International Maritime Organization (IMO), through its Women In Development (WID) strategy have, since 1989, pursued conscious programmes to increase the employment of women in the maritime sector globally.

5 IMO's Women in Development Programme

Shipping is a multi-trillion dollar industry. Over 90 % of the world's trade is carried by ships. Without this sector, the import and export of goods on the scale necessary for the modern world would not be possible. There are over 50,000 merchant ships trading internationally, transporting every kind of cargo. The world's fleet is

[5] See also "A Strategic Plan for the Development of the Merchant Marine Industry: Final Report" by the Merchant Marine Industry Team available at http://www.docstoc.com/docs/20788464/ASTRATEGIC-PLAN-FOR-THE-DEVELOPMENT-OF-THE-MERCHANT-MARINE-INDUSTRY; "Address at the Singapore International Maritime Awards" by R. Lim available at www.mpa.gov.sg/sites/global_navigation/news_center/speeches/speeches_detail.page?filename=sp110412b.xml; "Shipyard increases local jobs 35 % in seven years" by The Tribune available at http://www.tribune242.com/news/2013/feb/22/shipyard-increses-local-jobs-35-in-seven-years/.

registered in over 150 nations, manned by over 1.25 million seafarers of virtually every nationality (Pinnock 2009).

Less than 2 % of the world's 1.2 million seafarers are women (Belcher et al. 2003). The relevance of sea experience to many land-based jobs in the sector, also limits the ability of women to participate in the range of maritime-related jobs available ashore, beyond lower-level administrative positions (Tansey 2000).[6] From the shipowner/operator's standpoint, the principal objections to employing women at sea appear to center on the lack of adequate separate facilities for women on board and stringent physical requirements. The perception that seafaring is a man's job, has led to lack of training opportunities and work experience for women (Belcher et al. 2003).

The IMO has recognized the need for a highly-trained workforce in the maritime sector, to respond to the predicted global shortage of seafarers; to support port activities; administer maritime affairs, marine pollution prevention and control activities; and maritime education and training, among others. It has therefore developed its own strategy for the integration of women into the maritime sector, through its Women in Development Programme (WID), which commenced in 1989 (Tansey 2000).

The focus of the IMO WID strategy was the improvement of the access of women to all levels of training and employment in the maritime sector, through both mainstream programmes and gender-specific projects. The objectives of the programmes are to (Tansey 2000)[7]:

- Improve women's access to maritime training and technology;
- Increase the percentage of women at the senior management level within the maritime sector; and
- Promote women's economic self-reliance, including access to employment

Through its many phases, the IMO WID programme emphasized capacity building and provided gender-specific fellowships in response to the infrastructural and socio-cultural constraints which prevented women from having equal access to training and employment opportunities. It also promoted gender awareness in, and equal opportunities and advancement of, women in the maritime sector in general. The long-term objective was to encourage equity in the appointment and promotion of women to senior positions within the sector (IMO 2013; Tansey 2000).

Fellowships were provided to female professionals to pursue post-graduate studies at the World Maritime University (WMU) in Malmö, Sweden as well as the International Maritime Law Institute (IMLI) in Malta. To date, 421 women have been educated in M.Sc. degrees at WMU, and 242 in LL.M. degrees at IMLI. In the

[6] See also "The place of women in a men's world from a maritime university perspective" by C. Popescu and A. Varsami available at http://www.wseas.us/e-library/conferences/2010/Corfu/EDUCATION/EDUCATION-30.pdf.

[7] See also "Women in top jobs: WISTA-UK hears the stories from four women who have pushed the boundaries" available at http://www.allaboutshipping.co.uk/2013/09/22/women-in-top-jobs-wista-uk-hears-the-stories-from-four-women-who-have-pushed-the-boundaries.

case of WMU, the enrolment of women rose from less than 5 % in the late 1990s, to 30 % of present intake (WMU 2012). IMLI reserves 50 % of its places for female candidates. In the Caribbean, the WMU alumni stand at about 90, of which some 30 or 33 % are females, while 17 females have graduated from IMLI (Mitropoulos 2008).

The year 2014, marks 25 years of IMO's WID Programme and presents a convenient milestone to assess its impact on women in the maritime sector of the Caribbean. The above data, as well as testimonies of a few successful alumni, allow the intuitive conclusion that the WID Programme has been achieving its objectives by making inroads for women in this highly traditional and male-dominated industry. It is the view of the authors of this paper, that the tenure of the Programme and number of beneficiaries, provide the critical mass to attempt a more objective assessment of the extent to which the beneficiaries of the IMO WID Programme have been empowered to contribute meaningfully in the maritime sectors of their countries, and the stated goals of the IMO WID are being achieved. In particular, the development challenges facing the Caribbean, and the pivotal role that the maritime sector is set to play in the economic development of some countries, also support the need for such an assessment, for the following reasons:

- It would document and create greater awareness of the contribution of women to the maritime sector;
- It would support the promotion of the 'can-do' mentality among other women as well as policy makers, which could result in increasing the participation of women in the sector; and
- It would provide the opportunity to identify scope for improving the effectiveness of future IMO WID interventions.

The balance of this paper assesses the extent to which the IMO WID objectives are being achieved in the Caribbean, based on a survey of women employed in the maritime sector of the Region. It also identifies challenges faced, and proposes recommendations for the strengthening of future interventions aimed at attracting and promoting the advancement of women in the sector.

6 Methodology

The objectives of this research were fourfold:

1. to assess the effectiveness of the IMO WID Programme in the Caribbean, utilizing the hypothesis that beneficiaries of the Programme will hold senior positions in the maritime sector of their countries;
2. to provide an assessment of the contribution of women to the maritime sector of the Caribbean;
3. to ascertain the extent to which issues affecting women, identified in the literature review, prevail(ed) in the maritime sector of the Caribbean; and

4. to identify coping strategies employed and the extent to which recommendations to support the growth and development of other women in the sector provide any insight which can be beneficial to future planners of interventions in the sector.

Quantitative and qualitative research methodologies were used to achieve the objectives of the study. Questionnaires were administered to 60 females employed in supervisory, operational, middle and senior management positions in their organizations from the following eight (8) CARICOM countries: Anguilla, Antigua and Barbuda, Barbados, Belize, Guyana, Jamaica, Suriname and Trinidad and Tobago. In order to gain deeper insights on their coping strategies, recommendations and visions, some of the questionnaires were administered over the phone in guided interviews. A combination of quantitative and qualitative methods was, therefore, effectively utilised in this study.

Forty persons from eight (8) countries completed the questionnaires, which is a 67 % return. The questionnaire consisted of twenty four (24) items, which may be divided into four broad categories: (1) basic demographics (age, children, marital status); (2) professional data (type of job, position, tenure etc.); (3) challenges and coping strategies; and (4) recommendations/future actions. These data were used to support analysis of some of the issues which, based on the literature, impact female employment in the sector. Questions specific to some challenges faced, coping strategies employed, and the existence of gender equality policies in the work place, were developed to identify and confirm the working environment. The final questions sought to elicit the input of the participants as to vision and future actions.

7 Findings/Discussion

Demographic and Professional Analysis The first area of analysis pertained to the demographics (age, marital status, number of children and their age ranges) and the employment status of the participants. It was noted that the respondents were employed in a fairly broad spectrum of maritime organizations, in both public and private sectors.

Table 3 provides an analysis of the sample according to the age demographics. It will be noted that 52.5 % of the respondents were over the age of 45 and 87.5 % were 36 years and over. Table 4, which cross-tabulates age with position, shows that 26 (or 65 %) participants were employed in senior management positions in their organization, the majority (96 %) of which were 36 years and over. Only 12.5 % of the respondents were in the 27–35 age group, while the 18–26 age group is not represented at all. This may imply that females do not enter the maritime sector immediately out of secondary or tertiary institutions. This could be attributed to the lack of awareness of the potential of the maritime sector as a career option.

A cross-tabulation of tenure of employment in positions against age, reveals that more than 50 % of the persons in over-the-45-age category have been in their present position and therefore, the industry, for more than 10 years. This is confirmed when looking at the tenure in the industry in Table 5, where 61 % of those in senior management were also in the industry for more than 10 years and

Table 3 Age distribution of participants

	Frequency	Valid percent	Cumulative percent
27–35	5	12.5	12.5
36–44	14	35.0	47.5
45 and over	21	52.5	100.0
Total	40	100.0	100.0

Table 4 Age group/position in organisation cross tabulation

Participants		Position in organisation					Total
		Senior management	Middle management	Junior management	Operational	Employee	
Age group	27–35	1	1	0	0	3	5
	36–44	8	5	0	1	0	14
	45 and over	17	3	1	0	0	21
	Total	26	9	1	1	3	40

Table 5 Position in organisation and tenure of employment

Tenure	Position in organisation					Total
	Senior management	Middle management	Junior management	Operational	Employee	
Less than 1 year	1	0	0	0	0	1
1–4 years	3	3	0	0	0	6
5–10 years	6	1	1	1	1	10
Over 10 years	16	5	0	0	2	21
Total	26	9	1	1	3	40

in fact, some respondents indicated being in the industry for 20 and 30 years. It may be deduced that women, once entering the industry, often make a career of it, despite the challenges.

The analysis of the age of participants, against the number of children and the position held by the individuals, indicate that 14 (35 %) of the participants had no children, ten of which were over 36-years old, the age when it is deemed risky to have children. Seven (50 %) of the participants without children were over 45 years. Twenty-three of the participants (57 %) fell into the single, divorced, or separated categories. When considered together, these signal that women may be having challenges balancing work and family responsibilities.

Level of Educational Attainment and Position Ninety-five percent of the participants had attained tertiary level education and 87.5 % were employed in senior management or middle management positions. When educational attainment was

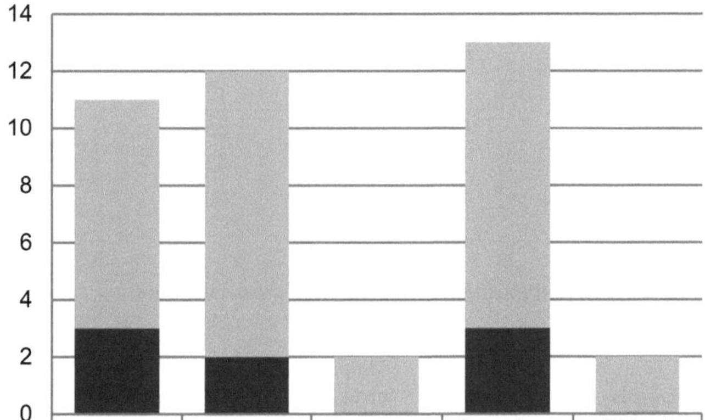

	WMU	OTHER	Other IMO	Combined IMO WID	Did not indicate
Senior Management	8	10	2	10	2
Middle Management	3	2	0	3	0

Fig. 1 Senior and middle management with maritime training

compared with positions held, it was noted that 85 % of the respondents with tertiary education were in management positions in their organization. It was further noted that 30 (75 %) of the participants had received maritime-specific training and these accounted for 90 % of the persons in senior and middle management positions (Fig. 1). This validates a major premise of the IMO WID, that education and training play a critical role in the empowerment of women.

The breakdown of institutions in which persons received maritime training, shows that 13 of the 30 persons (or 43 %) who indicated having received maritime training, had attended WMU, of which 11 were employed in middle and senior management positions, indicating a success rate of 84.6 %. Of the 14 (or 46 %) that indicated that their maritime training was from other sources than WMU, a more detailed analysis revealed that five were the beneficiaries of IMO short courses. This swells the spread of the IMO WID intervention to 18 of the 30 persons with maritime-specific training, and the positions in senior management to nearly 89 %.

An important finding is relative to the contribution to the sector. Women were found to be engaged in almost all aspects. Positions held included marine pilots; harbour master; maritime administrators; managers of port facilities; shipping agencies; shipping companies and ferry services; maritime educators; and maritime pollution prevention and enforcement. They were at the helm of port authorities, maritime administrations, coast guards, shipping agencies, and shipping companies.

Gender Equity Policies In the area of existence of gender equity policies in the workplace, 45 % indicated that there were policies, while the remaining 55 % either did not know (20 %) or said none existed (35 %). Sixteen percent of the respondents referred to the fact that government rules/policies applied and did not discriminate

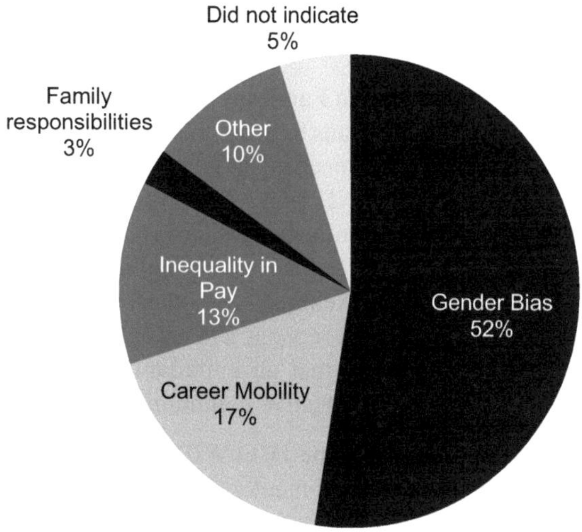

Fig. 2 Distribution of challenges faced by participants

between women and men. This may have a correlation to the number of government entities (57 %) covered by the survey. The majority (44 %) indicated that the employment and promotion processes were objective, with no differentiation between women and men, and the best qualified and experienced are employed. When this is added to the feedback relative to non-discriminatory government policies, it would appear that the general consensus is that organizational policies did not discriminate against females. Only a couple of respondents hinted at the practice of discrimination, even though there were no formal policies in this regard, and another spoke to promotion being dependent on whether one was 'liked'. However, as will be noted from the discussion below on challenges and strategies, gender discrimination featured prominently among the challenges in the industry.

Challenges and Strategies Figure 2 shows the breakdown of challenges faced by the participants. Over 50 % of the sample indicated they experienced gender bias in the workplace, which for the purpose of this survey, was defined as a preference to employ males. Career mobility and inequality in pay were the other significant challenges faced. Seven persons (17.5 %) indicated career mobility and five (12.5 %) inequality in pay. Family responsibility did not rank high among the challenges, accounting for only 3 %; neither did sexual harassment, at 2.5 %. Several respondents indicated multiple challenges, with the most common combination being gender bias and career mobility, followed by gender bias and inequality in pay.

In the face of challenges encountered in their organizations and the maritime sector in general, 46 % of the participants highlighted the acquisition of training and qualifications as their primary strategies for survival. Training included updating training, as well as improved qualifications. Other strategies included proving oneself and gaining respect through quality performance, hard work and persistence and generally, over achieving (43.7 %).

Recommendations to Facilitate Growth and Development of Women Analyses of the recommendations indicate that the participants believe networking would be the most significant mechanism to support the growth and development of women in the industry. The 21 participants (52.5 %) who recommended this, saw it as valuable for sharing information, ideas and best practices, and serving as a clearing-house for opportunities for employment in the maritime sector. This could take the form of conferences, seminars and other fora, where gender-specific issues can also be discussed. It would serve as a means of strengthening and supporting each other. It was also indicated that an important requirement in this regard would be the establishment of an effective communication network.

A critical plank of the IMO WID Programme over the last decade, has been to encourage the establishment of regional associations of professional maritime women, to create a forum for networking among female managers in the maritime and port sectors. Women in Maritime Associations (WiMAs) have been established in several regions of the world: Asia, Africa, and Latin America. None has, however, been established in the Caribbean.

In keeping with the importance given to training, as one of the strategies for overcoming challenges faced in the sector, 30 % of the participants recommended this as an important strategy to facilitate the growth and development of women in the sector. There was a clarion call from women in strategic positions in the maritime sector, to encourage and support the education and training of women and promote benefits for women. The idea being, that women who had advanced in their careers, need to do more to assist others and leverage their position to promote the advancement of the gender agenda.

Another major recommendation, is the need to establish national/regional associations and for women to join professional organizations (27.5 %). This reinforces the perception among the participants (77.5 %) of the need for networking, as the establishment of maritime associations of women professionals would be the ideal vehicle for such networking activities.

The mentoring of new entrants into the industry, as well as existing females, ranked fourth among the recommendations, with 22.5 % of the participants seeing this as important in the growth and development of women in the sector. There was the suggestion that senior women in the sector should identify women in junior positions to mentor.

Two recommendations could form best practices at the organizational or national/sector level. In the case of Belize Port Authority, a 'Women in Port' initiative was introduced in 2009, which allowed women in this sub-sector to meet and establish face-to-face contact, and it is presumed, discuss gender-related issues in the sector. The objective was to foster collaboration among women and thereby encourage their growth and development.

The other best practice, is the forum convened by the Jamaica Defence Coast Guard (JDFCG), as a part of the socialization of female recruits. It orients the recruit to gender-specific issues and how to survive in a male-dominated environment. The JDFCG appointed its first female head in 2013. It is the opinion of the authors of this paper, that the need to orient women to the industry on entrance, and sensitize them to the possible challenges they will face as females, is essential to their survival and ability to thrive.

Several other salient recommendations were put forward, some of which would form the Terms of Reference of any national or regional body to be established. These included the need to encourage other women: to perform at their best (another coping strategy) without compromising standards and morals; to choose maritime-related careers; to be team players; to participate in exchange programmes and visits; and to create awareness among women as to what the industry entails. The need to conduct a skills-gap assessment of the maritime sector, with a view to training women to fill identified gaps, was also indicated. There seems to be a need for women to be strong leaders, who are creative and determined in decision-making.

Vision for the Future of Women in the Industry The feedback relative to their vision for the women in the maritime sector, points to the awareness that not enough women are at the helm (32.5 %) in the sector, and a desire to see equality of treatment of women as it pertained to employment, opportunity, promotion and remuneration (27.5 %). The vision on equality of treatment is at odds with the findings in the area of gender equity policies (above), where 60 % indicated that existing policies in the organization did not address discrimination. This could point to a possible gap between policy and practice, or perception and reality, relative to gender equity, as well as the need for a gendered approach to policy development in the workplace.

Although not receiving majority support among the participants, there is nevertheless the shared vision of a future in the industry of women and men working alongside each other, to build the industry and collectively participate in the decision- and policy-making processes. An indicated prerequisite to this, was that women are not seen as the weaker sex, but individuals who can make significant contributions to the upliftment of the industry, in any capacity.

Most of the other visions overlapped with the recommendations made for the growth and development of women in the sector. There is, however, one vision that the researchers believe presents interesting food for thought. The participant envisioned the development of a specific code on mainstreaming women in the maritime sector at all levels, and believes that this will ensure 'genuine empowerment instead of tokenism'. This is interesting, particularly in the context of the Busan Declaration made in South Korea in April 2013[8] where the participants committed and agreed to, inter-alia "*Advocate, in [their] respective countries, the promotion for the adoption of policies and regulations which support access for*

[8] See also "Women in the maritime industry" by IMO available at http://www.imo.org/MediaCentre/HotTopics/women/Pages/default.aspx.

women to maritime education and the merchant marine professions". Experience has taught that the promotion of the adoption of national policies and regulations, are most effective when driven from the international level. Such a code which sets international standards for gender empowerment within the maritime sector could serve to foster best practices and boost the employment of women. Similar to the Maritime Labour Convention (ILO 2006), this Code could be regarded as the 'Maritime Women Bill of Rights.'

8 Conclusions and Recommendation

The survey of women who have risen to senior leadership positions in the maritime sector, has provided significant insight into the contribution of women to the maritime sector of the Caribbean and the important role of the IMO WID programme in their empowerment, in this regard. Women are now in senior management positions in a variety of maritime enterprises and several hold top positions. It is recommended that these achievements be highlighted at the Regional and national levels, to raise the profile of women in the maritime sector. This would serve to attract and inspire other women in the industry, by presenting role models. Greater awareness would also sensitize policy makers to the importance of integrating gender issues in the development strategy of their maritime sectors.

Below are some of the recommendations, which it is believed will contribute to the improvement of the future effectiveness of the IMO WID in the Caribbean, as well as general strategies for the empowerment of women in the maritime sector.

Effectiveness of IMO WID Programme in the Caribbean The discussion and analysis relative to educational attainment and position, confirm the important role of the IMO WID programme in empowering women to contribute to the maritime sector of the Caribbean. The fact that 89 % of the women who are beneficiaries of the IMO WID programme are employed in senior management positions, points to the achievement of one of the four major objectives of the Programme, namely, "to increase the percentage of women at the senior management level within the maritime sector." However, the job is not yet complete. Many of the women in the survey pointed to the need for education and training to improve women's qualifications and update their knowledge of the industry, as critical to their survival in the sector.

There is also scope for the programme to improve its contribution to the survival of women in the industry, by incorporating a gender-sensitization module in the syllabus of its mainstream courses and where possible, short courses. Such a module would identify what can be expected, provide knowledge of gender issues, and the work of the IMO WID, and best practices in social/interpersonal strategies, which can enhance survival.

As the way forward for the programme in the Region, the suggestion could be considered relative to the conduct of a skills-gap analysis, to identify future skills demand, which would serve to guide training (mainstream and short courses) interventions for women. This would be important, having regard to the maritime development plans of the States of the Caribbean, which could demand skill sets, not previously taken into consideration in the formulation of the IMO WID Programme.

Prevalence of Gender Issues in the Maritime Sector of Caribbean The findings of the survey confirmed as reality in the Caribbean, the global issues of gender bias in employment and promotion, career mobility and inequality in pay. Again, the acquisition of training and qualification is highlighted as a major strategy to address these issues. Importantly, there is also the need for organizational polices and national regulations to articulate and provide enforcement power to such measures. This recommendation comes against the background of the discussion on gender equity policy, where it was noted that despite 60 % of the respondents indicating the existence of organizational polices which did not discriminate against the employment and promotion of women, gender bias remained the primary challenge for women in the sector. The problem could therefore be the lack of effective enforcement mechanisms. It is further recommended that such mechanisms should ideally be driven at the international level. That is, an international code, establishing minimum standards for employment and/or empowerment of women in the maritime sector, along with appropriate 'control actions' to ensure compliance.

Coping Strategies and Recommendations to Support the Growth and Development of Women in the Maritime Sector of the Caribbean The acquisition of training and qualifications was identified as both a coping strategy, as well as a vehicle for the growth and development of women in the maritime sector, which confirms the strategy adopted by the IMO WID programme. Another major recommendation, is the need to establish national/regional associations. This would serve as an important vehicle to unite women in the sector as a cohesive force to promote change and facilitate development. It is therefore recommended that a professional association of maritime women (Women in Maritime Association) in the Caribbean be established, which would, *inter-alia*:

- be a primary forum for networking, through the hosting of conferences and seminars on gender issues and industry development;
- establish an effective communication network to facilitate ongoing dialogue and the sharing of ideas, and best practices among women in the sector;
- monitor standards and initiatives to encourage gender equity in employment, performance and qualifications opportunities, at all levels;
- promote the maritime sector as a viable career option for women in the Caribbean;
- identify and promote the job opportunities in the industry to facilitate career advancement of women; and
- foster the establishment of organizational mechanisms that orient and support women in the maritime sector.

Further study is recommended, which should cover all the States of the Caribbean and include males in the sector, to confirm the extent of the findings and to facilitate appropriate comparisons. This could be combined with the skills-gap assessment, to provide a more comprehensive picture of the needs of the Region, as a precursor to formulating future interventions.

References

Acevedo, S., Cebotari, A., Turner-Jones, T., Lindo, G., & Li, X. (2013). Caribbean small states: Challenges of high debt and low growth. Resource document. International Monetary Fund. http://www.imf.org/external/np/pp/eng/2013/022013b.pdf. Accessed 1 Apr 2014.

Belcher, P., Sampson, H., Thomas, M., Veiga, J., & Zhao, M. (2003). *Women seafarers: Global employment policies and practices*. Geneva: International Labour Office.

Bellony, A., Hoyos, A., & Nopo, H. (2010). Gender earnings gap in the Caribbean: Evidence from Barbados and Jamaica. Resource document. Inter-American Development Bank. http://publications.iadb.org/bitstream/handle/11319/1977/Gender%20Earnings%20Gaps%20in%20the%20Caribbean%3a%20Evidence%20from%20Barbados%20and%20Jamaica.pdf?sequence=1. Accessed 1 Apr 2014.

Bureau of Women's Affairs. (2011). Jamaica National Policy for Gender Equality (NPGE). http://www.jcdc.gov.jm/uploads/advisories/NPGE%20BOOKLET%20web.pdf. Accessed 1 Apr 2014.

CARICOM Secretariat. (2000). Empowering women for this millennium. www.caricom.org/jsp/speeches/cag_conference_barnett.jsp?null&prnf=1. Accessed 1 Apr 2014.

Commonwealth Secretariat. (2012). *Study to position Jamaica as a bunkering location in the Caribbean region: Final report*. London: Author.

Economic Commission for Latin America and the Caribbean. (2005). The millennium development goals: Latin America and the Caribbean perspective. www.eclac.org/publicaciones/xml/0/21540/chapter2.pdf. Accessed 1 Apr 2014.

Economic Commission for Latin America and the Caribbean. (2010). Caribbean synthesis review and appraisal report in the context of the 15th anniversary of the adoption of the Beijing declaration and platform for action. http://www.eclac.cl/publicaciones/xml/2/39542/LCARL.259.pdf. Accessed 1 Apr 2014.

Economic Commission for Latin America and the Caribbean. (2013). Implementation of the Cairo programme of action in the Caribbean (1994–2013): Evaluating progress and renewing commitment. http://caribbean.unfpa.org/webdav/site/caribbean/shared/publications/2013/L407_Background_document_for_Caribbean_Forum.pdf. Accessed 1 Apr 2014.

Gomes, C., & Chase, V. (in preparation). Progress in implementation of the Mauritius strategy: Caribbean regional synthesis report. ECLAC subregional headquarters for the Caribbean. http://www.sids2014.org/content/documents/250Synthesis%20Report%20Final%2020%20August%2020013.pdf. Accessed 1 Apr 2014.

ILO. (2006). *Maritime labour convention, 2006*. Genève: Author.

IMO. (2013). *Document TC 63/8, Integration of women in the maritime sector*. London: Author.

International Monetary Fund. (2013). Caribbean small states: Challenges of high debt and low growth. http://www.imf.org/external/np/pp/eng/2013/022013b.pdf. Accessed 1 Apr 2014.

Maniam, B., Russel, K., & Subramaniam, G. (2010). Gender inequality at the workplace: Time for a paradigm shift! *International Journal of Business Research, 10*(3), 161–166.

Mitropoulos, E. (2008). Empowering women in the maritime world. Resource document. IMO. http://www.imo.org/blast/mainframe.asp?topic_id=1698&doc_id=9135. Accessed 1 Apr 2014.

OECD. (2008). Gender and sustainable development: Maximising the economic, social and environmental role of women. http://www.oecd.org/social/40881538.pdf. Accessed 1 Apr 2014.
Parsan, N. (2012). The impact of globalization on African and Caribbean economies. Resource document. Embassy of the Republic of Trinidad and Tobago. http://www.ttembassy.org/index.php?mact=News,cntnt01,detail,0&cntnt01articleid=157&cntnt01origid=15&cntnt01detailtemplate=ttdetail&cntnt01returnid=70. Accessed 1 Apr 2014.
Pinnock, F. (2009). Women still an untapped resource for the shipping industry. *Caribbean Maritime, 8*, 32–33.
Tansey, P. (2000). Women on board: Ten years of the IMO women in development programme. Resource document. IMO. www.imo.org/blast/mainframe.asp?topic_id=406&doc_id=1082. Accessed 1 Apr 2014.
The Jamaica Gleaner. (2012). Caribbean women better educated but lower paid. www.jamaica-gleaner.com/gleaner/20121019/business/business9.html. Accessed 1 Apr 2014.
UN. (1995). The United Nations fourth world conference on women: Action for equality, development and peace: Platform for action. Beijing, China, September 1995. www.un.org/womenwatch/daw/beijing/platform/plat1.htm#statement. Accessed 1 Apr 2014.
UN. (2005). Taking action: Achieving gender equality and empowering women. www.unmillenniumprojec.org/document/gender-chapter79.pdf. Accessed 1 Apr 2014.
Wilson, N. (2011). Gender inequality still a major problem. Resource document. The Jamaica observer. http://www.jamaicaobserver.com/news/Gender-inequality-still-a-major-problem_9059484. Accessed 1 Apr 2014.
WMU. (2012). Facts 2012. http://wmu.se/sites/default/files/documents/files/Facts%202012%20wmu.pdf. Accessed 1 Apr 2014.

Women's Role in the Turkish and Global Maritime Industry

Ayşe Aslı Başak

Abstract Women have always had a blessed and heroic character, with a self-confident and powerful look in Turkish society since the ancient times of Turkish culture. Traditional issues have affected women's role in Turkish culture and lifestyle and, within the last 150 years, active working life, which began with industrial and technological innovations. Day by day, the social status of women in Turkey and job opportunities, have increased as the global shipping market expands. In the 1930s, Turkish women entered politics for the first time, one of the first suffrages in the world. The first female war pilot, *Sabiha Gökçen,* is from Turkey and she had the first flight in 1936. A thought occurred about Turkish women's capacity: "*If a Turkish woman can fly, why not to command a ship and pass over oceans?*". Yet, distinction and discrimination often block success. Approximately 60 years after the female war pilot, the maritime sector wanted to open a new door to young Turkish women. The belief about "*Women on ship bring bad luck!*" would finally move away and would give females chances to verify that management on vessels can also be performed by women captains and engineers. This paper includes history and real sea-life stories about/from Turkish maritime women and their achievements, which will highlight that having females on board does not bring any '*Bad luck*'.

Keywords Maritime culture • Maritime sector • Turkey • Turkish women

1 Introduction

In the legend of first women-on-board stories, many years ago, in the Middle Ages of Europe, women sailors Anne Bonney and Mary Reed had sailed on a merchant vessel as the first women working at sea, by pretending to be "*a man*", keeping their sexualities a secret (Akdogan 1956). Sea life was not easy to handle and had to be adapted for women pirates at the beginning. However, they had been able to deal with all difficulties and become the first women sailors on record.

A.A. Başak (✉)
Operation & Management Department, Cebi Maritime & Trading SA, Istanbul, Turkey
e-mail: asli.basak@nurship.com

© Springer-Verlag Berlin Heidelberg 2015

M. Kitada et al. (eds.), *Maritime Women: Global Leadership*, WMU Studies in Maritime Affairs 3, DOI 10.1007/978-3-662-45385-8_8

As another history of first women stories, Turkish women's capacity had begun to be realized by society as the result of their heroic success, which gave a different aspect to Turkish women's social status in ancient times. Economical, industrial and political changes affect women's role in society worldwide. At the beginning of 1930s, women had achieved the *suffrage* in politics in very few European countries (Kartal 2005). Prescient countries gave equal rights to women as much as men in social life and politics, and suffrage rights were given to "*Turkish women*".

Since technology and industry had been developing in 1930s, women began to participate in various jobs within many fields (Terzioglu 2007). The most significant case was the participation of women in the Turkish military as soldiers. Turkish women proved how brave they are, with being not only an ordinary soldier, but also being a "*War Pilot*" as would be honoured the "*First Woman War Pilot*", appellation given to *Mrs. Sabiha Gökçen* (TC HVKK 2012). Turkish women's capacity was realized again. Various jobs raised a number of "*firsts*", for Turkish women, in conjunction with their participating in new sectors. Another significant case came about 60 years after the "*first*" achievements of Turkish women and opened a new way to women's career path: the Maritime Sector.

Through the end of the twentieth century in Turkey, three female maritime students were accepted to the Maritime Faculty, achieving high marks in the University Entrance Exam. The first women to work on merchant vessels graduated as the youngest Turkish female officers and began to work with the rank of second Officer and third Officer on bulk carriers, LPG (Liquefied Petroleum Gas) tankers, chemical & product tankers, container & Ro–Ro vessels for many years, until one became the first female Captain in Turkey. Young Turkish women's job culture often reflects their heroic and blessed character. Turkish women seafarers working on board with their male colleagues do not compromise their gender identity, which is categorized as "*Reproducers*" with a manner of secured, confident, achieved and liberated character (Kitada 2013).

What has changed in the last 500 years around the globe since the first women pirates, Anne Bonney and Mary Read? The most visible change is working women's behaviours at sea, "*becoming a man*" or "*being a woman*". In this paper, research has been carried out on Turkish women seafarers and their real sea experiences. The life stories elucidate how Turkish women seafarers are working at sea without any sexual distinction and keeping it secret due to traditional and cultural issues, which have been faced since the first women seafarers in Turkey began working on board.

2 Research Methods

This research collected data from 25 Turkish Maritime women, including deck officers, engineer officers, masters and chief engineers, whose age range between 22 and 43 years. The data collection was conducted in the Turkish language and the author translated the data into English.

Firstly, an online survey was completed by women seafarers who still work at sea, in land-based jobs in Turkish maritime companies such as in Operation, Technical and Chartering Departments, and those who study in academics in Maritime Colleges in Turkey and worldwide.

The secondary method of the research included face-to-face interviews, which were carried out with 17 women seafarers, independent of the online survey. Interviews have been used for better understanding their sea experiences, with real life stories, including challenges, problems, achievements and recommendations from Turkish women seafarers. The history of women in the maritime sector, as well as women's role in Turkish Maritime Law, were discussed during the interviews. Meetings were held during the research period between June and December 2013. Most of the interviews were carried out over a routine lunch or dinner, a few were at social meetings and training sessions such as Class Societies' seminars and conferences, and the rest were private visits to their houses.

Research results give detailed information about the conditions of Turkish women seafarers at sea, and on land, and also describe the social status of women according to the Maritime Labour Law, a part of the Turkish domestic laws. Factors which affect women's working conditions, such as health problems and abuse cases, were also discussed, including their actual needs and the requirements that may be added to the Turkish Maritime Labour Law.

3 Women's Role in the Turkish Maritime Industry

3.1 *History of Women's Participation in the Turkish Maritime Sector*

Globally, women represent about 2 % of the world's seafaring workforce and few women seafarers prefer to work on Cargo vessels (ITF 2014). Figure 1 shows the ratio of male to women seafarers worldwide. Total seafarers constitute about 1.25 million, with only 24,500 women seafarers.

In Turkey in 2009, the registered ratio of men and women seafarers is respectively 99.95 and 0.05 %. The total number of male seafarers was 48,915, while only 210 were female seafarers (Aktug 2009). These results show that Turkey is still behind compared with the world trend in terms of women's participation in seafaring, but rates have been rising in recent years.

Istanbul University Engineering Faculty accepted the first female students to the department of Maritime Transportation in 1992. Maritime Transportation students did not even have any information about the department's compulsory on-board training period as a cadet, at least 12 months before graduating from school. It was only then, that they could become Oceangoing Watch-keeping Officers to work on board in upcoming years. As the interview result with Mrs. Saniye shows, when the first Turkish female maritime student commenced working on board as a deck cadet

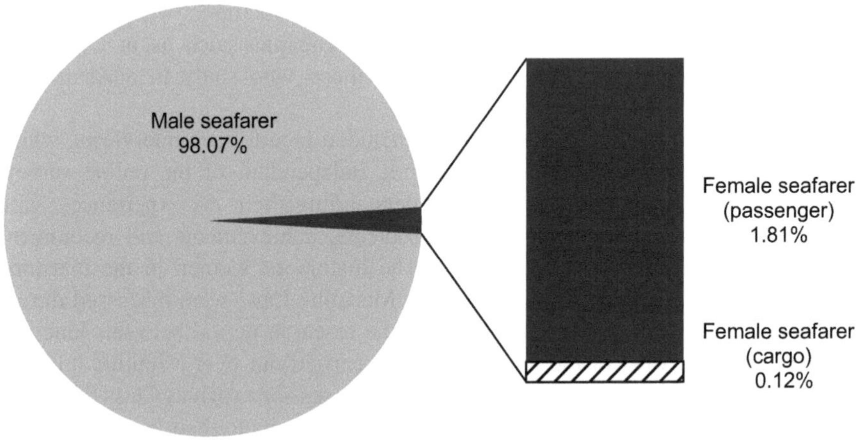

Fig. 1 The ratio of male to female seafarers. *Source*: Originally published by Drewry et al. (2009); published with kind permission of © Drewry Shipping Consultants. All rights reserved

in 1993, all companies were surprised and behaved prejudicially, because of the belief that "A w*oman on board brings bad luck*". Four years later though, this prejudice turned into a big amount of "*pride*", each day they had worked at sea.

A 24-year old Turkish female Oceangoing Watch-keeping Officer commenced her first voyage on a LPG tanker, which was a milestone in her career. It has already been very hard to work on board any type of Cargo vessel as a young lady; a LPG tanker was twice as hard. Mrs. Saniye says:

> "First, when the crew and seniors see a young lady on board, they get surprised, even up to not to be able to close their mouth and eyes! It was inevitable to feel the prejudice on your actions, but after only 4 months working on board, they realized and were also surprised, that the jobs to be done under my responsibility had been performing excellent, and so a new page in the Turkish Maritime sector has been opened; 'Attention Men! These ladies will take over your job!'." (Mrs. Saniye, 43 years old, Sea Experience: 2 years, Working at her own ship-brokering company)

The first women officers in Turkey became the first women Masters, year by year of their sea going experiences, on all oceans around the world. They did this against prejudice and various obstacles that occurred in their promotions. Stepping up their career paths so fast, opened doors to a new generation of young women: "*Why only be a Master? What about being a Chief Engineer?*"

In 1997, the Yildiz Technical University Naval Architecture and Marine Engineering Department, had accepted only one female student, who graduated in 2002 and started to work on board as the first female Engineer Officer on cargo ships, even on coasters. Mrs. Bahtiyar says:

> They got surprised when they first looked at me; surprised at twice when they heard that I am an Engineer Officer and will work on board as a 3rd Engineer. My first cadet vessel, a 1500 DWT coaster chemical tanker, had a very small cabin, working and living area for only 20 crew, and unfortunately no bathroom in the cabins; so the bathroom had been used in common by all crew except me. Luckily, the Chief Engineer gave me his cabin and bathroom during my training period, and he lived like a cadet when I was living comfortably in a Chief Engineer's luxurious life on board as an Engineer Cadet.

Being the first Turkish woman third Engineer, paved the way to being the first woman second Engineer for Mrs. Bahtiyar, within 2 years sea experience. By the achievements in her career at sea, she became popular in Marine Engineering and was offered many land-based jobs such as being the Designated Person Ashore, Technical Manager and Technical Superintendent as a Marine Surveyor through her excellent working references. The decision of leaving sea was very hard for a young woman that is addicted with her whole energy and love to the engineering job and working at sea; except a "*health*" reason which could not be underestimated in her situation. Health issues forced Mrs. Bahtiyar to choose a land-based job, to marry and to change her life.

As a third and most popular case for female students, acceptance to Maritime Faculties first occurred in 1999 at the Istanbul Technical University Maritime Faculty. When the first female students of the faculty graduated in 2004, all chose to go to sea and aimed to be Masters or Chief Engineers. Female students' percentage in the faculty has increased year by year, because maritime jobs had become popular as an opportunity for male and female students. In 2007, the faculty gave diplomas to 30 females and they began to work on Turkish and Foreigner Companies' Cargo vessels, even as still young and unexperienced officers. In 2014, the faculty had a total of 118 female students in the Marine and Engineering Departments (Istanbul Technical University 2012) and have over 250 female alumni, who cover the biggest percentage of the Turkish Maritime Sector (Basar 2013).

3.2 *Working Conditions and the Period of Turkish Women at Sea*

According to survey results, 48 % of women seafarers choose to work on board until the maximum age of 30–32, with an average 6–7 years sea experience (Table 1).

Another 52 % of the women prefer less sea experience, in order to work in land-based jobs, for various reasons. The main reason for leaving the sea depends on the issues of social/private life, such as marriages and having a child. A long-time working at sea may affect some women's health, due to stress on board, heavy working conditions and extreme working hours. However, various issues can effect women's decision to work at sea or on land. The main thought taken according to the survey and face-to-face interview is, as Mrs. Aylin said:

> I love my job on board and now on land. Although my social life was restricted during working on board, the experience that I gained was worth it. I am proud to represent my country and change the look of Turkey. I am also proud to pave the way for my sisters and my colleagues. (Mrs. Aylin, 32 years old, Sea Experience: 8 years, Rank: Oceangoing Master, Working in company as D.P.A. (Designated Person Ashore) of a Bulk Carrier Management)

Table 1 Working areas of women seafarers and average sea experiences

	The number of women	Percentage (%)	Average sea experience
On-board jobs	12	48	6–7 years
Land-based jobs	7	28	1–3 years
Academic jobs	6	24	1–5 years
Total	25	100	–

The decision to set up a family mostly forces women seafarers to choose their partners, over seafarers like themselves. A 32-year old woman seafarer, holding the license of Oceangoing Master, is working as Master of the ship with her husband, who is working as Chief Engineer on board. Working on the same ship also brought Chief Engineer Mrs. Deniz and her husband Master Mr. Engin together and they share not only the same ship, but the same life on a Turkish container ship. On-board life and working standards have became more convenient for women since technological improvements and facilities have increased. Since then, working at sea returned to a passion and addiction for women due to their success on job; even if they have already set up a family and had a baby, too. Here is what a container vessel's Master; a good wife and also mother says:

> I am married and I have a 3 month-old baby. I am working with my husband on the same ship; he is the Chief Engineer but I am the Master. Master of ship and Master of family... All crew adore my baby and love her too much! Yes, it is very difficult to work on board if you have a 3 month-old baby, especially during manoeuvring and in heavy seas... But I am happy. All my hearts – my baby, my husband and my sea – are with me. (Confidential, 32 years old, Sea Experience: 9 years, Rank: Oceangoing Master, Working at sea)

"*Mother Blessing*", care of women in Turkish culture, was always deemed a backbone of society and family structure. As much as women's role in society has become non-negligible, working life has also not changed; protection still continues on land, at sea, everywhere. Most of the maritime schools in Turkey made this case turn into "*Brotherhood*" structure under a protective mind of females including another Turkish tradition which rule would be affected by: "*hierarchy on board*". Maritime jobs in Turkey and working relations, have been constructed on "*mutual respect*" between subordinates and their seniors for many years. Somehow, the respect turned into an invisible brotherhood and became like a big family in the Turkish Maritime Sector. One of the 24-year old Oceangoing Watch-keeping Officers, Mrs. Banu says:

> "When I first embarked on the vessel as a cadet, everybody on board called me '*Sister*'. The Master's age was pretty old and he was as old as my father, and that's why he also called me 'Daughter'. I thought, 'Are we a family on board?' The answer was absolutely 'Yes!' I was the little sister and daughter of that family too, and I am always so glad of this protection. This is special for Turkish culture, I am proud of that."

To conclude, Turkish vessels have a safe and protective condition for women working on board due to cultural and traditional issues. Since technological improvements have increased, vessels' accommodation and working conditions became more comfortable for women seafarers. The face-to-face interviews with other Turkish women seafarers, showed that a woman on board mostly raises seafarers' quality of life on board and makes crew members more careful and approach each other kindly. This also maintains healthy relationships between crew members via creating a comfortable working atmosphere on board. The crew who sees that a woman can be successful in such types of demanding jobs, encourage her and his own siblings, relatives and other female students to study at the Maritime Faculty and to become a Captain or Chief Engineer, as an opportunity for a well-paid job.

In the meantime, widely-known disadvantages for women seafarers, compared with male colleagues, would be sexual harassment that women may face. As a result, women seafarers tend to feel weak and reluctant to continue their seafaring career (Thomas 2006). Unlike such global tendencies, this research revealed that Turkish women seafarers generally have safe working conditions on board. Nevertheless, it was reported that some Turkish women seafarers experienced hormonal deformation and physical fatigue due to extreme work patterns at sea. Seafarers have the right to be examined by a doctor at ports, during their contractual voyage, by the medical insurance provided by their companies and P&I Club in emergency health situations, according to the Maritime Labour Convention, 2006; which means women have the same rights on health issues as men working on board, even though body deformation is absolutely different. In the face-to-face interviews, women seafarers recommended that additional health protection rights must be provided to them, even when they are on annual leave and complete their contract on board.

3.3 Women's Role in Turkish and Global Maritime Law

On Turkish Flag vessels, all Turkish crew are employed according to the Turkish Maritime Labour Law, which came into force in 1967. However, seafarers got more effective rights on employment agreements through the Maritime Labour Convention, 2006 regulations. Turkish Maritime Labour Law still has not been revised and has continued to be studied by the Turkish Ministry of Transport and Maritime Affairs, according to International Labour Organization (ILO) global regulations (Turkish Ministry of Transport and Maritime Affairs 2013).

Globally, over the years, the ILO has maintained and developed a system of international labour standards aimed at promoting opportunities for women and men to obtain decent and productive work, in conditions of freedom, equity, security and dignity (ILO 2006). This makes the women seafarers equal among all seafarers in maritime laws and conventions and changes the term, "*sea men*" to "*women seafarers*".

In all conventions and regulations related to seamen and sea, women were included as "*seafarer*" to prevent gender discrimination. However, it is still written "*seamen*", which is translated as "*gemiadamı*" in Turkish language, Maritime Law, and Seafarers' Identity Cards. Women seafarers in Turkey ironically still have a "*Seamen's Book*" not a "*Seafarers' Register Book*".

$$\left.\begin{array}{ll}\underline{\text{Turkish Meaning :}} & \underline{\text{Gemi}} + \underline{\text{Adamı}} \\ \underline{\text{English Meaning :}} & \text{Ship} + \text{Man}\end{array}\right\}\ \text{Where is the definition of “Sea + Farer”?}$$

The expression of "*Female Captain*" still does not exist in the Turkish Maritime Law. The rights of female captains while working on board, have only been described generally as "*seafarer*" in the Turkish Maritime Labour Law, without any sexual distinction. For example, the law does not include the right of pregnancy while working on board. The main reason may be that women only work as officers, captains or engineers on board, not as ratings in Turkey. Turkish culture is far from the mind and view that women can work at sea as able seaman, ordinary seaman, oiler, cook, steward etc. Furthermore, the Turkish Maritime Labour Law has no expression about pregnancy and loss of health due to heavy working conditions, which may affect metabolism during the on-board working period of women. In particular, that is known as special women disabilities in Turkey.

According to women seafarers' recommendations in this research, the Turkish Maritime Law should exist in on-board working definitions and social rights, which are given specifically to women seafarers. Most of the Turkish women seafarers also think that it is only possible to gather under an organization between Turkish and global maritime communities in order to seek justice for their labour standards and rights.

4 Conclusion

Turkish women have always had a different role in society. Participation of women in the Turkish maritime industry opened a new discussion between the sector and seafarers. Prejudice and discussions have finally moved away, after Turkish women became successful in maritime jobs; on board and ashore. Working conditions at sea are affected by cultural difference. Turkish traditional factors create a well-based on-board working condition for women seafarers. Real life stories of female captains and engineers changed the idea of working on Turkish vessels, in which reflected the underestimated role of women. It is shifting towards protection and opportunities as a result of their success and professional ethics.

In spite of the advantages of women on board, they generally work under stress during their contracts. Family-based relationships would help to raise the working standards in welfare for Turkish maritime women. Unfortunately, sufficient support for women seafarers in the Turkish maritime sector is limited only to the level of statements. Lack of legislation on women seafarers' rights shows that global maritime culture and tradition are not ready to support women on board.

The Turkish maritime sector embraced the participation of women only recently, over the last 20 years. The rate of women is increasing day by day due to maritime jobs being more attractive for females with well-based working standards. Maintaining of a better on-board condition can be enhanced through the improvement of legislation. Employment of women will be able to advance more with encouragement of given rights by Law, in which traditional issues will be considered. The Turkish maritime sector can be a reference to the need for additional on-board facilities for women seafarers, and this should not be set out as barriers on women's career at sea.

References

Akdogan, R. (1956). Women pirates. *Turkish Sea Magazine*, 2/21, 10.

Aktug, S. (2009). Women's role at sea. Resource document. DenizHaber. http://www.denizhaber.com/HABER/17505/22/bayan-denizci-bayan-kaptan. Accessed 2 Dec 2013.

Basar, E. (2013). *Maritime schools in Turkey: 10th maritime education committee meeting*. Van: Turkish Ministry of Transport and Maritime Affairs Publishing.

Drewry, ILO, & ITF. (2009). *Manning 2009*. London: Drewry Shipping Consultants.

ILO. (2006). *Maritime labour convention, 2006*. Genève: Author.

Istanbul Technical University. (2012). *Faculty activity report*. Istanbul: Author.

ITF. (2014). Woman seafarers. http://www.itfseafarers.org/ITI-women-seafarers.cfm. Accessed 1 Nov 2013.

Kartal, C.B. (2005). *Getting suffrages and social rights for women in Turkey & municipality election in 1930* (Master of Science Thesis). Istanbul University Social Science Institute, Istanbul).

Kitada, M. (2013). Code of behaviour at sea: Women seafarers' shipboard identity management. *WMU Journal of Maritime Affairs, 12*(2), 213–227.

TC HVKK. (2012). Mirror of history: First woman war pilot in Turkey Sabiha Gökçen. http://www.hvkk.tsk.tr/tr/IcerikDetay.aspx?ID=34&IcerikID=86. Accessed 23 Oct 2013.

Terzioglu, Z. (2007). *Political rights of Turkish women in media (1930–1935)* (Master of Science Thesis). Marmara University Institute of Turkish Sciences, Istanbul.

Thomas, A. M. (2006). Sexual harassment in a residential occupation: The experiences of women seafarers. *Health Education Journal, 65*(2), 170–179.

Turkish Ministry of Transport and Maritime Affairs. (2013). *MLC 2006 activity report*. Istanbul: Turkish Ministry of Transport and Maritime Affairs Publishing.

Absent Mother Sailors: How Possible Is It to Do the Impossible?

Momoko Kitada

Abstract This paper examines how women seafarers on merchant cargo ships balance work and family life, particularly when they become a mother. Thirty-six women seafarers, including ten mothers, were interviewed. Their biggest concern was marriage and family, and they tend to face the issue of agency—individuals' capacity of making their own choices freely and acting independently. In other words, when marriage and family issues come into their lives, can women feel free to choose whether they continue seafaring or quit? In the sample, only five mothers either stayed at sea or returned to ship after the children were grown up. Those mothers who remained working at sea tended to encounter new challenges relating to their sense of motherhood, as well as their children's emotional relationship with the mothers. The study addresses the impact of mother's absence from home, both on mothers and their children. The paper concludes that it is not totally impossible for women seafarers to continue working at sea after having children, however, women's agency may be constantly challenged by their domestic gender roles, when they try to balance work and family life.

Keywords Agency • Breadwinner • Gender identity • Motherhood • Women seafarers • Work–life balance

1 Introduction

Historically, seafaring jobs have been dominated by men in many parts of the world. Only a few women on board navy ships, merchant vessels, or privateers were documented before World War I and there were still a limited number of women who worked at sea, mostly in the Navy during World Wars I and II (Aggrey 2000; Turley 1999). It was only the late 1970s when several maritime universities started to open doors for women to train officers on merchant ships. Women, as a potential source of qualified seafaring labour, have been discussed mainly for political and

M. Kitada (✉)
World Maritime University, Malmö, Sweden
e-mail: mk@wmu.se

© Springer-Verlag Berlin Heidelberg 2015

M. Kitada et al. (eds.), *Maritime Women: Global Leadership*, WMU Studies in Maritime Affairs 3, DOI 10.1007/978-3-662-45385-8_9

economic reasons. The International Maritime Organization (IMO) launched a programme called 'the Integration of Women in the Maritime Sector (IWMS)' in 1988, focusing on equal access to maritime training (IMO 1988). This strategy is now further strengthened by the UN Millennium Development Goal 3 (MDG 3): 'Promote gender equality and empower women' (UN 2000). In addition to the political motivation to employ more women in shipping, the shortage of qualified officers is anticipated to reach 13,000 officers worldwide, according to the BIMCO/ISF[1] Manpower Update, and the number will be either maintained or worsen in 2015 (BIMCO and ISF 2010). The shipping industry is facing an economic crisis unless they attract young people, including women, to train as future seafarers to operate ships for sustainable development.

Nevertheless, the gender balance of seafarers is still remarkably inclined towards men. Despite the scarce data about the number of women seafarers on merchant ships, an estimation made by IMO in 1992 suggests that women represent just one to two percent of the world's 1.25 million seafarers (Belcher et al. 2003). This percentage includes women workers in catering and hotel sections on board passenger ships and cruise vessels. When it comes to women seafarers on merchant cargo ships, the number drops significantly to 0.12 % (Drewry et al. 2009).

Aggrey (2000) highlights that one of the main obstacles for women in the maritime industry is associated with the difficulty of balancing work and family. This could be even more challenging for women seafarers who have to be away from their families for several months, while on board (Kitada 2012). How do women seafarers view their career paths in relation to marriage and family life? How does their seafaring experience influence their idea of marriage and family life? If women have chosen to continue seafaring after having children, how do they maintain their identity as mothers? This paper addresses how individual women seafarers make their own choices to manage their work and family issues and discusses women's agency in the case of women seafarers. The study further concerns the impact of mother's absence on the emotional relationship between mother and children.

2 Parallel Worlds Between Ship and Shore

Seafarers work and live on board a ship. In other words, the ship is a workplace as well as an everyday part of their private lives. Most seafarers on ocean-going vessels are likely to spend significant periods of time on board ships. It is usually several months on duty at sea and a couple of months off duty ashore. While they cannot see their families, lovers and friends, they often attempt to cut off their emotions from the land. Indeed, being emotional is one of the taboos in the occupational culture of seafaring, because emotions are regarded as negative

[1] BIMCO is the abbreviation of the Baltic and International Maritime Council based in Denmark, while ISF is the International Shipping Federation, located in UK.

elements of seafarers' qualities, which could adversely influence their teamwork at sea (Kitada 2011). Emotions are often associated with feminine qualities, therefore women seafarers tend to be extra-careful about their behaviour on board ships, not to be seen as feminine or 'girls' (Kitada 2013).

Such seafarers' lives do not end only at sea, but also extend to shore between their voyages. They return to another life based on shore, which is parallel to their sea life. Their time of living at sea and ashore is fragmented and they squeeze into the shore life which has existed without them. The temporal discontinuities of their linear stream of time could cause disharmony between their 'individual' time and 'family' time (Thomas and Bailey 2009). This problem is commonly acknowledged among seafarers, regardless of gender. Seafarers tend to find it awkward to return from ship to shore, as if they are interrupting their family members' peaceful life (Thomas and Bailey 2006).

The question may arise of when seafarers can feel rested and relaxed, if they are not allowed to express their emotions on board a ship and their presence may not be totally welcome at home on leave. Seafaring fathers should find it difficult in this working pattern, as they cannot linearly share their life with their family, without temporal discontinuities. In the case of seafaring mothers, it can be even more challenging in terms of their expected gender roles and their identity as a mother. How could these unstructured periods of seafarers' life-cycle between ship and shore, conflict with gender roles and identities of seafaring mothers? How do they fill the gap between their 'individual' and 'family' time, when they re-join the family waiting ashore?

3 Women's Agency in Balancing Work and Family

Seafaring is one of the extreme versions of horizontal gender segregation, similar to police (Holdaway and Parker 1998; Paoline 2003), firefighters (Yoder and Aniakudo 1995, 1996), and Navy (Newell et al. 1995). This literature describes mainly sexual harassment and gender discrimination at work and the same problems have been reported in the case of women seafarers (Belcher et al. 2003; Jo 2010). These women often struggle against masculine norms and values that oppress them; therefore, women's agency in gender-segregated occupations is constantly challenged. To deal with this situation, women seafarers tend to develop and utilise various identity management strategies and thus cope with gender-related problems (Kitada 2010, 2013). Aggrey (2000) argued that the challenges associated with women's gender roles, seem to have an impact on their perceptions of balancing work and family in the context of maritime industries.

When it comes to the work–life balance, women in full-time jobs tend to face the problem of choosing work or family, especially when they have children, as they are often expected to fulfill their expected gender roles within society (Klugman et al. 2014; Roeters and Craig 2014). Indeed, women today may not feel oppressed by men as much as they used to do. Individual choice, as well as responsibility, has been emphasised within neo-liberal discourse (Lyonette et al. 2011). Giddens

(1984) observes the phenomenon of social reflectivity, that an agent consciously adapts to the social structure in the process of socialization. Even so, it has been observed that, to a greater or lesser extent, the patterned arrangements of the social structure affect or limit the choices and opportunities available for them. In the contemporary labour market, increasing global integration and competition permit women to be the "weakest links" in global value chains in the informal economy (Chant and Pedwell 2008). Hence, women's agency—their individuals' capacity of making their own choices freely and acting independently—in terms of choosing mothering, may not be always one's ability to act and transform their circumstances, as patriarchal rules could be embedded in diverse institutions such as family, state, religion and labour markets (Charrad 2010). Even for the new younger generation, women's agency may not be always affordable, as the society still depends on a patriarchal structure, allowing men to be a ruler (Roeters and Craig 2014).

This paper explores the ways in which seafaring mothers construct the idea of mothering/motherhood and their identity as mothers, by managing two completely separate lives, seafaring and family. All the accounts on mothering and motherhood described in this paper, emerged from the interviewees of the study. The understandings of what is mothering/motherhood vary by individuals in terms of their experience, family, culture and religion. Though the sample of seafaring mothers was small, because the total population of women seafarers is very minor, as discussed earlier, it is important to give a voice to those who pioneered in balancing seafaring and family life, hence the new knowledge would serve young women seafarers who may find it difficult to cope with such challenges in their future careers.

4 The Setting for the Study

This research looks into women seafarers who wish to develop their career at sea, but face the issue of mothering, specifically the impact of absent mothers on the emotional relationship between mother and children. Hence, the study targeted women seafarers in their career paths, namely, female deck officers, engineers, or radio officers on merchant cargo ships. Cargo ships include oil and gas tankers, bulk carriers, Ro–Ro vessels, container ships, timber vessels and so on. These vessels are often operated by men and may have only one woman working on board. Other types of ships, for example, fishing boats, cruise ships, and yachts, were excluded from this research on women seafarers, due to the different nature of seafaring life patterns; and women on those ships do not necessarily develop their careers in the same way as women do on cargo ships. Navy Women were also excluded, as the public sector often offers a different employment pattern from the one in private sectors. Moreover, women seafarers on cargo ships are likely to share the same occupational culture (Kitada 2011), with a relatively small number of crew, typically just 18 people on a cargo vessel between 2,000 and 7,999 GT (JITI and Nippon Foundation 2010), sailing together from several weeks to months.

5 Methods

This study focuses on women seafarers' experiences of balancing work and family. The agency of choosing mothering is one of the biggest issues that women seafarers tend to face from the early stage of their seafaring careers. Their dilemmas on this specific topic are often not shared with anybody, even their closest family or friends, as they know that their difficulties are not easily understood by 'others' (Kitada 2010). Such untold truths of women seafarers' agency of choosing mothering, were studied by qualitative research methods 'which focus more on the subjective experiences and meanings of those being researched' (Maynard 1994).

The participants were recruited through snowball sampling and 36 women seafarers from six different countries joined the project. The participants were diverse in terms of their profiles. Their nationalities were largely Swedish (12), German (11) and Portuguese (9), as well as Japanese (2), Polish (1) and Ghanaian (1). Their ranks were from third mates to Captain/Chief Engineer; the length of their total sea time was between 6 months and 29 years; and their ages varied between 19 and 54 years old. Among the sample, ten women were mothers who used to work on board ships and the majority (26) were single or married/co-habited without children.

In-depth interviews were conducted as a primary data-collection method, in order to understand how women seafarers perceived the agency of choosing mothering and whether it is compatible with their seafaring careers. Whilst the majority of participants (30) were individually interviewed face-to-face as planned, other methods, such as a group interview (4), telephone interview (1) and e-mail interview (1), had to be utilised, due to feasibility during the fieldwork. A group interview took place when four women seafarers were all friends and gathered at once. A telephone interview was conducted with a newly introduced participant, only after the fieldwork trip to her country was completed. An e-mail interview was also alternated upon the request of a busy, yet enthusiastic woman seafarer, as it was the only way for her to participate in the research.

The interview data were recorded upon obtaining informed consent prior to the interviews. The average interview was approximately 2-hours long and the longest one took nearly 4 hours. The researcher transcribed the interview data, which were thereafter coded and analysed using the qualitative research software, NVivo. To ensure participants' confidentiality, all the individuals were assigned pseudonyms, which are found in the quoted texts in the paper. For the background information of the participants, their ages, job ranks, and country names are referenced after securing their permission in the paper. Such information is particularly important in order to explore the career stage of women seafarers and from the country they hail from, and whether that shapes their view on balancing their work and family lives. Although the author acknowledges the limitation of analysis by age, job rank, and country, as the data are limited, this paper does not intend to focus on comparison among the participants, but rather highlights women seafarers' difficult experiences of career choice.

6 Findings

Common Anticipation in Seafaring Careers All the women seafarers in the sample expressed a significant degree of anticipation in their future seafaring careers, when it comes to the matter of marriage and family planning. It was not always the question that the interviewer asked the participants, but rather the women seafarers themselves shared their views about the extremely difficult situation of having both seafaring careers and a family life. Young women seafarers were, in particular, motivated to become a Captain or a Chief Engineer in the future, however they also felt hesitant about not fulfilling their roles as mothers, if they pursued their dreams. A German deck trainee, Marina, stated:

> When you are in that situation, it would be totally different than only to think about the situation. Because when you have a baby, you also want to, I think, the feeling as a mother to a baby, I cannot imagine now. Because I am not in that situation. But I think when I have a baby, I would not say as a mother, 'Ok, you will take care of my baby, I will be far away for five months or something.' No, I think this is not really possible for me, it is impossible.—(Marina, Age 22, Deck officer trainee, German)

The title of this paper, "Absent mother sailors: How possible is it to do the impossible?" was derived from the voice of interviewees such as Marina. Same accounts emerged from other participants. Similarly, a Portuguese engineer, Brites, observed her woman seafarer friend who was no longer able to work on board because of her role as a mother. Brites felt it was a requirement for women to stay at home with a baby, as she described:

> Our friend...she has a child, a little girl....and she cannot go to sea again, because she needs to stay home.—(Brites, Age 34, Junior Engineer, Portuguese)

Women seafarers in some countries (e.g., Portugal), where gender division of work tends to be greater than other countries (e.g., Sweden), were likely to feel more obliged to their assigned gender roles, in particular, their roles as mothers. To stay at home with children was regarded as an unavoidable condition to fulfill the role as a mother, who is considered to take full responsibility of childrearing and they often cannot expect a contribution from the father. In other countries, such as Sweden, where the fathers' participation in childrearing is encouraged by the state (Seierstad and Healy 2012), women seafarers did not feel so much pressure in their role as mothers. It appeared to be rather a choice for women, whether they want to stay at home or not. A Swedish engineer, Julia, explained:

> After having babies (...) there is a woman, female Captain married an AB.[2] And he stopped sailing and took care of children, and she continues sailing. But I didn't want to be a kind of Mum. Emotionally, it would not be possible for me to still work on the ship, having children. Even [if] there is a father, I don't want to be a kind of mother.—(Julia, Age 34, Senior engineer, Swedish)

---

[2] AB stands for an able-bodied seaman who is categorised in rating ranks, not officers. Their jobs may not require them to have a license and they could serve as a helmsman and a lookout, etc. They are often skilful and multi-task on merchant ships.

For a Swedish engineer, Julia, it was her choice to quit seafaring in order to fulfill the role of a mother. Her idea of being a mother was not compatible with her seafaring career. She understood that her career path would continue by relocating herself from ship to shore and she kept working full-time in a shore-based maritime sector.

In fact, many women seafarers tend to see that it would be the most reasonable alternative for them, to switch their jobs from a ship-based to shore-based work. If one wishes to go to sea, even after they marry and/or have children, they tend to choose shorter voyage vessels such as ferries and coastal liners, or work as a pilot who guides a ship through dangerous or congested waters, like harbour ports or river mouths. Such patterns of seafaring jobs are still manageable for many women to work at sea, allowing them to go back home on a daily basis.

Nevertheless, the research shows that the norms, that women are naturally suitable for caring for children at home, predominantly exist in all the countries where the interviewees are based. Women seafarers seemed to find it very difficult to change such mindsets in their societies and the majority of them tended to quit seafaring when they encountered the situation where their gender roles in domestic spheres, pressure them to make a decision. Even if some women decided to stay at sea when they became pregnant, they could change their mind as soon as they saw their newborn babies. A Portuguese Captain, Vidonia, stated:

> I have to admit that I find it completely incompatible. When I disembarked 7 months pregnant, my idea was to continue at sea. However, the minute I looked at my baby I realized that I was being foolish and irresponsible. Children need care, emotional stability, a mum, a dad, lots of love, and if we decide to have kids, they have to be our biggest priority, above our own interests.—(Vidonia, Age 51, Captain, Portuguese)

Vidonia discovered a sense of motherhood when she first saw her baby in the hospital. This sense of motherhood was strongly associated with full responsibility as the mother of the baby and she described that it was not compatible with working as a seafarer. It was an immediate instinct as a mother who needs to protect her baby. A sense of motherhood described here, was more animal-like and inherent; however, this paper later argues another type of motherhood, which is something a mother 'acquires' during the time of childbearing.

Women seafarers in some cultures, on the other hand, told a different story. In some cultures, children are looked after by a large family, including extended families, and even a community to which she belongs. There was only one example in the sample, a Ghanaian woman Captain, Sisi. She stressed the idea in her culture that anyone who can earn for the family should work, regardless of gender. She could even hire a helper to do domestic work, with a relatively small investment. Hence, the need of fulfilling her gender roles can be easily satisfied and substituted by other available resources that she can access. In fact, potential breadwinners are expected and motivated to work for the family.

> In Ghana (. . .) one thing is honestly very easy to get help. I mean house help (. . .) to get a house boy, to get a house girl who help, you know, clean the house. So there is not much demand for the women apart from the cooking. But if you are lucky and you get a house girl who can cook very well, I mean who can make your stew or soup and things and put them in

> a fridge. (. . .) You come back in the evening and you just make rice or salad or something. So it's quite easy for women to actually pursue their dreams.—(Sisi, Age 52, Captain, Ghanaian)

Although Sisi's hard time of juggling her two lives, seafaring and family, will be presented later in this paper, it is apparent from this example that culture and social support for working women makes a big difference. The Republic of the Philippines is also known as a family-oriented society, focusing on communities and kin support networks (Peterson 1993), similar to Ghana. This research unfortunately does not have any sample from the Philippines, however a recent study on 'The Global Gender Gap', reported by the World Economic Forum (2013), shows that the Philippines was the fifth out of 136 countries in the Gender Gap Index, and women's economic participation and opportunity was highly regarded.

How Possible Is It to Keep Sailing While Leaving Children at Home? One may ask whether seafarers can bring their children on board their ships. It is possible for a spouse (i.e., wives)[3] and older children to travel together for a certain period of time on the same vessel where seafarers, at officer level, are working if the Captain permits. Babies and smaller children accompanied by adults may be allowed to visit the ship in port to see their father or mother for a short time. Notwithstanding, it is said that a seafarers' fate is that they cannot see their family once they are on board (Thomas et al. 2001, 2003). No matter what happens to their family, they should stay on board while on duty, which is a principle of seafaring jobs.

This poses a fundamental problem for women seafarers: how can they balance work and family? In many cultures, it is still unacceptable for women to be away from home for many months, especially when they have children. Dilemmas associated with their expected gender roles seem to be overwhelming and thus, many women seafarers, as discussed earlier, tend to quit their jobs when they have children.

Despite the challenges that women seafarers may have, there are several examples of women who continued to work on board a ship while leaving their children ashore. Thirty-six women seafarers were interviewed, including ten mothers who used to work on board ships. Of which, half quit seafaring after giving birth, while four of them continued working at sea, and one mother seafarer returned to sea when her child was grown up (Table 1).

Types of Seafaring Mothers Bearing in mind that there are not many women who actually remained working at sea after having children, this research highlights five examples of seafaring mothers and three types emerged. The first type was 'The mother of older kids'; a woman seafarer who returned to sea when her children were

[3] There is a long history in shipping that seafarers' wives travelled together with their seafaring husbands on war ships and merchant ships (Cordingly 2001). It is hardly heard that women seafarers bring their husbands on board, because it may draw unwanted attention from their male colleagues. Most women seafarers make efforts not to be seen as feminine while at sea, and need to prove their competence as professionals by working twice as hard as their male counterparts (Kitada 2013).

Table 1 The categories of ten mothers who used to work at sea

Type	Pseudonym	Nationality	Age	Rank/ department*	Length at sea (years)
The mother of older kids	Pamera	German	44	J/D	5
The breadwinner with no choice	Simone	German	53	R	10
	Karolina	Polish	52	S/D	14
The seafaring mother as her choice	Sisi	Ghanaian	52	Capt	19
	Rose	Portuguese	45	R	11
Those who quit and found a shore-based job	Yelena	Portuguese	41	Capt	7
	Vidonia	Portuguese	51	Capt	12
	Rute	Portuguese	47	R	10
	Julia	Swedish	34	S/E	10
	Rebecka	Swedish	44	S/D	15

*The abbreviations for rank/department: *Capt* captain, *S/D* senior deck officer, *J/D* junior deck officer, *S/E* senior engineer, *R* radio officer

grown up. The second type was called 'The breadwinner with no choice'; these women were in the circumstance that they had to earn enough money to feed the whole family. The third type was 'The seafaring mother as her choice', who decided to stay at sea while leaving her children at home. These three categories are explained with the following examples.

The first type, 'The mother of older kids', represents a woman seafarer who returned to sea when her child became old enough. There was only one sample which was found of this type. A German deck officer, Pamera, quit seafaring after giving birth and stayed with her daughter until she became 15 years old. Pamera recalled her memory that it was a big break for her and thrilling to go back to sea afterwards. Indeed, returning to sea after many years is equally difficult for male seafarers. Because of the introduction of new regulations, systems and technology, today's seafaring jobs could be quite different from the ones they experienced years ago. Seafarers are also expected to immediately perform well and show their competence on new ships. They tend to get extremely nervous before joining a new vessel. Furthermore, the renewal of licenses may cost time and money. Many seafarers who left sea are often reluctant to go back to seafaring, due to a number of constraints. Pamera, in the 'mother of older kids' type, explained, however, it was possible for her to have both lives, being a mother and a seafarer:

> When I had the mate certificate, I travelled one and a half years. And I made a big break, because I got pregnant. I stayed ashore nearly for 15 years. Then I got back [to sea]. It was a little bit different, but it was possible. (. . .) Good things to get a kid. Because you have a present to get the world addition to the one that you have now. Because it is really a second life, you will get. I like this experience very much. But I like both. (laugh)—(Pamera, Age 44, Junior deck officer, German)

Pamera's example, 'The mother of older kids' was, however, not commonly observed among both male and female seafarers due to the changes in regulations, systems and technology, as discussed earlier. The other types of seafaring mothers are 'The breadwinner with no choice' and 'The seafaring mother as her choice'. These two types of seafaring mothers made it possible to continue working at sea while leaving their small children. The difference between the two types was whether it was their choice or not.

'The breadwinner with no choice' is in the situation that women seafarers are the only ones in the family who can earn money and feed the rest of the family. Two samples out of five seafaring mothers in this research fit this type. A German radio officer, Simone, had a student husband and they decided that she would work on ships while her husband studied and took care of their baby. Simone signed off the ship and stayed at home when her husband was in the semester break and worked for a short period of time. It was the only option for Simone to continue seafaring while leaving her baby ashore, as she described:

> Our situation was that we had somebody who had to work for money. And my husband was studying. What shall I do? I have to go to sea. So I tried to minimise it. When the child was one year, I had been away for only four weeks a year. A year after, it was two months. So he grows. The longest voyage I did was five months. The very longest voyage I had. You see over the year it was not too much, I think. (...) It worked. It was to live.—(Simone, Age 53, Radio officer, German)

Another woman seafarer who had no choice but to continue working on board, was a Polish deck officer, Karolina. She did not return to her ship immediately after her child was born, however when the baby was 9 months, her husband lost his job because of an injury. Karolina, therefore, decided to work on the vessel with a shorter schedule, 2 weeks on and 2 weeks off. This working pattern allowed her to stay at home every 2 weeks until her child became 4 years old. Karolina explained that she got a lot of help from her parents while she was absent from home. She sometimes wondered why she was not at home with her child.

> When I was on board, usually my parents helped to take care of my daughter. (...) sometimes I was thinking, what I was doing here? Why I am not at home?—(Karolina, Age 52, Senior deck officer, Polish)

Karolina showed me a picture of her family during the interview, and her relationship with her children seemed nothing different from any other ordinary family.

The third type, 'The seafaring mother as her choice', on the other hand, includes two samples from the data of five seafaring mothers, and they stayed at sea for a relatively longer period of absence from home, compared to the other women seafarers. One seafaring mother, a Ghanaian Captain, continued serving at sea until she turned around 40 years old and another mother from Portugal stayed at sea until her oldest child became 10 years old. As a consequence of their long seafaring careers, there seemed to be an impact on their family relationship between a mother and children. A Ghanaian mother Captain, Sisi, described:

> I mean there might be at sea costs me love of my children. Because what happened was they got closer to their father. You know, because he was always there for them. So they got closer to their father rather than to me. It was Mummy, always the one who brought good things, you know, beautiful things from sea. (. . .) I missed the love of my children, their affection.—(Sisi, Age 52, Captain, Ghanaian)

Sisi confessed that seafaring cost her the love children have for their mother. She felt that her children did not love their mother in the same way as they did their father, because she did not stay close to them when she was sailing. The absence of mother became normal to the children and they developed a closer relationship with their father instead. The absent mother was, as a breadwinner, appreciated for bringing nice goods from abroad to the family, which made Sisi feel that her relationship with the children was "fake". Sisi illustrated her difficulty as a mother by describing her children's behaviours; when she told her children to do something, they asked their father for his confirmation; and when they cried, they chose their father:

> When you tell them to do something, they have to go and ask their father. You know, Mmm! I couldn't. . .I was jealous, you know. How? If I told them to do something, why should they go? And if they want to cry, they go to their father to cry. Why not come to me? I am your mum!—(Sisi, Age 52, Captain, Ghanaian)

Sisi's story highlights that the absence of the mother continues in her children's mind, even when she was at home. Her children were not able to develop the relationship with their mother the same as with their father, because they did not live and grow together. Sisi said, 'I love them, but they couldn't love me back, because I was not there for them.' Sisi, as a mother, was constantly thinking of her children as if she were in two worlds, ship and shore. Her children, on the other hand, lived in only one shore-based world, where their mother was not present. The gap between the mother and children grew, as time went by.

Another example of 'The seafaring mother as her choice' was a Portuguese radio officer, Rose, a mother of three children. Rose also did not give up seafaring and continued her sea career for 10 years after having children. By contrast to Sisi, who sacrificed the love of her children, Rose emphasised her identity as a mother throughout the interview. Rose described the difference of her emotions as a mother towards the two older sons and towards the youngest son. This gap was caused by how closely she watched her sons, which affected her sense of motherhood. Rose described:

> I didn't watch them growing up. My older two boys, I didn't watch them. (. . .) No, I was not here. So only when the oldest one was ten years old, I said myself, 'Well, I must end my career.' (. . .) The youngest one is six years old. Uh, very good difference between them. For this [youngest] one, I feel myself as a mother, because I was emotionally going on. The other ones, well, they were born and then I saw them in ten years old (. . .) the other one nine years old. It's very strange because in some ways I am not exactly a mother. Sometimes I am the oldest sister or even the sister around their age. So, we have problems with them making myself feel as a mother and say this is what Mama. . .Mother or Father wants to do. It's very difficult.—(Rose, Age 45, Radio officer, Portuguese)

Rose explained that her sense of motherhood was developed as she emotionally grew together by closely watching her youngest son. With two older children, however, she could not feel like a mother but rather a big sister or a sister around their age. This suggests that motherhood is not automatically embedded in the family relationship, but something to be "acquired" with confidence gained through intimate observations of one's children and the accumulation of shared lives. It can also be the knowledge for the mother that her continuous presence at home should privilege her as a knower of every single detail of her children. Without being there with the children, seafaring mothers might miss a big part of their family life and their identity as a mother can also be threatened. Rose's example provides a comparative analysis of a seafaring mother's sense of motherhood in relation to the child whose growth was observed and to the other children who were not.

7 Conclusion

This research looked into how women seafarers on merchant cargo ships perceive the issues of balancing work and family life. Young women seafarers in the early stage of their careers seemed to foresee the problem of continuing working at sea after marriage and particularly after having children. They felt it was unavoidable to make the ultimate decision of choosing work or family when the time came, and many seemed to accept their role as a mother. Choosing mothering is, however, made through the negotiation of women's agency under various social and economic pressures. Even when women seafarers decide to continue working on board ships, while leaving their children at home, a physical separation between the ship and home creates a number of challenges associated with their identity as a mother. This study indicates that the longer women seafarers work at sea, the more impact on their identity as a mother they experience in relation to their children.

Women's seafaring experience does not seem to equally influence the individual's idea of marriage and family life. Yet, problems still persist. A choice of mothering, therefore, is not simply women's agency through which individuals can act independently to make their own decisions without concerning the consequence on their relationship with their children. Though the sampling numbers were small, five seafaring mothers in the sample demonstrated that it is not totally impossible to continue working at sea after having children. In all the cases, women seafarers found a closest member of the family, often their own mothers and their husbands, to look after the children, while they were absent from home. Mothers in full-time jobs always face the issue of support in domestic work, including childrearing. Women seafarers, in this respect, must find a person whom they can trust and who can take the same responsibility as mothers do. Nevertheless, even if women seafarers successfully meet these conditions and do not give up working at sea, they seem to pay through the risk of sacrificing a part of their family lives because of their absence from home. Unstructured periods of seafarers' life cycle between ship and shore also tend to conflict with women's gender roles and prevent them fostering their identity as a mother. It is, therefore, not easy to fill the gap between their 'individual' and 'family' time when they re-join the family waiting ashore. This could bring further challenges to women's agency in choosing mothering.

Seafaring fathers, on the other hand, should face a similar problem, but to what extent their identity as a father can be threatened remains a question. It can be a further research recommendation that seafaring fathers are not an exception in this discussion. In fact, it is important to generate a discussion that it is problematic to impose on women to fulfill all the domestic roles and thus, give up their careers. Such arguments are helpful to raise awareness of women's unpaid work in the home as well as gender equality at work, across different industries.

Acknowledgements I extend my sincere appreciation to all the seafarers who participated in my research as well as Nippon Foundation, which funded the project.

References

Aggrey, H. A. (2000). *Women in the maritime industry: A review of female participation, and their role in maritime education and training (MET) in the 21st century* (Master's thesis). World Maritime University, Malmö.

Belcher, P., Sampson, H., Thomas, M., Veiga, J., & Zhao, M. (2003). *Women seafarers: Global employment policies and practices*. Geneva: International Labour Office.

BIMCO, & ISF. (2010). *Manpower 2010 update: The worldwide demand of and supply for seafarers*. Coventry: University of Warwick.

Chant, S., & Pedwell, C. (2008). *Women, gender and the informal economy: An assessment of ILO research and suggested ways forward*. Geneva: International Labour Office.

Charrad, M. M. (2010). Women's agency across cultures: Conceptualizing strengths and boundaries. *Women's Studies International Forum, 33*, 517–522.

Cordingly, D. (2001). *Heroines & Harlots: Women at sea in the great age of sail*. London: Pan Books.

Drewry, ILO, & ITF. (2009). *Manning 2009*. London: Drewry.

Giddens, A. (1984). *The constitution of society*. Cambridge: Polity Press.

Holdaway, S., & Parker, S. K. (1998). Policing women police: Uniform patrol, promotion and representation in the CID. *British Journal of Criminology, 38*(1), 40–60.

IMO. (1988). *The integration of women in the maritime sector (IWMS)*. London: Author.

JITI, & Nippon Foundation. (2010). *A study on the "Future global supply and demand for seafarers and possible measures to facilitate stakeholders to secure a quantity of quality seafarers"*. Tokyo: Japan International Transport Institute and the Nippon Foundation.

Jo, S. -H. (2010). *Why not women seafarers?: Towards a development strategy for the recruitment and retention of women seafarers in cargo ships with particular reference to the Republic of Korea* (Master's thesis). World Maritime University, Malmö.

Kitada, M. (2010). *Women seafarers and their identities* (Doctoral dissertation). School of Social Science, Cardiff University, Cardiff.

Kitada, M. (2011). Rethinking the occupational culture of seafaring: Challenges in the new era of cultural diversities. *Ocean Law, Society and Management, 3*, 80–97.

Kitada, M. (2012). Enabling the seafaring career to balance work and family life: From the perspective of women seafarers. *The Journal of Japan Society of Ocean Policy, 2*, 69–80.

Kitada, M. (2013). Code of behaviour at sea: Women seafarers' shipboard identity management. *WMU Journal of Maritime Affairs, 12*(2), 213–227.

Klugman, J., Hanmer, L., Twigg, S., McCleary-Sills, J., Hasan, T., & Bonilla, J. A. S. (2014). *Voice and agency: Empowering women and girls for shared prosperity*. Washington: World Bank Group.
Lyonette, C., Kaufman, G., & Crompton, R. (2011). We both need to work: Maternal employment, childcare and health care in Britain and the USA. *Work, Employment and Society, 25*(1), 34–50.
Maynard, M. (1994). Methods, practice and epistemology: The debate about feminism and research. In M. Maynard & J. Purvis (Eds.), *Researching women's lives from a feminist perspective* (pp. 10–26). London: Taylor & Francis.
Newell, C. E., Rosenfeld, P., & Culbertson, A. L. (1995). Sexual harassment experiences and equal opportunity perceptions of navy women. *Sex Roles, 32*(3–4), 159–168.
Paoline, E. A., III. (2003). Taking stock: Toward a richer understanding of police culture. *Journal of Criminal Justice, 31*, 199–214.
Peterson, J. T. (1993). Generalized extended family exchange: A case from the Philippines. *Journal of Marriage and the Family, 55*(3), 570–584.
Roeters, A., & Craig, L. (2014). Part-time work, women's work–life conflict, and job satisfaction: A cross-national comparison of Australia, the Netherlands, Germany, Sweden, and the United Kingdom. *International Journal of Comparative Sociology, 55*(3), 185–203. doi:10.1177/0020715214543541.
Seierstad, C., & Healy, G. (2012). Women's equality in the Scandinavian academy: A distant dream? *Work, Employment and Society, 26*(2), 296–313.
Thomas, M., & Bailey, N. (2006). Square pegs in round holes?: Leave periods and role displacement in UK-based seafaring families. *Work, Employment and Society, 20*(1), 129–149.
Thomas, M., & Bailey, N. (2009). Out of time: Work, temporal synchrony and families. *Sociology, 43*(4), 613–630.
Thomas, M., Sampson, H., & Zhao, M. (2001). Behind the scenes: Seafaring and family life. In *SIRC symposium proceedings 2* (pp. 117–143). Cardiff: Seafarers International Research Centre.
Thomas, M., Sampson, H., & Zhao, M. (2003). Finding a balance: Companies, seafarers and family life. *Maritime Policy and Management, 30*(1), 59–76.
Turley, H. (1999). *Rum, sodomy, and the lash: Piracy, sexuality, and masculine identity*. New York: New York University Press.
UN. (2000). *The UN millennium development goals*. New York: Author.
World Economic Forum. (2013). *The global gender gap report 2013*. Geneva: Author.
Yoder, J. D., & Aniakudo, P. (1995). The responses of African American women firefighters to gender harassment at work. *Sex Roles, 32*(3–4), 125–137.
Yoder, J. D., & Aniakudo, P. (1996). When pranks become harassment: The case of African American women firefighters. *Sex Roles, 35*(5–6), 253–270.

Part III
Maritime Education and Research: Impact of Women

Let Numbers Speak: Job Opportunities and International Exchange Programs for Female Maritime Cadets

Qi Chen

Abstract For 6 years, the Massachusetts Maritime Academy (MMA) of the USA has been conducting a student exchange program with Shanghai Maritime University (SMU) of China. Every spring term, about 20 cadets are selected from each institution and sent to the other campus to study for one semester. MMA, like many other traditional maritime schools, is a male-dominated institute, with the gender distribution being 12 % female cadets and 88 % male cadets. However, the cadets participating in the MMA exchange program have shown quite a different gender ratio with the female's participation rate, displaying a surge in the past 2 years. Furthermore, the female cadets tend to stand out in the job market upon graduation, especially in comparison to their male peers. This paper presents an analysis of what accounts for the success of selected female cadets, how they outperform in the international exchange programs, and their subsequent achievements in the job market by applying case-study methodology, school-wide surveys and the data collected over the course of 6 years. The findings indicate that the outstanding qualities of female cadets, such as language proficiency, cultural adaptability, flexibility, intuitive vision, and genuine curiosity and perseverance, are displayed and encouraged, allowing the women to reach their full potential. The school-wide cultural awareness and job market success, motivate more MMA female cadets to participate in the MMA-SMU exchange program.

Keywords Cultural adaptability • International Programs between Maritime Institutions • Language proficiency • Maritime woman

1 Introduction

Beginning during the spring term of 2009, the Massachusetts Maritime Academy (MMA) in the US launched a student exchange program with Shanghai Maritime University (SMU) of China. Every spring term, about 20 cadets are selected from each

Q. Chen (✉)
Massachusetts Maritime Academy, Buzzards Bay, MA, USA
e-mail: qchen@maritime.edu

© Springer-Verlag Berlin Heidelberg 2015

M. Kitada et al. (eds.), *Maritime Women: Global Leadership*, WMU Studies in Maritime Affairs 3, DOI 10.1007/978-3-662-45385-8_10

institution and sent to the other campus to study and gain experience. Since the exchange program is conducted in two countries that differ greatly in their culture, history, economic systems, social values and government structures, it imposes a huge challenge on the participating students to survive and be successful. Nevertheless, it has been well proved that MMA-SMU program provided students with strategies to move from shock to cross-cultural adaptability, which in turn, will make the students, as Hutchings et al. (2002) refer to, the new style employees who will be cosmopolitan, multilingual, multifaceted and be able to operate across national borders.

The MMA, like many other traditional maritime schools, is a male-dominated institute, with the gender distribution being 12 % female and 88 % male. However, the cadets participating in the MMA exchange program have shown quite a different gender ratio, averaging 17.2 % female cadets overall. Recently, the female participation rate has shown a surge, with 22.2 and 30.4 % respectively in the last 2 years. The female cadets, after being "gold gilded" with the China experience, tend to stand out in the job market upon graduation, especially in comparison to their male peers who have not participated in international programs. Furthermore, females benefit more from foreign language classes, as they tend to use social learning strategies, the techniques which involve more than one person in the language learning process (Ehrman and Oxford 1989). Language proficiency will also help them get better opportunities in the labour market (Beiser and Hou 2000), especially with multinational corporations which conduct business in other parts of the world.

This paper presents an analysis of what accounts for the success of selected female cadets, how they outperform male cadets in the international exchange program, and their subsequent achievements in the job market, by applying case study methodology, school-wide surveys and the data collected over the course of 6 years. The paper explains that in highly advanced society like US, economic development and capitalist relations are not necessarily detrimental to women in comparison to men. The research is in line with the works of scholars who proposed that "we must be wary of simplistically portraying men as winners and women as losers" (Moore 1988). For instance, Victoria Lockwood explains that women's position might be improved with capitalist development, using a case study of non-western women from the Tahitian islands, an overseas collectivity of the French Republic (Lockwood 2009). While the great majority of the literatures in the area still holds the conventional view that men benefit more than women, and women's position could even be deteriorating with capitalist development (Boserup 1970; Nash 1977).

2 Dramatic Increase in the Female Participation Rate in the Exchange Program

Since the year 2010, the Massachusetts Maritime Academy has sent cadets over to Shanghai Maritime University every spring term and accepted roughly the same number of Chinese students to study at the MMA campus. The following table

Table 1 Participation rate of MMA female cadets in the MMA-SMU exchange program

	2010	2011	2012	2013	2014
Female cadets	1	2	2	6	7
Total	11	16	17	27	23
% of females	9	12.5	11.8	22.2	30.4

gives us the numbers of the participating cadets from MMA with the gender distribution from the year of 2010–2014.

Table 1 shows a clear rise in the numbers of participating cadets of the MMA-SMU exchange program in the last 2 years, especially the female cadets. In 2014, the female cadets make up about one-third of the MMA exchange students studying at Shanghai Maritime University. Several reasons can help explain the increasing female participation rate in the program: the positive experiences of the first participating group of MMA students, their subsequent successes in the job market, school-wide cultural awareness in the academy, and the mutual understanding and world vision that results from the cultural exchange. In addition, the rapid economic growth in China during the past three decades has created great opportunities for both male and female maritime cadets. MMA cadets identify these benefits and actively pursue them.

2.1 *Cultural Awareness and World Vision*

The Massachusetts Maritime Academy is a principal maritime educational institute in the US, with a focus on excellent ocean-centric majors like Marine Engineering and Marine Transportation. However, as a state college, the great majority of cadets enrolled are from Massachusetts and other local areas in New England, a region in the North-Eastern corner of the United States. The academy has shown, more or less, the features of homogeneity and conservativeness. Thanks to the vision and courage of President Gurnon, MMA stepped out of its comfort zone in response to the proposal of SMU in China, and set up the MMA-SMU exchange program in 2008. The exchange program was the first international exchange program at MMA. Among all American maritime institutes, MMA is still the only institution which offers a successful international exchange program with Chinese maritime universities. The following school-wide survey of 109 cadets in 2011, show how the cadets perceived the program and how prepared they were in regards to international travel.

Table 2 indicates how extensively (or not quite) American students travelled outside the US and places they felt comfortable going to. Only a few American students had gone to Asian countries (except China), such as Israel, Jordan, India, and Japan and three had visited China, including one American-born Vietnamese. Around three-fourths of responding cadets made trips to Canada; a country that holds similar political, economic, social and cultural systems to the USA. And yet out of the 85 students who had visited Canada, all of them went to English-speaking areas like Toronto, Vancouver and Ottawa, and only one third had gone to French-speaking areas like Montreal and Quebec City. About 31 % of the respondents

Table 2 The world travelling by MMA cadets

Destination of travel	Percentage of survey participants (%)
China	3
Asian countries (except China)	7
European countries	31
Caribbean, South and Latin American countries	97
Canada	78

toured European countries, and the highly frequented destinations were Italy, Ireland, Portugal and England. To a great extent, this is due to the fact that many of the respondents are descendant of the British, Italian, Portuguese and Irish, can still speak the language, or have family members living in Europe. One cadet explained that his grandfather lived in a village outside of Rome and he has more than 20 Italian cousins.

The statistics in Table 2, also shows that nearly all of the MMA cadets paid visits to Caribbean, South and Latin American countries, such as Mexico, Barbados, Puerto Rica, Ecuador, Panama, Costa Rica and Tortola. That is mainly because cadets at MMA are required to take sea terms, and the countries in Caribbean, South and Latin American regions are usually the planned destination when the cadets take voyages with the school training ship.

Therefore, it is well expected that the MMA exchange students would unavoidably experience some "culture shock" when they go to China and try to blend into the new environment in such a swift period of time. The term, "culture shock", was first introduced by an anthropologist and economist, Kalervo Oberg, as a disease suffered by individuals living in a new environment. According to Oberg, culture shock resulted from the loss of well-known signs and symbols, causing individuals to experience anxiety, frustration and helplessness (Oberg 1960). To fully realize the stress MMA exchange cadets might face in China, the MMA-SMU program was designed in such a way which mitigates culture shock to the minimum. The effective measures include assigning one Chinese student and one American student as roommates, free selection of courses, extensive classes of language and culture, and cultural trips to enhance the understanding of the host country.

Table 3 presents the five major questions in the survey, taken in 2011 and 2013 respectively, and the answers the participating cadets selected. For each of the questions, the cadets had three choices, "positive", "negative" or "neutral", and gave one answer per question. They were also asked to provide further explanations to each of their choices.

In the surveys of both 2011 and 2013, a great majority of MMA cadets believed that the China program would have a positive impact on MMA, and none had negative opinions about Chinese students. With the development of the exchange program, there is a slight increase in positivity for all questions. Both Tables 2 and 3 clearly state that many MMA cadets have not gone far from where they were born and raised and were still uncomfortable with the unfamiliar. Most MMA cadets would prefer not to share a room with a visiting Chinese student. When being asked

Table 3 Answers to questionnaires (2011 and 2013)

Survey questions/answers	Positive (%)	Negative (%)	Neutral (%)	Year
The impact the China program would impose on MMA?	81.9	0.9	17.4	2011
	84.5	0.0	15.5	2013
How will the China program influence you?	33.0	2.8	64.2	2011
	39.0	1.5	59.5	2013
Do you want to go abroad for jobs or studies?	56.0	22.9	21.1	2011
	63.0	15.1	21.9	2013
What do you think of the Chinese students?	75.2	0.0	24.8	2011
	78.1	0.0	21.9	2013
Do you want to be the roommate of a Chinese cadet?	19.3	71.5	9.2	2011
	21.2	69.4	9.4	2013

the reason, several MMA students said that they would like to have a roommate who would be closer to themselves, with similar personalities, backgrounds, and hobbies. As one student put it, "I want to room with one of my friends."

It is also worth mentioning that over the course of 6 years, each group of Chinese exchange students brought qualifications of diligence, a strong work ethic, and determination to succeed, when they were selected and sent to the MMA campus. Though the Chinese students would experience culture shock and language barriers, they made extraordinary efforts to blend in and excel in the classroom. One MMA professor of Marine Engineering said: "It is a pleasure to have the Chinese students in my class. They work so hard and get the best grades." With the on-going exchange program, MMA cadets have become more culturally aware and keen on international affairs.

3 Positive Experience in China and Job Market Success for MMA Female Cadets

3.1 Positive Experience at SMU of China

Each year, the participating cadets from the academy gained very positive experiences during their stay in China. They believed the program helped them in the following three areas: developing good relations with Chinese people by experiencing the country first hand, putting them in more advantageous positions in different cultures and among different people, and meeting cadets of the same major from other countries. One student wrote in his report of the exchange program: "It is a great opportunity to meet people from other countries in similar fields of study." Another cadet said that "It allows exchange of cultures and offers a new unique experience. It also helps educate everyone in the school about the Chinese culture, not just those who get to go."

Many participating cadets from the first groups became strong advocates of the exchange program and promote the program in every possible way. The cadets present papers about the program and their own personal experiences at international and domestic maritime conferences, hold positions in the student council, serve as cadet officers of foreign exchange programs, give talks to cadets' parents, and encourage other MMA students to join the program.

The cadets from MMA have left a strong impression in China, especially the female cadets. The young women not only show their fine academic qualities by expressing their language proficiency, intuitive vision, and genuine curiosity and perseverance, but also their spirit and personality, through determination, cultural adaptability, flexibility, and the capability to overcome all difficulty, which goes beyond and above the expectations Chinese would have for females. Here is a good example: Myra was the only female cadet going to China in the first year. On top of being the best student in the class, averaging 85.2, while the class mean was an 82, Myra joined the soccer team as the eleventh member representing MMA to play against SMU and other university teams in Shanghai. It turns out that she scored the most in the games, and although she was once injured badly on the field and rushed to the hospital in an ambulance, her optimism and determination made a deep impression on her teammates, the Chinese cadets and the doctors who treated her in the hospital. One Chinese faculty at SMU exclaimed, "Wow, fragility, your name is not American women."

The female cadets from later years also maximized their time in China. They travelled extensively to gain first-hand experience of Chinese tradition, history, culture, and society. They sampled various types of Chinese foods, learned unique customs, met people from other parts of the world, and built life-long friendships.

The following table gives the grade report of the MMA female cadets studying at SMU, against the class mean of MMA exchange students who went to China in the same year.

Table 4 shows the average scores MMA female cadets earned for all the courses they took at SMU, and the class mean of all the male and female MMA exchange cadets of the same year. The female cadets received a higher course average each year except one. Just like what my department chair has observed over his 30 years teaching at MMA, "female cadets tend to be more persistent, hardworking and motivated. Under male-dominated areas like maritime, they would push harder to succeed, and show their male counterparts that they can be productive and successful. Male cadets are less attentive. I would rather teach an all female class."

3.2 Job Market Success for Female Exchange Cadets at MMA

At this point, we only have three groups of MMA cadets graduating from the academy after studying for one semester in China, and most received good job

Table 4 Grade report of MMA female cadets studying at SMU against class mean

	Year 2010	Year 2011	Year 2012	Year 2013
Female average	85.2	84.3	83.7	86
Class average	82	85.7	82.3	85.2

The score is based on the points cadets earn out of 100

offers upon graduation. For the purpose of this paper, we will focus on the jobs the female cadets entered after they were gold gilded with China experiences. We will look at the companies the female cadets received offers from in their senior year and how much their experiences in China contributed to the jobs and later promotions. We see three things clearly from the available data collected by the Office of Career and Professional Services of the academy: companies the females now work for tend to be large, with many international elements, a decent salary offer, and they are on a steady rising track of career development.

Myra, the first female who went to China in 2010, received a job with SpecTec upon her graduation as a regional sales manager. According to the front page of the company website, SpecTec is a premier provider of asset management solutions for the marine, offshore and energy, defence and yachting industries all over the world (SpecTec 2014). Her responsibility is to identify and evaluate sales opportunities in the United States, Canada, and Latin America. After working at SpecTec for two-and-half years, Myra switched to DNV GL Group, the world's largest ship and offshore classification society of the maritime industry, a leading technical advisor to the oil and gas industry, and a leading expert in the energy value chain, including renewables. The company has 16,000 employees across 300 sites, in more than 100 countries, and gains revenue of EUR 2,500 million/year. Myra works as Sales Support Manager and she loves her challenging and rewarding job.

The two female cadets from the second year of the exchange program, Shanna and Vanessa, were both hired by Canadian Steamer Lines (CSL) during the last semester of their senior year. They were assigned to work at the CSL shipyard in Jiangying, China.[1]

Danielle and Erin participated in the exchange program in the spring term of 2012 and graduated the summer of 2013. Danielle was offered a position as the Third Mate at Military Sealift Command (MSC). Military Sealift Command, part of US Navy forces, is the leading provider of ocean transportation for the Navy and the rest of the Department of Defence—operating approximately 110 ships daily around the globe.[2] Erin works at the General Dynamics Nassco as an entry-level superintendent and project manager. General Dynamics Nassco, located in San Diego Bay, California, is part of General Dynamics Marine Systems and has been constructing ships for commercial customers and the U.S. Navy since 1960.[3]

[1] Report from the Office Career and Professional Placement at Massachusetts Maritime Academy.

[2] For the information of Military Sealift Command, please see http://www.msc.navy.mil/. For cadet's job, please see report from the Office Career and Professional Placement at Massachusetts Maritime Academy.

[3] For information of General Dynamics Nassco, please see http://www.nassco.com/.

The five graduating female cadets received jobs from either American huge companies or multinational corporations, with branches all over the world. As Ferraro (2010) stated, it is crucial to understand cultural differences, value norms and language styles, even some non-verbal communication skills like body posture, hand gestures and facial expression between negotiating parties. This is because "when entering international negotiation, there are no longer shared values, interests, morals, behaviours and linguistic styles, all of which can greatly affect the process and outcome of the negotiation" (Ferraro 2010). To spend one semester in China obviously helps the female cadets obtain better understanding of the country, and those experiences were highly appreciated by the potential employers. In regard to the great jobs these female cadets received, President Gurnon of the academy made the following comments: "The unique international experience adds an extra level of value to the job applicants. Big companies would be greatly impressed when they see our qualified female cadets in a traditionally male-dominated institution, having the courage to travel to another country and be successful in a different environment."

The following graph presents the salary range of MMA seniors from the years 2011–2013.[4] There were 81 cadets in 2011, 93 cadets in 2012 and 108 cadets in 2013 who responded to the survey, respectively. The salaries were put into five different ranges; below $35,000, between $35,000 and $50,000, between $50,000 and $75,000, and between $75,000 and $100,000, and over $100,000. The vertical bars show the percentages of entry level salaries the responding cadets received for the year 2011, 2012 and 2013.

Figure 1 shows that about 50 % of MMA seniors have annual salaries that range from $50,000 to $75,000 for all the 3 years and well over 20 % earn in the $75,000–99,000 range. In 2013, 16 % received an initial offer of more than $100,000. Only three female exchange students out of the five responded to the surveys; two reported a salary range between $50,000–75,000 and the other $35,000–50,000.

In 2013, the salary ranges were further recorded by major and show that seniors from seagoing majors like Marine Engineering (ME) and Marine Transportation (MT) normally make more than non-seagoing majors, such as International Maritime Business (IMB), Emergency Management (EM), Marine Safety and Environmental Protections (MSEP) and Facility Engineering (FE). Among the 108 cadets that responded to the school survey, 63 of them were sea-going majors from ME and MT, and 45 were from the non-sea-going majors like IMB, EM, FE and MSEP. Figure 2 shows that for seagoing majors like ME, more than 60 % of the graduating cadets were offered $75,000 or more, and 80 % of the MT cadets more than $75,000. The great majority of non-sea-going majors cadets, like IMB, received less than $75,000, or even lower. These three female exchange cadets reporting to

[4] The data is recorded by the Office of Career and Professional Placement at MMA and based on the survey report the seniors returned. Salary reports of senior graduates from the Office of Career and Professional Placement at Massachusetts Maritime Academy (July 2011, July 2012, July 2013 and July 2013).

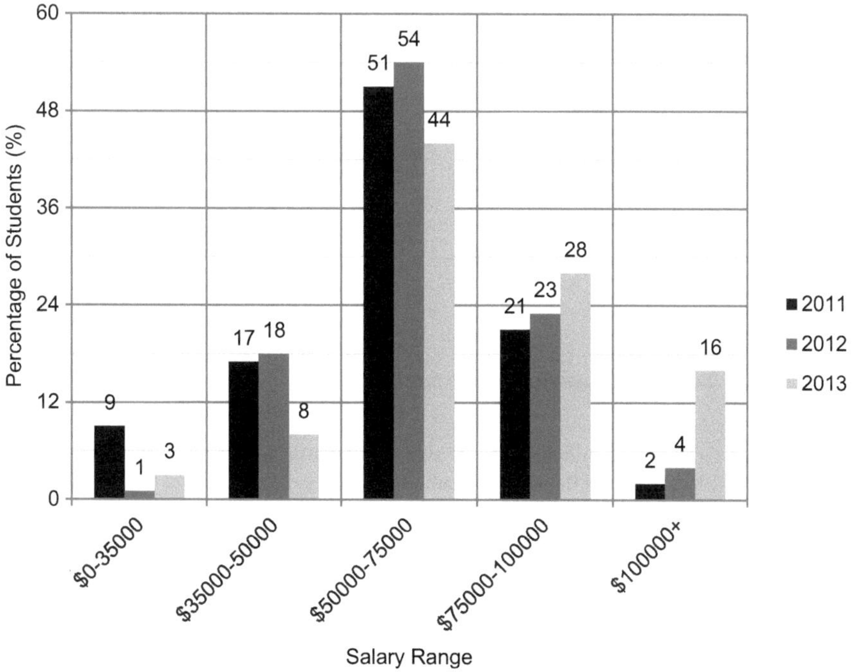

Fig. 1 Salary ranges seniors cadets received for the year 2011–2013

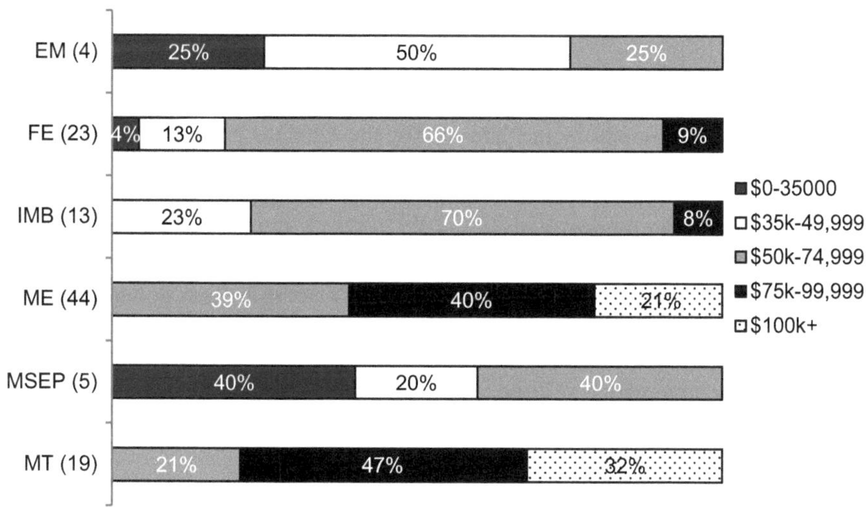

Fig. 2 Salary ranges by major in the senior class of 2013 in US dollars. The survey was conducted on 27 June 2013 and 108 responded

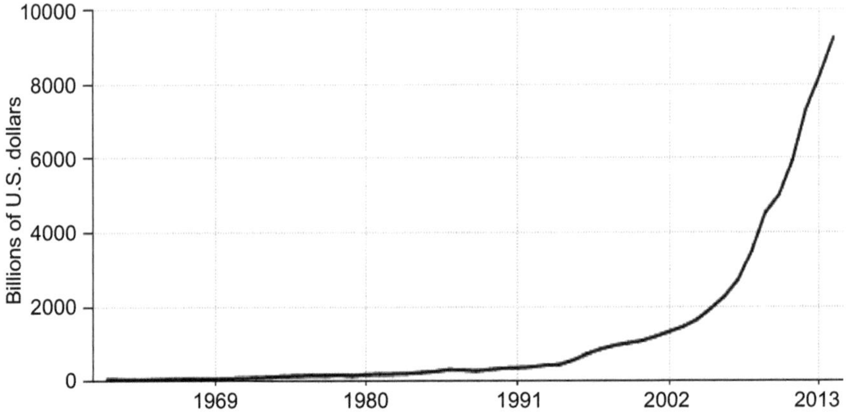

Fig. 3 China GDP and its growth between 1960 and 2013 in trillions of US dollars. *Source:* Originally published by World Bank (n.d.a); published with kind permission of © World Bank. All rights reserved

the survey happened to all be IMB majors and their earnings are definitely higher than the US national survey result, wherein women's earnings were only 76.9 % of men's earnings in 2006 (US Census Bureau referenced in Hoffman and Averett 2010).

4 Fast Economic Growth in China and Opportunities for Maritime Cadets

For three decades, China has developed tremendously, and despite the Asian financial economic crisis in the late 1990s, the Chinese economy continued to grow at rapid pace, with an average annual growth rate of almost 10 % between 1991 and 2010 (Chinability 2011). China's total international trade of goods in 2013 reached $3,982 billion, surpassing the USA's $3,848 billion, and made China the largest trading country in the world (Townhall Finance 2013). In 2012, China's GDP, valued at $8.358 trillion, surpassed Japan's $5.96 trillion dollar GDP and China became the second largest economy in the world, just next to the USA ($16.245 trillion) (World Bank n.d.b) (Fig. 3).

During the same period of time, there has been a dramatic development of the Chinese shipping industry. In 2013, eight Chinese ports were on the top ten list of the global cargo throughput rankings (Table 5).

China's shipping industry and container transportation has reached international standards, both in handling efficiency and building networks. In 2009, China reached 26.1 million TEUS in containerized cargo shipping, surpassing the USA, and has been ranked the largest exporter country of containerized cargo shipping

Table 5 Global cargo throughput rankings (in 10,000 T) in 2013

Ports	Port cargo throughput (10,000 T)
Ningbo-Zhoushan	80,978.00
Shanghai	77,600.00
Singapore	55,958.00
Tianjin	50,000.00
Guangzhou	45,512.00
Suzhou	45,430.00
Qingdao	45,000.00
Tangshan	44,620.00
Rotterdam	44,046.00
Dalian	40,840.00

Source: Originally published by China Shipping Database (2014); published with kind permission of © China Shipping Database. All rights reserved

ever since (World Shipping Council 2014). The Chinese government has not only set up massive shipping companies, like China Ocean Shipping Company (COSCO), but has also invested heavily in the water transport infrastructure, constructing new ports and rebuilding and enlarging older facilities.

Shanghai is the largest city in China and has become the centre of international finance and global shipping. Many international corporations set up branches in Shanghai and intend to hire personnel with training in their own field and with a world vision. The MMA cadets with China experiences would be considered as highly valued candidates to work for the international companies. For instance, a couple of years ago, an American waste management company (Wheelabrator Technologies) announced plans to construct five waste-to-energy facilities in the suburbs of Shanghai. This was in response to a Chinese government policy to increase the openness of its waste disposal market to foreign direct investment and to enhance efficiency and market mechanisms in the area. Wheelabrator Technologies intended to hire MMA cadets with China experience and with training in marine engineering and environment protection, to work in Shanghai, and would offer internships to MMA cadets even before graduation.

In recent years, Foremost Group, a New York-based shipping, trading, and finance enterprise, expanded its business to Asian countries, including Hong Kong and Shanghai. They contacted MMA in their search for a fleet manager or operations manager who speaks Mandarin Chinese. All potential job opportunities greatly encourage the MMA cadets to participate in the international exchange program and gain foreign experiences.

5 Conclusion

Looking at the available data, it is clear that the exchange students are given an edge over their peers. In regards to international experience that can easily be applied to future jobs, cadets who choose to take this opportunity find themselves much better candidates within a rapidly expanding job market. When combined with the females' statistically higher grades, it becomes an invaluable tool to help them stand out within the male-dominated field and gain, what Schneider and Barsoux (1997) refer to, the capacity to operate "across national borders somewhat like James Bond".

The international cooperation between two maritime institutes, such as that in the MMA-SMU student exchange program, would be very effective to help the participating cadets enhance their self-confidence, broaden their global visions and adapt to a new environment with ease and grace. The successful experiences of the MMA-SMU program are applicable not only to the maritime universities of USA and China, but also to the institutions which locate in other culturally diverse countries. When the participating cadets prove that they can survive and perform well in two completely different cultures, they demonstrate that they have all the necessary and sufficient skills to be successful within any type of job they are offered. And this is exactly what the potential employers are seeking of all graduating maritime cadets nowadays.

With the on-going development of the exchange program, and availability of additional data on the female cadets at MMA, more rigorous statistical analysis could be applied to the research, generating more significant conclusions. To do so, will unquestionably help us to see how the exchange program enhances cultural awareness, educates maritime cadets to embrace the differences, and fosters leadership qualifications of female cadets of maritime institutions.

References

Beiser, M., & Hou, F. (2000). Gender differences in language acquisition and employment consequences among Southeast Asian refugees in Canada. *Canadian Public Policy–Analyze de politiques*, *XXVI*(3), 311–330.

Boserup, E. (1970). *Women's role in economic development*. London: George Allen and Unwin.

China Shipping Database. (2014). Global port cargo throughput ranking. http://www.shippingdata.cn/free/item.do?toplmid=6354E42BC8844DB7B0874F603935CAAB&lmid=CCC4347CA99345E7B47A6AE90D7761BF. Accessed 1 Apr 2014.

Chinability. (2011). GDP growth in China 1952–2011. http://www.chinability.com/GDP.htm. Accessed 1 Apr 2014.

Ehrman, M., & Oxford, R. (1989). Effects of sex difference, career choice and psychological type on adult language learning strategies. *The Modern Language Journal, 73*(1), 1–13.

Ferraro, G. (2010). *The cultural dimension of international business*. Boston: Prentice Hall.

Hoffman, S. D., & Averett, S. L. (2010). *Women and economy: Family, work and pay*. Boston: Addison-Wesley.

Hutchings, K., Jackson, P., & McEllister, R. (2002). Exploiting the links between theory and practice: Developing students' cross-cultural understanding through an international study tour to China. *Higher Education Research & Development, 21*(1), 55–71.
Lockwood, V. (2009). The impact of development on women: The interplay of material conditions and gender ideology. In C. B. Brettell & C. F. Sargent (Eds.), *Gender in cross-cultural perspective* (pp. 510–524). New York: Prentice Hall.
Moore, H. (1988). *Feminism and anthropology*. Minneapolis: University of Minneapolis Press.
Nash, J. (1977). Women and development. *Development and Change, 8*, 161–182.
Oberg, K. (1960). Culture shock: Adjustment to new cultural environments. *Practical Anthropologist, 7*, 177–182.
Schneider, S., & Barsoux, J. (1997). *Managing across cultures*. Hertfordshire: Prentice Hall.
SpecTec. (2014). Overview. http://www.spectec.net/en. Accessed 1 Apr 2014.
Townhall Finance. (2013). China surpasses U.S. in international trade. http://finance.townhall.com/columnists/politicalcalculations/2013/02/13/china-surpasses-us-in-international-trade-n1511183/page/full. Accessed 1 Apr 2014.
World Bank. (n.d.a). China GDP 1960–2014. http://www.tradingeconomics.com/china/gdp. Accessed 1 April 2014.
World Bank. (n.d.b). Countries and economies: China GDP 2012, Japan GDP 2012 and USA GDP 2012. http://data.worldbank.org/country. Accessed 1 Apr 2014.
World Shipping Council. (2014). Trade statistics. http://www.worldshipping.org/about-the-industry/global-trade/trade-statistics. Accessed 1 Apr 2014.

Mind the Gap! Maritime Education for Gender-Equal Career Advancement

Maria Boström Cars and Cecilia Österman

Abstract Seafaring as an occupation, and the maritime community as a whole, is still a male-dominated industry. In order to encourage more women to engage in a career at sea, a number of campaigns have been launched by various stakeholders. Since gender gaps in education generally are larger in the developing world, while steadily closing in the developed countries, it is both understandable and appropriate that efforts largely have been directed towards enabling women in developing countries to engage in professional education and training, may it be maritime or other. However, is opening the door and encouraging women to participate in maritime training sufficient to keep and encourage women to embark on a maritime career? In this paper, we set out to examine how gender equality is addressed in the curricula of maritime education. A document analysis was performed, examining official study plans and curricula from eight maritime universities in Finland, Norway, Sweden and the Philippines; all nations ranked in the top five in the Global gender Gap Index. The results show that gender issues are not explicitly mentioned or addressed in these documents, indicating a lack of clear strategies for these matters. Educational institutions are important bearers of societal norms and values. Without effective gender-inclusive strategies and pedagogical and didactic approaches, there is a risk of reproducing inequality, instead of producing equality. Increasing numbers of female students will not alone close the gender gap in the maritime industry. Gender issues must be well defined, operationalised and included in educational policy and curricula-making at individual, structural as well as symbolical levels.

Keywords Equality • Gender gap • Maritime education • Women seafarers

M. Boström Cars (✉) • C. Österman
Kalmar Maritime Academy, Linnaeus University, Kalmar, Sweden
e-mail: maria.bostrom.cars@lnu.se

© Springer-Verlag Berlin Heidelberg 2015

M. Kitada et al. (eds.), *Maritime Women: Global Leadership*, WMU Studies in Maritime Affairs 3, DOI 10.1007/978-3-662-45385-8_11

1 Introduction

Seafaring as an occupation, has traditionally been, and to some extent still is, a profession that largely depends on experience. At an early age, youths were accepted on board to be guided, socialized—and sometimes bullied—into the working and living cultures of the sea. Over the past 150 years, nautical education has been formalized and generally incorporated into public education systems (Kennerley 2002). The educational content has since continued to evolve to meet the demands of the contemporary shipping industry, for a safe and efficient operation of ships. Baseline standards for training and certification across the world are established through the STCW Convention (IMO 2011) that was first adopted by the International Maritime Organization (IMO) in 1978 and revised in 1995 and 2010. Today, there are over 200 educational institutions, in over 80 countries, offering maritime education and training, ranging from basic safety and seamanship training, to the highest certification standard, now corresponding to academic degree level.

Despite some improvements in the area, both seafaring as an occupation and the maritime community as a whole, are still a male-dominated industry. In order to encourage more women to engage in a career at sea, a number of campaigns have been launched by various stakeholders in the sector. For example, the IMO Programme on the Integration of Women in the Maritime Sector (IWMS) to support women's participation in the maritime industry, has now celebrated its 25th year (IMO 2013). Specifically, the policy objectives of the programme were to:

- integrate women into mainstream maritime activities;
- improve women's access to maritime training and technology;
- increase the percentage of women at the senior-management level within the maritime sector;
- promote women's economic self-reliance, including access to employment; and
- consolidate the integration of women in the maritime sector as an integral element of IMO's technical co-operation activities.

Since seafaring no longer is a lifetime employment, but rather a stepping stone for a future career ashore, more women working on board will ultimately also increase the number of women at senior management level within the industry. Many organizations, such as marine insurers, classification societies and maritime administrations, regularly employ people with seagoing experience.

It is commonly held that gender gaps in education generally are larger in the developing world, while the gaps are steadily closing in the developed countries. Accordingly, it is arguably both understandable and appropriate, that efforts largely have been directed towards enabling women in developing countries to engage in professional education and training, may it be maritime or other. However, is opening the door and encouraging women to participate in maritime training sufficient? Educational institutions are important bearers of societal norms and values and without clear gender-inclusive strategies for curricula, pedagogy and classroom activities, there is an obvious risk of inequality being reproduced and consolidated, rather than equality being produced.

While gender-equal maritime education essentially, is a principle of individual fairness, it is also crucial to the legitimacy of the educational institutions. In the long term, it is also important for the development and competitiveness of the maritime industry and our society as a whole.

The Global Gender Gap Index was introduced in 2006 by the World Economic Forum in collaboration with Harvard University and University of California. The index measures the relative gaps between women and men across four key areas: health, education, economics and politics. In all, 136 countries are ranked on their gender gaps, depending on nearly 40 gender-related variables, reflecting legal and social factors that can affect gender disparity. The countries are thus ranked on their gender gaps and not on their development level or overall levels of education in the country (World Economic Forum 2013). The highest possible score is 1, representing equality and the lowest score is 0 for inequality.

In the latest Global Gender Gap Report, published in 2013, the five top-ranked countries with the smallest gender gaps are Iceland (0.8731), Finland (0.8421), Norway (0.8417), Sweden (0.8129) and the Philippines (0.7832). Since these five countries also have a longstanding tradition of seafaring, it would be fair to assume that structures and establishments for maritime education and training in these countries may pose as state-of-the-art in terms of gender-equality.

Hence, the purpose of the research study presented in this paper, set out to examine how gender equality is addressed in the curricula of contemporary maritime education, in the five top-ranked countries according to the Global Gender Gap Index in 2013 (World Economic Forum 2013). The overall aim is to contribute to the body of knowledge on gender-equal maritime education and training.

2 Research Design

The research study was initiated with a search for maritime academies and universities in the five countries. No university providing maritime education in Iceland could, however be found.[1] Once universities in the remaining four top-ranked countries were identified, current study plans and curricula of undergraduate programs in nautical science or comparable maritime education were searched for and downloaded from the internet during the autumn 2013. Only documents written in English, Swedish or Norwegian could be considered, due to the language barrier.

Study plans for the equivalent of Bachelor of Nautical Science for the following universities were analysed:

Finland: Åland University of Applied Sciences (2013) (Bachelor in Maritime Studies)

[1] Nevertheless, the University of Iceland offers programmes in Marine science and Fishery science, and there is also a Master of Coastal and Marine Management programme offered for the past 7 years at the University Centre of the Westfjords in Isafjordur.

	Novia University of Applied Sciences (Bachelor in Maritime Studies)
Norway:	Buskerud and Vestfold University College (2013) (Bachelor in Nautical Subjects)
	Aalesund University College (2013) (Bachelor in Nautical Subjects)
Sweden:	Chalmers University of Technology (2013) (BSc in Nautical Science)
	Kalmar Maritime Academy, Linnaeus University (BSc in Nautical Science)
Philippines:	PMMA—Philippine Merchant Marine Academy (2013) (BSc in Marine Transportation)
	PMMS—Philippine Merchant Marine School (2013) (BSc in Marine Transportation)

A content analysis was performed (Bryman and Bell 2007), where the documents were read, re-read, summarised and tabulated. In order to ensure a systematic procedure, an analytic framework was developed based on theories on gender-conscious pedagogy. Programme description, learning objectives and course content were controlled for any explicit reference to gender or equality issues. The analysis also included any pedagogical strategies cited in the study plans. Pedagogical strategies that include various teaching activities are important to make sure that different learning styles among the students are accounted for in the learning situation.

Naturally, analysing study plans alone will not provide a comprehensive image of reality. However, the topics mentioned in the study plans may serve as indicators of what is and what is not, considered important by the studied academic institutions.

3 Gender and Equality in Higher Education

The following section briefly presents the study's theoretical framework. First, the social construction of gender is problematized, followed by a section on gender and women in higher education and gender-conscious pedagogy.

3.1 Social Construction of Gender

In order to problematize gender differences, three processes in social construction of gender can be discerned; structural, individual and symbolical gender (Harding 1986). These aspects are always closely related, but vary in time and space.

Structural gender concerns organization and division of work. On a passenger ship for example, there are more male deck officers and marine engineers, while hotel and restaurant crew are women. Similarly, lecturers in academia are often men, while administrative staff tends to be dominated by women.

Individual gender represents the socially-constructed individual identity. Here, the values of the surrounding society are of great importance, since they strengthen one's own identity. For example, being a deck officer or a marine engineer, strengthens a male identity more than a female one. In forming individual gender, the communicative and interactive parts of the education process itself can be of importance. Hence, it is relevant to discuss whether an education offers a multitude of possibilities to strengthen individual identity, or focuses on predetermined patterns of identification.

Symbolical gender represents the meaning created by our establishments and systems of value. Symbolical gender is most prominent through language and a dichotomisation of epistemology, usually, in opposites attributed to either male or female gender, such as active/passive, logical/illogical, rational/irrational and so on. The language used, for example in educational materials, contributes to creation and recreation of gender on a symbolic level (von Wright 1999).

3.2 Gender and Women in Higher Education

The discourse of gender and women in higher education, is a key to understanding gender equality in the workplace. Previous research on gender issues in maritime education, specifically is scarce, but gender equality in higher education in general, is getting increasing attention. Previous empirical research indicates both a scientific-humanistic as well as a technical-care divide in higher education (Barone 2011). These divides are grounded both in curriculum content and subsequent career applications. Technically-oriented education programs tend to suit men better than women. Engineering educations and occupations are 'coded' in a masculine way. By entering this world as a woman, you are choosing a certain amount of resistance. Traditionally, 'hard' science and masculine attributes such as decisiveness and confidence are rewarded, while reflexivity and flexibility, attributes more female in character, are generally less highly praised (Berner 2003).

Furthermore, a student enrolling for a technically-oriented program may sign up not only for an education, but for an identity. A woman entering a male-dominated area often has to accept a totally new life, entailing new knowledge and information as well as a new culture, new jokes, pastimes and values. Generally, there is an overwhelming risk for the woman to feel out of place, inadequate, superfluous or like a mascot, thereby losing interest in the program (Aurell 2000). It is important that women in male-dominated programs develop useful coping strategies for these conditions, without losing their own identities.

3.3 Gender-Conscious Pedagogy

In his introduction to gender-conscious pedagogy for university teachers, Bondestam (2004) discusses five important areas for evaluating and furthering the discussion on gender issues in education:

- Students—what are their backgrounds, expectations and demands? Why do students choose different educational routes? Do women and men receive different grades? Which students drop out and which continue to postgraduate studies?;
- Course literature—do both women and men appear in the literature? In what way are they discussed? In what way are women and men described and explained? Is gender theory present in the literature, mandatory or per choice?;
- Instruction—do students encounter both female and male teachers? How do teachers approach female and male students? Do teaching activities cater for different types of learning styles? Do the active students dominate? How are silent students met and treated?;
- Examination—are exam questions gender-neutral? Does the chosen form of examination stimulate female as well as male students' learning? How is gender-sensitive feedback given to students?; and
- Course evaluation—how do students perceive the gender consciousness of the learning situation and that gender has been included in literature, instruction and examination? How do the students feel that the area of gender issues can be improved?

Gender-conscious teaching and learning are important general pedagogic actions to support gender equality in classroom activities. According to Bondestam (2004), gender aspects should be presented where it has relevance and where it reaches the individual student. Lewis (1990) recommends identifying natural moments of gender from the course, such as discussing course literature, building on a question from a student, or specific events, like a male takeover in the classroom. The overall objective is to create a general awareness of the situation.

4 Results

The results of this study, as it was designed, show that gender issues are not explicitly mentioned or addressed in any of the identified study and course plans, indicating a lack of clear strategies for these matters. Since content and learning objectives for maritime education largely are determined by the STCW convention, many similarities between the studied curricula could naturally be seen. For example, all study plans include references to maritime safety, ability to carry out watchkeeping duties and other professional responsibilities, as well as consideration for the marine and working environment. Notably, various kinds of cultural awareness studies are included either as specific courses, or at least mentioned among the learning objectives. This cultural awareness does, however, seem to be constrained to differences in national culture, or in some cases, differences between oriental and occidental cultures. References to the wider perspective of culture that encompasses, for instance, age, class, gender, religion, sexual orientation, that is commonly used by scholars in social sciences, is not visible.

Arguably, it is not possible to include all topics that are included in a Bachelor Programme. The results do, however, reveal that other matters that have been given special attention in the study plans include, for instance: knots and roperies (Novia University of Applied Sciences 2013), sexually-transmitted diseases and family planning (Commission on Higher Education 2013), and the automatic radar plotting aid (Linnaeus University and Kalmar Maritime Academy 2013).

The study plans are naturally expected to mirror the national legislation for higher education, but this compliance has not been investigated. With both authors coming from a background in Swedish academia, a discrepancy could, however, be noted. In accordance with the Swedish Higher Education Act (SFS 1992:1434, Chap. 1, 5§) that governs equal opportunities promotion, both universities have their own policies for including a gender perspective in education and research. These local policies seem not to be met, since study plans from both Swedish universities lack information on how the gender perspective is accommodated for in practice.

Including mention of gender issues in the study plan is, of course, a mere first step in the process of changing how women and men are looked upon and are expected to behave and perform. We, the authors, still argue that it is an important step to take and a way of making these issues visible to staff, as well as students. It is only when a problem is recognised as a problem, that we can start the task of solving it. And, it is only what is in the study plan; that the school is required to provide and will be audited on.

5 Discussion

The study presented in this paper is limited by its clear focus on the gender discourse and gender inclusive pedagogy. The study does not include other social categories such as age, class, ethnicity, religion and sexuality that are equally important, especially since these categories often coexist. But to enlighten such complexity would demand a different setting and is not within the scope of this study.

The content analysis of the official study plans yielded information on learning objectives, content and to some extent, pedagogical strategies. To obtain a more comprehensive view, it would have been desirable to complement the document analysis with, for instance, studies of course literature and course evaluations, as well as classroom interaction observations and interviews with students and staff. This is seen as a natural next step for further studies of gender equality in maritime education.

One of the most prominent findings to emerge, was that there seems to be a general 'gender blindness' in maritime education, perhaps as a result of the fact that the maritime industry historically has been largely dominated by men. This is not uncommon, especially in technically-oriented education and natural sciences (Hussenius et al. 2012). Bringing gender up on the agenda may range from difficult to unappreciated. Difficulties are occasionally reinforced by students, both female and male, who find gender discourse unnecessary and possibly even ridiculous. This can, however, be attributed to the previously discussed adaption of a new identity when entering a male-dominated education. It can be challenging to be 'one of the boys', while at the same time celebrating womanhood and initiatives of bringing gender issues up on the agenda. Similarly, this is seen also for women seafarers that enter the male-dominated work arena at sea. In a recent study of female seafarers (Kitada 2013), the results demonstrate how different strategies are used. Ideal types of strategies can be categorised as negotiators, constructors, maintainers, and reproducers. The strategies vary over time and most respondents in the study believed different strategies are needed on ship and ashore. This leads to a complex switching between identities. Kitada further identified three prominent subsets of norms and values on board ships: an emphasis on the hiding of emotions and feelings, the importance of jokes, and the prioritisation of the requirements of the job over the needs of individuals (Kitada 2013). These features of the seafaring culture reflect more masculine norms and values than in most shore-based cultures, placing demands primarily upon women seafarers to adjust, when entering the maritime work environment.

Gender awareness challenges stereotypical preconceptions, of which many of the students and teachers are bearers. Since gender stereotypes are highly resistant to change, gender segregation in education is highly resilient (Charles and Bradley 2002). Such stereotypes are easily reconciled with an 'equal but different' view, that finds widespread social acceptance and are difficult to contrast, because individuals do not perceive them as discriminatory. When making gender-coding visible and enlightening what effects it has on women, it means drawing attention to and putting women at the centre. This is an unusual and sometimes uncomfortable situation, that can be perceived as provocative by some (Hussenius et al. 2012). There is a common opinion that gender issues are irrelevant for certain subjects, if not impossible. Mathematics, chemistry and physics are examples of subjects where it is not unusual that this type of argument is presented; according to this way of thinking, there are no gender aspects of molecular studies, pump characteristic curves are gender neutral, the solution of a mathematical problem has nothing to do with gender, and so on. Therefore, it is necessary to make visible other tools for operationalising gender-inclusive policies and practices in the educational establishments. Beyond the need for formalisation of the inclusion of gender perspectives in curricula, Verdonk et al. (2009) argue that there is also a need for clear guidelines, incentives, disincentives and audits, in order for a structural embedding of gender in education. Furthermore, successful implementation of gender issues in education is entirely dependent on support from the leaders of the faculty. If gender expertise within the faculty is unavailable, schools are encouraged to consult external experts.

Increasing numbers of female students that choose a maritime education will not alone resolve gender bias in the maritime industry. Gender issues must be well defined, operationalised and included in educational policy and curricula-making at individual, structural, as well as symbolical levels. Without gender issues on the agenda, there is a risk of unnecessary reproduction of previous, and in some respects out-dated, values and tricks of the trade. Reflective practices upon her/his own position and how it could affect the education and relation to the students, may give the teacher useful insights and help create a more favourable learning environment for all students. This includes gender, but also class, ethnicity, age, nationality, sexuality and a number of other factors that affect the way in which a person views the world. A clear pedagogic platform can be developed and communicated to the students with regard to equality issues. Equality is not to treat everyone alike, but to create opportunities to gain knowledge, regardless of what the student in question brings of prior knowledge, values and experiences, and independent of whom the teacher is.

Gender issues span across the whole learning-situation. In order to make a difference, there needs to be awareness among teachers and other staff, as well as students. Other things that need to be taken into account are, for example, course literature, class-room presentations and everyday interaction between people at the schools. The challenge and paradox is that gender is a very sensitive area, but at the same time, almost invisible. Working to change existing structures is a matter of convincing others that there is a real problem, something that very well may be a difficult task. Since almost everyone sharing the same cultural background has a "silent agreement" to live by certain rules or expectations, depending on whether you are a woman or a man, it is often hard to accept that the differences, to a large extent, are constructions of a cultural and historical context, and not inherent and absolute abilities tied to sex. It is a concept that rocks the very foundations of what we perceive as reality, and not seldom uncomfortable for women as well as men.

The number of women in maritime education has increased over the last decades, but a reliance on the 'add women and stir' approach is unlikely to change existing hierarchies (Zuga 1999). Rather, it is needed to rethink contents and structure of education programmes, including governance, support and clear objectives in the study plans. Local projects and efforts can be of great importance, but they do not create structural change.

Mentioning gender issues specifically in study plans and curricula alone will not close the gender gap in the maritime industry. But, by highlighting the issues, there will be a natural need to address them at the level where it matters, in the interaction with students.

6 Conclusions

The results of this study show that gender issues are not a visibly integrated part of curricula in any of the eight universities studied. This fact is especially discouraging, since the universities were chosen from four of the countries with the highest Global Gender Gap Index, and thus could be assumed to represent state-of-the-art in this respect. Certainly, this study does not account for individual initiatives among students, teachers or other staff working to close the gender gap in education.

Leaving it to chance is, however, neither an effective nor reliable method of including gender awareness in maritime education. It needs to be formalised and most of all, it needs to have status as an important part of all education.

In order to resolve gender bias and close the gap in the maritime industry as a whole, gender-conscious pedagogical and didactic approaches must be well defined, operationalised and put into practice in educational policy and curricula making at individual, structural as well as symbolical levels.

References

Aalesund University. (2013). College/Bachelor i nautikk kull 2013. http://www.hials.no/nor/content/view/full/64486#. Accessed 1 Apr 2014.

Åland University of Applied Sciences. (2013). Sjöfart Läsåret 2013–2014. http://www.ha.ax/text.con?iPage=82&iLan=1. Accessed 1 Apr 2014.

Aurell, H. (2000). *Teknik på kvinnors vis – om villkor och möjligheter*. Stockholm: ESF-rådet.

Barone, C. (2011). Some things never change: Gender segregation in higher education across eight nations and three decades. *Sociology of Education, 84*(2), 157–176.

Berner, B. (2003). *Vem tillhör tekniken?: Kunskap och kön i teknikens värld*. Lund: Arkiv.

Bondestam, F. (2004). *Könsmedveten pedagogik för universitetslärare – en introduktion och bibliografi (Gender conscious pedagogy for university teachers – An introduction and bibliography)*. Stockholm: Liber.

Bryman, A., & Bell, E. (2007). *Business research methods*. New York: Oxford University Press.

Buskerud and Vestfold University College. (2013). Bachelor i nautikk. http://www.hbv.no/studietilbud/maritime-studier/bachelor-i-nautikk/. Accessed 1 Apr 2014.

Chalmers University of Technology. (2013). Sjökaptensprogrammet 180 hp (sjökaptensexamen). http://www.chalmers.se/sv/utbildning/program-pa-grundniva/Sidor/Sjokapten.aspx. Accessed 1 Apr 2014.

Charles, M., & Bradley, K. (2002). Equal but separate? A cross-national study of sex segregation in higher education. *American Sociological Review, 67*(4), 573–599.

Commission on Higher Education. (2013). *CMO No. 13, policies, standards and guidelines (PSG) for the Bachelor of Science in Maritime Transportation Program*. Philippines: Diliman.

Harding, S. (1986). *The science question in feminism*. Ithaca: Cornell University Press.

Hussenius, A., Andersson, K., & Gullberg, A. (2012). Integrerad undervisning om genus på lärarprogrammets ämneskurser. In A. Lundberg & A. Werner (Eds.), *Genusvetenskapens pedagogik och didaktik*. Göteborg: Nationella sekretariatet för genusforskning.

IMO. (2011). *STCW including 2010 Manila amendments: STCW convention and STCW code*. London: Author.

IMO. (2013). *Technical co-operation committee 63rd session, integration of women in the maritime sector*. London: Author.

Kennerley, A. (2002). Writing the history of merchant seafarer education, training and welfare: Retrospect and prospect. *Northern Mariner, 12*(2), 1–22.

Kitada, M. (2013). Code of behaviour at sea: Women seafarers' shipboard identity management. *WMU Journal of Maritime Affairs, 12*(2), 213–227.

Lewis, M. (1990). Interrupting patriarchy: Politics, resistance, and transformation in the feminist classroom. *Harvard Educational Review, 60*(4), 467–489.

Linnaeus University, & Kalmar Maritime Academy. (2013). Sjökapten 4-årigt program. http://lnu.se/institutioner/sjofartshogskolan/utbildningar/sjokapten-4-arigt-program-. Accessed 1 Apr 2014.

Novia University of Applied Sciences. (2013). Läroplaner 2013–2014: Sjöfart (270sp). http://ansokan.novia.fi/laroplaner2012v.html?id=3512. Accessed 1 Apr 2014.

Philippine Merchant Marine Academy. (2013). Bachelor of Science in Marine Transportation (BSMT). http://www.pmma.edu.ph/. Accessed 1 Apr 2014.

Philippine Merchant Marine School. (2013). Course description: Bachelor of Science in Marine Transportation (BSMT). http://www.pmms-online.com/page.php?p=4. Accessed 1 Apr 2014.

SFS (1992:1434) Högskolelagen (Swedish Higher Education Act).

Verdonk, P., Benschop, Y. W., de Haes, H. C., & Lagro-Janssen, T. L. (2009). From gender bias to gender awareness in medical education. *Advances in Health Sciences Education, 14*(1), 135–152.

von Wright, M. (1999). *Genus och text. När kan man tala om jämställdhet i fysikläromedel?* Stockholm: Skolverket.

World Economic Forum. (2013). *The global gender gap report 2013*. Geneva: Author.

Zuga, K. F. (1999). Addressing women's ways of knowing to improve the technology education environment for all students. *Journal of Technology Education, 10*(2), 57–71.

Are Women Contributing Equally to the Oceanography Science in Brazil?

Rozane Valente Marins and Juliana Berninger da Costa

Abstract Brazil has witnessed a huge increase in the number of articles published in international journals, has graduated more people, and displayed better science proxies. In Oceanography, Brazil has built up a complex system of science and technology, that today ranks 13th in the world in terms of scientific publications, according to the Thomson Reuters database; ahead of countries such as Holland and Russia. But this has not generally improved the gender equality in the field. An evaluation of gender in Brazilian oceanography is presented, as well as an investigation of the reasons for the low participation of women in the Brazilian political decisions today, regarding the future of the sea. Between 1995 and 2010, the percentage of women increased from 34 to 45 % in the leadership class, and from 41 to 52 % in the non-leadership class. But within its own class, the percentage of women leaders remained very similar during this period, varying from 29 to 26 %. In marine science, women leadership is even smaller, as viewed from recent initiatives such as the National Institutes of Science and Technology (INCTs) and the National Institute of Oceanic and Waterways Research (INPOH). Although some recent policies have promoted a more democratic selection of students to universities, and probably a better gender equality, specific mechanisms to improve women leadership in the young oceanography field, are still necessary.

Keywords Brazilian research network • Gender participation • Oceanography • Public policies

R.V. Marins (✉)
Coastal Biogeochemistry Laboratory of the Marine Science Institute, Federal University of Ceará, Fortaleza, Brazil
e-mail: rmarins@ufc.br

J.B. da Costa
Oceanography and Environmental Impacts Coordination Program – COIAM, National Council for Scientific and Technological Development (CNPq), Brasília, Brazil

© Springer-Verlag Berlin Heidelberg 2015

M. Kitada et al. (eds.), *Maritime Women: Global Leadership*, WMU Studies in Maritime Affairs 3, DOI 10.1007/978-3-662-45385-8_12

1 Introduction

From the first inventory of women in Oceanography, from 1997 to 2001 (Leta and Lewison 2003), researchers concluded that women received fewer fellowships to supplement their salaries, suggesting that gender-based discrimination occurred in the Brazilian peer-review process, although women published similar numbers of papers with similar impact factor, than those of men. But since then, Brazil has witnessed a huge increase in the number of articles published in international journals, graduated more people, and displayed better science proxies. Part of this progress was covered by more planning and scientometric[1] measures by the Brazilian scientific society and governmental agencies, that summarized the numbers of undergraduate, graduate, research groups and articles published in the different areas of knowledge. In the Oceanography field, Brazil has built up a complex system of science and technology, that today ranks 13th in the world in terms of scientific publications, according to the Thomson Reuters database; ahead of countries such as Holland and Russia. There are more than 100,000 active researchers in Brazil today, and a considerable number of scientists and engineers doing scientific and technological research of international standards (Pulizzi and Rezende 2010).

Some of the best known examples of success in Brazilian scientific research, are in areas where oceanography discipline can contribute significantly, such as oil drilling and production in deep waters by PETROBRAS, the Brazilian state oil company. But it is not clear if this new generation is improving gender equality, and it needs to be investigated.

Lacerda and Marins (2010) quantified the contribution of the Chemistry sector to the Oceanography field, which is a relatively recent scientific area in Brazil. The first undergraduate course in Oceanography was founded in 1970 in a remote area in the South of the country. Unfortunately, these authors did not summarize the gender contribution in their study.

In 2013, following national policies to improve the participation of the northeastern region of the country, and also women's involvement, in scientific decisions of the funding to oceanographic research and fellowships to marine researchers, R.V. Marins was elected as a member of the advisory committee of marine sciences of the National Council for Scientific and Technological Development (CNPq), and the opportunity to start an evaluation of gender in Brazilian oceanography was posed.

[1] Scientometrics is the area of study in measuring and analysing science, for example, by investigating the impact of journals and institutes in terms of scientific citations and mapping scientific fields.

2 Methods

The objective of this study is to evaluate gender equality in oceanography research and education in Brazil, by surveying the available data from CNPq, CAPES (the Coordenação de Aperfeiçoamento de Pessoal de Nível Superior)[2] from the Ministry of Education, and PPGMAR (Pesquisa e Pós-Graduação em Ciências do Mar),[3] also from Ministry of Education. From CNPq, the data emerged from the inventory of the absolute numbers of scholarships awarded in different researchers' levels (from technician to post-doc) and in different periods, January 2013 to January 2014 and after April 2014, when changes in the database were promoted by CNPq. From CAPES and PPGMAR, data on the number of undergraduate and graduate courses in Oceanography was accessed. To characterize the dynamic of students until 2011, the figures from the Brazilian oldest Oceanography course at the Federal University of Rio Grande (FURG), were computed.

Our approach has the intention to improve the discussion of gender in this particular scientific area. Also, this study aims to investigate reasons for the low participation of women in Brazilian political decisions about the sea's future, in an appropriate moment when Brazil's first presidential term by a woman is ending. The post-graduate courses in this period increased by 20 %, summing up 12 courses along the Brazilian coast, whereas the total area of Brazilian marine jurisdiction can reach 4,471,000 km^2, including the extended adjacent continental shelf.

3 Brazilian Science Numbers from Research Groups

From 1995 to 2010, an increase of 480 % of Brazilian researchers, in different areas of knowledge, was observed. Based on the research groups' database registered in CNPq, the number of researchers increased from 26,766 in 1995 to 128,668 in 2010

[2] CAPES (the Coordenação de Aperfeiçoamento de Pessoal de Nível Superior) is the Brazilian Federal Agency for the Support and Evaluation of Graduate Education. Founded in 1951, CAPES assists the Brazilian Ministry of Education in the formulation of national policies related to postgraduate study. Through CAPES, the Brazilian government provides beneficial services to the country's academic and educational community, promoting imaginative programmes both at home and abroad, and enabling the exchange of scientific and technological knowledge and skills. For further information, visit the websites, http://www.capes.gov.br and http://www.cambridgetrust.org/partners/capes-brazil.

[3] PPGMAR (Pesquisa e Pós-Graduação em Ciências do Mar) is a Research and Graduate Program in Marine Sciences. https://www.mar.mil.br/secirm/p-ppgmar.html.

researchers in all scientific areas. Simultaneously, women's participation increased 620 %. However, the proportion of women leadership in all areas of science remained low, from 11 % in 1995 to 13 % in 2010. Besides, when carefully observing the number of women in leadership positions relative to the number of female researchers, the total percentage of women leaders remained very similar from 1995 to 2010, varying from 29 to 26 % (Directorio dos Grupos de Pesquisa no Brasil Lattes n.d.). Plonsky and Saidel (2001) pointed out that the relative decrease in women leadership may be related to early retirement, following the fact that in Brazil, the minimum amount of working years required for a full salary pension for women is 25 years, whilst for men it is 30 years.

The frequent use of the maternity factor to explain the smaller participation of women in science, can be refuted when one observes that the average age of researchers is very similar between men and women. In 1995, the average age was 44 for men and 43 for women, remaining similar in 2010. The variability found between these years was insignificant (<1 % for men and 2 % for women).

4 Women in Brazilian Oceanography

Nowadays, there is a special program to improve the science network in Brazil, entitled National Institutes of Science and Technology (INCTs). This program was funded with nearly 130 million dollars, and a few thousands of scholarships to the selected 122 Institutes (but only seven of them work in marine science). The leadership among these seven marine science INCTs is composed of six men and only one woman. The low number of marine science representation in this national program, reflects the low percentage of research groups in the area. From the total research groups from 1995 to 2010, Oceanography, not considering related sciences like fisheries and aquaculture, represents less than 1 % of the different areas of knowledge (Directorio dos Grupos de Pesquisa no Brasil Lattes n.d.).

Recently, in order to help fill this gap, represented by the small numbers of excellence groups in marine sciences, and to improve the necessary capacity building in the field, the National Institute of Oceanic and Waterways Research (INPOH) was created by the Ministry of Science, Technology and Innovation. To organize and implement this new institute, there was a concern about geographic representation of scientific staff in charge of the administrative council, and to implement the research and technology lines of INPOH, which included a contribution from UNESCO. The staff is composed by 18 experienced researchers, however, only three of them are women.

Table 1 Percentage of gender distribution according to scholar level of researchers from 2000 to 2010 listed in the existing research groups in oceanography (Adapted from http://dgp.cnpq.br/censos/series_historicas/estudantes/index_estudantes.htm, accessed in January 2014)

	2000		2002		2004		2006		2008		2010	
Level	M	F	M	F	M	F	M	F	M	F	M	F
PhD	24.4	20.0	25.7	21.9	17.8	15.6	17.1	15.2	15.7	13.8	15.7	14.0
Master	36.5	33.9	30.7	30.0	20.1	19.9	19.5	19.1	18.6	18.2	17.3	16.8
Undergraduate	38.9	45.9	43.6	48.1	38.4	40.7	33.4	35.2	36.1	38.1	37.9	40.2
Others	0.3	0.3	0.0	0.0	23.8	23.8	30.0	30.5	29.6	29.8	29.1	29.0
Total	100.0	100.0	100.0	100.0	100.0	100.0	100.0	100.0	100.0	100.0	100.0	100.0

In December 2013, the most important national meeting of coordinators of Brazilian marine science undergraduate and graduate courses (sixth ENCOGRAD-MAR)[4] received 116 representatives of all research groups in marine science, registered in the CNPq database.[5] Forty-seven percent of the these groups were coordinated by women, being slightly higher in biological research (50 %), when compared to the chemical and physical oceanography, which together, represented 43 %.

The reasons why so few women are leaders of INCTs, and compose such a small number among the expert consultants in the organization of the new marine science federal institute, is not in consonance with the increase of women PhDs observed in research groups over the last 15 years evaluated.

Social policies to increase the entry of students from different social classes in the federal universities improved the access to scholarships for young students, including awards to young scientists (faculty students and technicians). The results of these affirmative polices are evident. A comparison of the percentage of this group, indicated as 'Others' (Table 1) in the research groups of CNPq, showed a ten times increase, from 0.3 % in 2000 to 29 % in 2010, and this increase is not different when the comparison includes gender. Also, women represented the majority in this group of faculty, students and technicians, indicated as 'Others' (about 60 %) during the entire period (Table 2) and the percentage in the highest level (PhD) of research improved, between 2000 and 2010, when from 49 % women to 56 %, as shown in Table 2. Here, the pattern shows better results than in the Plonsky and Saidel's (2001) study about gender, science and technology in Brazil during the 1990s, when the situation was the opposite, with 58 % being men.

[4] http://www.cdmb.furg.br/upload/arquivos/VI%20%20EnCoGrad_Mar_programacao%20preliminar.pdf.

[5] http://dgp.cnpq.br/diretorioc/.

Table 2 Percentage of gender within each scholar level of researchers from 2000 to 2010 listed in the existing research groups in oceanography (Adapted from http://dgp.cnpq.br/censos/series_historicas/estudantes/index_estudantes.htm, accessed in January 2014)

	2000		2002		2004		2006		2008		2010	
Level	M	F	M	F	M	F	M	F	M	F	M	F
PhD	50.9	49.1	48.2	51.8	47.2	52.8	45.6	54.4	44.9	55.1	44.3	55.7
Master	47.8	52.2	44.9	55.1	44.3	55.7	43.3	56.7	42.3	57.7	42.1	57.9
Undergraduate	41.8	58.2	41.9	58.1	42.6	57.4	41.5	58.5	40.5	59.5	40.1	59.9
Others	39.9	60.1	61.1	38.9	44.0	56.0	42.4	57.6	41.6	58.4	41.5	58.5
Total	45.9	54.1	44.3	55.7	44.0	56.0	42.8	57.2	41.8	58.2	41.5	58.5

The oldest oceanography undergraduate course in Brazil, which belongs to the Federal University of Rio Grande (FURG), and was founded in 1970, and has graduated, since the first class until 2011, circa 1,030 oceanographers. The gender distribution shows an increasing tendency of women participation, but not totally consolidated, as can be clearly observed in Fig. 1. In 2009, this University adopted the new national system evaluation exam to enter universities (ENEM),[6] which promoted a more democratic selection of students and probably improved gender equality.

A similar policy to open access to training abroad, was adopted by CNPq regarding research scholarships in different levels (Figs. 2 and 3). Between 2005 and 2011, the number of scholarships to work or study abroad decreased significantly, compared to the beginning of the decade. This probably led to the "Science without Borders" program which, since 2011, made possible the sending of over 40,000 students abroad, including undergraduates. Gender distribution of these scholarships was similar during most of the period 2001–2011. After, there was a slight increase in women participation.

The highest level of research scholarships in Brazil is called "Scientific Productivity", judged by a rigorous peer-reviewing process. Advisory committees are formed for all areas and researchers are ranked from the lowest "2" to the higher 1D, 1C, 1B and 1A. Normally, a researcher starts as rank 2 and may progressively rise up to 1A, which includes the best qualified researchers in the country. The system is considered highly trustable and rigorous, since besides the analysis of a high-level researchers committee, there are also invited *ad hoc* consultants to

[6] http://portal.mec.gov.br/.

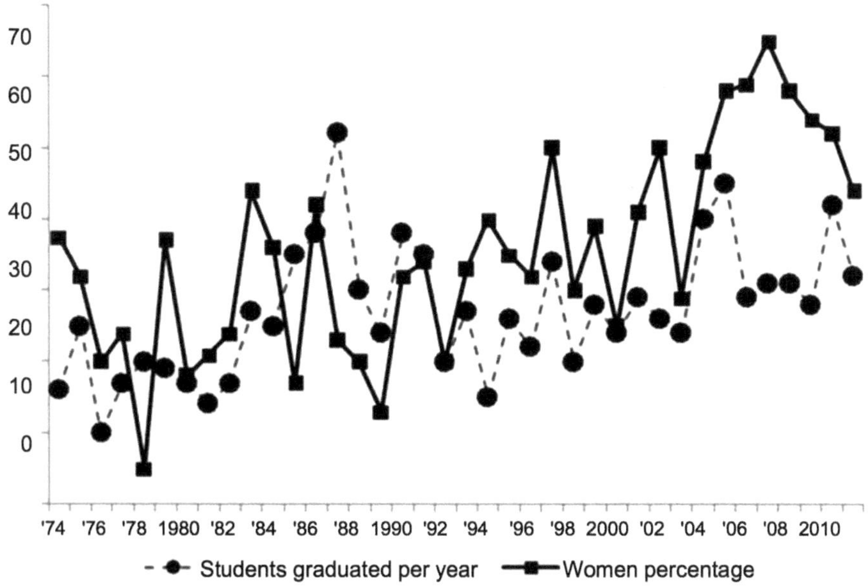

Fig. 1 Number of students graduated from the oldest oceanography course in Brazil and percentage of women in this group

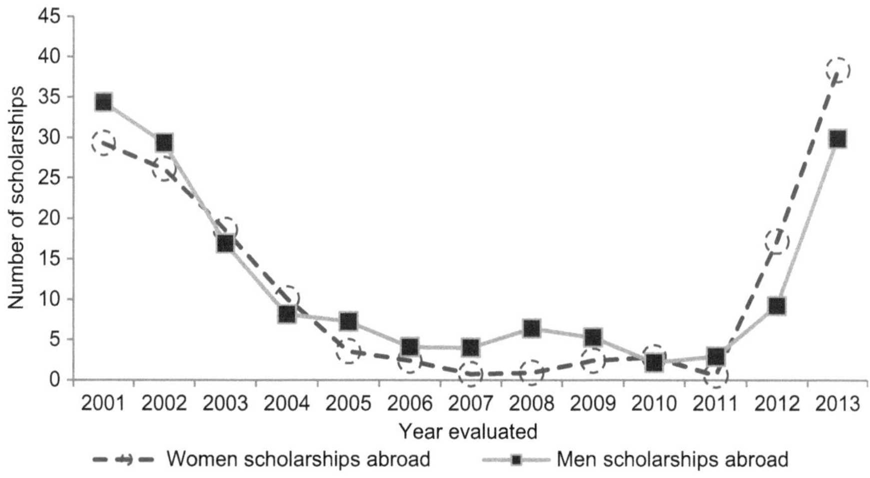

Fig. 2 Gender distribution, from 2001 to 2013, in the number of scholarships abroad distributed by CNPq

Fig. 3 Gender distribution, from 2001 to 2013, in the number of scholarships in the country distributed by CNPq

evaluate the submitted proposals. Alice Abreu, Emeritus professor at the Universidade Federal do Rio de Janeiro (UFRJ), explains that, despite the reliability of the system, it still reflects the supposed neutrality of science, therefore, gender is invisible, or has unknown meaning. While science is considered purely neutral and objective, it will still be difficult to introduce in scientific debate, factors such as gender equality (Academia Brasileira de Ciências 2014).

Contrary to all numbers presented above, when gender distribution is considered in the high-level scientific ranking ("Scientific Productivity"), there is an extremely low presence of women. Between 2001 and 2013, the percentage of women receiving scientific productivity grants never reached 30 % of the total approved grants (Fig. 4). It is evident, when comparing Figs. 2 and 3 with Fig. 4, that there is indeed inequality of gender, most probably derived from a cultural legacy, leading to this inequality of gender, among the top oceanographers in Brazil. These results are similar to the situation observed in other Latin America and Caribbean countries (Economic Commission for Latin America and the Caribbean 2013) but our work builds on mechanisms that progressively lead women from college level to the highest ranks of Brazilian research in Oceanography, showing an extremely strong

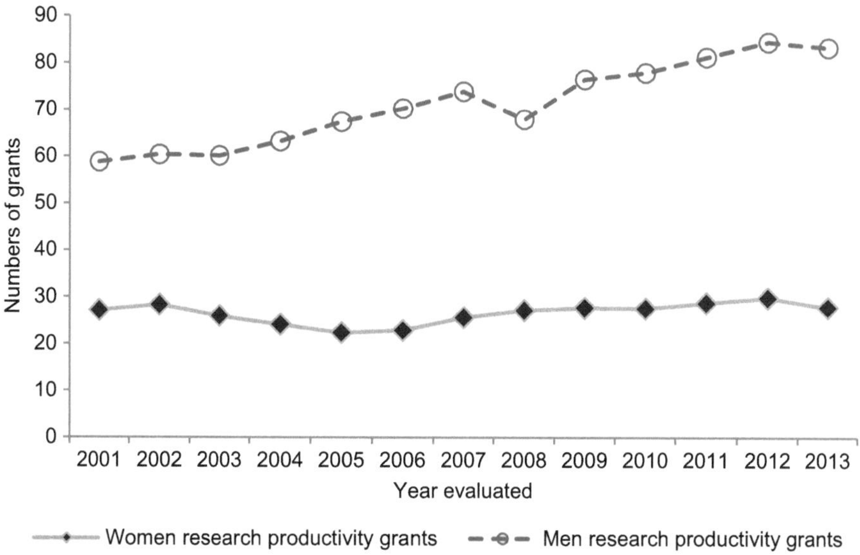

Fig. 4 Gender distribution, from 2001 to 2013, in the number of productivity grants distributed by CNPq

sieving process, that results in a very slow evolution of women participation in scientific leadership.

Similarly to what happens in the top of scientific research, and notwithstanding the result of affirmative public policies in increasing women participation in Oceanography at the university level, gender equality is also far from real when the non-qualified jobs in the marine area is analyzed. Schramm (2014) observed that, among fisheries workers in south Brazil, women working in the handling of captured fish, cleaning and preparing fishmeal for sale, as well as those working in collecting clams and even those working aboard fishery boats, are not officially considered as fishers by the Ministry of Fisheries; rather, they are included in the ministry statistics as fishermen wives.

Probably, even with time, the affirmative policies of access to university education and research grants may still not be able to increase women leadership, or gender equality, in the top ranks of oceanography in Brazil. In a recent symposium at the Brazilian Academy of Science (Academia Brasileira de Ciências 2013), Elisa P. Reis, an Academy's regional vice-president, commented that a lot of time was given to identifying women's difficulties and now it is time for action (Academia Brasileira de Ciências 2014). Therefore, new investments in capacity building and leadership programs, and even changing cultural legacies, will be necessary to abolish gender inequality in the higher ranks of Brazilian oceanographic research.

5 Conclusions

The large increase in the numbers of researchers in Brazilian science explains the good moment of the country's scientific productivity and participation in the international sphere. However, it does not show a strong consolidation of the good results regarding women. More leadership and specialists in the Oceanography field are highly necessary to fulfill the country's expectations and support its new economic scenario, which demands elevated quantities of resources, including marine natural resources. On the other hand, notwithstanding the existing public policies, specific mechanisms to improve women's participation and scientific leadership, in particular within the young oceanography field, are necessary, because this is still a small area inside the traditional areas of Brazilian science. However, the significant number of women with PhDs can help multiply results of the recent implemented policies and consolidating the welfare of Brazilian society with gender equality.

Acknowledgements We would thank for the great help of Prof. Dr. L.C. Krug, general coordinator of PPGMAR from the Brazilian Ministry of Education (MEC), who kindly provided his extensive database from PPGMAR and from FURG. We also thank CNPq for providing a grant during the writing of this research.

References

Academia Brasileira de Ciências. (2013). Simpósio fortalecendo a presença das mulheres na ciência Brasileira: Problemas e desafios. http://www.abc.org.br/article.php3?id_article=3059. Accessed 1 Apr 2014.

Academia Brasileira de Ciências. (2014). As conquistas da mulher brasileira na ciência. http://www.abc.org.br/article.php3?id_article=3181. Accessed 1 Apr 2014.

Directorio dos Grupos de Pesquisa no Brasil Lattes. (n.d.). Por liderança e sexo. http://lattes.cnpq.br/web/dgp/por-lideranca-e-sexo. Accessed 1 May 2014.

Economic Commission for Latin America and the Caribbean. (2013). *Women in the digital economy: Breaking through the equality threshold*. Genève: United Nation.

Lacerda, L. D., & Marins, R. V. (2010). Produção científica da área da química no desenvolvimento da Oceanografia no Brasil. *Química Nova, 33*(4), 1005–1013.

Leta, J., & Lewison, G. (2003). The contribution of women in Brazilian science: A case study in astronomy, immunology and oceanography. *Scientometrics, 57*(3), 339–353.

Plonsky, G. A., & Saidel, R. G. (2001). Gender, science and technology in Brazil. *Minerva, 39*(2), 217–238.
Pulizzi, F., & Rezende, S. M. (2010). Exciting times for Brazilian science. *Nature Materials, 9*, 532–533.
Schramm, F. P. (2014). Trabalhadoras do mar. Recourse document. Instituto Ciência Hoje. http://cienciahoje.uol.com.br/noticias2014/01/trabalhadoras-do-mar. Accessed 1 Jan 2014.

Education for Career-Building: How Women in the Maritime Industry Can Use Education to Improve Knowledge, Skills, Organizational Learning and Development, and Knowledge Transfer

Wilson Thoya Baya

Abstract The purpose of this paper is to discuss the role that education can play in improving the knowledge, skills, organizational learning and development, and knowledge transfer for women entering the maritime industry. The problem addressed by this paper is twofold: (a) the lamentably low number of women in the maritime industry and (b) the particular lack of women in leadership in the industry. This paper contains a discussion explaining how education can change the status quo for women in the maritime industry. One of the specific theoretical contributions of the paper is a model situating education between the social context and the employment context. Within this model, education can function to rectify gender inequalities that emerge from the social setting, and develop competencies that can allow women to enter the maritime industry in greater numbers, and also at leadership levels. A review of existing literature indicated that the mining, construction, and utility industries, which were also once dominated by men, have been able to increase the representation of women by weaving together education, the social context, and the employment context. Inspiration is taken from these three industries, to make recommendations to educational institutions serving the maritime industry. Finally, some specific pedagogical recommendations about best practices in maritime education, particularly in terms of leadership, are made. The conclusion is that educational industries serving the maritime industry can adopt a set of best practices in order to raise the representation of women in the maritime industry, particularly at leadership levels.

Keywords Gender equity • Male-dominated industries • Maritime education • Patriarchy

W.T. Baya (✉)
Bacha Maritime Movers – A Shipping Agency for U.S. Express Shipping Line, Mombasa, Kenya

The Institute of Chartered Shipbrokers, London, UK
e-mail: bayathoya@hotmail.com

© Springer-Verlag Berlin Heidelberg 2015

M. Kitada et al. (eds.), *Maritime Women: Global Leadership*, WMU Studies in Maritime Affairs 3, DOI 10.1007/978-3-662-45385-8_13

1 Introduction

Throughout the time I have spent working in the maritime industry in Kenya and elsewhere, I have noticed extreme gender inequity in the workplace. The maritime industry remains dominated by men, not only in terms of absolute numbers, but also in terms of the distribution of supervisory positions. However, over this same period of time, I have seen my home country of Kenya benefit tremendously from women's entry into many industries, and, just as promisingly, from women's assumption of supervisory and leadership roles that have long and unfairly been denied to them. This paper was motivated by the desire to address the well-known gender problem in the maritime industry, and issue a call to action to all colleagues, scholars, and policy-makers, who can make a difference.

The international maritime industry is aware of a particularly disturbing statistic. Horck (2010) notes that only about 2 % of the global seafaring workforce consists of women. This low participation rate of women in the global maritime industry is even worse than it appears, given that many women in the industry are not in positions of leadership or management. The main purpose of this paper is to identify the best practices that can allow women to play a more important role in the global maritime industry, both in terms of quantity (that is, relative representation in the workforce) and quality (that is, assumption of leadership and managerial positions).

For many years, women held the impression that it is forbidden to join the maritime industry, as men continued to conduct the maritime business and did not permit women to have access to the industry. It could have seemed like women were intruding on a sector that was in the control of men for centuries, and even in the present times, it has been difficult to break the status quo, when the majority of maritime nations still have minimal inclusion of women in the industry. Besides, there also exist cultural barriers that have acted as hindrances to women joining the industry. Today, the difficulty of having equal opportunities in the maritime industry presents a challenge for acquiring human progress, recognition, as well as respect for human rights.

The current global maritime situation seems bleak for women, despite the efforts of many stakeholders. Statistics carried out by the Seafarers' Rights International (SRI) for progressing seafarers' legal protection, indicates that approximately, 1.5 million seafarers work daily on a global fleet of more than 100,000 ships (Seafarers' Rights International n.d.). Another study by the International Labor Organization (ILO) puts the estimate at 1.2 million. In these approximations, women seafarers embody a very small percentage of the maritime workforce. The current statistics by the International Transport Workers' Federation (ITF), indicate that women comprise only 5 % of the global seafaring workforce, of which 94 % work as hotel staff on passenger ships (ferries and cruise ships), with the remaining 6 % working on cargo ships, such as tankers and container ships. In this minimal representation, the International Shipping Federation (ISF) states that women hold diverse positions which were once held predominantly by men, ranging from chief engineers, shipmasters, to other officer positions (BIMCO and ISF 2010). This proves that women have the ability to work on board any type of ship, at any position. With the current global demand for seafarers standing at 637,000 and 747,000 for officers and ratings respectively, as stated in the 2010 study carried out by the ISF, the maritime industry needs to put more emphasis on gender equity in training for maritime skills.

This paper calls attention to the role of education for career-building for women in the global maritime industry. It discusses four issues. First, it presents a model of the role that education plays in the lifecycle of female employment in the global maritime industry. This section looks at education as an important piece of the puzzle, but not the only piece. Before considering educational best practices as crucial tools for achieving more gender equity in the maritime industry, an exploration to enhance some understanding of how education fits alongside other factors, such as socialization, support, post-educational employment, and ongoing career advancement and development, is made. An understanding of the relationships between these different factors, will enable better design and implementation of educational practices that are more likely to achieve the intended goals of raising the percentage of women and women leading in the global maritime industry.

Second, the paper examines the role that education has historically played in generating opportunities and access for women in industries other than the global maritime industry. The maritime industry is certainly not the first, or only, industry in which women have been underrepresented, both in terms of general workforce participation and leadership. Likewise, many other industries have displayed gender inequity. The paper explains how education has been able to promote gender equity in other industries, that were once seemingly impervious to female participation and leadership.

Third, the paper examines the relationship between maritime education and maritime leadership. Grider (2013) indicates that one of the longstanding myths in our history, going back centuries, is that of natural captains, people who were born with the ability to manage themselves and others on the sea. This notion undermines the potential of women. This section of the paper explains how education can in fact develop leadership skills, that can enable women to thrive in the global maritime industry, just as their male counterparts.

In the fourth and final part, the paper unites the themes discussed into a single model of how education can generate equal opportunities and access for maritime women, in terms of gaining new knowledge and skills, organizational learning and development, and knowledge transfer, as applicable to leadership in the global maritime industry. In this part of the paper, the model presented at the beginning, explaining how education is perhaps the most vital link in increasing female participation and their leadership in the global maritime industry, is revisited.

2 A Model of the Role of Education

The purpose of the model presented below is to establish a basis for understanding (a) how and why women have been marginalized in the global maritime industry, and (b) what kinds of coordinated policies might be necessary to bring about

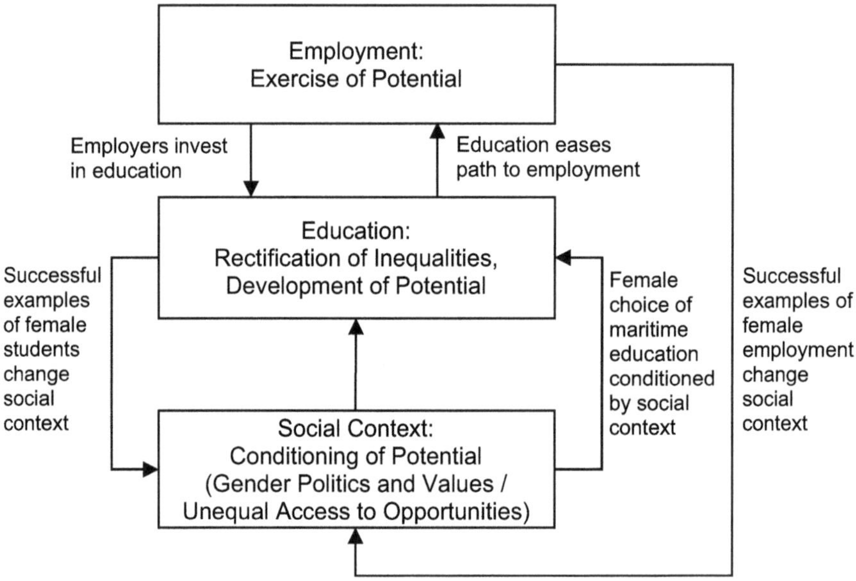

Fig. 1 Relationship between society, education, and employment. Education develops skills. Women with skills have an access to employment, hence change the societal biases levelled on women

changes in the status quo. The purpose of (b) is more important, because, if the position of women in the maritime industry is to change, there must be both a reconceptualization and a realignment of how social contexts, education, and employment coordinate to develop and promote female talent. Ultimately, in this sense, the model is a roadmap to the kinds of change necessary to address the gender issues in the global maritime industry (Fig. 1).

Education takes place within, and occasionally against, the context of larger social trends. Admittedly, this model is extremely simplified, but it is in general alignment with what the existing educational literature has to say about the relationships between social context, education, and employment. Each of these three areas can be understood in terms of potential. Based on some of the theories and findings explained later in the paper, it can be safely concluded that potential is something that is developed steadily over the lifecycle. In terms of women who could be potential members of the global maritime industry, or leaders within it, the lifecycle starts in the social context in which the woman is born. A review of the literature indicates that, in the vast majority of cases, there is an existing social bias against the participation of women in the global maritime industry (Grider 2013; Horck 2010; Pallis and Ng 2011). Some of these reasons are as follows. First, the global maritime industry often requires employees to be away from their families for long stretches of time, and women have historically been designated as caretakers of the family (Schultz 1990; Grider 2013). This situation has continued to portray the maritime industry as a men's world.

Second, the global maritime industry has been tainted with patriarchal ideas of men as hardy sailors and capable captains, carrying out physical work and exercising effective leadership of a kind, a situation Grider (2013) argues as a false claim.

Third, Grider (2013) notes the existence of many religious and social biases against the idea of an isolated workplace on a vessel that contains both men and women. This perception should place demands on the maritime industry to show cultural awareness and sensitivity, and promote leadership that induces cooperation and collaboration. In the model above, these kinds of ideas can be classified as part of the conditioning of potential; any given woman born anywhere on Earth has the same potential as a man to be a member of the global maritime industry, or a leader within it, but her social circumstances—particularly the gendered nature of those circumstances—constrain what she can or will do with that potential. The industry needs to understand that what is good for one sex is good for the other. The perception that some woman cannot perform certain duties should not reflect to the entire women population. Women ought to be hired for their skills and capabilities, and not only for their gender, or to provide diversity, or fill quotas.

Education develops potential (Morley 2007; Morley and Lugg 2009). In the case of women, education can fill in the deficiencies, or fight the negative conditioning of society vis-à-vis the female role in the global maritime industry. Education gives women the tools they need to overcome the counter-weights imposed on them by society (Morley 2007; Morley and Lugg 2009); in particular, education gives women knowledge, skills, organizational learning and development foundations, and knowledge-transfer abilities that can prepare them for employment, which is the actual exercise of potential. There are notable examples of women for whom education was the key to entering the global maritime industry, especially at higher responsibility levels than usually offered women in this industry. This relationship also goes the other way, as employers who are happy with graduates, make investments on their return through education. Thus, if maritime companies see that educated women are doing well in the workplace, they will directly and indirectly support maritime universities, such as the World Maritime University (WMU) and other institutions, in continuing to train the future maritime workforce.

Finally, is the reciprocal relationship that exists between social and employment contexts. As seen earlier, social context can determine employment practices, for example the kind of practices that discriminate against the promotion of women to positions of higher authority in the global maritime industry, or even against the hiring of women. However, when employers observe that women succeed at all levels in the workplace, then these examples change the social context. Whittock (2002) notes that social institutions begin to loosen their bias when they see that women are doing well.

This model provides an idea of how education sits between society and employment, playing the critical role of developing female potential and acting as the catalyst for gender equity in maritime employment. Having understood these relationships between society, education, and the global maritime workplace at a high level, the following part of the paper examines how education can break down barriers to entering workplaces, especially at positions of greater leadership.

3 The Role of Education: A Closer Look

In the title of this paper, maritime education is related to four specific characteristics: (a) knowledge, (b) skills, (c) organizational learning and development, and (d) knowledge transfer. The third section of the paper examines where the current paradigm of maritime education succeeds—and where it struggles—in each of these areas.

First, in terms of knowledge, maritime education can be given a high grade. Men and women are taught the exactly same subject matter, in the exactly same way. There is neither overt nor covert discrimination in pedagogy, curricula, or even admission standards. Therefore, the degree of knowledge acquisition for both women and men in the maritime industry is not the overriding issue.

In terms of skill, educational institutions should think more broadly about the special needs, constraints, and strengths of women in the global maritime industry. As pointed out by Horck (2010), women who enter the global maritime industry are more likely to leave before they have put in the time necessary to rise to higher levels of responsibility. Gekara (2009) notes the same observations. Some of the reasons contributing to this trend, as put forward by Dragomir et al. (2012) include: failure of the industry to consider women as having the same capabilities as their counterparts, sexual harassment, long times at sea, increased workload, fatigue, and complexity in handling mechanical equipment. Gills (2002) attributes the reasons to family factors such as pregnancy and marriage, or the lure of alternative attractive professions onshore. Incentives such as maternity leave, and shorter intervals of time at sea, could encourage more women into the industry and enable them to meet their family obligations as well.

This problem can be conceptualized as one of the skills; A particular set of vocational and emotional skills may be helpful for women to thrive in the transition from the educational environment to the workplace, and one of these skills has to do with managing the difficulties of a workplace that is still dominated by men and that can put significant stress on women's perception of themselves, thus making them self-conscious and self-doubting. It is important to point out that this issue is not one of knowledge; women who graduate from WMU and like institutions enter the workforce with the necessary vocational knowledge, but not necessarily the emotional and vocational skills that can sustain them, as they try to establish themselves in the global maritime industry.

Women empowerment is vital to the attainment of all goals associated with human rights development, equality, security, and safety. Even though a lot has been attained at the level of policy initiative on women empowerment and gender, quality implementation has not become effective and systematic, as expected. There is a significant gap between national level actions and global policies in dealing with the problems women undergo in the maritime industry. The results of failure to deal with gender equality issues in the maritime profession are felt by women all over the world. For instance, the continuing inequitable access to employment and education, the severe under-presentation in every decision-making aspect, as well as the unacceptable degrees of violence against women, factors seen by Weintrit (2011) as both life threatening and disempowering.

There ought to be a framework towards development elements that empowers women. This comprises the development of abilities and making sure there is access to necessary opportunities and resources. Others include the provision of leadership opportunities and roles in decision-making, and ensuring safety and security. Various groups and actors need to act to put in place these elements, which has to happen in a human rights approach framework. Couper (1999) argues that efforts to address these capabilities should start at a very early stage and should go on right through the life cycle.

Organizations such as IMO, ILO, and ITF have established initiatives that integrate women in the maritime industry. These institutions also offer training opportunities to match the requirements and needs of women. Governments must also play a role in developing and implementing policies that offer equitable access to education and health for boys and girls. Equal access to specialties, subjects, technology and science inclusive of communication technologies and new information, are vital. The teaching materials, curricula, and teacher training should be sensitive to gender, a factor seen by Magramo and Eler (2012) as crucial in guaranteeing that formal education contributes actively to women and girls' empowerment.

According to Zhao (1998), accessing critical opportunities and resources are vital to ascertain that women effectively maximize their abilities to benefit themselves, the community, their families and society. Securing abilities through education cannot be adequate in itself. Women have to access resources and opportunities through employment, research potential, and positions, to become part of the professional and academic associations. Even though women in the majority of nations are now dominating particular academic fields, and might even be more in numbers than men in attaining undergraduate and doctoral degrees, it does not translate to employment or academic careers and research positions. Equitable access to opportunities and economic resources are of particular significance for women's empowerment.

4 Learning from Other Male-Dominated Industries

A review of literature suggests that similar approaches have been taken by educational institutions that prepare women for careers in mining, construction, and utilities, all three of which were, until fairly recently, over 95 % male. Enormous strides have been taken in bringing female representation in these industries to over 10 %. This literature indicates that women who have entered these fields were better equipped with the emotional and vocational skills necessary to endure the initial period of adjustment and thus, place themselves in a position to advance through seniority (Gale 1994; Werthmann 2009; Dainty et al. 2000). These skills are often taught separately to women who are pursuing education in the mining, construction, and utilities fields. They are also paired with experiential learning opportunities which, according to Fielden et al. (2000), include those opportunities in which female students are paired with female mentors who have already achieved leadership success in these industries. By following these examples, educational institutions can play an important role in fighting the problem of female attrition in the global maritime industry.

Another useful practice from the mining industry in particular, is the role of pre-education. Non-profit institutions have done an excellent job of making young female students, often starting in primary school, aware of the existence of vocational opportunities in mining. If women start to think of themselves as being able to succeed in an industry long before they have entered a post-secondary institution, they might have an easier time enduring the initial period of adjustment (Agapiou 2002; Ng et al. 2009). The lesson to be learned for educational institutions that serve the global maritime industry, is to partner with non-profit organizations and other institutions that can publicize the existence and viability of global maritime careers for girls in primary and secondary schools. This approach has served the mining industry well. The factors of organizational learning and development, as well as knowledge transfer, can be considered under the heading of education and leadership, which constitutes the next section of the paper.

5 Education and Leadership

Gender equity in the global maritime industry, requires not only the increased hiring of women, but also the assumption of more leadership roles by women. In the past years, the concept of leadership has been treated as an innate capacity, or else as a complex set of skills and capabilities that cannot easily be taught. In contemporary times, precisely the opposite view prevails. Leadership has been extensively studied and broken down into discrete components that can be taught. One particularly influential model of leadership is that of Bass and Avolio (2011), who conducted extensive statistical testing to identify seven specific types of leadership. These types include:

- Idealized Influence: indicates whether you hold others' trust, maintain their faith and respect, show dedication to them, appeal to their hopes and dreams, and act as their role model;
- Inspirational motivation: measures the degree to which you provide a vision, use appropriate symbols and images to help others focus on their work, and try to make others feel their work is significant;
- Intellectual stimulation: shows the degree to which you encourage others to be creative in looking at old problems in new ways, create an environment that is tolerant of seemingly extreme positions, and nurture people to question their own values and beliefs and those of the organization;

- Individualized consideration: indicates the degree to which you show interest in others' well being, assign projects individually, and pay attention to those who seem less involved in the group;
- Contingent reward: shows the degree to which you tell others what to do in order to be rewarded, emphasize what you expect from them, and recognize their accomplishments;
- Management by exception: assesses whether you tell others the job requirements, are content with standard performance, and are a believer in "if it ain't broke, don't fix it."; and
- Laissez faire: measures whether you require little of others, are content to let things ride, and let others do their own thing.

With these seven types of leadership, how can the issue of teaching women leadership in maritime educational environments be approached? The first issue is determining whether leadership is actually being taught to male or female students. Leadership is a well-defined business concept with specific components, such as those identified in the research conducted by Bass and Avolio (2011). Leadership cannot be an afterthought in classes; it also cannot be taught in an anecdotal or non-precise way. Rather, maritime educational institutions should learn from business schools that are making leadership the centerpiece of classes, and that are also using experiential teaching methods (such as requiring students to go hiking or camping together in difficult conditions) to exercise and polish leadership. The most advanced and beneficial leadership courses are probably those in which leadership is scientifically dissected (whether into the seven components of the Bass and Avolio (2011) research, or into other leadership components that are recognized in the literature) and taught on a systematic basis, supplemented by experiential education. Once an institution has this kind of leadership pedagogy in place, one can think about how to adjust leadership training for women. Based on some of the factors discussed earlier in the paper, it is clear that many of the vocational problems women face in the global maritime industry—such as difficulty in managing teams of men—can be re-conceptualized as problems of leadership that can be taught in educational environments. In this way, education has an extremely important role to play in facilitating the ability of women to take leadership roles in the global maritime industry. Education can give women a systematic, intellectual, emotional, and experiential grounding in leadership that can, as transferred knowledge, carry over into their organizational development.

6 Conclusion

Female under-representation in the maritime industry is a global pressing problem, with the industry consisting of roughly 95 % men and 5 % women. This disparity is immense. However, there are good reasons to believe that education can play the role of a catalyst in promoting gender equity in the global maritime industry.

Institutions such as WMU have admitted an increasing proportion of women over the years. As the number and proportion of female graduates increase, there is a need to ensure that these graduates can influence the social settings from which they came. In simply being visible and serving as examples for girls and women from their home cultures, these graduates can convince families, religious institutions, and other important social collectives, to lower some of the biases and barriers in the path of female application to maritime institutions. Here, the role of WMU and other maritime educational institutions should be to hold local events and otherwise showcase the success of female graduates. Doing so can increase the pipeline of female applicants to maritime educational institutions, which in turn is likely to raise the proportion of women in the global maritime industry.

At the same time, maritime educational institutions should adopt some of the practices of educational institutions serving the mining, construction, and utilities industries, each of which was once just as inhospitable to women as the global maritime industry is to women today. These educational institutions have worked closely with non-profit organizations and other groups to ensure that young audiences—even girls in primary school—receive the message that there is room for them in male-dominated careers. If educational institutions can work together with other organizations, to ensure that young women hear about maritime careers as early as possible in their schooling, vocational commitment, educational preparation, and emotional preparation can be built in a more robust manner, long before these women enter a postgraduate institution such as WMU.

Another important point is to go beyond imparting maritime knowledge to female students. Female students need not only maritime knowledge, but also the special skills which are helpful to survive and thrive in a difficult vocational environment. It is evident from the examples of educational institutions serving the construction, mining, and utilities industries, that female students need to be given specific skills training in dealing with gendered issues on the job. Such skill training is likely to lower the percentage of women who drop out of the maritime industry, before they have a chance to advance.

If the percentage of women in the global maritime workforce is low, the percentage of women in leadership positions is even lower. Educational strategy should therefore focus specific attention on the question of how to place more women in leadership positions. Recommendations for best practices in this area are as follows: (a) teach leadership in formal courses, breaking leadership down into the specific and systematically teachable categories identified by Bass and Avolio (2011) or other researchers; (b) supplement leadership teaching with experiential leadership, for example in the form of simulated work environments or project-based leadership challenges; and (c) work with the ecosystem of partners (including female leaders in the maritime industry, maritime companies, government groups, alumni groups, and non-profit groups) in order to facilitate the transfer of women's leadership education into the actual work environment.

Women represent a strategic human resource that can address the challenges of shortages currently experienced in the seafaring industry. In order for the maritime industry to motivate women to join the sector, several steps ought to be taken that will be inclusive of seafaring active promotions, prospective career, positive experiences, and the willingness of companies recruiting women seafarers to diminish male domination in the industry. Shipping and crewing companies should implement policies that address sexual harassment and provide for maternity and pregnancy benefits for women seafarers. On the other hand, problems such as hostility from male crew members and unwillingness to recognize women seafarers for maritime jobs, sexual harassment incidents ranging from physical assault to verbal sexualized comments, should be addressed effectively by shipping companies. This is to ensure a continuous retention of present women seafarers, as well as women seafarers' recruitment in the future, and a progressive perspective of the global maritime industry.

References

Agapiou, A. (2002). Perceptions of gender roles and attitudes toward work among male and female operatives in the Scottish construction industry. *Construction Management & Economics, 20*(8), 697–705.

Bass, B. M., & Avolio, B. J. (2011). Multifactor leadership questionnaire. Resource document. Mind Garden. http://www.mindgarden.com/products/mlq.htm#overview. Accessed 26 Dec 2013.

BIMCO, & ISF (2010). *Manpower 2010 update: The worldwide demand of and supply for seafarers*. Coventry: University of Warwick.

Couper, A. D. (1999). *Voyages of abuse seafarers, human rights and international shipping*. London: Pluto.

Dainty, A. R., Bagilhole, B. M., & Neale, R. H. (2000). A grounded theory of women's career under-achievement in large UK construction companies. *Construction Management & Economics, 18*(2), 239–250.

Dragomir, C., Baftranca, G., & Surugiu, F. (2012). Motivation of joining women in the maritime sector. *Maritime Transport & Navigation Journal, 3*(3), 2–79.

Fielden, S. L., Davidson, M. J., Gale, A. W., & Davey, C. L. (2000). Women in construction: The untapped resource. *Construction Management & Economics, 18*(1), 113–121.

Gale, A. W. (1994). Women in non-traditional occupations: The construction industry. *Women in Management Review, 9*(2), 3–14.

Gekara, V. (2009). Understanding attrition in UK maritime education and training. *Globalisation, Societies and Education, 7*(2), 217–232.

Gills, D. (2002). *Women and work in globalising Asia*. London: Routledge.

Grider, J. (2013). Sailors, states, and employers in the construction of masculine maritime identity. *Politics, Groups, and Identities, 1*(2), 225–229.

Horck, J. (2010). The gender perspective in maritime education and training. *WMU Journal of Maritime Affairs, 9*(1), 93–119.

Magramo, M., & Eler, G. (2012). Women seafarers: Solution to shortage of competent officers? *International Journal on Marine Navigation and Safety of Sea Transportation, 6*(3), 397–400.

Morley, L. (2007). Sister-matic: Gender mainstreaming in higher education. *Teaching in Higher Education, 12*(5–6), 607–620.

Morley, L., & Lugg, R. (2009). Mapping meritocracy: Intersecting gender, poverty and higher educational opportunity structures. *Higher Education Policy, 22*(1), 37–60.

Ng, A. K., Koo, A. C., & Ho, W. C. (2009). The motivations and added values of embarking on postgraduate professional education: Evidences from the maritime industry. *Transport Policy, 16*(5), 251–258.

Pallis, A. A., & Ng, A. K. (2011). Pursuing maritime education: An empirical study of students' profiles, motivations and expectations. *Maritime Policy & Management, 38*(4), 369–393.
Schultz, T. P. (1990). Women's changing participation in the labor force: A world perspective. *Economic Development and Cultural Change, 38*(3), 457–488.
Seafarers' Rights International. (n.d.). Welcome to Seafarers' Rights International. http://seafarersrights.org/. Accessed 1 Apr 2014.
Weintrit, A. (2011). *Human resources and crew resource management marine navigation and safety of sea transportation*. Boca Raton: CRC Press.
Werthmann, K. (2009). Working in a boom-town: Female perspectives on gold-mining in Burkina Faso. *Resources Policy, 34*(1), 18–23.
Whittock, M. (2002). Women's experiences of non-traditional employment: Is gender equality in this area a possibility? *Construction Management & Economics, 20*(5), 449–456.
Zhao, M. (1998). *Women seafarers in the EC: A preliminary report based on German and UK case studies*. Cardiff: Seafarers International Research Centre.

Part IV
Global Leadership for Maritime Women

Women Leadership in Maritime Law Firms: The Antwerp Case

Anniek Wouters

Abstract Antwerp's maritime law firms exhibit low female participation and leadership. Women occupy solely 20 % of Antwerp's maritime lawyers, the percentage of female partners being a negligible 8 %. This is striking, as currently, female trainees at the Antwerp bar outnumber their male counterparts. The same applies to law graduates at the University of Antwerp (UA). This paper explores factors contributing to and perpetuating the gender gap. The first phase of the research revealed the existence of a substantive pool of qualified female lawyer trainees and pointed to high female attrition rates. The second phase of the research involved both qualitative and quantitative methods with Antwerp's 15 maritime law firms, through in-depth interviews and questionnaires, modelled after the 2010 National Association of Women Lawyers (NAWL) Survey on the retention and promotion of women in law firms. This paper argues that male lawyers tend to be more satisfied with career development opportunities. Although female participation has increased, female attrition rates are significant. The majority of female maritime lawyers are below 40 years old. Blatant discrimination is nearly absent, though a majority of interviewed women witnessed gender stereotyping. Historic reasons, such as the traditionally male-dominated dynamics inherent to the shipping industry and the lawyer's profession, have an impact. Nevertheless, the paper argues that the main factors perpetuating low female participation, remain work-life imbalance, lack of opportunities to work on a part-time basis, lack of child-care amenities, lack of female mentors and role models, lack of female networking and support groups, low emphasis on and lack of incentives to increase diversity, subjective advancement and hiring standards, and the small scale of the firms, increasing the importance of "alikeness". Lastly, the paper renders empowerment strategies for both individuals and firms.

Keywords Empowerment strategy • Female attrition • Gender bias • Maritime law firms • Women leadership

A. Wouters (✉)
Roosendaal Keyzer Lawyers, Antwerp, Belgium
e-mail: anniek.wouters@roosendaal-keyzer.be

© Springer-Verlag Berlin Heidelberg 2015

M. Kitada et al. (eds.), *Maritime Women: Global Leadership*, WMU Studies in Maritime Affairs 3, DOI 10.1007/978-3-662-45385-8_14

1 Introduction

This paper explores women's participation and leadership in maritime law firms. Literature is available on both female participation in law firms and in the maritime business in general. However, research on female maritime lawyers is lacking, hence the focus of this paper.

The research's geographical focus entails Antwerp. The city harbors Belgium's single most important port in terms of size and trade. Consequently, Belgium's main practice and development of maritime law comes about in Antwerp. The material focus of this research entails the profession of maritime lawyers, practicing at the Antwerp bar. Given the homogenous built-in male character of Antwerp's maritime lawyers, the focus on women should not obscure other dimensions though, such as race and ethnicity.

The first section of this paper sets out findings derived from previous research regarding female participation and leadership, regarding both the shipping industry in general and private law practices. The second section sets out the quantitative research conducted. Several data were collected in order to gauge the precise extent of female participation and leadership in maritime law firms. The qualitative research of Section 3 combines hypotheses derived from the literature review and the quantitative research. A questionnaire was disseminated to Antwerp's maritime lawyers, examining whether these hypotheses apply to them. Section 4 of the paper contains the results emerging from the questionnaires. Finally, Section 5 lists the implications and attempts to convey paths for improvement.

2 Theoretical Framework

2.1 Trends and Evolutions

The Shipping Industry: A Traditionally Male-Dominated Sector For centuries, the maritime business has been exclusively under men's control. Women solely make up 2 % of the world's seafaring workforce (ITF 2012). Gender discriminatory practices exist at all levels of the occupational hierarchy and within individual job categories in the shipping sector (Narbutas 2004). The ratio of men in management positions, to that of women, is four-to-one in the following five categories of maritime companies: ship repairs, brokering firms, logistics/warehousing, clearing/forwarding and port administration (Onwuegbuchunam 2011).

Several factors have contributed to low female participation and continue to do so (Dragomir and Surugiu 2012). These include traditional gender roles, as women traditionally met resistance to working outside the home in the maritime business, which requires substantive travel and contacts with the seafaring culture (Dragomir et al. 2012). Further, differences in, inter alia, physical strength and adequate separate facilities for women, contributed to low female participation (Horck 2008).

The literature on maritime women has mainly focused on female under-representation regarding seafarer-, technical-, and engineering-related jobs. Women in the maritime business tend to take up differing career paths than men (Dragomir et al. 2012). They opt, relatively more often, for shore-based career paths, such as maritime law (Popescu and Varsami 2010). Maritime private law practices are not immune to the plight though. Similar constraints act as a constraint on the representation of women in shore-based maritime jobs. As maritime law cases involve dealing with these almost exclusively male enterprises and practices, the paper hypothesizes spill-over effects, inducing fewer women willing to embark on a career in maritime law firms.

Nevertheless, during the past decades, efforts have been made to enhance women's participation in the maritime workforce. As the quantitative research demonstrates, access for women to a career at the Antwerp bar has increased dramatically, to the point where women now make up more than half of the new lawyer trainees.[1] Yet, it seems, this trend has not manifested itself for Antwerp's maritime law firms.

Erosion of Blatant Discrimination for Lawyers: Still Gaps Between Principles and Practice Blatant or overt gender discrimination has eroded, and opportunities for female lawyers have dramatically increased. Still, substantial gaps exist between gender equality principles and practice (Rhode 2012). Too often, women do not advance to leadership levels. Despite the absence of blatant discrimination, women hold less influential and prestigious jobs, advance more slowly, and are less likely to benefit from job changes and transfers than men. Advancement and pay structure, career development opportunities and performance appraisal, are more geared to the advantage of men (Brett and Stroh 1997). Female lawyers exhibit similar overall career satisfaction as men, though they experience greater dissatisfaction with dimensions of practice relevant to leadership opportunities (Dinovitzer et al. 2004). Even when given autonomy and control, women in self-employed status are still unequal to men in terms of authority, power and income (Onwuegbuchunam 2011).

The absence of overt discrimination makes it difficult to perceive factors contributing to female under-representation. Also, it results in a lack of consensus on whether there is a serious problem. The status and comfort of the privileged groups seem to unconsciously perpetuate the gender bias (Rhode 2012). Privileged groups tend to attribute ethnic and gender differences in leadership to differences in choices, capabilities and commitment, that a firm has limited ability or responsibility to influence. However, these mechanisms probably do not fully explain the gap between gender equality principles and practices. Attrition rates among female lawyers are twice as high as among comparable males, and men's likelihood of

[1] According to figures provided by Y. Nauwelaerts, vice-president of the Antwerp bar.

making partner is much greater (Rhode 2012). As much of the disadvantage facing women does not involve demonstrably or overt discrimination, it will prove very arduous for them to establish that they were treated adversely, based on gender. Social patterns that produce contemporary gender obstacles, can often not be adequately captured by legal definitions of discrimination. Finally, institutions are not given incentives to address gender biases, so they might want to refrain from collecting information revealing patterns of exclusion.

2.2 *Contributing Factors*

Conforming to Male Standards Leading women tend to conform to male standards. Numerical dominance shapes the culture and dominant roles which one should conform to, until a numerical minority reaches a critical mass (Brickman 2008). Women's first strategy to survive in a male-dominated environment consists of gender neutrality and striving for alikeness (Horck 2008). Women settle into male norms, as alikeness is a key parameter for men to appoint women to leading positions. Indeed, early female attorney leaders described conforming their appearance to traditional norms, and refraining from being a "shouter of women's rights" (Rhode 2012). In order to settle in, women do not always show their full capacity and competence. They are oftentimes pressured to assimilate to prevailing norms, instead of, inter alia, taking on a more feminine approach or pursuing a part-time career.

The Influence of Traditional Gender Roles Cultural and social attitudes towards what constitutes a male or female job and gender inequality in education and training, mainly cause occupational segregation (ILO 2007). Shipping is traditionally seen as a risky, male job and access to education and training was, until recently, limited for women. Strongly held traditional beliefs and stereotypes have a significant role to play when it comes to appointing and promoting decisions. Women were erroneously thought to have limited abilities, impairing them from adequately coping with the demands of some job specifications (Onwuegbuchunam 2011). Gender stereotypes thus impede women from pursuing leadership tracks. Public opinion agrees that the pursuit and exercise of power is inconsistent with traditional notions of femininity, causing women's discomfort with it (Chanow and Stiller Rikleen 2012).

Despite significant progress, women are still oftentimes perceived as less competent. On most qualities associated with leadership, such as assertiveness, competitiveness, self-promotion and business development, women are rated lower than men (Rhode 2012). Regarding performance evaluations, similar descriptions of performance result in lower ratings for women (Biernat et al. 2011). Also, women are often held to higher standards through gender stereotypes.

Cognitive Biases Account for and Reinforce Traditional Stereotypes It makes people more likely to accept, notice and recall information that confirms their prior assumptions (Rhode 2012). Mothers, as opposed to fathers, are immediately assumed to be less available and committed. Lawyers will more easily remember the times when a working mother left early, than the times when she stayed late (Rhode 2012).

Traditionally male-dominated professions exhibit patterns and workplace structures rooted in traditional gender roles, advantaging those willing to work 'sweatshop hours'. Law firms' escalating workplace demands and inflexible practice structures, impede female leadership, as long hours make it unattractive to many women, especially since women still continue to shoulder the major burden of domestic work (The Bureau of Labor Statistics of the U.S. Department of Labor 2004). Law is known as a sleep-deprived profession, contributing to lawyers' disproportionate rates of stress. Female lawyers who temporarily step out of the workforce, or reduce their workload, are often permanently derailed by that decision (Rhode 2012).

Perception of a Problem and Priority Given the comfort and status of the privileged group, their members typically do not perceive the need to include minorities (ABA Commission on Women in the Profession 2006). Ethnic and gender differences in leadership are attributed to differences in choices, capabilities and commitment and that one has limited ability or responsibility to influence. Private practices generally blame the small pool of qualified candidates. Such attitudes help account for the relatively low priority that most legal employers attach to efforts aimed at increasing female participation (Meyers 2004). Next, such attitudes understate the extent to which unconscious stereotypes and workplace structures disadvantage women (Rhode 2012).

In-Group Favouritism Individuals feel preferences for members of their own group. Individuals who are similar in important respects, such as gender, are more likely to allocate loyalty, opportunities, rewards, cooperation, favorable evaluation and mentoring to similar others (Rhode 2012). Dissimilar individuals face hurdles to develop social capital, i.e., access to advice, support, sponsorship, client development activities and desirable assignments (Kay and Wallace 2009). Women are often being left out of pitches for client business and relegated to 'workhorse' positions. The allocation of work and client development opportunities is often influenced by in-group favoritism. The latter is particularly harmful for lawyers, as in law firms, the capacity to bring in substantial business is quintessential for leadership. Many firms still operate without formal standards of evaluation, hiring and promotions. Lack of these objective standards tends to reinforce in-group favouritism. Consequently, men are disproportionately encouraged to leadership tracks when firms channel talented junior lawyers (Rhode 2012).

Next, the paper argues that in-group favoritism could be compounded by beliefs that diversity can heighten conflict and communication problems. It is easier to work with people who are similar in important respects. This may be particularly true for the maritime sector, where one has to deal with parties established all over the world. Differences among parties in the shipping industry—linguistic, gender and cultural—can engender casualties, caused by arduous communication (Horck 2008).

The Fundamental Role of Mentors, Role Models and Support The support and inclusion provided by mentors and role models are crucial for participation and leadership. Minorities often report isolation and marginalization, whereas women often experience exclusion from "old boy networks" (Rhode 2012). Mentoring is the single most effective means to eradicate a sense of isolation (McWilliams 2007). Well-designed initiatives evaluating and rewarding mentoring activities substantially improve female retention rates (Schipani et al. 2009). For example, the appointment of upper-class mentors to guide women, and ensuring that qualified female midshipmen be given command officer positions, proved crucial to women's inclusion at the US Maritime Academy (Brickman 2008). Having relatives working in the maritime business, substantially enhances the likelihood of embarking on a maritime career. As networks and affinity groups stimulate female participation, one should not underestimate the potential impact of initiatives like the Maritime Women: Global Leadership Conference, hosted by the World Maritime University in 2014.

These examples point out that it is critical for organizations to have sufficient women at senior levels, addressing their time and commitment to assist others on the way up. A growing number of organizations have formal mentoring programs. However, it is key to have adequate rewards or monitoring, to ensure effectiveness of these programs. When evaluated and monitored, formal mentoring has substantially improved female retention rates (Rhode 2012). It must be kept in mind however, that relationships which develop naturally are preferable, as they avoid mismatching and do not simply yield advisors, but sponsors. Men are more likely to have such sponsors and to have their help in promotions. The sponsor goes beyond giving feedback and advice and uses his or her influence to advocate for the mentee. Female subordinates are sometimes not being sufficiently invested in, due to assumptions about commitment, capabilities and low likeliness of staying (Ibarra et al. 2010). Without such sponsorship, women are less likely to be appointed to top roles and are more reluctant to go for them.

2.3 *Strategies and Remedies*

It seems crucial for women to divert time to actively seeking and developing relationships with mentors who can open doors at leadership levels (Scharf et al. 2004). Secondly, women need to be clear about their goals and seek challenging assignments. One can always take into account the existence of unconscious biases and exclusionary networks. Firms have an important role in developing strategies as well. What is crucial is a commitment for promoting diversity from the top. A commitment to implementing diversity should be reflected in organizational policies and priorities (Catalyst 1996, 1998). Firms should design effective and objective systems of evaluation, rewards and allocation of professional development opportunities (Rhode 2012). Individuals should be held accountable for the results. The most successful approach entails task forces or committees with diverse and influential members who enjoy credibility and hold a stake in the results (Dobbin and Kalev 2007). Lastly, studies suggest that affirmative action is needed in order to achieve substantive female participation. If one defines equality as sameness, one assumes women's adjustment to the status quo. The latter only confirms that it is a place for men, run by men. The US Maritime Academy has given special attention and training for women that male peers did not receive, which proved critical for women (Brickman 2008). On the downside, male colleagues often perceive affirmative action as providing undeserved special privileges, thus entailing the potential for resentment (Rhode 2012).

The turn for diversity may even be triggered by external events. For instance, one factor stimulating United States law firms to increase female participation, has come from their clients, whom made it an important operating point (Bentsi-Enchill 2006). By making it a factor in allocating work, they are compelling legal employers to implement diversity (Rhode 2012).

3 Research Methods

Quantitative and qualitative research methods were applied through questionnaires and in-depth interviews in order to gauge the precise extent of female under-representation in Antwerp's maritime law firms. Data collected from the Law graduate program at the University of Antwerp (UA) demonstrate that the percentage of women graduating has dramatically increased over the past decades (see Table 1). Female graduates now outnumber their male peers. The percentage of women enrolling at the UA's law faculty comprises 60 % (Table 1).

As highlighted Table 2, female students graduating from the Advanced Master in Transport and Maritime Law of the UA, make up 50 % regarding the academic year 2013–2014. In the previous 2 academic years, they made up, respectively, 72 and 75 %.

Female students tend to surpass their male peers in terms of grades. However, concerning the highest performers, female students are under-represented. Moreover, as one climbs higher up the academic ladder, from assistantships to PhD's, to

Table 1 Enrollment numbers and percentages, General Master in Law at the University of Antwerp

Year	Men	Women	Total
2012–2013	915 (40 %)	1,389 (60 %)	2,304
2013–2014	969 (41 %)	1,419 (59 %)	2,388

Table 2 Enrollment percentages, Advanced Master in Transport & Maritime Law at the University of Antwerp

Year	Men (%)	Women (%)
2009–2010	65	35
2010–2011	39	61
2011–2012	25	75
2012–2013	29	71
2013–2014	50	50

independent academic staff, the percentage of women decreases steadily (Wyckaert 2006).

Furthermore, data collected from the Bar association indicate that women still form a minority regarding the total number of lawyers. Nevertheless, their participation is steadily growing. Currently, first-year female trainees outnumber their male counterparts in Antwerp. Although empirical evidence is lacking, female attrition rates are presumed to be significantly higher than those of male colleagues. In the fall 2013, 63 female trainees and 45 male trainees, embarked on their legal career at the Antwerp bar. Fifty-eight percent of the first-year trainees thus consist of women. The combined percentages of first- to third-year trainees currently registered at the Antwerp bar, demonstrates a ratio of 189 female trainees (63 %), compared to 113 male trainees (37 %). The Flemish Bar reports there were in total, 5,814 male lawyers (58 %) and 4,280 female lawyers (42 %) active in Flanders in 2012. Since 2000, 473 (51 %) female lawyers, compared to 470 male lawyers (49 %), have quit practicing at the Antwerp bar. Given that the participation of women has only recently dramatically increased, these percentages suggest that attrition rates among young women are disproportionately high. This is consistent with Dutch research pointing towards highest attrition rates among female lawyers below the age of 35 (De Haas 2006).

Lastly, data were collected regarding Antwerp's 15 maritime law firms (Table 3). Only those who made maritime law their main area of practice were included. Lawyers within these firms, whom are not practicing maritime law as their main area of practice, were filtered out. Consequently, the ratio of male to female maritime lawyers entails 68–17, i.e., 80–20 %. The percentage of female maritime lawyers is markedly lower than the percentage of female lawyers prevailing in firms practicing other branches of law. The ratio of male to female partners at said maritime firms imparts yet another picture, being 34 male partners to 3 female partners. Only a baffling 8 % of the maritime women break through to partnership.

Hypotheses were derived from the literature review in Section 1, on female underrepresentation in the maritime sector and on impediments to female lawyers' leadership. A questionnaire was developed aimed at testing whether the combined hypotheses apply to the maritime law firms in Antwerp. The questionnaire was partly modelled after the 2010 National Association of Women Lawyers (NAWL) Survey on the retention and promotion of women in law firms (Scharf and Sanders Netties 2004; Scharf et al. 2009). In particular, the questionnaire tested for the following (Scharf and Flom 2010).

Table 3 Maritime law firms in Antwerp

Firm	Male lawyers	Female lawyers	Male partners	Female partners
1. Roosendaal Keyzer	8	1	4	0
2. Fransen Luyten	7	1	3	0
3. Ambos	3	1	1	1
4. Van Doosselaere	6	0	2	0
5. Ponet	7	1	3	0
6. Van Hemelen, Bettens & De Cocker	5	0	3	0
7. Clijmans	2	1	1	0
8. Navius	2	0	2	0
9. Kegels Co	6	3	2	0
10. Elegis	5	1	3	0
11. Marcon Rubens	7	3	4	0
12. Metis	2	3	1	2
13. D'Hoine & McKay	4	2	2	0
14. In-port lawyers	2	0	1	0
15. Goemans & De Scheemaecker	2	1	2	0
Total	68	17	34	3
Percentage	80 %	20 %	92 %	8 %

First, the rationale for female under-representation was questioned. Particular interest is drawn by whether lawyers attribute gender differences to inherently female or external factors. It was investigated whether female under-representation is attributed to factors such as availability, capabilities and commitment. Secondly, the extent to which traditional gender roles help account for and reinforce low female participation, were examined. It was also explored whether workplace structures and demands are rooted in traditional gender roles, and whether they are flexible. Availability of flexible work hours, part-time work and child-care facilities were investigated. Also, the extent to which there are objective standards for appraisal, hiring and rewards were gauged. Third, it was explored whether (female) role models, mentors and support networks are provided. Fourth, it was examined to what extent the shipping environment, i.e., clients, in which participating lawyers operate, is still male dominated. It was gauged whether female participation is a requisite for profitability and whether clients compel for diversity. Fifth, the extent to which women are currently "rainmakers" within Antwerp's maritime law firms was inquired, as well as the opportunities given to them to achieve such status. Opportunities given to develop client relations, levels of responsibility and opportunities given to advance to, inter alia, partnership, were measured. Furthermore, the extent to which women are held to higher standards and perceived to be less competent was examined. It was also explored whether female participants report having to conform to male standards and work environments, and even having to prove themselves. Lastly, the perception of low female participation is a problem and the priority attached to remedying the problem was gauged.

The questionnaire was disseminated to nearly 60 Maritime Lawyers in Antwerp, out of which 31 participated. The response rate was 52 %. The percentage of women participating was 32 %, or 10 females. Most questionnaires were conducted in writing, whereas a few occurred orally, so as to give some nuances.

Two female participants (20 %) advanced to partnership. The results thus reflect a selection bias, given that only 8 % of all Antwerp's female maritime lawyers advanced to partnership during their professional career. Next, only two female participants are above the age of 40. Of the remaining 7 women, 4 are below the age of 27 and 3 constitute trainees. One female participant had already completely quit practicing due to a burn-out, whereas two of the women below age 27 are about to quit practice within a year.

The percentage of participating men entails 68 %, or 21 male attorneys. Eight participants are above the age of 40, or nearly 40 %. Again, a selection bias was present, given that the response rate among the younger male attorneys was considerably higher. In reality, more male lawyers are above the age of 40 than suggested by the results.

4 Findings

4.1 General Observations

The results suggest that the majority (80 %) of the female maritime attorneys are below the age of 40, compared to 60 % of the males. However, the male percentage is believed to be even lower, given the selection bias towards young male participants. This suggests that women have only recently begun joining maritime firms in greater numbers. Some of the in-depth interviews with older lawyers confirmed the changing dynamic. Likewise, it suggests that female attrition rates are substantially higher than those of male counterparts. A half of the female participants below the age of 30 said that they would be withdrawing from a career as a maritime lawyer within a year. Some participants pointed out that female trainees often tend to quit after a few years, either switching to other branches of law, or embarking on an in-house legal career. This suggestion is plausible, given the high percentages of female law graduates and female trainees at the bar, gradually decreasing as these women progress in their careers. The high attrition rates among young, female, maritime lawyers is not easy to explain, as most of these women do not have family lives yet. Dutch research suggests that these withdrawing women display a lack of self-confidence, which is indispensable for the lawyer's profession (De Haas 2006). This paper argues that although future empirical research is required, one cannot only blame women.

A second observation concerns the large number of female respondents, i.e., 40 %, having relatives working as a maritime lawyer. Apparently, it lowers the threshold of embarking on a maritime legal career. The same may apply to men, though this was not examined.

4.2 Prevailing Beliefs on Reasons Accounting for and Perpetuating Low Female Participation

Regarding the rationale for low female participation in maritime law firms, 70 % of the participants put forward work-life imbalance as a main impediment. Twenty-two percent report the demanding nature of the lawyer's profession to be a main determinant. One respondent pointed out: "Maritime law can be more demanding than most other branches of the law". This undoubtedly refers to surveys on board vessels, as well as regularly having to arrest vessels beyond normal working hours. As one female associate pointed out: "The first time I assisted a survey on board a vessel (under the supervision of the Nautical Commission), I was wearing a dress instead of trousers, which wasn't particularly appropriate for climbing the vessel's rope ladders in front of (only) men." Further, it is striking that 40 % of female participants point to their intrinsic characteristics, such as being more caring and exhibiting softer communication patterns, as opposed to only 10 % of the men. The men tended to be very cautious in their replies, and to a lesser extent report that women's intrinsic characteristics contribute to low female participation. However, the traditional perception seems to prevail that women are less fit for the profession of a lawyer. Indeed, the main reason for female under-representation put forward, concerns the demanding nature of the profession, the deadlines, the stress and the irregular working hours. This assumes that women tend to cope less easily with work-life imbalances as well as demanding work environments. Either that, or they are less willing to cope with it.

Forty percent of the participants pointed to other rationale, the most common being that the shipping environment is a traditionally male sector. In that regard, low female participation in maritime law firms is seen as an extension or a reflection of the maritime industry as a whole. As one woman stated quite strikingly: "It's a man's world". Yet another widely known reason entails maritime law to be a niche sector. This accounts for a limited number of vacancies and graduates interested in the maritime sector. It is argued that the maritime world is quite unknown to most lawyers in Belgium, unless one retrieves a link through business encounters, relatives, sports and hobbies.

A negligible 10 % of the men persistently believe that a small pool of qualified candidates can be held accountable for low female ratios. This is striking, given the large number of female law graduates.

Men and women tend to differ on the extent to which they believe gender differences in leadership and partnership are mainly attributable to differences in choices, capabilities and commitment, that the firm has limited ability or responsibility to influence. Quite notably, women on average rate the above attributes to be 4 on a scale from 1 (disagree) to 10 (agree), whereas men, on average, assigned a 6. In other words women, to a larger extent, believe that firms can do more in order to ensure female participation. This paper argues that differences in perception such as these, may continue to perpetuate low female participation.

4.3 Nature of Clients

Although a trend towards more female clients was discerned, nearly 80 % of the participants represent a very large majority of male clients. This is seen as a reflection of the traditionally male shipping industry in which the participants operate. This paper argues that female participation has not been made an operating point for male clients in allocating work to Antwerp's maritime law firms. The rather homogenous male clients' profile thus contributes to diversity being less a prerequisite for profitability. One participant remarked: "It remains a man's world."

4.4 Overall Career Satisfaction and Professional Development Opportunities

When rating the opportunities given to advance within their firm, i.e., become partner, men on average allocated a 6.6 on a scale from 1 (low) to 10 (high) Female participants, on average, attributed a 6.3. Men on average, rate the level of responsibility at a 7.9; whereas women rate this level to be a 7.2. Men judge the opportunities given to develop and manage client relations to be a 6.8; whereas women assigned, on average, a 5.

It must be noted, however, that the female results are skewed due to two female partners assigning the maximum. Merely taking into account the average rates, draws a distorted picture. When one looks at the median rates, the discrepancy with the male results is more blatant. The median woman rates were her opportunities to advance at 5, her level of responsibility at 6, and her opportunities to develop and manage client relations, a deep 4.

Male participants assign themselves, on average a 4.5, when asked whether they consider themselves a "rain-maker". On average, females only assign themselves a 2.6. Despite some opportunities given to women to develop client relations, the evidence thus reveals that men continue bringing in the substantial amount of business. This is disappointing, as bringing in business is crucial for advancement in a private law firm. This paper argues that this trend is compounded by the male features of the maritime business as a whole.

Overall career satisfaction of both sexes seems to be positive. Female perceptions of professional development opportunities are rather positive, albeit to a lesser extent than men. Nevertheless, this is contradicted by the empirical evidence at hand. Indeed, female partnership remains disproportionately low, as well as the reality of women bringing in substantial business. Firstly, the results are affected by a selection bias, given the overrepresentation of female partners among the participants. Next, it is argued that the female perceptions are perhaps overly optimistic, given the discrepancy with reality. This is consistent with the overall gap between principles of equality and reality. The limitations, resulting from any other factors and dynamics which were not investigated within the scope of this research, are also noted.

4.5 Mentors, Role Models and Support Networks

Only one female participant reported never having received support from a mentor. Of the remaining female participants, 90 % enjoyed the support of a male mentor. More female mentors and role models are required to enhance female participation, as well as initiatives evaluating the mentoring activities. Furthermore, it is argued that perhaps another kind of mentoring is required, as male mentors referred to being involuntarily assigned as mentors. Indeed, Belgian law requires all trainees to fulfill a 3-year traineeship under the close supervision of an older, qualified attorney in the same firm, a so-called "patron" (De Haas 2006).

In general, support networks are largely lacking. A few female respondents mentioned such a network, for example, the Women International Shipping & Trading Association (WISTA). However, low participation of Antwerp's female maritime lawyers, the international focus, as well as the lack of a specific legal focus, impairs a substantive impact. It is argued that local initiatives are critical.

4.6 Perception of a Problem and Priority Attached

On average, male participants rate the importance of increasing diversity 4 on a scale of 1 (low) to 10 (high). Female participants on average, allocated a 6.8. The perception of a problem and the priority attached, remains lower among men, which is reflected in the firm's policies. This has to be improved, as the firm's policies are critical in molding female participation. In that regard, men on average, allocated a mere 3.6 out of 10 when asked to what extent the top of the firm is committed to increasing female participation.

4.7 Experienced Gender Bias and Discrimination

Although none of the female respondents have experienced overt discrimination, 50 % have witnessed inappropriate conduct of male maritime lawyers, from a gender perspective. Gender stereotyping in a verbal form is the most commonly reported conduct, with 30 % of participants having encountered it. Ten percent of female participants report having experienced either impolite conduct towards women, gender stereotyping in jokes, or verbal sexually inappropriate conduct. For instance, one participant explained that: "One of the partners commented, after an unsuccessful business encounter with a woman, that it was the last time he would take on a woman aboard his ship." Notably, 20 % have experienced physical sexually inappropriate conduct. Quoting one female participant: "Sadly I had to quit my job, as my boss wanted more than a strictly professional relationship." There is a clear divide however, in the types of inappropriate conduct, taking into account age categories. Comfortingly, only the older female participants report physically sexual conduct, whereas the younger age categories have only experienced gender stereotyping. This points to the issue becoming even more difficult to detect in the form of covert gender discrimination. For instance, one female associate stated: "From the moment I became a mother, I did not receive any more bonuses, although the partners are satisfied with my work."

Now we will turn to the gender biases affecting job appraisal that female participants experienced, as well as female professional conduct in a male environment. Women rate the extent to which they are being held to higher standards than male colleagues at 5.7 out of 10, on average. The necessity of conforming to traditional/male standards when working in a male environment, was rated on average, 6.3. Lastly, the importance of alikeness and humor for professional development in a male environment was rated 7.3. These results suggest that although women to a certain extent adhere to traditional norms and endeavor to fit in, there is some scope for individual female behavior styles.

4.8 Firm Policies

The results regarding firm policies about leave, child-care facilities, flexible working time and advancement of part-time workers, were somewhat surprising. Female participants rated the opportunities for flexible work hours very favourably; 8.3 on average. The male participants were somewhat more negative, giving on average, a 6.8. The same trend applies to the firm policies about leave, where women and men respectively rated on average 7.3 and 6.2. The firm's advancement of partners or associates who are not working on a full-time schedule, was rated on average, 6.2 by women and 4.2 by men.

It is striking that women tend to rate these opportunities more favorably than men, given that precisely the need of such opportunities is being held to constitute major impediments to female participation. The author argues that the small scale of Antwerp's maritime law firms enables a margin for flexible work hours. Smaller teams, as opposed to large corporate structures, can be more understanding and empathetic towards personal needs for flexible work hours.

This paper argues that male participants tend to rate these opportunities more negatively for themselves and, to a lesser extent, perceive the need to rely on child-care facilities. It is relatively less considered as an option by men, hence why they rate the scope for child-care facilities more negatively. As one male partner mentioned: "It would not make sense to become a partner not working on a full-time schedule."

Consequently, it is argued that this is an area where efforts to enhance female participation, such as broadening the scope for part-time work, could have trickle-down effects for male lawyers as well. Such efforts could enhance working conditions, benefiting men as well. Surely, men must suffer from work-life imbalances as well. However, currently only women seem to be more willing to take a professional step back in order to remediate these imbalances.

On a side-note, it is questioned whether female participants perceived the firm's policies about commitment to diversity, leave and advancement of associates working on a part-time schedule, slightly too optimistically. After all, the discrepancy between perceptions and reality is blatant. The percentage of female partners, as well as women working on a part-time schedule, remains negligible. Intervening factors, as well as the selection bias of female partners, could account for the discrepancy as well. As one female participant remarked: "When hiring new trainees, the partner made a comment that they would prefer a male trainee, as they would not be on maternity leave anytime soon."

Further, the results demonstrate the need of child-care policies. Both female and male participants rated these policies on average a 3. Several participants pointed out that such policies are non-existent within their firm. It is argued that the small scale of Antwerp's maritime law firms may be the main culprit. Although the small scale allows for flexible work hours, the scale simply is not large enough to make economical, the bearing of child-care policies, such as on-site care. Even when given opportunities to work flexible hours and advance when working on a part-time schedule, it must still be practically feasible.

4.9 Lack of Formal, Objective Standards of Appraisal, Promotion and Hiring

The processes of hiring, evaluations and promotions do not adhere to formal, set, objective or written standards. Female participants rate these standards to be even more subjective, giving a 3 on average, whereas men on average, allocated a 4. The small scale of Antwerp's maritime law firms impedes the feasibility of formal strategies. All scrutinized firms are small, the two largest firms consisting of only

9 maritime lawyers. This is regrettable, as formal, set and objective standards are critical in reducing the scope for unconscious gender stereotyping and increasing female participation (Rhode 2012). The small scale of Antwerp's maritime law firms therefore induces 'alikeness' behavior and in-group favoritism, unconsciously impeding higher female participation. One female participant mentioned in this regard: "The men in the office often get the opportunity to go to seminars abroad. I have never been given this opportunity." Arguably, this is one of the reasons why larger Antwerp law firms, practicing other branches of law, exhibit higher female participation ratios. This is arguably so due to objective standards of evaluation, hiring and promotion. As one participant rather poignantly remarked: "During my job interview, both attorneys, in a humorous way, stressed that they would prefer hiring men, as this would benefit the likelihood of winning the annual football game, against a competing Dutch maritime law firm."

The small scale of the firms compounds gender issues in other regards as well. Inter alia, for small firms it is not economically feasible to establish on-site child care facilities, to implement formal diversity strategies, or to establish gender task forces. Also, it is argued that small firms do not perceive diversity to be a prerequisite for profitability, not having the clients urging them to increase diversity either.

5 Conclusions

5.1 Overall Balance

The overall balance appears rather promising. Women are increasingly joining maritime law firms. The clients, rather homogenous male shipping companies, are slowly opening up to women as well. The participating men were very cautious and replied to the questionnaire in a rather gender-neutral manner. No overt discrimination was reported. Also, women judged their career opportunities rather positively, albeit less positively than the men. Opportunities for flexible work hours and leave were judged very well.

On the downside, men continue bringing in the substantial business. Men, to a lesser extent, perceive the need to increase female participation. The small scale of the firms impedes development and implementation of gender strategies. Correspondingly, standards of appraisal, hiring and promotions do not adhere to formal and objective processes. This leaves the door open for unconscious gender biases in these small, niche, male-dominated firms. The traditional perception seems to prevail that women are less fit for the demanding profession of a lawyer. Attrition rates among young, female lawyers are disproportionately high. A half of the female participants have experienced inappropriate conduct from a gender perspective, mainly gender stereotyping in comments.

5.2 *Subtle Patterns of Gender Bias*

The discrepancy between principles and practice is noteworthy. One could call into question the positive overall picture emerging from the questionnaires. First, it is argued that the selection bias towards female partners is the main culprit. A disproportionately high percentage of partners among the female participants inflated the results concerning professional development opportunities. Second, the discrepancy is consistent with previous research. Indeed, it is common for factors contributing to low female participation to be difficult to perceive.

Previous research describes modern patterns of gender bias to be highly subtle. For instance, male supervisors judged male attorneys on Wall Street more favorably than female attorneys, on ratings that mattered for promotion. However, narrative comments showed either no gender effects or greater favorability toward women (Biernat et al. 2011). Correspondingly, the male maritime lawyers were very cautious not to display any overt gender bias in responding to the questionnaires. Female professional development capabilities were rated with rather great favorability. However, subtle and unconscious gender biases may persist, i.e., resulting in discrepancies between the reported principles and reality.

5.3 *Strategies*

The paper now elaborates on strategies for Antwerp maritime law firms to adopt, in order to enable more substantive female participation and leadership.

Female maritime lawyers should actively seek relationships that surpass formal mentorship, to sponsorship. A local support network should be established (Weisberg 2004). Female lawyers who decided to step out of the lawyer labor force should continue being professionally active. Volunteering, occasional paying projects and re-enter programs, can all aid the transition back (Rhode 2012). This could be crucial in developing the much needed support and role models in order to ensure that maritime female lawyers reach a critical mass.

The development and implementation of both evaluating and rewarding systems regarding the 3-year "patron"-ship is critical. The same applies to developing and enforcing formal standards and processes of evaluation, hiring and promotions. Firms should develop strategies and policies on, inter alia, child care and advancement of lawyers not working on a full-time schedule. This would benefit male lawyers as well. As long as the men feel there is no scope for leave and part-time schedules, the bulk of the household burden will continue to fall on women's shoulders, practically impeding women's advancement. One could consider establishing nurseries at the court house or in its vicinity, as well as longer income guarantees after giving birth (Van der Schueren 2006). Next, the top of the firm should be severely committed to increasing diversity, i.e., by implementing diversity strategies. As the small scale of Antwerp's maritime law firms renders the feasibility and profitability of abovementioned formal policies unlikely, one should consider an overarching committee or task force, with representatives of each firm.

References

ABA Commission on Women in the Profession. (2006). Visible invisibility: Women of color in law firms 19. http://www.google.be/url?sa=t&rct=j&q=&esrc=s&frm=1&source=web&cd=1&ved=0CB4QFjAA&url=http%3A%2F%2Fwww.americanbar.org%2Fcontent%2Fdam%2Faba%2Fmarketing%2Fwomen%2Fvisible_invisibility_fortune500_executive_summary.authcheckdam.pdf&ei=Sp_sU_ayEojX7AbAoYDQCA&usg=AFQjCNFGetbgJWjrrAaPlRZq1OlW5SrUTQ&sig2=jWuTlvGZU54XiW8ltHySag&bvm=bv.72938740,d.bGE. Accessed 14 Aug 2014.

Bentsi-Enchill, J. (2006). Inclusion or illusion? Determining if a law firm is really committed to diversity. *Women Law Journal, 91*, 10.

Biernat, M., Tocci, M. J., & Williams, J. C. (2011). The language of performance evaluations gender-based shifts in content and consistency of judgment. *Social Psychological and Personality Science, 3*(2), 186–192.

Brett, J., & Stroh, L. K. (1997). Jumping ship: Who benefits from an external labor market strategy? *Journal of Applied Psychology, 82*(3), 331–341.

Brickman, J. P. (2008). Maritime education and training of women: Their impact on the program at the United States Merchant Marine Academy. Resource document. Dokuz Eylül Üniversitesi. http://web.deu.edu.tr/maritime/imla2008/Papers/32.pdf. Accessed 1 Apr 2014.

Catalyst. (1996). *Women in corporate leadership: Progress and prospects*. New York: Author.

Catalyst. (1998). *Advancing women in business – The catalyst guide: Best practices from the corporate leaders*. New York: Author.

Chanow, L. B., & Stiller Rikleen, L. (2012). Power in law: Lessons from the 2011 women's power summit on law and leadership. Resource document. Center for women in law. http://www.utexas.edu/law/wp/wp-content/uploads/centers/cwil/Summit_White_Paper-FINAL.pdf. Accessed 1 Apr 2014.

De Haas, M. (2006). Werkstress en uitval van jonge vrouwelijke advocaten. *Ad Rem Themanummer 2006, Vrouwen aan de balie*, 28–34.

Dinovitzer, R., Garth, B., Sander, R., Sterling, J., & Wilder, G. (2004). After the JD: First results of a national study of legal careers. Resource document. The National Association for Law Placement Foundation for Law Career Research and Education, the American Bar Foundation. http://www.americanbarfoundation.org/uploads/cms/documents/ajd.pdf. Accessed 1 Apr 2014.

Dobbin, F., & Kalev, A. (2007). The architecture of inclusion: Evidence from corporate diversity programs. *Harvard Journal of Law & Gender, 30*(2), 283–284.

Dragomir, C., & Surugiu, F. (2012). Seafarer women – Perception of the seafaring career. In *Proceedings of the 2nd International Conference on Economics, Political and Law Science (EPLS' 13): Advances in Fiscal, Political and Law Science, Brasov, Romania, 1–3 June, 2013*, 15–18.

Dragomir, C., Batrinca, G., & Surugiu, F. (2012). Motivation of joining women in the maritime sector. *Maritime Transport & Navigation Journal, 3*, 3.

Horck, J. (2008). Cultural and gender diversities affecting the ship/port interface: Maritime education and training efforts to bridge diversity gaps. In: *1st International Ship-Port-Interface Conference: The Human Element, ISPIC 2008, Bremen, Germany, 19–21 May 2008*, 1–15.

Ibarra, H., Carter, N. M., & Silva, C. (2010). Why men still get more promotions than women. *Harvard Business Review, 88*(9), 80–85.

ILO. (2007). *ABC of women workers' rights and gender equality*. Geneva: International Labour Office.

ITF. (2012). Inside the issues: Women seafarers. http://www.itfseafarers.org/ITI-women-seafarers.cfm. Accessed 1 Apr 2014.

Kay, F. M., & Wallace, J. E. (2009). Mentors as social capital: Gender, mentors and career rewards in law practice. *Sociological Inquiry, 79*(4), 418–452.

McWilliams, K. T. (2007). Role models I have known – And why they are vital. *Women Law Journal, 92*, 12–13.

Meyers, L. M. (2004). Firms must address perceptions of gender bias. *Women Lawyers Journal, 89*, 20.

Narbutas, J. (2004). Women in the maritime industry. *SPC Women in Fisheries International Bulletin, 14*, 23–25.

Onwuegbuchunam, D. E. (2011). Gender discrimination in the Nigeria's maritime industry. *International Journal of Development Digest, 2*, 15–26.

Popescu, C., & Varsami, A. E. (2010). The place of women in a men's world from a maritime university perspective. In *Proceedings of the 7th WSEAS International Conference on Engineering Education: Latest Trends on Engineering Education, World Scientific and Engineering Academy and Society (WSEAS), Corfu Island, Greece, 22–24 July, 2010*, 182–186.

Rhode, D. L. (2012). Women and the path to leadership. *Michigan State Law Review, 12*(4), 1439–1468.

Scharf, S. A., & Flom, B. M. (2010). Report of the 2010 NAWL Survey on the retention and promotion of women in law firms. *Women Law Journal, 95*, 10–18.

Scharf, S. A., Masters, L. S., Berner, N. G., & Robertson, C. J. (2004). Through the glass ceiling: Best practices for women lawyers and their firms. *Women Law Journal, 89*, 7.

Scharf, S. A., Oblander, C. T., Trost, M., & Tipton, E. (2009). Report of the 2009 NAWL Survey on the status of women in law firms. *Women Law Journal, 94*, 8–15.

Scharf, S. A., & Sanders Netties, Z. (2004). Benchmarking for success: Introducing NAWL assessment questionnaires: Tools for retention and advancement of women in private practice. *Women Law Journal, 89*, 14.

Schipani, C. A., Dworkin, T. M., Kwolek-Folland, A., & Maure, V. G. (2009). Pathways for women to obtain positions of organizational leadership: The significance of mentoring and networking. *Duke Journal of Gender Law & Policy, 89*(16), 98–103.

The Bureau of Labor Statistics of the U.S. Department of Labor. (2004). American Time Use Survey—2004 results announced by BLS. http://www.bls.gov/news.release/archives/atus_09202005.pdf. Accessed 14 Aug 2014.

Van der Schueren, A. (2006). Vrouwen aan de balie doorgelicht. *Ad Rem Themanummer 2006, Vrouwen aan de balie*, 7–8.

Weisberg, A. (2004). Advancing women in law firms: A blueprint for success. *Women Law Journal, 89*, 10.

Wyckaert, M. (2006). De togata kijkt in de spiegel: Vrouwelijk gekleurde bedenkingen over het glazen plafond in het advocatenberoep. *Ad Rem Themanummer 2006, Vrouwen aan de balie*, 15–20.

Women Are Better Leaders Than They Think: Gender Differences in the Self-Assessment of Leadership Skills in the Maritime Industry

Olga Delgado Ortega, Kjell Ivar Øvergård, and Veronica Henden

Abstract It is highly desirable that women and men have the same access to maritime training and work aboard ships. Gender stereotypes affect judgment of competence in women and men differently. This study investigated female and male maritime officers' ability to evaluate their leadership skills. A 360° leader evaluation survey obtained both self-assessments and co-worker assessments of maritime officers' leadership (both positive and negative) skills, using the MLQ-5X leadership questionnaire. Results from 17 female and 30 male maritime officers shows an interaction between gender and errors in self-evaluation (tendency to over-estimate or under-estimate) of leadership skills. Female leaders tended to underrate their actual leadership skills, while male maritime officers tended to overrate their leadership skills relative to the evaluations of their co-workers. For negative leadership skills, female maritime officers over-estimated the level of negative leadership skill they had, while male leaders under-estimated their level of negative leadership skills. For positive leadership skills, the opposite relation was present (women under-estimated and men over-estimated the level of positive leadership skills). These results point—for the first time—to a gender difference in the evaluation of leadership skills in the maritime domain. An overtly critical attitude towards one's own leadership skills might be a factor in explaining why many women choose to abstain from high-status positions in the maritime industry. Maritime leadership training can be made more inclusive by focusing on gender differences in the (self)-evaluation of leadership skills.

Keywords Gender differences • Leadership • Maritime officers • Self-assessment • Stereotypes • Women seafarers

---

O.D. Ortega (✉)
Departament de Ciències i Enginyeria Nàutiques, Universitat Politècnica de Catalunya, Facultat de Nàutica de Barcelona, Barcelona, Spain
e-mail: odelgado@cen.upc.edu

K.I. Øvergård • V. Henden
Department of Maritime Technology and Innovation, Buskerud and Vestfold University College, Borre, Norway

© Springer-Verlag Berlin Heidelberg 2015

M. Kitada et al. (eds.), *Maritime Women: Global Leadership*, WMU Studies in Maritime Affairs 3, DOI 10.1007/978-3-662-45385-8_15

1 Introduction

The vast majority of leaders in the maritime industry are men. However, the proportion of women seafarers is increasing. In the modernized work environment of today, it is preferable if women and men are given the same opportunities to access training and work positions in the maritime sector. There is general agreement in recognizing that women face more barriers and difficulties than men, to occupy positions associated with responsibility. The challenge of attracting women leaders to the maritime industry has already been addressed by resolution number 14 "*Promotion of the participation of women in the maritime industry*" where participants at the Diplomatic conference on the STCW convention in Manila expressed their support to facilitate more women to participate in the maritime sector by developing long- and medium-term plans to integrate them in the field (IMO 2011). To allow for an increased participation of women in the maritime professions, we need to identify possible barriers that can hinder women in applying for a maritime education and profession. Our goal is to identify whether there exist gender differences in the self-evaluation (sic. self-esteem) of leadership skills. Self-evaluation, or self-esteem, is important for any person that would like to hold a job that requires skill and competence. Persons with little belief in themselves, would, according to common sense, be less likely to apply for a job for which they felt they were not competent. Hence, understanding how female officers rate themselves as leaders relative to their male peers, would be of interest, to understand the possible psychosocial barriers that keep women from seeking a profession in the maritime industry.

1.1 Gender Differences in Leadership

Early studies indicated that there might be differences in leadership between women and men (Bowman et al. 1965). Some authors claim that women lack the necessary managerial skills and traits (Henning and Jardin 1977 referenced in Eagly and Johannesen-Schmidt 2001). Furthering the assumption that women are less competent leaders, Mansfield (2006) writes that women are inherently less competitive, do not like taking unnecessary risks and are more likely to let their emotions affect them in their decisions. Henceforth, according to Mansfield's premises, women are less suited to become leaders in a competitive world.

On the other hand, some argue that women's leadership is actually more effective in contemporary society (Helgesen 1990). Women tend to be *more* participative and democratic and *less* autocratic and directive than men (Eagly and Johnson 1990). Further, women score higher than men in the Multidimensional Leadership Questionnaire (MLQ) leadership subscales 'Idealized Influence' (charisma), 'Inspirational Motivation', 'Individual Consideration', and 'Contingent Reward', while men score higher on 'Management-by-Exception' and 'Laissez-

Faire' (Eagly and Johannesen-Schmidt 2001). However, other studies have not shown such clear differences (Komives 1991; Maher 1997; Kent et al. 2010). And, furthering the disagreement, several researchers argue that there is little or no association between gender and leadership styles (van Engen 2001; Kent et al. 2010).

The ambiguity in results may be due to the importance of the social context in which leadership is exercised (Rosener 1990; Druskat 1994). In "traditional" bureaucratic, rigid and historically male-dominated organizations, such as the maritime sector, gender differences are masked because women must adapt to the norms and dominant male expectations in this type of organizations. By contrast, in "non-traditional" organizations, women would feel more willing to display their true leadership style—given that there exist such differences. These discussions indicate that there is no general agreement between researchers on whether women and men adopt different leadership styles (Eagly and Johannesen-Schmidt 2001).

1.2 Leadership Effectiveness and Gender

When it comes to the effectiveness of women or men leaders, there are not clear differences between women and men. However both female and male leaders are slightly more effective in leadership roles that were congruent with their gender (Eagly et al. 1995). The differences between female and male leaders—to the extent that there are any—is nicely summed up by "women are no less effective at leadership, committed to their jobs, or motivated for leadership roles than men. However, women are less likely to self-promote and negotiate than men" (Northouse 2013). In essence, women are just as effective as men, but they will seek to improve their own position to a somewhat lesser extent than men.

1.3 Gender Differences in Evaluation of Competence and Leadership Skills

Today, women and men are becoming more equal, respectively, when it comes to choice of education and occupation. Nonetheless, there still exists a tendency to evaluate women and men's competence differently. Many researchers believe that discrimination and biased evaluation is the main reason why women are looked at as less competent and less likely to be prominent leaders (Beyer 1990; Eagly and Karau 2002; Eagly et al. 1992; Heilman et al. 2004). Also, stereotypes are believed to be a major cause of why women and men are judged unequally. Stereotypes have also been shown to influence self-esteem and also how the different genders are expected to behave in female- and male-type jobs (Minter et al. 2005).

A meta-analysis, based upon 136 studies investigating gender differences in leadership, found that the stereotypical perception of women as more interpersonally-oriented leaders and men as more task-oriented ones, was observed in laboratory settings, but not in organizational contexts (Eagly and Johnson 1990). Studies evaluating the assessment or evaluation of leadership behaviours have found that women who led in what was perceived to be a masculine manner, tended to be devaluated relative to male leaders (Eagly et al. 1992). If a woman is performing equally well as a man would do in a masculine-typed job, the woman can still be given a biased judgment, based upon the cultural stereotypes that assume women are not supposed to act and behave the same way as men. This kind of behaviour from a woman can elicit negative consequences and evaluations, such as lack of social approval and the exclusion of women from the same opportunities as men (Heilman et al. 2004).

Interestingly, women do not only face discrimination from men, but also from women. For example, women who are assessed by other women in a hiring process, are less likely to be hired. This effect is not present when the assessors are men (Biernat and Fuegen 2001). It is easy to think that since women know about the existing cultural prejudice, they would be able to correct for the bias. However, women tend to set higher standards for other women. Also, a further bias is that both women and men were more willing to hire women if the decision were associated with low risk and small consequences, but quickly changed towards favouring men if the consequences were more serious (Biernat and Fuegen 2001).

1.4 Self-Evaluation of Leadership Skills

The perception of tasks as feminine or masculine seems to affect self-evaluation of task performance. Self-consistency theory (Beyer 1990) anticipates that men, as a result of high esteem in masculine tasks, will overestimate their actual competence. However, when it comes to feminine tasks, men are more accurate in their self-evaluation (Beyer 1990). For women, the situation is somewhat different. Women tend to underestimate themselves in masculine tasks and have more accurate expectations about the feminine and neutral tasks (Beyer 1990; Eagly et al. 1992). Hence, the accuracy of the self-evaluation of women and men will depend on whether the task is seen as representing a feminine or a masculine trait.

For example, imagine a child crying after a fall during play in the kindergarten. An adult who works at the kindergarten picks up the child to comfort it. Comforting children is a stereotypically feminine task, and the evaluation of the task would depend on whether there was a man or a woman who performed the task. A man doing this task would be evaluated as more empathic than a woman doing the same task. This is an example of *Shifting standards*, and it occurs when individuals have different beliefs about opposing groups (Biernat and Manis 1994). The consequence is that different groups can be evaluated using different standards. Research shows that women and men are evaluated using different standards in many occupations (Biernat and Vescio 2002; Wennerås and Wold 1997). Thus, feedback involving "good work" to a woman may not be "good work" for a man (Biernat and Fuegen 2001).

Women tend to be held to a lower standard than men, however, at the same time, women are held to a higher confirmatory standard (Biernat and Fuegen 2001). Higher confirmatory standard means that women must perform better than men to achieve the same level of evaluation, hence, to be evaluated with the same level of competence, women must work harder (Biernat et al. 2010).

1.5 Relevance to Maritime Industry

There are reasons to believe that there are different standards for evaluating the competence of women and men in the maritime sector. This is particularly so because working as a seafarer has—and still is—been portrayed as a masculine work arena. Existing gender beliefs will influence both male's and females' expectations for themselves, and both groups will compare their own performance relative to the opposite gender (Correll 2004). Females and males will also apply different standards to evaluate their own task competence, because of existing gender status beliefs (Correll 2001). Consequently, since males are viewed as the more competent gender in masculine-typed work tasks, males are more likely to seek greater challenges in education and work. Meanwhile, women may also seek greater challenges, just to be evaluated to the low standard of her gender, and have to work more for the same achievement as her male peer.

IMO has indicated an interest in increasing the participation of women in the maritime sector, "... to endeavor considering ways to identify and overcome, at an international level, the existing constraints ... so that women can participate fully and without hindrance in seafaring activities..." (IMO 2011). Our contribution to this aim is to investigate how female and male leaders evaluate their own level of leadership skills. The general aim is to identify to what extent female officers under- or over-estimate their leadership skills relative to male officers.

1.6 Hypotheses

This paper investigates the following hypotheses:

Hypothesis 1: Women will underestimate their overall leadership skills level while men will overestimate their overall leadership skills level, relative to the ratings given by their co-workers.

Since maritime leadership is associated with a masculine trait, we hypothesise, following self-consistency theory (Beyer 1990), that women will be more critical towards their own skills. Further, we expect that this effect will be dependent upon whether the leadership skills in question are positive (i.e., supportive, rewarding, and so on) or negative (i.e. punitive, after-the-fact, or of a non-leadership type). These effects are further operationalised in hypothesis 2a and 2b below:

Hypothesis 2a: Female officers will show a tendency to overestimate their own level of negative leadership skills while male officers will underestimate their own level of negative skills, relative to the ratings given by their co-workers.

Hypothesis 2b: Female officers will tend to underestimate their own level of positive leadership skills while male officers will tend to overestimate their own level of positive leadership skills, relative to the ratings given by their co-workers.

2 Method

2.1 Research Design

Parts of the data set (30 male and 3 female maritime officers) are based on a recent doctoral research project (Delgado 2012). Additional data from 14 female officers was sampled for this study, using a similar data collection method as in the initial doctoral project.

Data collection took the form of a 360-degree evaluation of leadership using the MLQ-5X questionnaire, which will be explained in the Sect. 2.4. A total of 47 leaders assessed their own leadership scores and they where also rated on the same questionnaire by their co-workers (between 2 and 6 co-workers). Because effective leadership is based on the effect the leader has on their co-workers, we chose to use the colleagues' evaluation as an indicator of the leader's actual skills.

2.2 Participants

A total of 47 maritime officers, consisting of 17 women and 30 men, participated. The female officers ranged from 28 to 48 years of age (Mean = 35.5 years, SD = 3.9) while the male officers ranged from 29 to 58 years of age (Mean = 40.6, SD = 7.3). The officers were mainly of Spanish (n = 26) or Portuguese (n = 16) nationality. The remainder of the participants were Norwegian, Argentinean and Dutch.

2.3 Sampling Strategy

Participants were recruited using social nets and professional contacts. Participants were asked by e-mail or by phone calls, to answer voluntarily the Multifactor Leadership Questionnaire on-line.

2.4 The Multifactor Leadership Questionnaire

The Multifactor Leadership Questionnaire (MLQ—also known as MLQ-5X for short) measures a broad range of leadership types (Bass and Riggio 2006). MLQ has been extensively researched and validated, it has been found to be valid across cultures and types of organizations, and is used in much leadership research.

The MLQ has evolved over the last 25 years, with numerous investigations of leaders in public and private organizations, from CEOs of major corporations, to non-supervisory project leaders. The MLQ 5X is a 45-item, 360-degree multi-rater leadership measure. Respondents rate the regularity of an occurrence on a likert-scale (0 = never, 4 = always). MLQ categorises leaders as having either transformational, transactional or laissez-faire leadership styles. While transactional leadership, in the best case, makes followers reach the expected, transformational leadership is to work in a way that inspires followers to reach beyond the expected (Bass and Riggio 2006). Transformational leadership is also known to be associated with wellbeing and the increased positive mental health of the follower (Arnold et al. 2007). It may also help to satisfy the needs of Maslow's hierarchy of needs (Burns 1978). The transactional leader leads by giving something that the follower wants in exchange for the desired work task (Bass 1996).

As already discussed, this study sought to distinguish "positive" from "negative" leaders. Thus, we chose certain positive and negative facets from MLQ to create aggregated measures of positive and negative leadership, disregarding whether they belonged to different styles or not.

2.5 Positive Leadership Skills

The following six characteristics describe positive leadership skills (i.e., where showing more of these skills is associated with being a better leader) (Bass 1997):

Idealized Attributes (IA). The leader demonstrates integrity through her/his attributes and virtues, gaining the respect and trust of her/his team.

Idealized Behaviour (IB). The degree to which the leader illustrates a good example by her/his own behaviour.

Individualised Consideration (IC). The leader treats the employees as individuals, recognising that they have their own abilities, needs and aspirations. Using the followers' own goals, the leader tries to create growth by choosing the projects best suited, as well as mentoring/coaching along the way.

Intellectual Stimulation (IS). Old assumptions, traditions and beliefs are questioned in order to stimulate new perspectives and procedures. Open-mindedness and reasoning is encouraged of follower's before decision-making takes place. The leader will also reinforces the followers' potential for innovation and creative thinking, by reframing problems and questioning assumptions. In this process, it is important that no answers are seen as stupid or that the mistakes of the individual follower are not made fun of.

Inspirational Motivation (IM). The leader presents an optimistic, attractive and attainable vision for the future that helps the followers to raise the anticipation of themselves. By the best means, the vision can ultimately be envisioned for the followers themselves and in that manner, a healthy attitude emerges.

Contingent reward (CR). The leader ensures that work objectives are defined and clarified and contingently rewards behaviours that are in accordance with fulfilling these goals.

2.6 Negative Leadership Skills

The subscales we considered as negative leadership skills, were the three characteristics presented below (Bass 1997):

Management by Exception, Active (MbEA) involves the leader monitoring the work situation, looking for potential problems, and thereby is able to anticipate oncoming mistakes and can take corrective actions. The leader's focus is on errors and avoiding these, rather than improving existing processes.

Management by Exception, Passive (MbEP) is a negative leadership characteristic where the leader does not intervene in organisational processes before problems become apparent and serious.

Laissez-Faire (LF) is a type of non-leadership, where the leader avoids responsibilities and does not make decisions. The leader is basically passive avoidant.

2.7 Calculation of Total Leadership Score

Total Leadership Scores (TLS) were calculated by reversing the scale of the negative scores and then summing up all leadership scores (both positive and negative). The Total Leadership Score (TLS) was calculated according to the following formula:

$$TLS = (IA + IB + IC + IS + IM + CR) + (4\text{-}MbEA) + (4\text{-}MbEP) + (4\text{-}LF)$$

Based on the formula above, the total leadership score is an un-weighted average of the positive leadership skills (IA, IB, IC, IS, IM and CR) and the reversed negative leadership skills (MbEA, MbEp and LF). This ensures that high scores on positive leadership skills and low scores on negative skills, contribute positively to the overall leadership score.

3 Results

Categorisation of effect sizes in this paper follows Cohen's classification of effect sizes for mean differences between groups (Cohen 1988). The categories are *small* ($d < 0.30$), *medium* ($0.30 < d < 0.80$) and *large* ($0.80 < d$). Due to the fact that we have *a priori* direction-specific hypotheses, we have used planned comparisons involving one-sided null-hypothesis tests (see e.g., Ryan 1959 for a discussion).

3.1 Overall Leadership Score

Female officers ($\overline{x} = 2.818, \sigma = 0.363$) tended overall to be rated slightly higher by their co-workers than their male counterparts ($\overline{x} = 2.61, \sigma = 0.506$). This effect was of a medium size (($t_{(45)} = -1.493, \overline{x}_{\text{diff}} = -0.209$, 95 % CI of $\overline{x}_{\text{diff}}[-0.438, 0.021]$, $d = 0.474$, one-tailed $p = 0.072$) but the effect was not statistically significant (i.e., the type I error level was higher than the commonly accepted 0.05 level).

When it came to the officers' self-evaluation relative to their co-worker's evaluation (calculated as Self-rating—Co-worker's rating), female officers ($\overline{x} = -1.33$, $\sigma = 2.55$) tended to underestimate their own overall leadership skills compared to their male counterparts ($\overline{x} = 0.371, \sigma = 2.96$). The difference between the women and men officers was of medium size in the predicted directions ($\overline{x}_{\text{diff}} = -1.705$, 95 %CI of $\overline{x}_{\text{diff}}[-3.11, -0.298]$, $t_{(45)} = 1.993$, $d = 0.595$, one-tailed $p = 0.026$). Female officers scored themselves, on average, lower than their co-workers, while male officers marginally scored themselves higher than the rating by their co-workers. These findings are in accordance with predictions of hypothesis 1.

3.2 Negative Leadership Skills

The co-workers rated female ($\overline{x} = 3.75, \sigma = 1.03$) or male ($\overline{x} = 3.89, \sigma = 1.67$) officers with a statistically non-differentiable level of negative leadership skills. The effect size was small, to the extent of being negligible ($t_{(45)} = 0.30$, $\overline{x}_{\text{diff}} = 0.134$, 95 % CI of $\overline{x}_{\text{diff}}[-0.602, 0.870]$, $d = 0.097$, one-tailed $p = 0.383$). Thus, on the whole, female and male officers were on average rated by their co-workers to have the same level of negative leadership skills.

However, when it came to the officers' self-evaluation relative to their co-worker's evaluation (calculated as Self-rating—Co-worker's rating), female officers ($\overline{x} = 0.808, \sigma = 1.195$) tended to greatly overestimate their own level of negative leadership skills, compared to their male counterparts ($\overline{x} = -0.119$, $\sigma = 0.930$). The difference between female and male officers was of medium size in the predicted directions ($\overline{x}_{\text{diff}} = -0.926$, 95 %CI of $\overline{x}_{\text{diff}}[-1.44, -0.41]$, $t_{(45)} = -2.957, d = 0.595$, one-tailed $p < 0.003$). Female officers scored themselves, on average, higher on negative leadership skills than their co-workers, while male officers marginally scored themselves lower than the rating by their co-workers. These findings are in accordance with predictions of hypothesis 2a.

3.3 Positive Leadership Skills

There was a statistically significant difference on positive leadership skills between female ($\bar{x} = 2.853$, $\sigma = 0.475$) and male ($\bar{x} = 2.562$, $\sigma = 0.504$) officers. The effect size was ($t_{(45)} = -1.937$, $\bar{x}_{\text{diff}} = -0.29$, 95 % CI of $\bar{x}_{\text{diff}}[-0.537, -0.044]$, $d = 0.593$, one-sided $p < 0.03$). Female officers were, on average, rated higher by their co-workers on positive leadership skills than the male officers.

When it came to the officers' self-evaluation relative to their co-worker's evaluation (calculated as Self-rating—Co-worker's rating), female officers ($\bar{x} = -0.527$, $\sigma = 2.253$) tended to underestimate their own level of positive leadership skills compared to their male counterparts ($\bar{x} = 0.252$, $\sigma = 2.36$). The difference between female and male officers was small but in the predicted direction ($t_{(45)} = 1.104$, $\bar{x}_{\text{diff}} = 0.779$, one-sided 95 % CI of $\bar{x}_{\text{diff}}[-0.382, 1.940]$, $d = 0.33$, one-sided $p = 0.138$). These findings are in the same direction as the predictions of hypothesis 2b, but the observed effect is too small for us to reject the null hypothesis.

3.4 Interaction Effect of Gender and Valence of Leadership Skill

After observing that the differences between the leader's self-rating and the co-workers rating is dependent upon gender and the valence (the negative or positive value attributed to a leadership skill) of the leadership skills in question, we evaluated the possibility of an interaction effect (as would be expected based upon hypothesis 1 to 2a and 2b). A repeated measures ANOVA, with gender as a within-group factor, was calculated. The results showed that even in our small sample, there are indications of an interaction effect ($F_{(1,\ 45)} = 3.973$, $p = 0.052$, $\eta_p^2 = 0.081$). The interaction effect is shown in Fig. 1.

As can be seen in Fig. 1, the crossing of the lines indicates an interaction effect between gender and valence of leadership skills that is also supported by the statistical results. Note that the means of female officers are further away from the horizontal line and in the opposite direction of the means of the male officers.

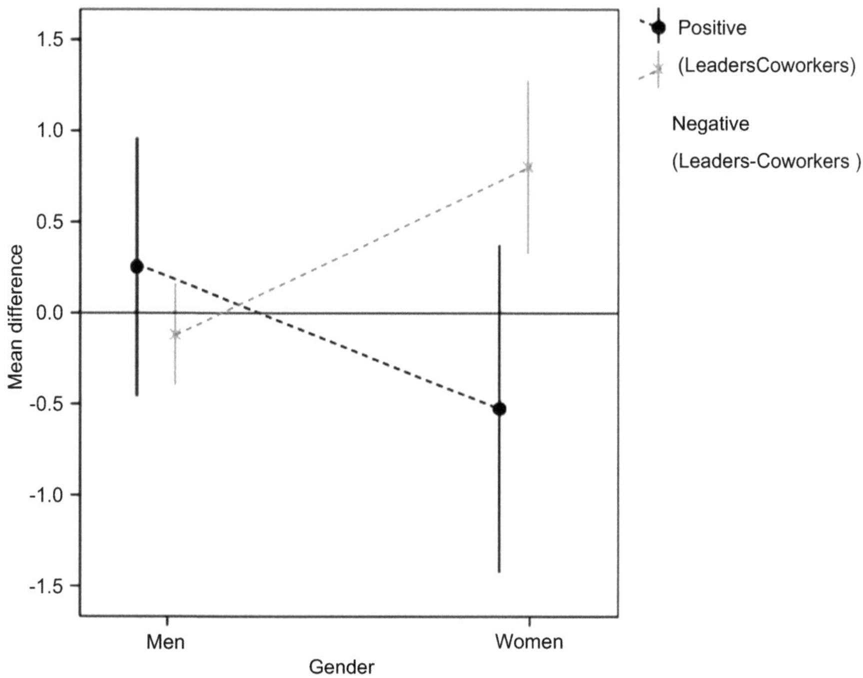

Fig. 1 Effect of gender and valence on self-evaluation of leadership skills. Means for female and male officers on positive leadership skills (*circle*) and negative leadership skills (*cross*). *Error bars* are ±1.645 standard errors (90 % CI) of the mean. The *dashed lines* indicate the change between two conditions. The whole *horizontal line* at 0 shows the position where there would be no difference between the co-workers and the leader's evaluation of leadership skills

4 Discussion

The goal of this study was to examine how maritime officers evaluate and are evaluated by co-workers, relative to positive- and negative-leadership skills. We predicted that since working as a maritime officer is culturally and historically characterized as a masculine-typed job, women would underestimate their positive leadership skills, while over-estimating their negative leadership skills compared to their male colleagues. Results from 17 female and 30 male maritime officers show an interaction between gender and errors in self-evaluation (tendency to over-estimate or under-estimate) of leadership skills. Female leaders tended to underrate their actual leadership skills, while male maritime officers tended to overrate their leadership skills relative to the evaluations of their co-workers;—this is in accordance with our hypothesis 1. For negative leadership skills, female maritime officers over-estimated the level of negative leadership skill they had, while male leaders under-estimated their level of negative leadership skills, in accordance with expectations in hypothesis 2a. For positive leadership skills, the opposite relation was present (women under-estimated and men over-estimated the level of positive leadership skills) and this was also in accordance with expectations in hypothesis 2b.

So, what can be the nature behind our results? The maritime profession is historically and culturally associated with masculine norms and behaviour, and the tendency for female officers to underestimate their leadership skills, as seen in our study, is in accordance with research showing that women tend to under-estimate themselves in masculine tasks (Beyer 1990; Eagly et al. 1992). The biased self-assessment can thereby originate from females and males, using different standards to evaluate their own competence (Correll 2001).

However, our findings, that women were rated marginally higher than men on overall leadership skills, and got significantly better scores on positive leadership skills than men by their co-workers (no difference on negative leadership scores), are in opposition to the studies which have found that men tend to be favoured over women as leaders, especially in occupations characterized by masculine traits (Beyer 1990; Eagly et al. 1992), and that individuals tend to assess women leaders more negatively than the comparable male leaders (Eagly et al. 1992). Also, other research has found that women who do just as well as men in a masculine-typed job, elicit more negative evaluations (Heilman et al. 2004). The observed discrepancy in our study may be caused by an authentic difference between the female and male participants in our study—it might be that the women that have chosen a maritime career at sea are extraordinarily well-suited for this type of job—meaning that the selection of female officers may be even stricter than for men, due to a tendency for women to have a higher confirmatory bias for proving competence (Biernat and Fuegen 2001). Still, the observed differences between female and male officers where at best small, except for positive leadership skills that had a moderate effect size. So, even if this is a possible factor in explaining the difference, drawing conclusions on the causes behind the observed effect, based on our initial study, is premature. Still, the overall effect observed in our study, that women tend to underestimate their own leadership skills relative to the assessments made by their co-workers, is in accordance with other research. We should focus on how this finding could impact on the inclusion of female officers in maritime professions.

For an individual who wants to pursue a career path in the maritime domain, they would want to feel that he/she is competent enough to perform the required tasks. However, individuals are affected differently by gender stereotypes when assessing their own behaviour (Minter et al. 2005). As previously mentioned, positive feedback should increase the level of self-assessment (Correll 2004). Research performed by Correll (2001) suggests that when women are assessing their own performance, they depend more on feedback given on their competence than their male colleagues, and will continue to set low standards for themselves if they do not receive confirmations on their competence. However, Biernat and Vescio (2002) state that because women and men are assessed to different standards, women are more likely to receive positive nonverbal feedback if they perform well, but even if the performance was good, women are less likely to get career-enhancing opportunities, such as men. If women do not receive the positive feedback they need to feel confident in their performance, they will continue to feel less adequate. This lack of self-esteem will have a negative effect on their self-evaluation, thus leading to an underestimation of their positive leadership skills and overestimation of their negative leadership skills. Thus, allowing for improved feedback during leadership training, as well as a benchmarking of leadership behaviour, could be a factor in improving female officers' self-assessment and thereby their willingness to pursue a maritime career.

4.1 Limitations of This Study

The present study is limited by the fact that we cannot clearly identify causes of the observed effects, as gender stereotypes and shifting standards can affect the leaders as well as the co-workers, or both. We acknowledge this limitation, as only experimental research allows for generalized causal inference (Shadish et al. 2002). We would claim that it is necessary to identify the extent of a phenomenon before one proceeds to an investigation of the causes of the phenomenon. To that extent, we have found results that are in accordance with other research as well as finding some results that are in need of further research to be fully understood. Future studies that seek to identify the causes of differences in evaluation and self-evaluation of competence ought, to the greatest extent possible, to use an experimental design, allowing for causal inferences.

Another limitation resulting from the limited number of women seafarers in the maritime industry, is the limited number of participants. As inferences made from statistics are based upon assumptions that the samples are representative for the respective populations (of female and male officers), we can say that our inferences and conclusions are probably more correct for female officers, as we sampled a much larger proportion of female officers than we did for male officers. Since our research is focused on findings regarding women, we would argue that the reduced number of participants in our study would not reduce the validity of our conclusions regarding female officer's self-assessment of leadership. Future research could be improved by using a stratified sampling strategy (Henry 1990), where the proportion of female vs. male officers would be reflected in the sizes of the samples.

This study also used a convenience sampling method. Participants were asked by the first author (Olga Delgado Ortega) to participate in the study. We acknowledge that this non-random sampling method might create bias in our results, and we would like to see this limitation amended by using random stratified sampling, where female and male maritime officers are randomly drawn (e.g., from lists of employees at maritime organisations).

Also, the fact that participants who might refuse to participate could introduce a bias, since participants in the study can be expected to be more positively oriented to our research than those that refused. Since we do not have demographic data from those that refused to participate, we cannot test for this possibility. Future research could solve this by using the randomised stratified sampling (Henry 1990) mentioned above, and by using necessary statistical evaluation to identify possible differences between those that accept, and those that refuse to participate, in future studies.

The respondents' ability and fluency in English could also have affected the reliability of our study. Most of the respondents' mother tongue was not English. However, English is a working language in the maritime industry and the respondents should therefore be able to respond adequately to a questionnaire in English. Furthermore, it is not expected that the reliability of the difference between female and male seafarers would be affected by a potential lack of English proficiency, as each group would be expected to have an equal proficiency.

4.2 Future Research

Future research should elucidate why women are affected, and to which degree they are influenced, by gender stereotypes. It would, for example, be interesting to compare results from the male-typed maritime leadership with results from female-typed professions, such as nursing jobs. This would allow us to further understand the impact of whether a task is seen as male- or female-typed, and how it would affect the evaluation of competence (Minter et al. 2005).

Another area, which would be interesting to test, is whether female and male officers are evaluated differently when they perform the same leadership tasks/ behaviours. Recent experimental research has indicated that such differences in evaluation of leadership skills exists in the maritime industry (Loiko 2014) but more research is needed to identify the characteristics that cause differences in the evaluation of women's and men's leadership skills.

The overall aim of leadership research in the maritime domain, should be to identify effective measures to improve the participation of women in maritime education and the profession (IMO 2011). Of interest, would be to identify whether improving feedback during leadership training (Correll 2001) would improve female officer's confidence in their leadership skills. Additionally, following Correll (2001), it would be interesting to see if the use of benchmarking of leadership behaviour between women and men could reduce the observed error in female officers' self-assessment of leadership skills. Identifying and implementing these measures might increase women's willingness to pursue a maritime career.

5 Conclusion

This study has documented that female maritime officers tend to underestimate their own leadership skills. The opposite effect is observed for male maritime officers. The main contribution of this study is to identify and describe the extent to which women underestimate their own leadership skills. Theory and previous research give reason to believe that gender stereotypes and shifting standards for evaluating skills and competence, is a factor in explaining the observed effect. However, we cannot at the present say whether this is due to stereotypes affecting the leaders' self-assessment, or the co-workers' assessments, or both.

References

Arnold, A. K., Turner, N., Barling, J., Kelloway, E. K., & McKee, M. C. (2007). Transformational leadership and psychological well-being: The mediating role of meaningful work. *Journal of Occupational Health Psychology, 12*(3), 193–203.

Bass, B. M. (1996). *A new paradigm of leadership: An inquiry into transformational leadership.* Binghamton, New York: US Army Research Institute for the Behavioral and Social Science.

Bass, B. M. (1997). Does the transactional-transformational leadership paradigm transcend organizational and national boundaries? *American Psychologist, 52*(2), 130–139.

Bass, B. M., & Riggio, R. (2006). *Transformational leadership.* New Jersey: Lawrence Erlbaum.

Beyer, S. (1990). Gender differences in accuracy of self-evaluations of performance. *Journal of Personality and Social Psychology, 59*(5), 960–970.

Biernat, M., & Fuegen, K. (2001). Shifting standards and the evaluations of competence: Complexity in gender-based judgment and decision making. *Journal of Social Issues, 57*(4), 707–724.

Biernat, M., Fuegen, K., & Kobrynowicz, D. (2010). Shifting standards and the inference of incompetence: Effects of formal and informal evaluation tools. *Personality and Social Psychology Bulletin, 36*(7), 855–868.

Biernat, M., & Manis, M. (1994). Shifting standards and stereotype-based judgments. *Journal of Personality and Social Psychology, 66*(1), 5–20.

Biernat, M., & Vescio, T. K. (2002). She swings, she hits, she's great, she's benched: Implications of gender-based shifting standards for judgment and behavior. *Personality and Social Psychology Bulletin, 28*(66), 66–77.

Bowman, G. W., Worthy, N. B., & Grayson, S. A. (1965). Problems in review: Are women executive people? *Harvard Business Review, 43*(3), 15–28.

Burns, J. M. (1978). *Leadership.* New York: Harper & Row.

Cohen, J. (1988). *Statistical power analysis for the behavioral sciences.* Mahwah: Lawrence Erlbaum.

Correll, S. J. (2001). Gender and the career choice process: The role of biased self-assessments. *American Journal of Sociology, 106*(6), 1691–1730.

Correll, S. J. (2004). Constraints into preferences: Gender, status and emerging career aspirations. *American Sociological Review, 69*(93), 93–113.

Delgado, O. (2012). Improvement areas of seafarers' leadership. *Maritime Transport V Proceedings*, 149–170.

Druskat, V. (1994). Gender and leadership style: Transformational and transactional leadership in the Roman Catholic Church. *Leadership Quarterly, 5*(2), 99–119.

Eagly, A., & Johannesen-Schmidt, M. (2001). The leadership styles of women and men. *Journal of Social Issues, 57*(4), 781–797.

Eagly, A., & Johnson, B. (1990). Gender and leadership style: A meta-analysis. *Psychological Bulletin, 108*(2), 233–256.

Eagly, A. H., & Karau, S. J. (2002). Role congruity theory of prejudice female leaders. *Psychological Review, 109*(3), 573–598.

Eagly, A. H., Karau, S. J., & Makhijani, M. G. (1995). Gender and the effectiveness of leaders: A meta-analysis. *Psychological Bulletin, 117*(1), 125–145.

Eagly, A. H., Makhijani, M. G., & Klonsky, B. G. (1992). Gender and the evaluation of leaders: A meta-analysis. *Psychological Bulletin, 111*(1), 3–22.
Heilman, M. E., Wallen, A. S., Fuchs, D., & Tamkins, M. M. (2004). Penalties for success: Reactions to women who succeed at male gender-typed tasks. *Journal of Applied Psychology, 89*(3), 416–427.
Helgesen, S. (1990). *The female advantage: Women's ways of leadership*. New York: Doubleday.
Henry, G. T. (1990). *Practical sampling*. London: Sage Publications.
IMO. (2011). *STCW including 2010 Manila amendments: STCW Convention and STCW Code*. London: Author.
Kent, T. W., Blair, C. A., Rudd, H. F., & Schuele, U. (2010). Gender differences and transformational leadership behavior: Do both German men and women lead in the same way? *International Journal of Leadership Studies, 6*(1), 52–66.
Komives, S. (1991). Gender differences in the relationship of hall directors' transformational and transactional leadership and achieving styles. *Journal of College Student Development, 32*, 155–165.
Loiko, A. (2014). *Does gender stereotypes exist in evaluation of maritime leadership behaviors?* (Bachelor Thesis). Buskerud and Vestfold University College, Borre.
Maher, K. (1997). Gender-related stereotypes of transformational and transactional leadership. *Sex Roles, 37*(3–4), 209–225.
Mansfield, H. (2006). *Manliness*. New Haven: Yale University Press.
Minter, R. M., Gruppen, L. D., Napolitano, K. S., & Gauger, P. G. (2005). Gender differences in self-assessment of surgical resident. *The American Journal of Surgery, 189*(6), 647–650.
Northouse, P. G. (2013). *Leadership: theory and practice*. Thousand Oaks: Sage Publication.
Rosener, J. (1990). Ways women lead. *Harvard Business Review, 68*(6), 119–125.
Ryan, T. A. (1959). Multiple comparisons in psychological research. *Psychological Bulletin, 56* (1), 26–47.
Shadish, W. R., Cook, T. D., & Campbell, D. T. (2002). *Experimental and quasi-experimental designs for generalized causal inference*. Boston, MA: Houghton-Mifflin.
van Engen, M. L., van der Leeden, R., & Willemsen, T. M. (2001). Gender, context and leadership styles: A field study. *Journal of Occupational and Organisational Psychology, 74*(5), 581–598.
Wennerås, C., & Wold, A. (1997). Nepotism and sexism in peer-review. *Nature, 387*, 341–343.

How to Cope with Second-Generation Gender Bias in Male-Dominated Occupations

Pınar Özdemir and Taner Albayrak

Abstract It is often discussed that if a person works in a job dominated by the opposite gender, gender-related challenges are likely to arise. For example, women tend to experience difficulties in male-dominated occupations, because they have to cope with the bias set for them because of their gender. It may be less difficult to eliminate bias the women directly face, but additional action must be taken to cope with the so-called second-generation gender bias, which means, unlike intentional and obvious (first-generation) gender bias, invisible customs and practices in an organization that look neutral, but appear to hold women back and prevent them from reaching their full potential. On the other hand, rising to top positions is hard in male-dominated sectors, because of not only the bias in question, but also the glass ceiling that is always there for them. In this study, the hardships women are likely to meet in male-dominated occupations are taken into consideration with an emphasis on the maritime sector and a model to overcome second-generation gender bias and break the glass ceiling that is preventing women from rising to top positions, is suggested. The model, which is a combination of mentoring and participative leadership, is outlined after examining the steps taken to promote the roles of women in the maritime sector.

Keywords Career paths • Double binds • Mentoring • Participative leadership • Second-generation gender bias

1 Introduction

The research conducted by Blades and Pearson (2005), which covered occupations available for the European members of the OECD and the United States and obtained in 2004, show that at least half of all working women are in 11 of the 110 occupations, while half of the men work in more than 20 of them. This suggests that women tend to enter a more restricted range of professions than men

P. Özdemir (✉) • T. Albayrak
Maritime Faculty, Piri Reis University, Istanbul, Turkey
e-mail: pozdemir@pirireis.edu.tr

© Springer-Verlag Berlin Heidelberg 2015

M. Kitada et al. (eds.), *Maritime Women: Global Leadership*, WMU Studies in Maritime Affairs 3, DOI 10.1007/978-3-662-45385-8_16

do. According to the same data, the number of men working in the maritime sector is 52 times more than the number of women working in the same sector.

Women who work in male-dominated occupations tend to 'face challenges that differ from those who work in more gender-balanced and female-dominated occupations. These challenges affect their retention and career success. The challenges women face in attempting to penetrate successfully, and persevere in historically male-dominated work environments, emanate from traditional gender hierarchies and norms that prevail in the family and society' (Martin and Barnard 2013). Despite gender equality and empowerment, the household unit tends to have a traditional structure in general, that makes males the dominant gender. 'Women who defy conventional female career patterns and choose to pursue careers in male-dominated occupations, often return to careers that accommodate their roles as primary care-givers better' (Martin and Barnard 2013).

The research (Warren 2009) has found that 'talent-management systems in male-dominated jobs are frequently vulnerable to pro-male biases, that inevitably result in less diverse employee pools. Because senior leadership teams, which tend to be dominated by men, set the tone for talent management norms, masculine stereotypes can creep into human resource tools. Employees who meet criteria (potentially based on masculine stereotypes) are selected for promotion and/or tapped as future leaders and/or offered developmental opportunities. Because male-dominated industries and occupations tend to be particularly vulnerable to masculine stereotypes due to lack of diversity, women may find excelling in these industries or occupations to be particularly difficult' (Catalyst 2013).

2 Second Generation Gender Bias

Unlike first-generation gender discrimination, which is intentional acts of bias against women, women in today's workforce, especially those working in traditionally male-dominated fields such as the maritime environment, are experiencing a much more camouflaged foe-second-generation gender biases that are impeding their advancement and adding stress to their lives. 'According to researchers (Trefault et al. 2011) at the Center for Gender in Organizations (CGO), second-generation gender biases are "work cultures and practices that appear neutral and natural on their face", yet they reflect masculine values and life situations of men who have been dominant in the development of traditional work settings. These deeply entrenched gender-biased dynamics exist in our culture, norms, and organizational practices and directly affect hiring decisions, promotion, and salaries' (Carter 2011). Second-generation gender bias involves 'social practices and patterns of interaction among groups within workplace, that, over time, exclude non-dominant groups. Exclusion is frequently difficult to trace directly to intentional, discrete actions of particular actors, and may sometimes be visible only in the aggregate' (Sturm 2001).

Second-generation bias does not 'necessarily produce direct, immediate harm to any individual. Rather, it creates a context in which women fail to thrive or reach their full potential. Feeling less connected to one's male colleagues, being advised to take a staff role to accommodate family, finding oneself excluded from consideration for key positions—all these situations reflect work structures and practices that put women at a disadvantage' (Ibarra et al. 2013).

An article published in Harvard Business Review in September, 2013 (Ibarra et al. 2013) does not focus on deliberate exclusion of women, but focuses on investigating "second-generation" forms of gender bias as the primary cause of women's persistent underrepresentation in leadership roles. 'This bias erects powerful, but subtle and often invisible barriers for women, that arise from cultural assumptions and organized structures, practices and patterns of interaction that inadvertently benefit men, while putting women at a disadvantage' (Ibarra et al. 2013). According to Ibarra et al. (2013), invisible barriers for women include: a paucity of role models for women; gendered career paths and gendered work; women's lack of access to networks and sponsors; and double binds.

A Paucity of Role Models for Women There are not many women role models for the women. This discourages women from working in male-dominated occupations. They have no one to depend on when they need advice or support. What's more, they think they will be hindered by the glass ceiling, and no matter how hard they work, they won't be promoted to top positions.

Gendered Career Paths and Gendered Work Once there were not as many women in the work force as there are now. At that time, all the organizational structures and work force were designed to meet the needs of men. There is a tendency in the organizations to reward the heroic work, usually performed by men, and undervalue the backstage work usually done by women.

'These practices were not designed to be discriminatory, but their cumulative effect disadvantages women and a vicious cycle ensues: Men appear to be best suited to leadership roles, and this perception propels more of them to seek and attain such positions, thus reinforcing the notion that they are simply better leaders' (Ibarra et al. 2013).

Women's Lack of Access to Networks and Sponsors Networks in an organization are particularly important for people aiming for top positions. Unfortunately, women have a lesser chance to access influential networks in male-dominated organizations. This prevents them from reaching prominent people and getting important information beforehand. They are less likely to find sponsors or mentors in the organizations, because people have a tendency to choose the people of the same gender to work with and to sponsor.

Double Binds Some features are closely linked by the genders and positions in an organization. The qualities linked to the men are decisiveness, assertiveness and independence, which are also connotated with the leaders. On the other hand, the features linked by the women are niceness, unselfishness and altruism, which contradict the qualities a leader is supposed to have.

Ibarra et al. (2013) state that 'women who excel in traditionally male domains, are often viewed as competent, but less likable than their male counterparts. Behaviours, which are seen as self-confidence and assertiveness in men, often appear arrogant or abrasive in women'. On the other hand, women behaving in a feminine style in positions of authority are liked, but not respected.

'For women, the difficulty of penetrating historically male-dominated occupations, coupled with the unwillingness to accommodate them in those occupations, makes the environment unattractive for enticing substantial numbers of women into these fields and retaining them there. Further, a lack of understanding of the challenges that women face, and how they cope in these environments, may add to the poor integration and advancement of women in historically male-dominated occupations' (Martin and Barnard 2013).

3 Challenges Faced by Women in the Maritime Sector

Working on board a ship is one of the most challenging jobs a woman does, due to its traditional nature as a male-dominated occupation. There are 1.25 million sailors in the world and only 2 % of them are women. Of this number, 51.2 % come from OECD countries. In the remaining 48.8 %, women in Eastern European countries have a 23.6 % share, while women in Far Eastern countries represent 13.7 % and those in Latin America, Africa and Middle East countries have a 11.5 % share (Deniz Haber Ajansı 2006).

As in all other male-dominated jobs, women in the maritime sector tend to experience a number of challenges, some of which arise from the bias, and some of which do not. In the scope of this study, an online search was made to identify problems of women working in the maritime sector. A wide range of interviews given by the women in the maritime sector were searched through the internet and scanned to determine what the underlying problems they are likely to meet. As a result, ten major challenges, which are listed below, have been revealed:

1. Not being able to rise to the top positions;
2. Not getting the same salary as the men in the same positions;
3. Having to work more than the men do to be promoted;
4. Being employed in restricted areas or in the areas they are not educated for;
5. Being given less on-the-job training opportunities;
6. Not having a strong network, as the men have;
7. Not having the solidarity and network due to the insufficient number of women in the sector, so not getting the benefits of them, as the men do;
8. Insufficient mentorship opportunities to integrate women into the field;
9. Not being able to perform organizational citizenship behaviours as much as men can, due to the fact that they are primary caregivers in the family; and
10. Suffering from work overloads and time management problems.

It was seen that the challenges the women in the maritime sector are likely to suffer from, are not different from the ones that women working in any male-dominated sectors are likely to encounter. What makes the situation worse for the women in the maritime sector, may be the special circumstances of their work place. Working on board a ship, which means being away from home for a long time, is difficult, even for men.

As the number of the women working in the maritime sector increases, some steps are taken to solve these challenges. For example, IMO takes specific measures, through its strategic planning and at the operational level of technical co-operation, to promote the increased participation of women in the maritime sector. The Programme for the Integration of Women in the Maritime Sector (IWMS) remains the primary vehicle for supporting the UN Millennium Development Goal 3 to "Promote gender equality and empower women". IMO is making a concerted effort to help the industry move on from the tradition which takes shipping as a male-dominated industry, to help women achieve a representation within it, that is more in keeping with twenty-first century expectations. This programme, which aims for the integration of women in the maritime sector, has a primary objective to encourage IMO member states to open the doors of their maritime institutes to enable women to train alongside men and so acquire the high level of competence that the maritime industry demands (IMO 2013).

In a recent conference held in Busan, South Korea, the declaration of intent towards the development of a Global Strategy for Women Seafarers was adopted. The conference adopted the Bussan Declaration,[1] in which the participants agreed to forge partnerships and solicit support of government agencies, as well as international and regional bodies, to facilitate the implementation of a Global Strategy for Women Seafarers (IMO 2013). There are some international and regional associations established to serve the same purpose.[2] The common purpose of all these associations is to promote education, training and career opportunities for women linked to the maritime sector, advocate gender equity, increase the recognition of social responsibilities relating to women in the maritime sector, and promote cooperation, friendship and understanding through the exchange of knowledge and the dissemination of information (Secretariat of the Pacific Community n.d.).

[1] http://www.imo.org/MediaCentre/HotTopics/women/Documents/BUSAN%20DECLARATION (Revised1)%20(3).pdf.

[2] They are, for example, UN Atlas of the Oceans: Role of Women; Arab International Women's Maritime Forum for Middle East and North Africa; Women in Maritime Associations—Asia (WIMA–Asia); Women in Maritime Philippines (WIMAPHIL); International Women's Maritime Forum for MENA and Africa; Association for Women in Maritime, East and Southern Africa (WOMESA); Pacific Women in Maritime Association (PacWIMA); Network for Professional Women in the Maritime and Port Sectors of the West and Central Africa Region; Papua New Guinea Women in Maritime Association (PNGWIMA); and Women's International Shipping & Trading Association (WISTA).

4 Suggestions

There is an on-going change in the world, deriving from globalization, advancements in technology and an increase in consideration of people and the environment. These may add or decrease the hardships experienced by the women in the maritime sector. Nevertheless, it seems that gender bias against women is not easy to change, because the expected roles of women, as in most societies, are still experiencing a slow process of changing the norms of caregivers and mothers. To eliminate the bias against women and hardships they encounter, and to bring the women to the positions they deserve, a model can be designed. This model is a combination of 'mentoring' and 'participative leadership'.

4.1 Mentoring

'Mentoring is to support and encourage people to manage their own learning, in order that they may maximize their potential, develop their skills, improve their performance and become the person they want to be' (Parsloe 2008). A mentor is a person who gives another person help and advice over a period of time, and often also teaches them how to do their job (McIntosh 2013).

As the definitions suggest, a good mentor gives not only help and advice to an intern, but also the opportunity to learn the experiences and knowledge of an expert in the field. Leaders are also mentors and they have the responsibility of training the leaders of the future. Furthermore, organizations recognize that workforce demographics have changed dramatically in recent years, as women and members of different minority groups, who hold few positions of social power, have joined the workforce in greater numbers, especially in developing countries. 'In addition, technology has automated traditional employee functions and continues to affect on-the-job performance, altering the way people see themselves within the corporate structure' (Management Mentors 2013).

All these changes, and the changes in the structure of organizations, make it necessary to make some changes in the orientation period of the newcomers to an organization. Mentoring, along with the buddy system and coaching, is a key to adapt the interns to their career and to the organization, and train them for the top positions. Besides, mentoring is a win-win activity, which contributes positively to both sides, so both the company and the intern benefit from the process (Koçel 2013).

On the other hand, not all the employees in a company can benefit from the mentoring to the same extent, since mentors tend to choose people resembling themselves (Robbins and Judge 2013). This may put the women in a disadvantageous position in male-dominated organizations, as there are not a lot of women in top positions. Only 11 % of the executive officers in male-dominated occupations are women (Catalyst 2013). This restricts the number of women from whom interns can get mentorship to rise to higher positions.

4.2 *Participative Leadership*

The other solution suggested to help women to rise to leading positions, is to make use of participative leadership. Companies are becoming more and more flexible. Now that organizations do not depend on the traditional hierarchy any more, it may be hard to direct and coordinate the efforts of the people to the target of the company. Quality of the work also changes and that means most of the work in the twenty-first century will be more intellectual than physical (Hartog and Koopman 2002). All the change in the structure of the companies and in the quality of the work, requires a change in the leadership style. It is agreed that there is not only one best leadership style that can be applied in all situations. Considering all the leadership styles, participative leadership seems to be more suitable for women working in male-dominated jobs, one of which is maritime, to eliminate second-generation gender bias, crack and break the glass ceiling, and rise to top positions. 'The myth about participative leadership is that it is a feminine leadership style, as studies have shown that women leaders have a higher tendency to use a participative leadership style, while males typically use an authoritative leadership style' (Goode 2014).

In participative leadership, the leader, rather than taking autocratic decisions, seeks to involve other people in the process, possibly including subordinates, peers, superiors and other stakeholders. There are many potential benefits of participative leadership (Changing Minds n.d.), some of which include:

- Involvement in decision-making improves the understanding of the issues involved by those who must carry out the decisions;
- People are more committed to actions where they have been involved in the relevant decision-making;
- People are less competitive and more collaborative when they are working on joint goals;
- When people make decisions together, the social commitment to one another is greater and thus increases their commitment to the decision; and
- Several people deciding together, make better decisions than one person does alone.

Participative leadership, practised fully, will help the women improve organizational citizenship behaviours, provide them with decision-making experience, and prepare them for prospective leading positions.

4.3 Participative Leadership in Mentoring Groups

As is seen, both mentoring and participative leadership have been considered helpful to promote the position of women in male-dominated jobs. In this study, a combination of these two solutions is suggested: employing participative leadership in the mentoring groups established in the organization.

In the ideal practice, a person with more experience and at a higher position, can be the mentor of another person. But in the situations like those in male-dominated organizations, where there are not enough women in top positions to mentor the women in lower positions, mentoring teams consisting of three people, two of whom are men, can be formed. The members of the team, guided by a leader, that is the mentor, may be given some jobs, which require them to work in closer connection with each other than they do in the normal work-setting, share all the data they have, and coordinate. This may cause them to create a network among the three, which may be the basis of a greater network in the organization in which a woman can take part in the future. This practice may also give way to solidarity, where the members of the group can help each other in situations where mentoring is necessary. Therefore, the team may become a kind of self-supporting and mentoring team at the end.

The goal of this team will not only be a mentor-mentee relationship, but also helping the mentees overcoming the second-generation gender bias. To realize this, the mentor in charge of the team will both guide the mentees in and out of the organization and create cases in which the mentees will be required to share their ideas, to reach a consensus and reach a decision on the subject given. Apart from this, the teams established in this way in an organization, can get together at certain intervals to discuss certain issues. During these meetings, mentoring team members are encouraged to make use of participative leadership skills. By doing so, the women in the teams will not only be trained for higher positions, but also learn how to overcome the second-generation gender bias. On the other hand, the men in the team will be stripped off the second-generation gender bias, thus making the activity a win-win situation. Because they will be working together, they will get to know the abilities and skills of the other gender better. The team spirit will also help them overcome the bias.

Once decision-makers feel confident that women are starting to be accepted into the network in the organization and can function as effectively as men can, they will give them greater responsibilities. Psychologists note a vicious cycle: If bias against women as managers restricts women's access to higher management positions, they are shut out from the chance to demonstrate their ability to handle line responsibility and further build their leadership skills (American Psychological Association 2006). This practice will also help women to overcome four types of obstacles that they say they face, which are not being heard and listened to, not being accepted as an equal or as part of the 'in' group, establishing credibility, and stereotyped expectations of women's behaviour (Groysberg and Bell 2013).

The maritime sector is an occupation which attracts more and more women, year by year. Maritime jobs are generally more demanding and less indulging than any other male-dominated ones. In particular, women seafarers work on board a ship, which can be a dynamic and harsh place and there are less opportunities for them to get help in case they need it. Therefore, it requires both physically and mentally tough people, requires leadership skills and swift decision making qualities and is less tolerant for gender differences. That being the case, it requires more leadership training activities for women. The model suggested above can be used to meet these demands. Mentoring teams, like the ones mentioned above, may be formed in both shore-based and sea-going posts (ashore and afloat units) in the maritime sector. The prospective women leaders can benefit from such a training a lot, and this practice may both help women to achieve their goals, and men to overcome the bias against women.

5 Conclusion

The number of women is increasing in the work force. They are getting more and more interested in all kinds of jobs, and male-dominated ones are no exception. Various literature suggest that there are still a number of gender-related challenges in these occupations. First is the fact that women tend to have a lot of responsibilities at home. Second, women have to fight for eliminating the gender bias, whether seen or unseen, and third, women strategically need to cope with the hardships of working in male-dominated areas and unwillingness to accommodate them in those occupations, which might be the result of their considering the job as their domain historically, and superstitious traditions run long and deep.

Of these, the most important one is the bias against women. The first thing they must do is to beat the bias against them. Whether seen or unseen, whether first or second generation, biases are the most important obstacles on their journey to break and go through the glass ceiling. Only by breaking that bias, and adopting cooperative roles to support each other, can they be heard in male-dominated occupations such as maritime jobs. Working on board a ship is considered to be one of the most challenging jobs a woman can do, so it is especially vital for the women in this sector to be aware of all these difficulties and take measures against them.

There are some steps taken to ease these difficulties. In this paper, a model is suggested to cope with these challenges and to prepare the women for future leading positions. The model, which is a combination of mentoring and participative leadership, is expected to give women a chance to eliminate second-generation gender bias and to compete in equal terms with men for leadership positions.

Women need to be empowered in this way, to prove themselves as equally valuable team members, and take a step towards overcoming the difficulties they face in their journey to top positions in male-dominated occupations, including the maritime sector. The main challenges the maritime sector faces today are tight labour market conditions, high drop-out rates from industry, a lack of recruitment at basic levels, un-coordinated approach by employers, and a lack of interest among young people. Wider employment of women in the maritime sector, especially in the shipping business, will definitely contribute to decreasing these problems. Women employees, who perceive a high degree of empowerment, will be motivated to serve organizations and leaders that provide opportunities for the feelings of competence and control. Since empowerment is evidence that the organization shows high expectations on them to independently carry out tasks, and that the contributions that they make will benefit the organization, women are willing to build high quality relationship with their leaders/supervisors, for overall success and effectiveness of the organization.

This article is mainly based on the long-term experience of the authors in the maritime sector, in the navy and merchant marine fleet, personal observations and interviews with seagoing and shore-based female officers. It suggests further research to collect evidence of second-generation gender bias, from the various parts of the maritime sector.

References

American Psychological Association. (2006). When the boss is a woman. http://www.apa.org/research/action/boss.+aspx. Accessed 10 Dec 2013.

Blades, D., & Pearson, M. (2005). Women and me in OECD countries, occupations of men and women. Resource document. Organisation for Economic Co-operation and Development. http://www.oecd.org/std/37962502.pdf. Accessed 16 Dec 2013.

Carter, S. B. (2011). The invisible barrier: Second generation gender discrimination: The new face of gender bias and how we can stop it. Resource document. Psychology today. http://www.psychologytoday.com/blog/high-octane-women/201104/the-invisible-barrier-second-generation-gender-discrimination. Accessed 13 Dec 2013.

Catalyst. (2013). Women in male-dominated industries and occupations in U.S. and Canada. http://www.catalyst.org/knowledge/women-male-dominated-industries-and-occupations-us-and-canada. Accessed 11 Dec 2013.

Changing Minds. (n.d.). Participative leadership. http://changingminds.org/disciplines/leadership/styles/participative_leadership.htm. Accessed 11 Dec 2013.

Deniz Haber Ajansı. (2006). Seyir defterinde kadin imzasi. http://www.denizhaber.com.tr/seyir-defterinde-kadin-imzasi-haber-3283.htm. Accessed 16 Dec 2013.

Goode, E. (2014). How participative leadership can improve your organization. Resource document. Hub Pages. http://ericgoode.hubpages.com/hub/Participative-Leadeship. Accessed 16 May 2014.

Groysberg, B., & Bell, D. (2013). Dysfunction in the boardroom: Understanding the persistent gender gap at the highest. *Harvard Business Review, 91*(6), 88–97.

Hartog, D. N., & Koopman, P. L. (2002). Leadership in organizations. In N. Anderson, D. S. Ones, H. K. Sinangil, & C. Viswesvaran (Eds.), *Handbook of industrial, work and organizational psychology* (Organizational psychology, Vol. 2, pp. 166–187). Thousand Oaks: Sage Publications.

Ibarra, H., Ely, J. R., & Kolb, D. (2013). Women rising: The unseen barriers. *Harvard Business Review, 91*(9), 60–66.

IMO. (2013). Women in the maritime industry. http://www.imo.org/MediaCentre/HotTopics/women/Pages/default.aspx. Accessed 12 Dec 2013.

Koçel, T. (2013). *İşletme Yöneticiliği*. İstanbul: Beta Yayınları.
Management Mentors. (2013). Why do organizations implement formal mentoring programs? http://www.management-mentors.com/resources/corporate-mentoring-programs-faqs/. Accessed 11 Dec 2013.
Martin, P., & Barnard, A. (2013). The experience of women in male-dominated occupations: A constructivist grounded theory inquiry. *SA Journal of Industrial Psychology, 39*(2), 1–12.
McIntosh, C. (Ed.). (2013). *Cambridge advanced learner's dictionary*. Singapore: Cambridge University Press.
Parsloe, E. (2008). What is Mentoring? Resource document. The Oxford School of Coaching & Mentoring. http://www.mentorset.org.uk/pages/mentoring.htm. Accessed 13 Dec 2013.
Robbins, S. P., & Judge, T. A. (2013). *Örgütsel Davranış*. In İ. Erdem (Ed.). İstanbul: Nobel Yayınları.
Secretariat of the Pacific Community. (n.d.). Regional Maritime Programme. http://www.spc.int/maritime/index.php?option=com_content&task=view&id=40&Itemid=33. Accessed 12 Dec 2013.
Sturm, S. (2001). Second generation employment discrimination: A structural approach. *Columbia Law Review, 101*(3), 458–568.
Trefault, S., Merrill-Sands, D., Kolb, D., & Carter, S. (2011). Closing the women's leadership gap: Who can help? Resource document. Simmons College. http://www.simmons.edu/som/docs/insights_32_v6.pdf. Accessed 1 Apr 2014.
Warren, A. K. (2009). Cascading gender biases, compounding effects: An assessment of talent management systems. Resource document. Catalyst. http://www.catalyst.org/knowledge/cascading-gender-biases-compounding-effects-assessment-talent-management-systems. Accessed 1 Apr 2014.

Women in Shipping: Navigating to the Top

Karin Orsel

Abstract Shipping—the world's second oldest industry and the first global business. It has been the engine of trade throughout the millennium, and the source of pride, industry and employment. Until recently, it has been an almost entirely male domain.

2014 marks the 40th anniversary of the Women's International Shipping and Trading Association (WISTA). WISTA is a networking organization for women at the management level in the maritime industry.

WISTA's mission and vision is to facilitate the exchange of contacts, information and experiences amongst our members, promote the education of our members, and to develop business contacts around the world.

Keywords Career/business opportunities • Global network • Mentorship • Support maritime industry • WISTA • Women at management level

Shipping—the world's second oldest industry and the first global business. It has been the engine of trade throughout the millennium, and the source of pride, industry and employment. Until recently, it has been an almost entirely male domain. But in the past 50 years, there has been a shift and opportunities for women to participate in this exciting, dynamic industry are created and increasing every day.

2014 marks the 40th anniversary of the Women's International Shipping and Trading Association (WISTA). WISTA is a networking organization for women at the management level in the maritime industry. It was founded in the United Kingdom in 1974 when a handful of women brokers active in the tanker market from Germany and the United Kingdom met in London over lunch. Through the years, this became an annual event and contacts from overseas were invited to join

K. Orsel (✉)
WISTA International, Groningen, The Netherlands

MF Shipping Group, Farmsum/Delfzijl, The Netherlands

International Chamber of Shipping, Groningen, The Netherlands
e-mail: kyorsel@mfgroup.nl

© Springer-Verlag Berlin Heidelberg 2015

M. Kitada et al. (eds.), *Maritime Women: Global Leadership*, WMU Studies in Maritime Affairs 3, DOI 10.1007/978-3-662-45385-8_17

the meeting. The group expanded throughout the world to include women from other areas of shipping and trading.

In 1981, the annual lunch turned into an annual international conference, the first of which was held in Hamburg, Germany. Since that time, an annual international conference has been held in 20 different countries, including Norway, Sweden, Holland, Greece, England, France, the United States, Canada and Singapore. The 2014 conference will be held in Cyprus.

WISTA's mission and vision is to facilitate the exchange of contacts, information and experiences amongst our members, promote the education of our members, and to develop business contacts around the world. WISTA is active in 33 countries (called National WISTA Associations or NWAs) and has more than 2,000 individual members worldwide. It represents all working fields and segments of the maritime industry. Its membership consists of seafarers, ship owners, ship managers, ship agents, ship brokers, ship suppliers, ship financers, advisors, consultants, civil servants and maritime lawyers, to name some.

WISTA is governed by an Executive Committee (ExCo) which is responsible for adherence to the organization's bylaws and finances. ExCo is elected by the NWAs and is responsible to the members. Its current President is Karin Orsel, who is CEO of MF Shipping Group in the Netherlands. An effort is made to ensure that the composition of the Executive Committee is reflective of WISTA's members and is geographically diverse. ExCo meets regularly to discuss how to increase WISTA's profile worldwide and expand opportunities for women in the maritime industry.

Operating in a male-dominated industry could be daunting without the ability to network with other professionals who are experiencing the same challenges and opportunities. WISTA provides its members with access to a global network of women in the industry, replete with business and international career opportunities. WISTA is also cooperating with the International Maritime Organization, World Maritime University, International Chamber of Shipping, INTERTANKO, InterManager, International Transport Federation, Youngship International, the International Association of Ports and Harbors, and BIMCO, all with the goal of raising WISTA's profile and the visibility of women in shipping, along with providing more opportunities for WISTA members to network and grow their businesses.

WISTA is committed to demonstrating leadership in the shipping industry and nurturing the next generation of women in shipping. WISTA has various mentorship programs in place, including its cooperation with Youngship International, where WISTA members are the mentors and Youngship members the mentees. This program was developed by WISTA Norway and has been made available to National WISTA Associations around the world. WISTA encourages maritime peers to undertake the challenge of being a role model and mentor.

WISTA is in the process of building its roster of global Ambassadors. As the name implies, these leading industry figures share the goal of women's success in the maritime field, and are willing to communicate that message in the various venues they occupy. Current Ambassadors include Ms. Lisa Raitt, Minister of Transport for Canada; Ms. Catharina Elmsater-Svard, Minister for Infrastructure,

Sweden; Ms. Anna Wypych-Namiotko, IMO representative in Poland; Ms. Elisabeth Grieg, CEO of Grieg International in Norway; Ms Joyce Bawa Mogtari, Deputy Minister of Transport, Ghana; Ms. Tineke Netelenbos, Chairman of the Royal Association of Netherlands Shipowners; and Admiral Mary Landry, Director of Incident Management & Preparedness Policy at the U.S. Coast Guard, amongst others.

WISTA also recognizes leadership in promoting the advancement of women with its Personality of the Year Award. Recipients have included Captain Carmen Dewilde of Belgium, Katharina Stanzel of INTERTANKO, Mfon Ekong Usoro of Nigeria, Suzanne Williams of the United Kingdom and Pamela Conover of Carnival Corporation. NWAs recognize within their countries, women of excellence who contribute to the industry.

WISTA also supports and mentors women who have chosen an education at a maritime academy or other university. If a student wants a mentor, WISTA will find them one. In the United States, WISTA is an active sponsor and supporter of the "Women on the Water" Conference, organized by the U.S. Maritime Administration, and held annually with female maritime academy students from the federal and six state maritime academies in the United States. The WOW Conference generally attracts over 200 female cadets. WISTA members attend and lecture at these events, as well as meet with students who are interested in industry opportunities.

WISTA members are regular guest speakers at international industry events and commonly invite maritime students to attend. WISTA also helps improve its members' competencies via knowledge sharing and organizing workshops on personal development. These are particularly evident in NWA activities and range from updates on regulatory issues to management skill development.

WISTA itself is preparing for its 40th Anniversary celebration at its International Conference in Cyprus in October 2014, by developing a series of profiles, "I am WISTA," highlighting the women of WISTA and WISTA activities. The Cyprus Conference, attracting international speakers, will include Captain Kuba Szymanski of InterManager, Michael Bodouroglu of Allseas, Katharina Stanzel of INTERTANKO, Themis Papadopoulos of Interorient Navigation, Sofia Fürstenberg of Maersk, Jim Lawrence of Marine Money International, and Philippos Philis of Lemissoler Group.

As part of the 40th anniversary celebration, WISTA UK has launched a shipping photographic and essay competition related to its *Came by Ship* campaign. A vehicle for raising awareness of the role that shipping plays in the lives of our global society, *Came by Ship* will reach an international audience and communicate the message that more than 90 % of the world's goods travel by ship.

Another milestone this year is the 20th anniversary of WISTA Nigeria. They will be observing this important step by hosting an event at the Musical Society of Nigeria in Lagos, where Monica Mbanefo of IMO fame will deliver remarks on Women Empowerment. This will be followed by a celebration, including fireworks.

Throughout its history, WISTA has received enthusiastic support from the maritime industry. In addition to its strategic alliances, companies such as The

Marshall Islands Ship Registry, MF Shipping Group, Tototheo Group, Deloitte, Clyde & Co, The American Club and Blank Rome LLP, have been sponsors of WISTA and its activities. Their executive leadership has participated in WISTA events and been speakers at its many fora.

WISTA stays connected through its monthly newsletter. NWAs also commonly generate their own newsletters highlighting their activities. There is also an intentional move to spotlight WISTA members, sharing their stories about success and challenges in shipping.

WISTA is also active in its many communities. From beach cleanups, to fundraisers for seafarer welfare groups, and shoebox Christmases, WISTA connects locally as well as globally. Two years ago, WISTA enabled a woman photojournalist to travel around the world on cargo ships to create a video documentary about life aboard ships.

As WISTA matures, it is playing an increasingly visible role on the global shipping stage. Through its strategic alliances, WISTA is reaching most sectors of the industry with levels of involvement that range from education to projects and programs. WISTA continues to grow, with NWAs being formed every year on all continents as the demand for a networking organization dedicated to facilitating the careers of women in shipping grows.

WISTA faces the same challenges confronting the maritime industry. Attracting young people into the field is at the top of most executives' list. In order to be successful, the maritime industry must more fully embrace the use of social media to excite the next generation and engage their attention to shipping as a career choice. WISTA is endeavoring to address this core issue through reaching out to existing and potential members at all levels through LinkedIn, Facebook and Twitter, as well as at industry conferences where WISTA members speak.

It is commonly acknowledged that corporations and boards are more successful when there exists women as leaders. Shipping lags behind most industries, simply based on the historic career path into the maritime industry. Certain aspects of shipping, in years past, were not well suited to women, as they required extreme manual labor. Many of these barriers have been reduced due to the mechanization of shipping. Another barrier was the all-male maritime academy structure. This, too, was eliminated in the last few decades, and the percentage of women accepted into maritime academies grows each year. This has improved the ratio of women to men in the field—but there is a long way to equality.

WISTA tries to make a difference by encouraging its industry partners and associations to work and address issues together. Over the past 40 years, the employment of women in our industry has increased (both ashore and afloat), as well as for women in top management and Board positions. But there is still a long way to go in many regions of the world. There is a known shortage of qualified people—let us make use of the 50 % of the workforce (women) that are available and more than willing to enter our industry.

In today's global maritime industry, there is room for growth and opportunity. Let's work together to cultivate women as candidates for inclusion in the best industry in the world!

Part V
Sustainable Issues in Shipping: Women's Contribution

Chinese Women Seafarers: Past, Present and Prospects

Pengfei Zhang and Minghua Zhao

Abstract The global maritime industry plays an important role in international trade, the world economy, global stability and civil society as a whole. Both the IMO and the ILO have made great efforts to promote women's employment in the maritime transportation sector. However, until now, less than 2 % of the global seafarers are women. In China, the government has advocated women's rights, liberation and gender equality since the communists came into government in 1949. Chinese women have been encouraged to be employed in the traditionally male-dominant industries, such as mining, construction and seafaring. China feels proud of its strong track record of placing women on board commercial vessels as captains, chief engineers, radio officers and as navigating seafarers in various other positions. But, the glory has long become a history of the past. Now, in the twenty-first century, the number of navigating women seafarers in China has become extremely small. Training women as seafarers has drawn both praise and criticism from both scholars and practitioners in the industry. This paper takes the approach of a case study and analyses the key issues concerning the training and recruitment of women seafarers in China today. The rich empirical data presented, provides a clear picture of Chinese women seafarers today.

Keywords Chinese • Maritime • Seafarers • Women

1 Introduction

Since the founding of communist China in 1949, especially during the planned economy in Mao's time, Chinese women have been strongly encouraged to take employment in the traditionally male-dominant industries, such as mining, construction and transport. In shipping, women have been recruited and trained as seafarers since the 1960s and several women seafarers have been recognised as making distinctive contributions to the country's maritime industry as 'female heroines'.

P. Zhang (✉) • M. Zhao
China Maritime Centre, Greenwich Maritime Institute, University of Greenwich, London, UK
e-mail: shippinglaw@126.com

© Springer-Verlag Berlin Heidelberg 2015

M. Kitada et al. (eds.), *Maritime Women: Global Leadership*, WMU Studies in Maritime Affairs 3, DOI 10.1007/978-3-662-45385-8_18

However, within the past half century, the number of Chinese women seafarers remains small and women cadets still find it difficult to find ships to sail on after graduating from maritime education and training institutions. This paper aims to examine the recruitment, training and employment of women seafarers in China in the last six decades, with attention placed on relevant issues in the twenty-first century, through a case study of the small number of women cadets in Shanghai Maritime University (SMU), the country's only maritime education and training (MET) institution which opens its doors to women for nautical studies. The paper also explores the socioeconomic, political and cultural factors responsible for the lack of development of women's participation in this sector of the maritime economy in the country.

This paper has four main sections. After this brief introduction, the discussion moves to a section with a global view on women's participation in seafaring where some historical 'facts' and institutional efforts are discussed, both at the international and the national levels. Then, another section provides a brief historical review of women seafarers in China, from the 1950s up to the end of the twentieth century. The third section is the core of this study. It examines and evaluates, in detail, the Women Seafarers Project in Shanghai, focusing on women seafarers in the twenty-first century and the scrutiny covers several key aspects of women seafarers' recruitment and employment including motivation, enrolment, ship culture and conditions. The attitudes and behaviours of shipping companies are also examined here. After that, one section is devoted to an analysis of the prospects for women seafarers in China. Finally, the paper wraps up with a brief summary of the main points discussed and an in-depth discussion and analysis of the key barriers blocking women's participation in seafaring in the country. It concludes with recommendations calling for urgent change in national legislation and regulation, policies and practices in shipping companies, in order to advance women's rights interests in shipping and seafaring in China.

2 Background

Seafaring has been predominantly a male industry all over the world. The maritime industry had developed its own culture "which denied or precluded a female presence, except under controlled conditions" (Appleby 2013). In many coastal communities, people were profoundly superstitious about women on board. They believed that women on board ships would be a 'potential source of malevolence or bad luck'. In North Carolina, for example, some folklore asserts that if a man meets a woman while on his way to his fish, he will not catch any fish (White 1964).[1]

Worldwide, according to a 'land mark ILO study' conducted by a group of researchers in Cardiff University (ILO 2003), it was only after World War II, in the

[1] Indeed, such superstation remains strong in some fishing and seafaring villages in the twenty-first century. Zhao et al. (2014) reports in their study of women's role in English fisheries conducted in 2011 that even women fisheries officers in the region are still careful 'not to touch the fisherman's boat' for fear of 'bringing bad luck' to his trip.

mid-1940s, that women began to appear regularly as crew members aboard cargo ships—"most often on Swedish ships as stewardesses, cooks and radio officers" (Belcher et al. 2003). The first group of women cadets were recruited in the late 1960s and this was mainly in response to the drop in numbers of young male recruits in Europe. For some 15 years, from the mid-1980s, the shipping world lost interest in recruiting women, as it faced mounting structural problems of flagging out, over-capacity, declining freight rates and new sources of male seafarers in Southeast Asia and Eastern Europe. Women were still recruited as officer cadets in Europe, but since the overall levels of training in this region were declining, no particular interest was attached to women. Since the late 1990s, however, the international fleet has experienced an increasing shortage of competent officers. This has inspired a growing interest in recruiting and training women seafarers as a possible solution (Magramo and Eler 2012; Belcher et al. 2003; ILO 2001).

The United Nations (UN) and its two specialised agencies—the International Maritime Organization (IMO) and the International Labour Organization (ILO)—have made great efforts in promoting women's participation in shipping and seafaring. Since the early 1970s, the UN has established clear goals "to end discrimination against women and to ensure their equal participation in society" (UN 1985). In 1989, the IMO implemented the programme 'Women in Development (WID)', with the following objectives (Tansey 2000):

- to integrate women into mainstream maritime activities;
- to improve women's access to maritime training and technology;
- to increase the percentage of women at the senior management level within the maritime sector; and
- to promote women's economic self-reliance, including access to employment.

Since then, the IMO has made various efforts to encourage the entry of women into the merchant seafaring profession. In 1995, for example, the IMO adopted the 1995 amendments to the International Convention on Standards of Training, Certification and Watchkeeping for Seafarers, 1978 (IMO 1995). Resolution 14 to the amendments sheds particular light on the "promotion of the participation of women in the maritime industry". The Resolution notes that Governments are invited:

- to give special consideration to securing equal access by men and women in all sectors of the maritime industry; and
- to highlight the role of women in the seafaring profession and to promote their greater participation in maritime training and at all levels in the maritime industry.

The IMO's Long-and-Medium-Term Plan has established the aims of promoting the participation of women in the maritime sector. In 2010, the Manila Diplomatic Conference called for increasing concerns over the aims and reemphasized the role of women as a valuable resource (IMO 2011). In April 2013, the IMO adopted the Busan Declaration[2] during the Regional Conference on the Development of a

[2] http://www.imo.org/MediaCentre/HotTopics/women/Documents/BUSAN%20DECLARATION(Revised1)%20(3).pdf.

Global Strategy for Women Seafarers. The Declaration encourages all participants to "forge partnerships and solicit support of government agencies, as well as international and regional bodies, to facilitate the implementation of a Global Strategy for Women Seafarers" (IMO 2013).

The ILO has also been very active in promoting women's participation in shipping as seafarers. In 2001, the ILO adopted a resolution[3] which addresses gender issues at the 29th Session of the Joint Maritime Commission. This resolution encourages the shipping industry "to take positive steps to act against any aspect of discrimination based on gender" (ILO 2001). Following the Resolution, the ILO initiated a study, led by Belcher et al. (2003), on women seafarers for "discussion at a future meeting of the commission". The study was undertaken with a view "to establishing appropriate standards and guidance for the industry to provide women seafarers with a realistic opportunity to maintain a career at sea". Based on this study, the ILO adopted another resolution[4] concerning the promotion of opportunities for women seafarers. This resolution requests "the Director-General to give due priority in the use of resources, to examining measures which can further promote career opportunities and appropriate working and living conditions for women seafarers" (ILO 2006b). All these efforts have led to a series of requirements regarding the improvement of the work and living conditions for women on board of commercial ships, as prescribed in the ILO's Maritime Labour Convention 2006 (ILO 2006a). For example, Paragraph 9 (b) of Standard A 3.1, which requires "separate sleeping rooms shall be provided for men and for women". In addition, 11 (a) of Standard A 3.1 requires "separate sanitary facilities being provided for men and for women".

In China, there was no legal prohibitions explicitly against women working aboard ships. On the contrary, since the 1960s, the Chinese government has always encouraged women to participate in the maritime sector, particularly in Mao's time under the planned economy. However, with half a century gone, the number of Chinese women seafarers has not grown as much as it has been wished. In reality and in practice, Chinese women seafarers face various hindrances or obstacles and have found it difficult to develop a career at sea.

3 Chinese Women Seafarers Before the Twenty-First Century

In early China, as in many other countries, work roles were traditionally divided according to gender. Women usually worked inside the home and men outside (Hinsch 2011). A deep-rooted sense of Chinese people was that the home was the

[3] http://www.ilo.org/public/libdoc/ilo/2001/101B09_3_engl.pdf.

[4] http://www.ilo.org/wcmsp5/groups/public/---ed_norm/---normes/documents/publication/wcms_088130.pdf.

center of female labour, such as cooking on the stove, washing clothes and caring for children. 'Men ploughing and women weaving' (*nan geng nv zhi*) was an ideal description of a Chinese traditional family. However, this labour division had been primarily shaped by Confucian moral and social philosophy, which was the "dominant cosmology and familial ethic for more than 2000 years" in China (Abbott et al. 1995). This philosophy advocates 'men's power and dominance over women' and supports women's subordinate status in social and culture life (Nie 2011).

In modern China, women have a long history of struggle against discrimination. Since the early twentieth century, many women's organizations have appeared in China. These organizations launched campaigns and engaged in activities calling for women's rights, liberation and gender equality (Lu 2004). When the communists came into government in 1949, Mao was determined that the new China would strive to establish a brand new relationship between men and women, by completely getting rid of Confucianism, the core of the traditional Chinese social norms. To promote gender equality, Mao exclaimed a strong egalitarian slogan: "women hold half the sky" (Wang 2011). Since then, the world began to witness a significant increase of Chinese women's participation in various sectors of the economy traditionally occupied by men, such as in construction, mining and shipping.

While the new ideology has paved the way for change by eliminating the old tradition, the development of the shipping industry in China has provided new job opportunities for women. In the 1950s, women began to be recruited in marine schools to be trained as seafarers, primarily to sail ships on inland waters. Since the early 1960s, China has started to establish its own ocean-going fleet and there has been a steady increase of the number of seafarers on board of the country's commercial vessels. However, the supply has not always met the demand. As a possible solution to the shortage of seafaring labour, women were encouraged to study in maritime colleges and then work aboard ships, inland and ocean going. In the two decades of the 1960s and the 1970s, women seafarers were found sailing on the Yangzi River (*changjiang*) and in 1974, the world was excited to see the *Fengtao*, the world's first women-officers-only Chinese cargo ship trading in international waters (Belcher et al. 2003). Some of these women seafarers have earned high distinctions and are considered as 'heroines' in the Chinese maritime industry. For example, Qingfen Kong, the first-ever female captain in China's ocean shipping, was highly praised "by the leader of Chinese government" (Zhuo 2008). Yafu Wang, the first, and the only female chief engineer in China, received the same honour and esteem. She was even promoted to hold a high-ranking official post in China's shipping industry (Sheng and Ke 2009). In order to pursue a seafaring profession, many women seafarers, including these two, even had to miss the opportunity to get married. Both Kong and Wang have won high respect in China because they have contributed their whole youth to the country's maritime industry (Liang 2009).

However, these women seafarers were in very small numbers and their career as professional seafarers did not last long. In the 1980s and 1990s, with the introduction of economic reform which promotes market forces, gender equality had received less attention than before. At the same time, the demand for seafarers in China during this period apparently declined in general (Li 2010). This was primarily due to the reform measures adopted by shipping companies which emphasised productivity and efficiency, and hence began to shed 'surplus' seafarers. At the same time, shipboard technology, such as automation and computerisation, developed so rapidly that shipping companies responded quickly by adopting the technology as it had proved effective in reducing crew size, hence good potential to increase profits in the shipping business (Zhao 2002). The overall business and political-ideological environment in China became such that it became pointless to encourage women to take part in seafaring during this period. In addition, the 'strategy' of placing women on board ships had turned out not as successfully as it seemed. In reality, among the very small number of women seafarers, less than half had stayed at sea for a relatively long time. The majority of them had to give up their career, primarily because of marriage and family.

4 Research Methods

This paper has drawn on the authors' shared research interest and experiences in their study of Chinese seafarers. Most of the empirical data presented in this paper comes from a larger research project on seafarers' rights in China, which is led by Zhang. The mixed method has been adopted in gathering the primary data used in supporting this paper. Fieldwork has been carried out in Shanghai, Dalian and a number of other Chinese coastal cities, where more than 100 interviews were conducted with officials in maritime administration, shipping managers, lecturers in MET institutions, managers of crewing agencies, male and female seafarers, officials of seafarers' trade unions and other stakeholders. The case study approach was taken, as the core of this study, in analysing the recruitment and employment of women cadets in the Shanghai Maritime University (SMU). Both qualitative and quantitative data were collected from semi-structured interviews with six lecturers and 20 female students, as well as a questionnaire survey of 170 students (70 female and 100 male) registered for nautical studies at the university. As noted earlier, most of the empirical data presented in this paper has been drawn on Zhang's fieldwork in China in 2013, but references have also been made to Zhao's research, including her earlier field trips in the country.

5 Chinese Women Seafarers in the Twenty-First Century: A Case Study from Shanghai

There are at least 75 MET institutions in China, with an annual capacity of over 30,000 cadets in total (MOT 2013). The number is strong, but none were willing to enrol female student for nautical or marine engineering studies. The situation remained the same until 2000 when a 'dramatic' event occurred in Shanghai. As if to celebrate the coming of the new millennium, SMU announced that it would start to recruit female students for nautical studies. The training programme tailored for female students has been called the Women Seafarers Project (WSP).

The WSP has made a historic breakthrough. Although this was only a single case, the significance of the WSP at SMU lies in that the project has fundamentally changed the condition of seafarers recruitment which had set the rule that 'no female student in maritime studies' for over 20 years in China from the 1980s. In September 2000, 30 female students were enrolled for nautical studies at the SMU Merchant Shipping School. This cohort was mixed in ten classes, and trained side by side with a much larger cohort of male students (n = 270). The recruitment of female students for seafaring training was considered an important event, and their first training on board was widely reported in local and national media (SOHU 2003; SINA 2009).

Fourteen years have passed and as many as 356 female students have been trained by the WSP at SMU. As of January 2014, the SMU continues with its WSP and the university remains the only MET institution in China which opens its door to women for training to become seafarers. What has happened to these women cadets and seafarers, during and after their training at SMU? Have other MET institutions followed the model initiated in Shanghai and recruited more women for training to be seafarers? The rest of the paper will attempt to answer these questions.

5.1 *Enrolment of Female Nautical Students*

Since 2000, the SMU has regularly recruited and trained female students in nautical studies. Considering the hard working conditions in the engine room, the WSP only recruits female students for nautical studies. The marine engineering study keeps its door closed to women. Until 2014, there have been 356 female students enrolled in nautical studies and 255 graduated. Figure 1 describes the SMU enrolment of students for nautical studies by year of admission and the data clearly indicates that the number of female students is roughly one-tenth of that of their male counterparts.

The SMU has officially declared that the aims of the WSP are to educate and train women seafarers for international fleets, and to encourage women to participate in this traditionally male-dominated sector of the maritime industry. In Zhao's

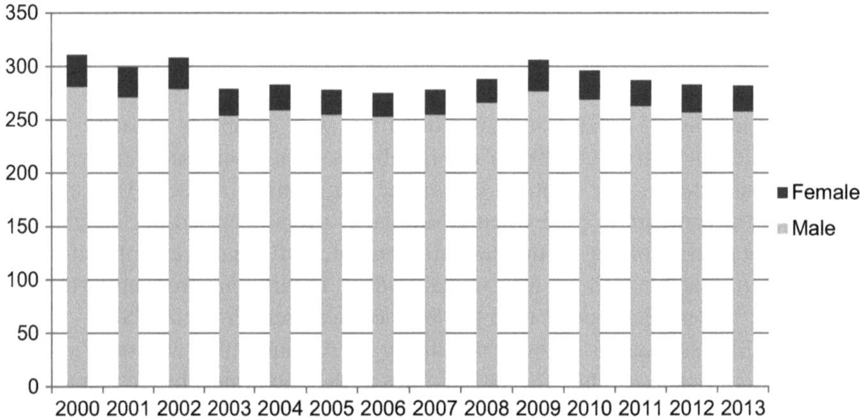

Fig. 1 SMU enrolment for nautical studies by year of admission by gender (2000–2013)

interview with the then senior management of the School of Nautical Studies at SMU in 2001, while this objective was clearly noted, there was also a demonstration of a desire for international prestige, as he said:

> I must mention another reason for us to decide to recruit women cadets. Some two or three years ago, we attended maritime events organised by the IMO in Japan and in the Philippines. In both, they showcased their women cadets. They look really smart and beautiful, really outstanding. We were feeling bad. Our country is a big country and we have the socialist tradition to have women working in the traditionally male-dominated industries. But, now, we are lagging behind. We must catch up so that we can also showcase our women seafarers at future IMO events. .... We discussed these thoughts with the leaders at Shanghai Municipality and got their support to go ahead.

In addition, some cultural consideration was actually also behind the thought for the recruitment of women seafarers in Shanghai, as Zhang found in his field research in 2013 in Shanghai. Back in the 1990s, with the dramatic development of the Chinese maritime industry, including port facilities, a rapidly increasing number of vessels called at Chinese ports. This imposed increasing pressure on the Vessel Traffic Service (VTS) in many ports. The VTS in many ports were short of telephone operators to coordinate the arrival and departure of international ships. "Many people considered that women would be most suitable to perform the duties in the call centre of VTS. Compared with the stiff and harsh orders from a man, a female voice may inspire different feelings for seafarers, and seafarers are more likely to follow the instructions from the VTS call centre" as recalled by a senior lecturer at SMU in the interview. So, the feminine quality or women's 'soft' voice was also used to help rationalise the proposal to recruit women as seafarers. Given that VTS operators need to have the background of nautical studies, in 2000, the School of Nautical Studies at SMU recruited the first group of female students and the recruitment has continued for 14 years since then.

It has been hoped that the WSP in Shanghai would inspire other MET institutions in other parts of the country to follow suit, hence more women would be encouraged to join the industry as seafarers. Unfortunately, the innovative actions initiated in Shanghai have not been modelled after by any other MET institutions in China. The SMU remains the only university that keeps its door open to women who aspire to sail at sea.

5.2 Employment of Female Nautical Graduates

As of January 2014, 255 women students (out of the 356 recruits) have graduated under the auspices of the WSP at SMU. This indicates a completion rate of 72 %. Indeed, a great expectation has been placed on these female students. Unfortunately, the reality is very different. Very few female graduates from the programme have been engaged in seafaring professions. The most recent head count of women seafarers in navigation is virtually a handful, at six (to be discussed later in the paper).

Why? A range of problems are to be addressed. First of all, it was the resistance of the ship owners and shipping managers that has been identified as the greatest problem for the female graduates to find seafaring posts. Most of the female students have reported difficulties in finding jobs with shipping companies after graduation from the SMU, in spite of the strong support from the Nautical School at the SMU (this will be further discussed later in the paper). Besides, the unexpected competition in job hunting was also a problem. This problem has not only prevented these women from finding seafaring jobs, but also blocked their way in finding the posts they thought they had been trained for. Many of the female students have indeed applied for posts as VTS operators. However, the VTS operators are government official positions. Only those who pass the national civil service examination can apply for these positions. In China, the admission to government civil servant posts is extremely competitive. According to the report by the SMU's Employment Guidance Centre, only two female students have landed posts as VTS operators in Zhenjiang port.

Furthermore, the low rate of completion of training is also part of the problem. Among the total 255 graduates, only 32 students have completed all the training requirements, passed the final exams and obtained their certificates as qualified seafarers. The number of women who have regularly worked on board ships is actually no more than six, as noted above. Most of the female graduates recruited by the WSP have actually found land-based jobs in shipping companies, government agencies, port facilities and so on. Figure 2 indicates the distribution of employment directions of female nautical graduates from the SMU since 2000.

The above figures show that only a handful of the female graduates are engaged in seafaring. Many, however, have found posts in various sectors of the maritime industry, as VTS operators, pilots, PSC inspectors, ship agents, ship brokers, freight forwarders and so on. A closer examination would find, even for the six women seafarers, that their employment conditions are different from the conditions for 'standard' seafarers, that is, male seafarers. First, these women seafarers are all

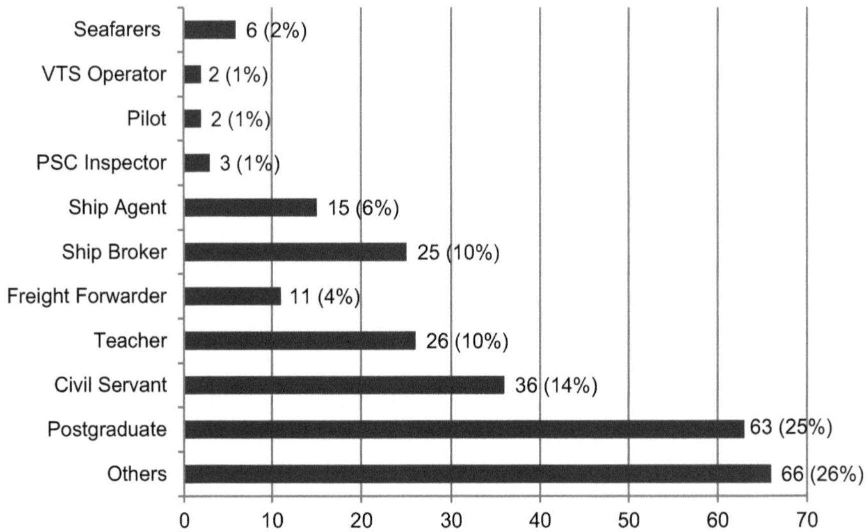

Fig. 2 Distribution of employment sectors of female nautical graduates (2000–2013)

employees in the SMU, rather than in a trading shipping company. Although they have registered as qualified seafarers, they all have another status as lecturers in the Merchant Shipping School. They have been working on board regularly, but that is just to maintain and renew their certificates, the same as many male lecturers in the School. Secondly, unlike most seafarers who work on board merchant ships, these women seafarers often only work on training ships. Their work and living environment, the relationships of the crew members and so on, are different from that aboard merchant ships. Thirdly, similar to their predecessors, the 'heroines' in the 1960s/1970s, some of them have been 'drafted' to perform duties primarily for national prestige. For instance, two of these women have been placed on board of the well-known scientific research ship '*Xue Long*' (Snow Dragon) and navigated through the Antarctic and Arctic. These expeditions make them very famous in China and they receive honourable distinctions.

In spite of all these problems, recruiting female nautical students has become one unique feature of the SMU, bringing it honour, respect and good reputation. This is well-known in the Chinese maritime industry, and the SMU has received both applause and criticism. Many people consider that the SMU has made a historic breakthrough by regularly recruiting female nautical students for so many years. The general perception is that the WSP not only contributes to the improvement of gender equality, but also helps more women to participate in the seafaring profession (Xie 2013). On the other hand, the SMU has also been criticized as having encouraged female students to study a course which does not offer a bright employment prospect. As an instructor of SMU explained in the interview in the summer of 2013:

> We have to admit that those female nautical graduates do not have good employment prospects. Therefore, the majority of them have to participate in professions which are not relevant to maritime. Accordingly, the nautical knowledge they have studied would become totally useless in their daily work. I always tell my students to learn not only nautical knowledge, but also as much other knowledge as possible. Otherwise, they do not have competitiveness to find a job on land. Therefore, we have received various criticism and complaints, and we have also been suggested to cancel the WSP programme. (Interview WSF01-SMU 2013)

This interview echoes almost the same words in Zhao's interview, conducted with a number of senior lecturers in the same School at the start of the WSP at SMU, 14 years ago. The Head of School shared his concerns about the prospects of his female students' future employment as he said:

> This is our first time to train women as deck officers, on a trial basis. But, we must be responsible for these girls. We must make sure that what they learn from us will be useful when looking for jobs in the labour market after graduation. So, we have tailor-made their curriculum, and they are required to take double courses. This means, while they register with us to do nautical studies, they also need to take a lot of other courses, such as business management, finance and so on. This is to guarantee that these girls would be able to find jobs in another sector, if they can't find ships to sail. We are fully aware that shipping companies may not welcome women aboard. (Interview WSF02-SMU 2013)

This is disappointing, as it clearly indicates a serious lack of progress regarding women's participation in seafaring, if not in shipping as a whole. The situation remains largely the same today as it was 14 years ago.

5.3 *Motivations to Become Seafarers*

Why have these young women decided to join the seafarers training? An investigation was conducted among 70 female nautical students of the SMU in 2013, trying to find the answer. According to this study, these female students have reported several main reasons for them to choose to join the training. The expectation for higher income has been listed at the top of their motivations. In China, compared with many jobs on land, working at sea usually offers good pay, although Chinese seafarers' wages are amongst the lowest when compared internationally (Alderton et al. 2004). Secondly, there is fierce competition in the Chinese college entrance examination, in particular for popular majors such as IT, finance, investment management and business studies. By contrast, nautical studies are an unusual speciality, and there are not so many students competing for entrance. More importantly, seafaring has long lost its popularity with young people in coastal cities and provinces since the mid-1990s. Maritime study therefore has much less competition, hence it is more attractive to some applicants, especially those from rural areas. Thirdly, the tuition fees for nautical studies are much lower due to the subsidies provided by the government, as an incentive to attract more applicants. The seafaring training course is therefore particularly preferable for many students from poor families in inland rural provinces. It is worth noting that two other

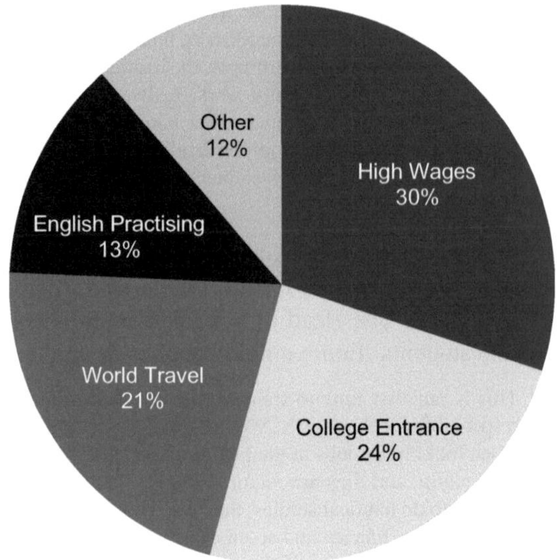

Fig. 3 Major reasons for choosing nautical studies among female students (2013)

motivations, 'free world travel' and 'opportunities to practise English' are also reported as important factors in attracting for these young women. Figure 3 presents the identified major motivations when these female students decided to choose the course of nautical studies.

Caution must be taken when interpreting the data here. The survey was conducted amongst the young women students who did not actually have experiences of working at sea. So, the reported motivations such as 'higher wages', and 'free travel (to see the world)', are based more on perception or even imagination, rather than real knowledge about the sea.

5.4 Attitudes Towards Seafaring as an Occupation

The attitudes towards seafaring as an occupation also vary among these female students. Surprisingly, the above-mentioned investigation also indicates that there is a high proportion of female students holding positive attitudes towards seafaring as a profession. Figure 4 indicates the different attitudes towards seafaring as an occupation among the same female students. The majority of them (78 %) were willing to choose seafaring as an occupation if they had the opportunity. Only a very small proportion of students (9 %) had negative attitudes towards seafaring as a profession.

Several reasons contribute to such an overwhelmingly positive attitude towards seafaring as a profession. Firstly, with the rapid development of technology and the high level of automation on board today's ocean-going ships, seafaring as a profession no longer requires intensive labour or physical strength. Most women

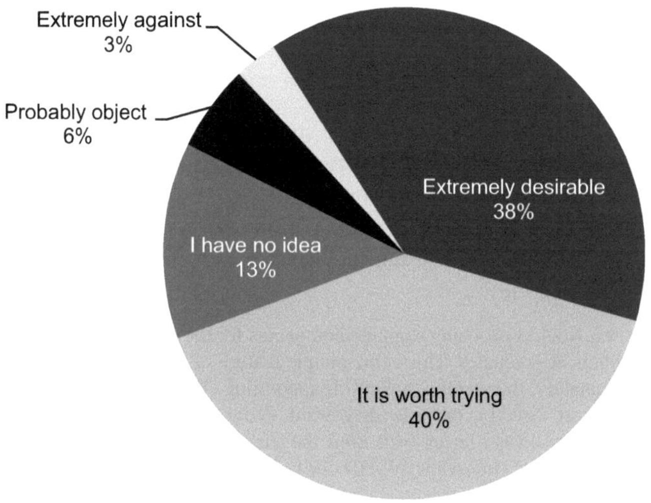

Fig. 4 Attitudes towards seafaring as an occupation among female nautical students (2013)

are physically and intelligently strong enough to perform the duties on board as deck officers. Secondly, nowadays, college graduates in China are facing extremely strong competition in finding job opportunities. The problem is even worse for female nautical students, who do not have much competitive advantage to get a job on land. Therefore, a seafaring occupation would be a good choice for them. Thirdly, in recent years, the SMU have been very active in promoting women seafarers, placing them in prominent positions. These promotional activities may help convince the female students that women are more likely to be successful on board than men. A 20-year-old female nautical student explained in the interview in the summer:

> I would like to work on board as a seafarer if I have the opportunity. The majority of my female classmates have the same aspiration as me. We think it is very cool to stand on the bridge wearing a uniform and with binoculars in hand. Furthermore, we can travel to many places without any cost. We have read the stories of the women seafarers in our university. They set brilliant examples for us and inspire us very much. However, we know that very few shipping companies are willing to employ female seafarers. We hope they open more positions for us. (Interview WSF03-SMU 2013)

While the reason to choose nautical studies varies, a seafaring occupation remains very popular among female students. As a matter of fact, many of them expressed very strong desires to work on board ships. Therefore, the fact that more recruitment opportunities should be made for female students after their graduation, is of great importance.

5.5 Shipping Companies' Attitudes Towards Recruiting Women Seafarers

Despite the efforts made by the female students, as well as the SMU, Chinese shipping companies are still very conservative in recruiting women seafarers. Most female nautical graduates are even unable to find a shipping company for their graduation practice. The SMU has made various efforts to promote female graduates' employment opportunities, but the effect is very limited. A lecturer in SMU explained in the interview:

> Every year, we would visit many shipping companies for the employment opportunities of our female nautical graduates. This is the unique feature of the SMU, so we want to do it better. Unfortunately, the result is always disappointing. The shipping companies seldom reject our request directly, because they want to take in more male graduates from us. However, they always let us wait until the girls give up their hope and find other land-based alternatives. (Interview WSF04-SMU 2013)

Why are shipping companies unwilling to recruit women seafarers? There are many factors contributing to shipping companies' negative action in recruiting women seafarers. Firstly, the supply of male seafarers in China is sufficient to meet the demand of shipping companies. Although sometimes they experience a shortage of senior officers, the companies can relieve the shortage by temporarily increasing seafarers' wages, hence attracting more (male) seafarers or as an incentive for the existing officers to stay at sea longer. Secondly, having women seafarers on board is considered to possibly lead to higher costs for shipping companies. The Maritime Labour Convention 2006 (ILO 2006a) and other international conventions, have prescribed special requirements for women seafarers, such as separate sleeping rooms and bathrooms. In addition, ship owners may have to provide women seafarers with women-specific materials and supplies such as sanitary towels and family planning pills. Therefore, most ship owners are reluctant to employ women seafarers that may cost them a bit more. Thirdly, the number of qualified women seafarers is too small for shipping companies to recruit competent women seafarers regularly as a normal practice. Besides, in the eye of many ship owners and shipping managers, "women seafarers would bring about extra troubles for crew management on board..... The management of an all-male-crew is much easier than to handle a mixed-gender crew," as a senior crewing manager in a major state-owned ship management company explained in the interview. He went further to say that:

> In recent years, we have received many suggestions to recruit female nautical graduates. Some suggestions come from high-ranking leaders of the SMU. We have discussed this matter at internal meetings many times. However, the proposal of recruiting female seafarers is always objected by the majority of meeting members. The primary reason is that no one wants to take the responsibility to make a decision. We do not know what may happen if a women is working on board among a group of male seafarers. We have heard some incidents in some other shipping companies which were associated with women seafarers on board. We do not want to make the same mistakes. (Interview WSF05-SMU 2013)

Indeed, shipping companies expressed concerns, as they believe that 'women seafarers at sea sometimes may also cause troubles and inconveniences to other male seafarers.' They reported, "(W)hen the crew members are male only, the relationship between crew members are relatively pure and simple. The relations may change significantly when a woman joins the group. In addition, many inconveniences may occur because these male seafarers have to share the same space with women." These concerns were further reported by a 36-year-old third engineer who shared his experience and opinion in the interview,

> I have once worked with a Singapore female seafarer, and she is the second officer. Before the lady joined us, everything on board was fine and peaceful. However, after her coming, many things changed, and troubles occurred. For example, all crew shared the same laundry room. We normally put the washed clothes on the clothes lines in the laundry room with heating facility. However, the lady always put her underwear together with ours. Many colleagues reported that they felt nervous and uncomfortable about that. Furthermore, we could no longer strip to the waist in the common rooms. In addition, afterwards two senior officers were jealous of each other because of the lady. Therefore, the matter was reported to the crewing manager as an incident, and she was called back to the company immediately. (Interview WSF06-SMU 2013)

This 'incident' suggests a ship culture very unfriendly to women seafarers. The problem was primarily with the attitudes and the behaviours of some male crew members. Ironically, it was the woman seafarer that got the punishment.

6 Prospects of Women Seafarers in China: A Discussion

The evidence discussed in this paper clearly indicates that there is still a long way to go before Chinese women seafarers can enjoy fair treatment and have fair employment opportunities on board. The Chinese government has implemented a series of national laws and regulations to protect women's employment rights. For example, since 1992, China has implemented the Law on Protection of Women's Rights of the PRC (LPWR 1992). According to Article 21 and Article 22, Chinese women are entitled to the same right to work as men. In addition, an employer should not refuse to employ women, nor to set additional restrictions for women on account of gender difference. The same provisions have been reemphasised in a number of other laws and regulations, for example, in Article 13 of the Chinese Labour Law (CLL) 1995 and Article 27 of the Chinese Employment Promotion Law 2008.

Although there is no legislation explicitly against women's participation in seafaring and other traditionally male-dominant sectors of the economy, there are a number of regulations which in effect restrict women's employment opportunity. For example, according to Article 59 of the Chinese Labour Law, women should avoid working in underground mining or other work with Grade IV physical intensity.[5] Article 60 of the CLL makes a further restriction by noting that menstruating women should be prevented from working in a place with high altitude,

[5] Grade IV physical intensity means within 8 h the average energy consumption of a labourer reaches 2,700 calories and the net labour time reaches 370 min

low temperature or cold water, or other work with Grade III physical intensity.[6] In addition, women must have special protection during menstruation, pregnancy, childbirth and maternity periods. Although intended to protect women's rights and interests, these provisions, in practice, tend to deter many employers from recruiting female workers, including women seafarers. One senior recruiting manager in a major shipping company explained his company's recruitment policy and practice as follows:

> If we recruit women seafarers, we have to consider a series of issues, including women's physical labour conditions, women's physiological condition and their maternity requirements. We know that women have equal employment rights. According to the Chinese Labour Law, we have the responsibility to provide equal employment opportunities for women. However, we are entitled to reject women's applications based on the restriction provisions in law, and we can say that our rejection is to protect their legal rights under the Chinese law. (Interview WSF07-SMU 2013)

The 'rationale' given by this shipping manager is largely representative of the attitudes in the industry (Li 2012). There is, therefore, much to improve in the Chinese legal system to enable and empower women's participation in shipping and seafaring in China.

7 Conclusion

Working on board ships is vastly different from that in land-based industries. The relevant provisions must take into account the characteristics of work conducted by women seafarers. Furthermore, although many provisions state that women have equal employment rights with men, these provisions lack details and are too general for enforcement. To ensure women seafarers can benefit from the law, more specific provisions should be stipulated. Meanwhile, punitive measures should be available to ensure that it is not easy for employers to violate these provisions.

On the other hand, the fact that only a limited number of women seafarers are available in the labour market, is another factor which restricts their employment opportunities. Although, at the global level, the number of women seafarers is increasing (Belcher et al. 2003), women tend to be scattered in different ships. In most cases, there is only one female working among a group of male seafarers. Under this circumstance, the woman is extremely isolated, hence more vulnerable to sexual harassment or other kinds of serious threats. If women seafarers are on board as a group, they may help each other and may be able to defend their rights together. In addition, shipping companies are often reluctant to change their crewing practice for one female seafarer. However, if there are a group of women

[6] Grade III physical intensity means within 8 h the average energy consumption of a labourer reaches 1,764 calories and the net labour time reaches 350 min.

seafarers at their disposal, it is expected that they are willing to change their 'manning' strategy.

In addition, the maritime industry needs more incentives to employ women seafarers. Under the current legal environment, shipping companies do not have enough incentive to recruit women aboard. In their view, women seafarers on board can only bring about more troubles for crew management, including for instance, sexual harassment, assault or other abuses. On the other hand, employing women seafarers implies additional cost for the shipping company. According to international standards, a ship with women seafarers on board should be equipped with special facilities and supplies. Shipping companies generally care more for profit. They usually do not need to take women into consideration unless they suffer from a serious shortage of seafaring labour from the conventional sources, that is, the male and foreign seafarers.

Therefore, it would be insufficient just to appeal that women seafarers should have access to more employment opportunities. Radical measures must be taken to facilitate change; change in attitude, behaviour, policy and practice. Specifically, efforts must be made in the three aspects in order to improve the conditions for women seafarers in China. Firstly, gender equality is an important indicator of social justice of the society. The government should take pragmatic actions to promote employment opportunities for women seafarers. For example, the government can provide incentives for shipping companies by offering preferential taxation. Secondly, society can call for trade unions, social communities and organizations to provide more support for women seafarers' employment. On one hand, women seafarers should be provided with adequate training to ensure they are sufficiently competent and can take on all the responsibilities on board. On the other hand, there should be a mechanism that shipping companies are provided with financial support for employing women seafarers. This support is to make up the additional cost incurred because of employing women on board. Thirdly, the maritime industry should establish its Corporate Social Responsibility (CSR), which promotes gender equality in the profession. Shipping companies that are active in employing women seafarers should have the entitlement for better reputation and prestige. As a result, they will have more opportunities to promote better business than those who ignore their corporate social responsibilities, including fair recruitment and treatment of women seafarers.

References

Abbott, D., Zheng, F., & Meredith, W. (1995). An evolving redefinition of the fatherhood role in the People's Republic of China. In M. Das & V. Gupta (Eds.), *Gender roles and family analysis* (pp. 191–202). New Delhi: M D Publications Pvt Ltd.

Alderton, T., Bloor, M., Kahveci, E., Lane, T., Sampson, H., Thomas, M., et al. (2004). *The global seafarer: Living and working conditions in a globalized industry*. Geneva: International Labour Office.

Appleby, J. C. (2013). *Women and English piracy, 1540–1720: Partners and victims of crime*. Woodbridge: The Boydell Press.
Belcher, P., Sampson, H., Thomas, M., Veiga, J., & Zhao, M. (2003). *Women seafarers: Global employment policies and practices*. Geneva: International Labour Office.
Hinsch, B. (2011). *Women in early imperial China*. Plymouth: Rowman & Littlefield Publishing Group, Inc.
ILO. (2001). *The impact on seafarers' living and working conditions of changes in the structure of shipping industry: Report for discussion at the 29th Session of the Joint Maritime Commission*. Geneva: International Labour Office.
ILO. (2003). Women seafarers: Fighting against the tide? As on land, so by sea: Women join the ranks of seafarers. http://www.ilo.org/global/publications/magazines-and-journals/world-of-work-magazine/articles/WCMS_081322/lang-en/index.htm. Accessed 20 Apr 2014.
ILO. (2006a). *Maritime Labour Convention, 2006*. Genève: Author.
ILO. (2006b). *Resolutions adopted by the International Labour Conference at its 94th (Maritime) Session*. Geneva: International Labour Office.
IMO. (1995). *The 1995 amendments to the International Convention on Standards of Training, Certification and Watchkeeping for Seafarers, 1978*. London: Author.
IMO. (2011). *STCW including 2010 Manila amendments: STCW Convention and STCW Code*. London: Author.
IMO. (2013). Women in the maritime industry. http://www.imo.org/MediaCentre/HotTopics/women/Pages/default.aspx. Accessed 18 Jan 2014.
Li, J. (2012). The gloomy prospect for female students in nautical studies. Resource document. Renren Net. http://blog.renren.com/blog/249955840/797881994. Accessed 7 Sep 2014.
Li, S. (2010). The retrospect of new China's seafarers' export business. *China Water Transportation, 11*, 14–15.
Liang, B. (2009). Heroines in China: The narrative of three women seafarers. *Ocean World, 11*, 23–24.
LPWR. (1992). The law on protection of women's rights. http://www.china.com.cn/chinese/zhuanti/jtbl/1058275.htm. Accessed 23 Jan 2014.
Lu, M. (2004). The awakening of Chinese women and women's movements in the early twentieth century. In J. Tao, B. Zheng, & S. L. Mow (Eds.), *Holding up half the sky: Chinese women past, present, and future* (pp. 55–70). New York: Feminist Press at the City University of New York.
Magramo, M., & Eler, G. (2012). Women seafarers: Solution to shortage of competent officers? *International Journal on Marine Navigation and Safety of Sea Transportation, 6*(3), 397–400.
MOT. (2013). The opening of Chinese Seafarers' Conference 2013 in Shanghai. http://www.moc.gov.cn/zhuzhan/jiaotongxinwen/xinwenredian/201306xinwen/201306/t20130626_1438603.html. Accessed 22 Apr 2014.
Nie, J. (2011). *Medical ethics in China: A transcultural interpretation*. Oxon: Routledge.
Sheng, W., & Ke, B. (2009). Yafu, Wang: The first women chief engineer in new China. *World Shipping, 1*, 12–13.
SINA. (2009). The video recording the first group female nautical students on training ship. http://video.sina.com.cn/v/b/21134575-1237213390.html. Accessed 22 Apr 2014.
SOHU. (2003). The first group female nautical students on training ship. http://news.sohu.com/62/78/news207187862.shtml. Accessed 22 Apr 2014.
Tansey, P. (2000). Women on board – Ten years of the IMO Women in Development Programme. Recourse document. IMO. http://www.imo.org/blast/mainframe.asp?topic_id = 406&doc_id = 1082. Accessed 23 Jan 2014.
UN. (1985). World Conference to Review and Appraise the Achievements of the United Nations Decade for Women: Equality, Development and Peace. http://www.un-documents.net/nfl-intr.htm. Accessed 23 Jan 2014.

Wang, T. (2011). Towards a proper relation between men and women: Beyond masculinism and feminism. In R. Fan (Ed.), *The Renaissance of Confucianism in contemporary China* (pp. 91–108). New York: Springer.
White, N. I. (1964). *The Frank C. Brown collection of North Carolina folklore*. Durham: Duke University Press.
Xie, L. (2013). Very few Chinese women seafarers. http://www.matouwang.com/news/detail.htm?id=1325. Accessed 22 Jan 2014.
Zhao, M. (2002). The consequences of China's socialist market economy for seafarers. *Work, Employment and Society: A Journal of the British Sociological Association, 16*(1), 171–183.
Zhao, M., Tyzack, M., Anderson, R., & Onoakpovike, E. (2014). Women in English fisheries: Roles, contributions, barriers and prospects. In J. Urquhart, T. G. Acott, D. Symes, & M. Zhao (Eds.), *Social issues in sustainable fisheries management* (pp. 233–254). Dordrecht: MARE Publication Series.
Zhuo, D. (2008). The story of old pictures: The first group of women seafarers in new China. *China Maritime, 3*, 99.

Sustainable Development Issues in Shipping: Women, the Under-Represented Human Resource

Colin J. Stevenson

Abstract This paper questions why there are relatively low numbers of women in the shipping industry, at a time when there is still a critical shortage of seafarers in general. This should provide an ideal opportunity for more women to enter the industry. The reasons why this is apparently not the case, are examined. For the purpose of this paper, the main reference is to the shortage of officers in the deep-sea trades. Received wisdom is that the industry is still not suitable for women, with the stereotype of a seafarer being male, when other industries have moved on from this perception. This gender stereotyping, together with widespread discrimination in many sections of the seagoing industry, is a broad concern. Several aspects of the role of a seafarer are examined, amongst which will be the satisfaction of human needs as applied to women, the attitude of employers to women, and barriers that might be an impediment to choosing this career. Also suggested is the possibility that, because of insufficient information about the opportunities, women's perceptions might in themselves be creating an imaginary barrier. The final part of the paper makes some suggestions that might be implemented as a means of increasing women at sea and addressing the imbalance of genders on board ship.

Keywords Attitudes • Barriers • Career • Human needs • Stereotyping • Women

1 Introduction

The International Maritime Organization (IMO) and International Labour Organization (ILO), have both passed resolutions supporting promoting women in the maritime sector. Resolution 14 of the IMO's International Convention on Standards of Training, Certification and Watchkeeping for Seafarers 1978 (IMO 2011) and a resolution adopted by the ILO at its International Labour Conference 2006, refer (ILO 2006).

IMO and ILO can implement the international conventions, but they have no authority to impose regulations relating to employment, beyond the requirement by the applicable conventions for the qualifications on board.

C.J. Stevenson (✉)
C J Maritime Training and Consultancy, Lee-on-the-Solent, UK
e-mail: cjmaritime@yahoo.co.uk

© Springer-Verlag Berlin Heidelberg 2015
M. Kitada et al. (eds.), *Maritime Women: Global Leadership*, WMU Studies in Maritime Affairs 3, DOI 10.1007/978-3-662-45385-8_19

References to "the maritime industry" often imply that this comprises a single entity, rather than a number of national and international companies competing commercially in international trade. These companies also compete for seafarers internationally, in a pool that is insufficient to supply the numbers required to man all ships. This makes regulating the industry, beyond international convention, impossible.

This paper is directed predominantly toward the problem of why there are so few women at sea on foreign-going vessels and how the numbers might be increased. The discussion applies mainly to the shortage of women officers in the deep-sea trades. The cruise industry employs a significant number of women at sea, but these are mainly service providers for passengers, hairdressers, shopkeepers, etc. The contention here is that women on foreign-going vessels are faced with challenges that would not apply to the service providers on cruise ships. The offshore industry does not have the same shortfall of officers, as it is attractive to foreign-going officers, mainly because of higher salaries and better leave allowances. As the offshore industry has grown, so the movement from deep sea to offshore, has exacerbated the shortage on foreign-going vessels.

It is a recognised fact that there is a considerable shortfall of officers at sea, as shown by successive updates to the BIMCO/ISF Manpower Study (BIMCO and ISF 2010). The low numbers of women at sea are difficult to explain at a time when the manpower shortage opens up greater opportunities to take up a seafaring career. It would appear to be the ideal time for a young woman to go to sea, with shipping/manning companies finding it more and more difficult to attract suitable candidates to the career. On-board conditions are now very good, with single en-suite accommodation, air conditioning and the availability of regular communication with family and friends via the internet.

This paper examines the possible issues and barriers that might be impacting upon the comparatively low numbers of women at sea today, and the consequential loss of this valuable human resource.

By investigating what would attract women to the career, and what would satisfy their needs, and by understanding the actual and perceived barriers, it might be possible to provide an employment package that would attract greater numbers of women. The provision of a more attractive working environment can only aid in the recruitment and retention of women.

2 Current Awareness

The industry has still not learnt the lessons of the past. In the maritime industry, when freight rates are low, the first action of many employers is to stop training, relying on poaching trained officers from others. This has always been the way but, with the current shortage of trained seafarers and fewer people entering the industry, it has become more difficult to rely on attracting trained seafarers from others. It is also difficult to identify alternative sources of seafarers, although current wisdom predicts that Africa might become the next major source of seafarer supply.

The lack of women at sea has not gone unnoticed. The Seafarers International Research Centre's (SIRC) Symposium of 2003 in Cardiff, presented some research findings that addressed these problems in several papers, in particular the article of Thomas (2004). This paper is based upon research into just this very topic, the lack of numbers of women seafarers. There are several quotes in her paper that illustrate the negative mind-set of some, possibly many, shipping companies to employing women on ships. However, there are some very positive comments to counterbalance this negativity. In the same year, the ILO published a study, again highlighting the shortage of women at sea (Belcher et al. 2003). The problem is also recognised in the Philippines, as shown by an article in Transnav (Magramo and Eler 2012).

Research published in 1999 examined officer retention in the maritime industry (Stevenson 1999). An extensive questionnaire was the primary data collection vehicle and a total of 809 usable returns were received. The number of women completing the questionnaire was negligible, so it was impossible to extract any meaningful results from the data. The suggestion here is that a similar research project, aimed specifically at women at sea and to those considering a career at sea, might help understanding of women's needs for a career.

In spite of the recognition of the problem, and the IMO and ILO resolutions, the number of women attracted to a seafaring career remains very low. What is even more remarkable is the lack of meaningful research examining this issue. The problem has been identified, but little has been put in place to improve the situation.

3 Satisfaction of Human Needs

In the shipping industry, the shipowner is profit-motivated and the seafarer is satisfaction motivated, and it is the balancing of these two apparently contradictory factors, that must be achieved to aid recruitment and to improve retention. According to Roy (1990), in his work on social observations and needs theories, there is a close association between satisfaction and social harmony and this is an imperative to the efficiency and safe running of a ship. It is therefore necessary to identify those factors that are of the greatest importance to those at sea. Failure to understand these factors will not assist in improving the numbers of women attracted to the industry. This applies not only to their job satisfaction, but that of the satisfaction of their human needs. Is it possible that one of the main reasons that women do not choose a seafaring career, is the perception that their needs might not be met in the male-dominated environment that is shipboard life?

Most modern proponents of Needs Theories have based their initial thinking upon the Step Hierarchy of Needs (Maslow 1970). Moving from the lowest step, Survival Needs, through Safety Needs, Belongingness and Love Needs, Esteem Needs to the top step, Self-Actualisation, his proposition was that the lower step, or need, must be first satisfied before moving on to the next step.

In a review of many studies, Wahba and Bridwell (1976), came to the conclusion that there is no clear evidence that human needs can be classified in five distinct categories, or that these categories are structured in a specific hierarchy. They do agree that there is some evidence for the existence of possibly two types of needs, namely maintenance and growth needs. The former include Maslow's first two steps and the latter, his top three steps.

Hertzberg (1966) in his research enumerated 'Motivators' and 'Hygiene' factors, stating that satisfaction of these is necessary to provide complete job satisfaction. There is some similarity between this theory and that of Maslow, with his step hierarchy of needs. More recent researchers have found, as with Maslow, that there is broad agreement on the existence of these factors, but that they vary from person to person and group to group. In the context here, there might be a wide variance between genders.

Galtung (1990) indicated that there is a clear difference between material satisfiers and non-material satisfiers which, if carried over to the ship and the seafarer, could be on the one hand for example, the difference between provision of leisure facilities, and on the other the choice of sailing with seafarers from one's own country of origin or domicile, or as a woman sailing with other women.

Mitchell (1990) suggested that the existence of a variable hierarchy gives rise to two fundamental questions. Firstly, does a needs' hierarchy vary from person to person or group to group according to variations in age, gender, education, culture, etc., or is it fixed and universal? This is one of the few references to gender amongst these researchers.

A study of shipboard Deck Officers (Stevenson 1999) refers to Aspiration Needs which are defined in the research as: "Those factors, the satisfaction of which an individual considers necessary and indispensable to life, happiness, success and self-fulfilment." The findings of the research took a further step in the theory of human needs, by showing clearly that Aspiration Needs are not fixed and universal for all. The notional division of Aspiration Needs into many different classifications or groups, as postulated by many researchers such as Lederer et al. (1980), Silver (1987) and Chevalier (1990), is superseded by the identification from the research that they are not found in a specific rigid hierarchy, but may change from individual to individual and are influenced by both the age of the individual and by their nationality. Again, with reference to this paper, they might equally be influenced by gender.

However, what was identified in the research is that there is a further division of Aspiration Needs, not in the way that past researchers have classified them, but as 'Professional' and 'Personal', and showed that the first remain constant within the national group regardless of age, and that the second are influenced by both age and nationality. It is therefore a reasonable assumption that these might also be influenced by gender. The understanding that some individual factors of Aspiration Needs may be considered as either 'Professional' or 'Personal', provides the employer with valuable knowledge that might assist in the composition of multi-national and mixed-gender crews, when formulating employment contracts.

The proposition here, is that it is entirely possible that there might be a measurable difference in needs between genders. If this is true, then by identifying those Aspiration Needs that are applicable to women, this might be reflected in the employment package offered by an employer, by providing the satisfiers to these identified needs. Research into the needs of women at sea might provide valuable information in understanding the current disincentives to women in pursuing the career and so assist in recruitment.

4 Research

Developing technology and the many recent requirements of international law, have changed and expanded the job function of an officer on board ship. The job of officers at sea has evolved more and more into a multi-functional job, requiring multi-tasking.

A research study from the United States (Igalhalikar et al. 2014) investigated human brain connectivity and this confirmed many long-held stereotypes about behavioural differences between the sexes. It stated that men "see and do" while "women are more intuitive and collaborative". It also states, "A man is more likely superior at learning and performing a single task, while women have better memories and are more collaborative in terms of arriving at a solution that works for everybody". The conclusion is that men are better at focusing and women at multitasking. A possible extension to these findings might be that women are less confrontational and would possibly make better team players; if this can be confirmed by research, then there is a strong suggestion that employing more women on board ship might reduce interpersonal conflict and by extension improve efficiency. This study gives an indication of the advantages that women might bring to the role of a ship's officer.

Research carried out at SIRC for the ILO (Belcher et al. 2003) looked at 17 training institutions with a combined student body of 6,518 of which 647 were women, approximately 10 % and of these, only 33 % enrolled in engineering courses. This appears to indicate that the perception that women cannot carry out the engineering job function at sea is still very much a perception held by those in training. Another finding from this study stated that a number of lecturers were unenthusiastic in teaching women or recommending a career at sea to them. Other findings included; some men had problems taking orders from a woman, employers stated that women performed better than men, and that prejudice runs through every stage of the recruitment and training process.

The 10 % of women in this study does not reflect the percentage currently employed at sea, and the reason for this was not addressed in the study. It is possible that there must be an even greater drop-out rate for women trainees than that for men, but whether this is so, or at what stage this occurs, is not known. Research into this issue would be useful to further understanding of the problem.

5 Barriers

Family Life The main problem that exists for all those that go to sea, is that of living a life totally different from that in a normal shore-based occupation. This assumes a greater significance for women, relating to family and children.

It is commonly accepted by training officers that an employee staying with a company for 5–7 years will make a minimal return on training investment (ROI). If this is so, then a female cadet joining at 17/18 will be qualified at the officer-of-the-watch level by the time they are 20, and a further five years' service will bring them to 25. Research from the University of Southampton (Bhrolchain and Beaujouen 2012) found that the average age for UK and French women to have their first child is 28. Add to this, the figures from the UK Office of National Statistics (2012) that 49 % of women giving birth in the UK were age 30 and over, it would appear to indicate that the family barrier is not insurmountable for women wishing to embark upon a seafaring career.

Cross-Cultural Issues in a Multi-National Crew This is definitely a real barrier and disincentive to women going to sea. There appears to be a serious problem relating to multi-national crews, mainly because of the attitude toward women of some nationalities informed by their own cultures. Young female cadets relate horrendous stories of how they have been treated on board. They are often treated as second-class citizens, on a level with the non-officer members of the crew.

It is unlikely that there will be any immediate changes in the attitudes toward women in some cultures and this is just something that employers will have to accept. However, this barrier might be mitigated by more selective personnel appointments and taking care not to send women on board vessels crewed with nationals that have a cultural anti-female attitude. The work by Hofstede (1980) might serve as a useful guide to human resource management in the context of harmony on board ship.

Harassment It is often quoted and seen in research papers that women can be disruptive on board ship. The men see them as targets, again excluding passenger ships and ferries, and there is often only a single woman on board, or at best two or three.

Reported instances of males attempting to access female accommodation, banging on doors, constant ringing of the telephone and regular sexual innuendos, are examples of unacceptable behaviour in a civilised society and is symptomatic of a group that has a disproportionate representation of one sex within the group, or in this case, crew. Instances of this behaviour would be markedly reduced if there were a larger representation of women in the crew, another indication of the advantages of employing more women on board ship. Employers must see the dual advantage of targeting a larger recruitment pool and at the same time reducing this disruptive anti-social behaviour.

If the behaviour mentioned above is rife, then it is largely a managerial fault on the part of the company, master and senior officers. Clear guidelines to all, as to what is acceptable with regard to behaviour in a mixed-gender crew, would radically reduce these incidents. It should be made clear to any women having reservations about selecting a career at sea, that they do not have to accept sexual harassment and it is the duty of the company and the master to make it quite clear to all that any such behaviour would not be tolerated.

Perceived Barriers These are far more difficult to evaluate as factors discouraging women to go to sea. However, it would be an interesting area for research to find if the perceptions of the life understood by women career-seekers are in fact creating barriers that do not exist. The perception of life at sea is often created at the interview stage, when the interviewer is less than honest about the career, or less than enthusiastic about recruiting women. The idea promoted by some recruitment officers of going to sea to see the world is still frequently articulated as an incentive to join, when the truth is far from this. Fast turn-around times in port, reduced crew numbers, and security issues in many ports, are just some of the barriers to being able to get ashore in port today.

Recruitment must be an honest process and it is possible that some recruitment officers have not experienced life at sea themselves and might have little idea of the actualities of life on board ship. This is particularly pertinent to women applicants, as they will already possess many more reservations than males about the career.

It is also possible that the opportunities for a seagoing career are not widely enough known to women. Many are still unaware of this career choice and, if they are aware, they are dissuaded from following it by the perception that it is not a career for women. This can be put down in part to the preconceived reservations that are still held by shipping companies and training/recruitment officers with regard to having women on their ships. Until employers put their preconceived ideas aside this will continue to act as a disincentive.

6 The Current Situation

There is little doubt that there have been some positives in shipping companies that have embraced the idea of employing women at sea. It is often quoted that women work harder than men and appear to be more committed to the job. This appears to be a result of having to convince a predominantly male-dominated crew that they are capable of doing the job as well as a man. An example of what appears to be a barrier has been overcome to the advantage of those employers that have employed women. However, in the current climate of low seafarer supply, targeting women would considerably widen the pool from which seafarers might be recruited.

The SIRC symposium in 2003 also stated that women often have a positive effect in a workplace (SIRC 2003). People that might behave in a heavily masculine way tend to temper their behaviour and language when in the presence of women.

In other words, the on-board society reflects the norm ashore if women are present on board. The opposite to this is shown by feedback from some women at sea who claim that they have had to adapt to many of the norms of male behaviour in order to be accepted. Adopting aggressive behaviour and bad language are two such examples.

The stereotype of a seafarer is still dominantly male and this is a barrier to women in choosing a career and a concern to all who believe in equal opportunities in the workplace. Employers are still not committed to the idea of women on their ships. This of course does not apply to ferries and cruise ships but, in a shipping company trading deep sea, there is a continued reluctance to accept more than a token female representation in the crew.

Equally, the actual job at sea is stereotyped as a historical fact and many employers have not moved to correct this. This has been perpetuated by the argument that women do not have the physical strength to carry out the requirements of the job on board ship. With the evolution of technology and the development of systems this is no longer an argument that can be supported.

It is apparent from feedback received that some recruitment officers have attitudes pertaining to employing women that are steeped in the stereotype mentioned earlier. They interview women with little enthusiasm or real wish to employ them and have preconceived ideas as to their value on board. They feel that because of the family issue there is little chance of a female cadet staying for long and as such, women are a risk to training investment and will have a negative effect on their training budget. It is suggested here that this is a perceived barrier brought about by negative and uninformed thinking on the part of employers.

7 Addressing the Balance

Some of the barriers that do exist can be partially mitigated by management procedures and selective appointments to a vessel. By this it is meant ensuring that one woman is not the lone female on board and that, in the case of a mixed nationality crew, she is not the only person from her country.

There are other possible avenues to explore to further address the problem and the following suggestions might assist in mitigating the problem.

All Female Crews The possibility of an all-female crew should be examined. A shipping company could use this as a recruitment tool to attract quality female applicants. By selecting applicants to be trained specifically for one or two vessels it would remove many of the concerns that might exist by those considering the career. Initially, it might be necessary to have male senior officers if there are no women in the company to fill the positions but, once the training of this specific group has commenced, in around 5 years the majority of on-board positions could be filled by these recruits. This might also be an attraction to women already qualified in the industry as many current senior women officers also suffer from male chauvinism and discrimination on board, even in senior positions.

One of the problems facing newly-qualified officers is getting employment in an industry that prefers experience. If a forward-looking shipowner elected to employ an all-women crew there would be a requirement to maintain a future supply of officers. They might recruit the estimated numbers of women required and they might be sent to a training establishment as a dedicated group. The contract could stipulate a minimum term for staying in the company on all female-crewed vessels in return for tuition fee payment and a modest stipend whilst under training. The advantages are several. The trainees would be introduced to the company culture, many of the early problems of women entrants in mixed classes at training establishments would not exist and employment at the end of the successful training period would be guaranteed.

Additionally, the satisfiers for any identified needs that differ from males might be more easily provided in both the employment package and in the provision of different or additional facilities on board ship.

Family-Operated Vessels Another possibility is to take the example of the barge crews in Europe that operate on the major rivers Maas, Rhine, Weser, Elbe, etc. These are often operated by families and maybe this could be extended to merchant vessels trading worldwide. A forward-thinking shipping company might recruit couples that both have qualifications. As far back as the 1950s some Scandinavian vessels had, for example, a male navigating officer whose wife was a stewardess. In these modern times might it be possible to employ a couple with the wife qualified as a navigator and the husband a cook? There are no obvious barriers to this being a perfectly workable employment practice. A number of couples operating the vessel seem to be a possible benefit to the company whilst reducing the on-board tensions and problems that exist with only one or two women in the crew.

8 Conclusions

The fact that there are relatively few women at sea is an established fact. Also it seems apparent that, due to the shortage of seafarers and slowly changing attitudes, the opportunity for women to go to sea has never been better. It might be possible that some of the perceived barriers might not be as important a disincentive as commonly thought.

From the lack of women taking up the career it would seem that employers have not realised that women might be a partial solution to their employment problems. In general, there has been little thought given to the needs and expectations of women in order to improve recruitment and retention. Employers need to have a better understanding of the expectations of women entrants.

The role of research cannot be emphasised too strongly. The main area for future research might be to investigate the human needs of women who are already at sea and of those planning to take up a career. The basic needs of adequate salary, safety, food and shelter are obviously supplied, but what additional provision could the employers offer to attract women to the industry? If it is possible to identify the major needs of women and their expectations in pursuing this career then this information might be beneficial in offering a different employment package and additional on-board facilities.

Changing the employment package does not necessarily mean adding costs to the employer as it might be possible to substitute satisfaction of some male needs existing in a current employment package, and identified as less important by females, by those that are essential to females.

There is without doubt an urgent need to address some of the questions raised here if the sea-going side of the industry is to attract more women to seafaring. With the continuing shortage of officers at sea now is the ideal time to take advantage of this under-represented human resource.

References

Belcher, P., Sampson, H., Thomas, M., Veiga, J., & Zhao, M. (2003). *Women seafarers: Global employment policies and practices*. Geneva: International Labour Office.

Bhrolchain, M., & Beaujouen, E. (2012). Fertility postponement is largely due to rising educational enrolment. *Population Studies, 66*(3), 311–327.

BIMCO, & ISF. (2010). *Manpower 2010 update: The worldwide demand of and supply for seafarers*. Coventry: University of Warwick.

Chevalier, M. (1990). Needs-based decision-making in conflict: Human needs theory. In J. Burton (Ed.), *Conflict: Human needs theory*. Basingstoke: Palgrave Macmillan.

Galtung, J. (1990). The basic needs approach. In J. Burton (Ed.), *Conflict: Human needs theory*. Basingstoke: Palgrave Macmillan.

Hertzberg, F. (1966). *Work and the nature of man*. Cleveland: World Publishing Company.

Hofstede, G. (1980). *Culture's consequences: International differences in work-related value*. Beverly Hills: Sage Publications.

Igalhalikar, M., Smith, A., Parker, D., Satterthwaite, T. D., Elliott, M. A., Ruparel, K., et al. (2014). Sex differences in the structural connectome of the human brain. *Proceedings of National Academy of Sciences, 111*(2), 823–828.

ILO. (2006). *Resolution II concerning the promotion of opportunities for women seafarers*. Geneva: International Labour Office.

IMO. (2011). *STCW including 2010 Manila amendments: STCW convention and STCW code*. London: Author.

Lederer, K., Galtung, J., & Antal, D. (1980). *Human needs: A contribution to the current debate*. Cambridge, MA: Oelgeschlager, Gunn & Hain.

Magramo, M., & Eler, G. (2012). Women seafarers: Solution to shortage of officers? *International Journal on Marine Navigation & Safety at Sea, 6*(3), 397–400.

Maslow, A. H. (1970). *Motivation and personality*. New York: Harper and Row.

Mitchell, C. (1990). Necessitous man and conflict resolution: More basic questions about basic human needs theory. In J. Burton (Ed.), *Conflict: Human needs theory*. Basingstoke: Palgrave Macmillan.

Roy, R. (1990). Social conflicts and needs theories: Some observations. In J. Burton (Ed.), *Conflict: Human needs theory*. Basingstoke: Palgrave Macmillan.

Silver, P. F. (1987). Job satisfaction and dissatisfaction revisited. *Educational and Psychological Research, 7*(1), 1–20.

SIRC. (2003). *Proceedings of SIRC's third symposium*. Cardiff: Cardiff University.

Stevenson, C. J. (1999). *Labour retention in a global industry: Ships' deck officers* (Doctoral dissertation). Nottingham Trent University, Nottingham.

Thomas, M. (2004). Get yourself a proper job girlie!: Recruitment, retention and women seafarers. *Maritime Policy & Management, 31*(4), 309–318.

United Kingdom Office of National Statistics. (2012). Live births in England and Wales by characteristics of mother, 2012. http://www.ons.gov.uk/ons/rel/vsob1/characteristics-of-Mother-1--england-and-wales/2012/sb-characteristics-of-mother-1--2012.html. Accessed 1 Apr 2014.

Wahba, M. A., & Bridwell, L. G. (1976). Maslow reconsidered: A review of research on the need hierarchy theory. *Organisational Behaviour and Human Performance, 15*, 212–240.

Improving the Current Regime for Ship Safety Inspections: Opportunities for Technology Research and Women Employment

Marlene Calderón, Diana Illing, Ingrid Schipperen, and Pedro Antão

Abstract The new inspection regime that entered into force in 2011, allowed the Paris Memorandum of Understanding (MOU) to change the target of inspecting 25 % of individual ships calling at each Member State, to a system based on the ship-risk profile. The latter combines a set of generic and historical factors (e.g., ship's type and age, number of deficiencies and detentions, performance of ISM companies) that assists the work of port state control inspectors. Despite those improvements, prioritising ships for safety inspection is still a challenge, not only for authorities, but also to other stakeholders such as classification societies, ship owners, managers and operators. This paper introduces the recently EU-funded project SAFEPEC—Innovative risk-based tools for ship safety inspection. It aims at decreasing the current workload on surveyors through the development of a software prototype that enables the interoperability and coherent interpretation of the different inspection data sources that are available. Additionally, SAFEPEC will develop sensor systems for long-distance monitoring, tracking of failures and collection of near-real-time data from critical ship areas, such as the hull structure and shipboard equipment. As in the entire maritime community, the area of ship inspections is male dominated, although there is a slight shift seen. A small literature review and a survey among both males and females working in the maritime world, showed that both the physical aspects of the job and the difficulties to balance work and family, might still be reasons for females to avoid this work. The new technologies developed within the SAFEPEC project can help to increase job opportunities for women in the future.

M. Calderón (✉)
Maritime and Technology Faculty, Southampton Solent University, Hampshire, UK
e-mail: marlene.calderon@solent.ac.uk

D. Illing
IHS Global SAS, South Englewood, CO, USA

I. Schipperen
TNO – Nederlandse Organisatie Voor Toegepast Natuurwetenschappelijk Onderzoek, Delft, The Netherlands

P. Antão
Glintt Inov, Global Intelligent Technologies, Lisbon, Portugal

© Springer-Verlag Berlin Heidelberg 2015
M. Kitada et al. (eds.), *Maritime Women: Global Leadership*, WMU Studies in Maritime Affairs 3, DOI 10.1007/978-3-662-45385-8_20

Keywords Gender and technology • Inspection data • Port state control • Remote surveying • Women inspectors

1 Introduction

Few studies have investigated the effectiveness of the different inspections methods applied by the stakeholders and what can be learnt or extrapolated from the inspection data gathered by them. Consequently, it is yet uncertain to what extent the current inspection regime is efficiently tackling poor quality vessels and thereby contributing to an increase of safety culture in shipping. This obviously passes for an actual reduction and/or elimination of hazardous incidents, including no-conformities, near misses and accidents.

This paper is comprised of four main sections. The first section briefly examines the improvements and challenges of the current port state control regime, namely the EU regime and Paris MOU.[1] In this way, a brief historical overview is presented to show how the system evolved since its inception in the late 1970s.

In the second section, the paper discusses the EU FP7 project SAFEPEC, that aims at improving the current port state control inspection regime, as well as individual stakeholders' practices for real-time monitoring and integration of data related to ship safety status. The term stakeholders here, applies to the EU maritime administrations responsible for ship inspection, ship owners, ship operators, shipyards, ship equipment manufacturers and research centres.

Third, the paper presents the results from a pilot questionnaire survey in which a group of maritime specialists participated. The survey was conducted in January 2014. The last section offers a reflection about how remote sensing technologies, such as those developed by SAFEPEC, would open new job opportunities to specialists, mainly women engineers and seafarers, who are now still underrepresented in the maritime world.

2 The Port State Control Regime: Improvements and Challenges

The fundamental objective of the Paris Memorandum of Understanding (MOU) is to reduce substandard shipping. The current Port State Control (PSC) regime originated in 1978 through the adoption of the Merchant Shipping Convention[2] by eight North Sea states (Özçayir 2001). Following the Amoco Cadiz accident, the demand for

[1] The Paris MOU is the organization, consisting of maritime Administrations from 27 member states (Belgium, Bulgaria, Canada, Croatia, Cyprus, Denmark, Estonia, Finland, France, Germany, Greece, Iceland, Ireland, Italy, Latvia, Lithuania, Malta, the Netherlands, Norway, Poland, Portugal, Romania, the Russian Federation, Slovenia, Spain, Sweden and the United Kingdom). They annually inspect more than 18,000 foreign ships in the Paris MoU ports.

[2] The instrument is known as the International Labour Organization (ILO) Convention No. 147.

Table 1 Historical overview of the Port State Control Regime

2014	The Tokyo MOU introduces the New Inspection Regime (NIR) for the selection of ships
2013	The Directive 2009/16/EC on port state control is amended in order to add the MLC compliance
2011	Paris MOU introduces the NIR on port state control. EU adopts the Directive 2009/16/EC on port state control
2000	The Black Sea MOU is signed for the Black sea region. The inspection quota is 15 %
1999	The Abuja MOU is signed for the West and Central Africa Region. The inspection quota is 15 %
1998	The Indian Ocean MOU is signed for the Indian Ocean Region. The inspection quota is 10 %
1997	The Mediterranean MOU is signed for the Mediterranean Region. The inspection quota is 15 %
1996	The Caribbean MOU is signed for the Caribbean Region. The inspection quota is 15 %
1995	IMO adopts Resolution A.787(19) on procedures for port state control
1994	The US launches its own Port State Control Programme and develops a risk-based boarding matrix that establishes a history of poor performance based on the identification of ships, owners, flags and classification societies. Vessels that pose the higher risks are boarded with greater frequency and have greater operational controls imposed
1993	OCIMF introduces a Ship Inspection Reporting (SIRE) scheme in an attempt to reduce the number of ship inspections carried out by its members. The Tokyo MOU is signed for the Asia-Pacific Region (Tokyo MOU). The inspection quota is 75 %
1992	The Acuerdo De Viña del Mar Agreement on port state control, also known as Latin American Agreement is signed. The inspection quota is 15 %. IMO establishes the Flag State Implementation (FSI) Subcommittee to improve governments' performance
1982	The Paris MOU is adopted and signed by the maritime authorities of 14 states. For the first time, a regular and systematic control of ships is exercised by a regional group of port states which are parties to the relevant conventions. The MOUs provide for a total number of inspections, expressed in terms of a percentage, that each of the State Party to the relevant MOU shall conduct. The Member States agree to inspect 25 % of the estimated number of individual foreign merchant ships which enter their ports during a 12 month period
1978	The Hague Memorandum of Understanding is signed by eight North Sea countries

stricter regulations increased in Europe, to the extent that in 1982, a group of 14 states agreed to apply a common regime for ship safety inspection, today known as the Paris MOU. It was aimed at overseeing the compliance with a set of International Maritime Organization (IMO) Conventions, to which the states were signatories.

The regime, considered 'interim' at the time of its implementation, has nowadays grown substantially, not only in terms of the number of regions that emulate a similar kind of agreement, but also with respect to the harmonisation of the methods applied for targeting vessels and verifying compliance with international established standards for the protection of human life, environment and businesses (Cariou et al. 2008).

Table 2 New Inspection Regime—targeting scheme used by the Paris and Tokyo MOUs

Ship performance factors	Ship age Ship type The number of past ship deficiencies The number of past ship detentions
Stakeholders performance factors	Performance of the flag of the ship Performance of the recognised organisation (RO) Performance of the company responsible for the ship safety management (ISM)

Table 1 provides a brief overview of the historical evolution of the PSC mechanism. As can be seen, it has evolved from a quota-based regime[3] to a risk-based inspection regime, where a set of factors are used to estimate the ship-risk profile. Accordingly, the targeting scheme, used for ships inspection by the Paris and Tokyo MOUs,[4] depends on two groups of factors, as presented in Table 2. The first group are characteristics related to the ship performance: age, type, number of previous deficiencies and detentions. The second group is based on the (related detention rate) performance of those stakeholders that can greatly influence the ship operational condition: the flag of registry, the organisation that classes the ship and the company that conducts the ship-safety management.

The United States Coast Guard (USCG) was the first regime that adopted risk-profile criteria (in 1994) to evaluate the performance of the ship and stakeholders. More than 15 years later, the Paris and Tokyo MOUs superseded the USCG criteria, with the adoption of the 'New Inspection Regime' in 2011 and 2014, respectively. Nonetheless, today, the three regimes are at the forefront of the other PSC regimes and maintain somewhat comparable data about ship, flag and class performance. The detention rate is the key indicator, so far applied, to evaluate the safety culture of ships, flag states and classification societies.

Following the Erika and Prestige accidents, the European Maritime Safety Agency (EMSA) was established in 2003. Currently, EMSA is tasked with the auditing of Recognised Organisations (ROs) which carry out the inspection, survey and certification of ships on behalf of Member States. EMSA also operates THETIS,[5] a centralised database that maintains the results of the PSC inspection of foreign ships calling at EU ports. Relevant European Commission (EC) Directives, in the context of the PSC regime, adopted since EMSA's inception, are the following:

[3] MS under the Paris MOU agreed to inspect 25 % of the estimated number of individual foreign merchant ships which enter their ports during a 12 month period.

[4] The Tokyo MOU is the organization, consisting of maritime Administrations from 19 member states (Australia, Canada, Chile, China, Fiji, Hong Kong (China), Indonesia, Japan, Republic of Korea, Malaysia, the Marshall Islands, New Zealand, Papua New Guinea, the Philippines, the Russian Federation, Singapore, Thailand, Vanuatu and Vietnam) with cooperators and observers. In 2013, 31,018 inspections were carried out on ships registered under 98 flags.

[5] Port State Control database.

- Directive 2009/16/EC on port state control.
- Directive 2013/38/EU amending Directive 2009/16/EC.
- Directive 213/54/EU concerning certain flag State responsibilities for compliance with and enforcement of the Maritime Labour Convention 2006.

Most statistics suggest that the risk-based criteria mentioned above, work well and have encouraged stakeholders to increase their feeling of responsibility. Studies demonstrate that the number of deficiencies for the same ship, generally reduces each time it is inspected (Cariou et al. 2008). Furthermore, the cost of insurance claims for ships inspected can be significantly reduced (Knapp and Frances 2010). However, there is some criticism too, namely, on the part of the oil majors, on how effective PSC inspections are, given the stringent requirements to which they are already subject, such as the Tanker Management Self-Assessment set up by Oil Companies International Marine Forum. Consequently, inspections for the tanker sector have been recognised as being excessive and ‘overlapping by the various stakeholders’ (Knapp and Frances 2010).[6]

Another constraint, is the human subjectivity attributed to PSC inspectors. In other words, the decision to detain a ship or not relies heavily on their professional judgement. On many occasions, PSC inspectors have been criticised for limiting their role to documentary inspection. In fact, the analysis conducted by Knapp and van de Velden (2009), suggested that treatment of vessels across ports varies. Therefore, efforts are needed towards the harmonisation of inspections procedures, training of inspectors and integration of datasets across MOU regions.

The US Coast Guard (USCG) has been particularly successful in detecting wrong practices during the issuing of safety equipment certificates, and for the first time in history, has sued an inspector that issued an International Oil Pollution Prevention (IOPP) Certificate, even though he knew the Oil Water Separator was not operable, as required by MARPOL (Norris 2011). However, much more is required. For instance, risk profiling in the future should not only focus on the ship, but also on the shipping companies and their efforts in developing integrated systems for recording and analysing data about incidents, including near misses. For instance, it would be interesting to calculate the accident rate of the company, as proposed by some authors (Heij and Knapp 2011). Thus, newer indicators for safe ship operation can be developed.

[6] See also paper “Inspection and control in regulating the occupational health and safety in the tanker industry: The perspective of the regulated” by S. Bhattacharya presented at the University of Aberdeen’s Work, Employment & Society (WES) Conference, University of Aberdeen, Aberdeen, Scotland, UK, 12–14 September, 2007.

3 The SAFEPEC Project

It is in the context described above, that the European Commission, under its Seventh Framework Programme (FP7) for Research and Development, invited the shipping community, including stakeholders from Recognised Organisations, Maritime Administrations, Shipyards and Research Centres, to carry out projects that can contribute to optimising the current regime for ship-safety inspection. The SAFEPEC project—Innovative risk-based tools for ship safety inspection—has been granted funding and it is due to start after the summer of 2014. This section provides an overview of the project.

3.1 Aims and Approach

The overall objective of the SAFEPEC project is to provide stakeholders with a more rationalised and harmonised approach to performing inspections; thus proper and timely measures are adopted in order to reduce the risk of ship's structure and equipment failure. This approach will be based in risk-based methods, specially developed for the project, with the definitive aim of facilitating not only the inspection regime implemented by maritime safety authorities, but also to support the maintenance programs scheduled by ship owners and repair yards.

The product(s) developed within SAFEPEC will be tested and demonstrated in the following types of ships:

- Liquefied Natural Gas (LNG) ships
- Cruise ships
- Roll-on/Roll-off vessels
- General cargo ships
- High speed vessels

SAFEPEC will examine current best practices for risk-based inspection, carried out in other high-risk industries such as aviation, nuclear and refinery, in order to determine those practices that could be easily adapted and applied in the shipping sector, and mainly in those ship types selected above.

SAFEPEC will conduct a cross-analysis of the existing data sources from the maritime industry, in order to link the causes of incidents (casualties and near miss cases) with the reports available from past inspections conducted by the different stakeholders.

Such an approach surely will require the definition of new parameters; in other words, an interoperable information architecture for data exchange between the existing databases. This will contribute towards the development of a more harmonised risk-based approach for ship inspection and maintenance. A major benefit of the approach would be the reduction of ship lifecycle costs; this because inspection and repair intervals would be based upon the early detection of failures in critical areas of the ship. In other words, by combining failure occurrence probability and consequences, rather than on arbitrary inspection periods.

Additionally, the project will address the health and safety issues related to conducting inspections, by introducing instrumentation-based e-inspection. In this way, the proposed risk-based approach will reduce the number of required inspections and inspection locations, without jeopardising the reliability of the results. Hence, the work load on surveyors can decrease significantly.

3.2 Stakeholder Involvement

Port authorities, classification societies, flag states, ship owners and insurance companies, are just a few of the stakeholders with particular interest in this topic. As presented before, the new risk-based, port state control regime is already implemented. The SAFEPEC project can provide the stakeholders with means to reduce the costs of inspections without compromising the safety levels, and meanwhile improve their own Port State Control profile or flag state profile. SAFEPEC offers the opportunity to go from the past major accident-driven legislation, to proactive security. Within SAFEPEC, the project's innovative developments will be performed in close partnership with key stakeholders, through workshops, consultation forums and other initiatives, with the aim of bringing together diverse views and opinions about the usefulness of the products developed.

3.3 Research Development

It is necessary to understand the research challenges that the SAPEPEC project brings. The crucial one is, "How to move from raw data to wisdom?". In order to understand this, two main research aspects are explained below.

3.3.1 A Framework for Information Architecture

The lack of data is still today, one of the presented reasons for model simplification, use of expert opinion, or simply for not updating the existing data. In the present technological era, it is difficult to understand these limitations, since every organization collects huge amounts of data on a daily basis. However, data, *per se*, does not constitute knowledge.

Although, there are certain situations were data is unavailable, due to confidentiality reasons, reality shows that more than the problem of missing data, there is also an absence of standards and definition of best practices for the structured collection and recording of information. This is something that seriously impacts the ability of analysis/prediction of given phenomena and contains technological development. The shipping industry is not immune to these issues. Different stakeholders use different information formats, taxonomies and standards.

Within SAFEPEC, this problem will be tackled by developing new standards and taxonomies for interoperability. This will allow different stakeholders to exchange information with higher quality and fewer problems than what is achievable today.

Furthermore, a data model will be developed which will harmonize data structures from the e-navigation field with registered requirements from the ship inspection area. This will thereby enable transfer of ship inspection data between the parties involved in the process and linking this data to other uses, e.g., in ship operation or maintenance.

Thus, this project constitutes a golden opportunity to combine different data sources, ranging from inspection, accident/incident/near misses, flag state, ISM companies shipyards, etc., and standardize and integrate these data sources into a single information architecture.

3.3.2 An Improved Framework for Risk-Based Inspection

The translation of the data to shipping inspection information, requires the development of an integrated risk-based inspection framework. Therefore, several models will be developed within the project. In the *casualty* model, the different underlying causes of an accident (human error, mechanical failure, weather related, etc.) will be identified and a Bayesian Belief Network (BBN)[7] model will be developed in order to establish the hierarchy of the causes (Mascaro et al. 2010). Based on the relation between accidental events and underlying causes, a *vulnerability* model will be developed, taking also into account influence parameters like safety culture, compliance culture, training, and inspection techniques. For the *consequence*, it will develop a generic model for the identification and assignment of consequences, taking into account characteristics such as ship type, cargo volume, number of crew, etc. Finally, for the *inspection*, a model will be developed describing a probabilistic relationship between the inspection observation and the actual state of the ship, and by taking into account factors influencing inspection quality.

The *inspection* model will be integrated with sensor technologies, for near-real-time ship condition (particularly in critical equipment and hull areas subjected to high stress or bending moments). The abovementioned models will be combined, to rank a given ship according to its risk and using BBN models, the risk can be computed, conditional on inspection outcomes.

The application of a new risk-based model for improving the current inspections procedures can greatly facilitate the process of assigning risks during the ship

[7] It is a kind of probability theories and represents the relationship between propositions or variables, for modelling decision-making under uncertainty.

maintenance planning process. Ship yards, in particular, can benefit from such a model, because it allows for computing probabilities for a ship structure or equipment to fail, in the future. These inputs are likely to change the routine of ship operators and shipyards in relation to how often repairs are required at a respective cost. In sum, such models will contribute to preventive maintenance actions to be adopted by operators, yards and classification societies.

3.4 Technological Development

SAFEPEC will not only adopt a risk-based inspection approach, but also make use of technology to facilitate remote inspection. Technological improvements will be demonstrated *in situ* to the stakeholders (in ship and ashore), thus providing to the maritime industry the opportunity to evaluate its operational benefits.

Furthermore, based on these technological improvements, it will be possible to provide legislative recommendations, grounded in cost-benefit analysis. This will be performed by following the Formal Safety Assessment steps. For the developed scenarios, the variation of risk, before and after the implementation of the developed technologies, will be quantified. Based on the results obtained throughout the different workshop demonstrations with the different stakeholders, it will be possible to estimate the individual benefits of the project outcomes per stakeholder.

So how can this new approach of shipping inspection help create other job opportunities, especially also for the now still much absent females in this line of work. To understand, it must first be investigated what the main reasons today are for females to avoid this area. The next paragraph provides some discussion on that topic, based on a small literature review and a survey amongst both males and females working in the area.

4 Exploring the Role of Women in Ship Safety Inspection

4.1 Women in Technical Courses

It is interesting to see that while the human sex ratio at birth is approximately 107 boys to 100 girls, only 1–2 % of the global workforce of seafarers are women (Tansey 2000). It has nothing to do with the intelligence of women. When looking at the amount of university graduates in six European countries (Poulsen 2003), it is seen that women form approximately 42–61 % of all university graduates. Although the percentage of women completing a Doctorate (PhD) is slightly lower, somewhere between 32 and 42 %, this is still considerable. But these are the figures for all tertiary education, while the employment in the maritime world is mainly technical. Looking at the figures for technical studies, the participation of women is much lower. Poulsen (2003) has researched the distribution of women over different subjects of education in Austria and for technical subjects, the percentage of women is between 5 and 24 %, with engineering at the low end. The experience in the Netherlands is no different, with an average of 20 % women at the Delft university, ranging from 6 to 10 % for mechanical and maritime engineering or aerospace engineering, to 30–40 % for the more female-oriented architecture or industrial design. In Germany, the German Ministry for Education and Research is trying to increase the very low share of women at universities in the so-called MINT-subjects (Mathematics, IT, Natural sciences, Technology/engineering), with specific campaigns to attract women for these subjects—it has become a national effort.

Where does this lack of involvement of women in the technical areas come from? There are several explanations. The first one is cultural-based. Already in our early childhood, we are confronted with the fact that toys for girls are mainly based on domestic duties and beauty, while boys are encouraged to build things and play outside the house. And during our educational and professional career, a girl normally has to prove herself twice as much if she wants to pick the more technical and science subjects. Then there are the physical aspects. Technical areas are still associated with physical heavy work and 'getting dirty'. A third factor is the lack of female role models. All of this does not encourage women to choose a career path in a technical area.

4.2 *Women in Shipping*

Is there only bad news? No, the involvement of females is growing, albeit slowly. A large increase in the participation of women was seen in the last decades in the cruise industry. In the mid 1980s, only 5 % of personnel on board cruise ships were female, whereas at the beginning of this century, this has grown to 18–20 %. But also here we see that although these females are employed in the shipping industry, most of them are involved in the hotel and catering service, while only 0.5 % is in the technical maritime professions. Zhao (2001a, b) investigated the reasons for these females to work on board. Most of the women from the western world, which make up 50 % of all the females in this business, want to meet new cultures and see the world. For the women originating from other areas in the world, the financial aspects are the main motivation. The shipping industry to them, offers the opportunity to escape poverty.

It is interesting to see that females in the cruising industry are more generally accepted by their male colleagues than in other maritime sectors. This is probably due to the fact that they are still involved in more female-oriented work. The stereotypical characterisation remains. There is also a large difference between males and females in the amount of time they want to spend on board. Most females state that after a few years, they want to seek on-shore jobs and start a family. Combining a family with work on board is not what they want. So the females themselves help to preserve the cultural differences between the genders. On the other hand, combining family and work is easier in an onshore job. That is probably the reason why the amount of women in onshore maritime jobs, such as port services, naval architecture, and national maritime affairs, is higher.

In a report published by the United Nations University (Taeb 2005), the effect of the technology advancement on women's employment in the area of science and technology is described. As an example, it is stated that in China, before the arrival of technological advancements, only 1 % of the employers in the metal industry were female. Now, due to the presence of new technologies, this figure has increased to 28 %. The new technologies made the work less physically demanding, so more suitable for women. So summarising all of the above, it seems that there are a few main reasons why there are so few women to be found in the maritime industries:

1. Cultural bias and tradition;
2. Physical hard work; and
3. Often work away from home

The first reason cannot be changed in a short time, and frankly, it is up to the women of this world to change that. By encouraging girls in our vicinity and showing them that they can do whatever they want, the females working in the maritime industry can act as role models, slowly changing the stereotypical characterisation of what is the female role in the world. Next to that, women participation programmes, such as that of IMO and certain maritime colleges, can help.

The latter two reasons can be influenced more easily. We are living in an era in which the technological advancements are ever growing. Technological tools can be used to make a lot of work physically less demanding. Furthermore, the information and communication technologies make it possible, to a certain extent, to work away from the actual location of your work.

4.3 A Pilot Survey About Female Participation in Ship Inspection

During the preparation of this paper, a questionnaire was designed and used on a pilot basis, to collect the views from a group of specialists in the maritime field. A description of the survey and results are presented below.

4.3.1 Brief Description of the Survey's Aim, Sample and Questionnaire

The survey aimed at collecting the participant's perceptions on the role of women in the maritime sector. Both genders were invited to participate in the survey and share anecdotes and life-experiences about their entry to the sector, as well as their

Table 3 Characteristics of the sample

Sex	
Female	13
Male	9
Maritime subsector	
Ship design/construction	1
Ship operations/shipping	3
Marine-related equipment	1
Other services	17
Job position	
Scientist/researcher	6
Inspector	1
Other	12
Professional experience	
Average in years	7.5

satisfaction with their roles. Taking into account the impossibility to collect accurate figures about the number of women inspectors, participants were asked to provide a rough estimation of both gender's shares.

The survey contained a total of 15 questions. Although the survey was initially designed for female participants, it was later decided to include male participants, too. In this way, the perceived views of men about their female colleagues' contribution could be also investigated. The questionnaire was sent to all participants in advance and with some of the participants, a phone interview followed. The reason for sending the questionnaire in advance was to give the interviewee time to prepare answers, especially the quantitative questions of this survey. All in all, 69 questionnaires were sent out to the potential interviewees. Only six interviews were conducted by phone because of time reasons, and 13 filled questionnaires were received by email. In some cases, phone calls were made to the participants in order to clarify some of the statements provided by them. Anonymity was ensured to the participants and no names of people or companies are referred to in this paper. The characteristics of the sample are summarised in Table 3. As can be seen, more participants were women working in the maritime services and only one person worked in ship design/construction. On average, the participants worked 7.5 years in this business, with the lowest time of 5 years and the longest time of 11 years. Therefore, it can be stated that most participants had significant experience in the field.

4.3.2 Women Unbalance in the Maritime Industry: *Male Culture*

One key question asked to the participants was: *'Do you consider the maritime sector to be a men's world? If YES, why and what do you think are the obstacles for women to work in the industry?'* The overwhelming majority (17 out of 19) replied that the sector is indeed of men's domain. Few participants (2 out of 19) did not consider that maritime business as men dominated.

Very interesting were the comments and opinions given by the participants. Although most of the participants agreed that gender unbalance has in the past been definitely the case, they also mentioned that the situation is changing gradually now. Tradition was considered the major reason why this business is seen as a male dominated. Most participants highlighted that the situation is particularly different in onshore jobs where the conditions are more favourable for women with families, and the female share is much higher than at sea.

Furthermore, it was stated that areas like shipping, where a strong physical condition is required, are very male dominated and only a very few women work in these areas. In this respect, one of the obstacles for women employed on board ships was the lack of shower facilities for ladies. This kind of statement is later challenged by some of the anecdotes provided by women during the survey.

Below are some of the explanations given to the question, *'why and what are the perceived obstacles for women to work in the maritime sector?'* As can be appreciated, more participants confirmed that working on board ships is very demanding for women and is not always compatible with children and family. One participant expressed that no discrimination is felt in the consulting services.

> As a tradition and appearance when you first enter the sector, yes, it is a men's world. Main obstacle is the prejudice that people (employers and male colleagues) have that **a woman is not 'strong' enough to handle the tasks**. For on board occupation, old ships, shared shower facilities on those ships are other obstacles that make the choice of employer fewer in number for women. [bold added]
>
> It was always seen as a men's world. Maybe it is not the most attractive industry for woman. In certain areas of this industry **the main obstacle may be the time availability work/ family** (when being away from home). [bold added]
>
> Yes, it all begins with the education already. Most technical areas are men's worlds and the maritime sector is one of the more male oriented. Obstacles that I can see: **as a female you have to prove yourself more.** People tend to see you at first as the secretary. Furthermore, the job normally requires quite some travelling, that might be difficult for females in a family situation. [bold added]
>
> Yes, it is traditionally a men's word mainly because, **the work on the board of ships is physically too heavy for a woman**, including for a watch-keeping officer. In addition, she . . .has to take care for children and her family. There is no problem for a woman to work in the other maritime sectors. [bold added]
>
> It definitely has been a man's world, because in past times the job was very hard and physically strenuous, but this has already changed, and so today I see no real obstacles.
>
> No – not on the consulting side of the market

One of the respondents considered that seafaring life is currently discouraging male workers too, so this may be interpreted that not only culture, but incentives are missing to engage a seafaring career.

> It is a male dominated work environment. One of the prerogatives to work ashore is quite often a Master or Chief Engineer license plus a certain professional experience in shipping. Women are now much more appreciated in the shipping industry than 15 years ago but still the **female attendance to nautical colleges is at small numbers**. My guess is that younger women are much more aware of the constraints especially in

social life that are accompanied to the jobs in shipping. It appears from discussions with females that they see a difficulty of having a reasonable work/live balance when being employed on ships. And in fact **the social conditions under which shipping takes place are also the reason why a lot of males are leaving the ships to join jobs a shore**. [bold added]

4.3.3 Estimated Share of Women Unbalance in the Maritime Sector

Another important question was about gender share, as follows: '*What is your guess about the percentage of male/female: In the maritime industry? In your company?*' On average, the estimated percentage given for women working in the maritime business was in the range of 12 %, with 30 % being the highest guess, and 3 % the lowest.

The picture gets a little different when it comes to the company the respondents are working in. The average result was 32 % of females working in the business. This number has to be taken with care, as not all participants had time to prepare this question. The stated numbers on the female share within the organization was very often a "hard" and little reliable number that has to be obtained from the human resource departments or just counting the smaller specialised departments. The lowest number was stated was 5 %. It was given by port specialists; therefore, this figure may well change, for example, in ports that outsource e.g., terminal operations and other jobs that are very male dominated. The highest percentage given on that question was 60 %.

To the question '*Do you see any differences in the share of women in different fields of the maritime industry?*', the majority (15 out of 19) confirmed with a 'yes' that really there might be differences in the share of women among different fields in the maritime industry. The other participants did not have an opinion on this question.

4.3.4 Perceived Obstacles for the Career Development of Women Within the Maritime Sector

The time required to work and the educational backgrounds, were mentioned as the main obstacles for increasing the number of women in the sector. It is important to mention here that the Working Time Directive, 2003/88/EC [8] does not apply to specific sectors, and work at sea is one of them.

To the question: '*Are time demands one of the constraints for women to work in these fields?*', there were not visible differences in the replies, some of them (8 out

[8] 93/104/EC of 23 November 1993 was repealed by EU Directive 2003/88/EC of 4 November 2003. It provides EU workers the right to a minimum number of holidays each year, rest breaks, and rest of at least 11 h in any 24 h; restricts excessive night work; a day off after a weeks work; and provides for a right to work no more than 48 h per week.

of 19) answered "yes" and another group (5 out of 19) answered "no", and the remaining (4 out of 19) said "maybe". One participant added that time demands is not a constraint, as long women do not have children. Another participant thought that time may be a constraint, mainly due to personal protection, as some women may be afraid of driving on their own during night hours, for instance, to the port in case of a ship accident.

The replies to the question concerning the educational background, *'Could the educational background be a reason for the high share of men employed in this industry?'* generated marked views. The majority of participants answered this question with "yes" (10 out of 19), and the other stated a "no" (5 out of 19). Four interviewees answered with "maybe" and two participants did not have an opinion on this. An analysis of the qualitative answers that were provided to this question, highlights the following:

- All engineering-related jobs are significantly male-dominated and they include the jobs at ports where a very strong physical condition is required. Often, it was mentioned that this gender unbalance already starts at university where many more males usually study engineering subjects, compared to female students. A German participant mentioned that this situation very much reflects the situation in Germany, where so called MINT subjects (Mathematics, IT, Nature science and Technical subjects) are mainly studied by male students. Another participant, who was a former seafarer and is now working as scientist, also mentioned that in some countries, women were not allowed to be admitted on seafaring operations for a long time.
- In contrast, many fields like administration in the port, or in maritime-related companies and in logistics, have a very high female share. This situation seems to turn again, the higher the job positions are. Management positions are also, in the maritime world, a real male-dominated business, with almost no women accompanying such positions. In science, there appears to be a very equal share of males and females, probably due to the better conditions that science generally offers for women.
- Another impression that one participant shared, was that women would rather work on liners than on other kind of ships, due to the timely operation of liners, that make it easier for women to combine work and family life.

The question on *'How many female PSCOs (Port State Control Officers) do you know?'* received ten answers, four of them stating they do not know any PSCO, the others stated they knew from two to five. Surprisingly, nearly half of the participants did not know what was meant by this question.

Concerning the number of maritime scientists, it is possible to state that there are many: *'Do you know any female maritime scientists, and if yes, do you know something about their contribution to the industry?'* Most respondents (14 out of 19) stated that they knew some, or at least one female scientists; few (3 out of 19) did not know a maritime female scientist. Qualitative comments for this question included:

. . .in research and logistics there are many women. In our organization about 50 %. . .

. . .(I know) . . ., chairman Port of Los Angeles. She is biologists by education, and the environmental questions in maritime business are also thanks to her on top of the agenda.

There are not even so many maritime male scientists I know of. I think there are many (female), at least on the way to become a scientist.

4.3.5 Maritime Women Anecdotes

Question 12 was the one that respondents mainly enjoyed and where amazing histories were given. *'Can you share your personal experience/anecdote as a woman maritime professional?'* Below is a compilation of the seven responses obtained to this question. Most of them revealed a sort of gender discrimination, stereotype and gender-role conception. Two of the responses also show certain reluctance on both parts: the boss and employee, with regard to top job positions. Contrarily to male workers, females are expected to show their abilities. Two out of seven participants suggested that maritime women are not an issue.

After graduating from university, I went for a job interview to a tanker company which had never before employed any female officers on board. I was sitting in a big room with all the superintendents, DPA, HR manager who were all graduated from the same university and had the same background. **I was asked so many questions** which in my opinion showed their concern whether I could handle on board life or not, such as seasickness, sleeping and waking up weird hours. All these things can be problems for anybody. **Seasickness is not something unique for women as far as I know**. None of my fellow male graduates would get to this kind of interview. At the moment it is getting better, however, **there are still concerns of decision makers when it comes to promote a female to a position for instance**. Nobody wants to put his hand under the stone with no real ground for this. [bold added]

In 1994 I embarked as deck cadet in a Portuguese ship, being a single woman on board. For the first 3 months I had difficulties in communicating with the boatswain but after a very challenging period everything went well. I also worked as water clerk in a shipping agency, being the first woman doing that in the Lisbon port area. **When I tried to get the job, my boss said that he preferred a man but that I could try for 3 months. I worked there for almost four years**, but then I had a baby and it became very difficult to be available 24 hours per day to assist the ships if needed. After a short period in another shipping agency but with a desk job, I worked for 8 years in the maritime administration and since 2009 in my current position. [bold added]

One time I went with my female colleague to a ship. **The males on board first clearly thought we were just two ladies asking for route directions or something.** When we mentioned that we were there to talk about the issue they had, everybody looked surprised and the setting changed. Although when we really wanted to walk through the ship some gentleman was send first to see if everything was reachable and safe for us. Something I have not experienced when I went to ships with a male colleague. [bold added]

I consider female scientists hard workers and as such they deserve to be recognized and given top positions. However, for some reason, most women lack confidence on themselves and when they are given such opportunity is not rare to find women that are not willing to embark in positions with higher responsibilities and higher salaries just because they think the position may demand tasks above their perceived abilities. In fine, **female workers need to be trained in leadership**. In this way, both, the female worker and company can benefit of the potential of women professionals. [bold added]

I have no special experience. Only on some occasions, e.g. meetings or related events, it is always being the only one or part of **few women in the crowd**. [bold added]

Generally I can say, if you know your subject and are not one of these girlie women, you are quickly accepted by the men in this business. They do check you in the beginning, but **once you have proved some knowledge and some social competence, you are accepted**. [bold added]

My personal experience is very variable but, I still remember the favourite sentence of one of my lecturers in the university that, **Mathematics and Technical sciences are not proper area for a head with a long hair**. [bold added]

I have worked with several women, and it has in most cases a positive experience; like with man. And when I don't like somebody, **it doesn't matter whether female or male**. [bold added -a male participant stated this]

Not experienced any situation that you would not have experienced also in another situation.

4.3.6 Job Satisfaction of Maritime Women

The statements presented in the previous sections give an idea about the development that is taking place. While it is true that in most occasions, female workers are often being discriminated against in the maritime field, there is some hope that this situation is also changing.

Participants were asked *'How they would rate their satisfaction on a scale from 1 to 10 with 10 being the highest satisfaction level'*. In general, the satisfaction level was very high. A total of 14 people answered the question. The most common rating was between 9 and 10. None of the participants expressed dissatisfaction. The lowest ratings came from two women with a rating of 5 and 6.5 respectively, which displays not dissatisfaction, but rather neutrality. However, what the question did not allow to be explored, was what factors were related or contributed to the respondents to choose a low level of satisfaction (e.g., salary).

In the questions asked to women about whether they would think about changing to another industry with a higher female share, most women (four out of five) answered with "no". Two female respondents explained that if she ever thought of changing into another business, then a higher share would not definitely be the reason. Another comment from a female participant stated:

...We have to get young people into the business. Once the woman are in this industry they are very satisfied, at least what I have heard of the women I know.

Over the question addressed to male participants, where they were asked to assess the growing involvement of women into the maritime industry on a scale of 1 to 10, where 1 is very negative, 5 is neutral and 10 positively high. The average rating was 8, which is positive. One participant explicitly stated a 5, as he stated that he is very neutral about the gender. Only one participant did not answer this question, and wrote n.a.

5 The SAFEPEC Project: Employment Opportunities for Women

As seen in both the literature review and the survey, there are a few reasons that keep coming up when looking at the underrepresentation of women in the shipping inspection business. Shipping inspection is seen as an area which requires a 'strong' person and it puts high demands on the surveyors' work/private balance. Addressing these issues might provide better opportunities for women. The SAFEPEC project indirectly does this. Inspection will not only be done by a human being, but sensors, such as strain gauges and cameras, will continuously monitor the health status of the ship. This information will be transferred to shore where risk-based techniques are applied to identify risk areas. So, after implementation of this approach, the inspector has continuous remote access to the condition of the ship. The actual inspection, which can never be fully replaced by technology, thus becomes far more efficient and targeted. The area of ship inspection is one in which there are now only a few women involved, but that could provide increased opportunities for women. In the UK Maritime and Coast Guard Agency, for example, two out of 105 inspectors are women. Nevertheless, one of the female surveyors is in charge of a Marine Office and responsible for nine male surveyors.[9] Ship inspection is still a physically demanding job, with lots of climbing around in ships and work having to be done, of course, at the ship itself. Within the EU SAFEPEC project, the aim is to provide stakeholders with a more rationalised and harmonised approach to perform ship inspections. Thus, proper and timely measures are adopted in order to reduce the risk of ship's structure and equipment failure. This will be achieved by adopting a risk-based inspection approach and by making use of technology to facilitate remote inspection.

This offers new opportunities for women. With these new inspection techniques, it would be possible to split the inspection task into a fully on-shore job in which an inspector bases her report on the health status of the ship on the remote information of the hardware installed on the ship, and the risk-prediction models and the actual on-board inspection, could be done by someone else. Even if the inspector also performs the on-board inspection, this will be less strenuous due to the more targeted inspections possible due to the information gathered beforehand from the remote sensor network. The presence of the remote sensing techniques will also make it easier for personnel on board, and the ship owner, to accept the judgement of the inspector. Although this is of benefit to all inspectors, it will in particular help females, who are normally less accepted on board.

[9] Email communication with P. Dolby on the 7th February 2014.

6 Conclusions

The port state control regime first adopted in the 1970s marked a new era, because it focused the states' attention on prevention, rather than response policies. The initiative was so important that it was rapidly followed by other regions, including the US, that in 1994 implemented a similar scheme. In recent years, the port state control regime has undergone major improvements, as risk methods have been incorporated to select and inspect ships. However, new methods need to be developed for risk profiling. In the future, it should not only focus on the ship, but also in the shipping companies. Not only the detention rate, but newer indicators can be developed. Heij and Knapp (2011) suggested using the 'accident rate' of a ship management company as a new indicator. However, more interesting would be developing, for instance, a qualitative (or nominal) indicator that takes into account not just the accidents, but also the near misses and non-conformities recorded by the company. In conformity with the safety pyramid or triangle, the higher the number of near misses and non-conformities recorded by a shipping company, then the higher the company's commitment needs to be, to increase its safety culture and reduce accidents (Borg 2002). The SAFEPEC project can bring new knowledge, because it will analyse historical incident data and correlate them with ship inspection data. In this way, relevant mathematical models will be developed to identify and analyse precursors and factors that can potentially lead to serious accidents.

Concerning the survey, the overall and not too surprising result, showed that the maritime business is still today seen as a purely man's world. Nearly 90 % (17 out of 19) of the interviewees answered with "yes" when they were asked whether they think the maritime industry is a man's world. It was also independent of the industry the interviewees worked in, e.g., a more technical-related area, in science, or in an administrative area. The other striking result—a real highlight—is that though this business is seen as a man's world, the women who work in this field were very satisfied with their jobs. The total average of the level of satisfaction given by both genders, was rated at 8.5. Women rating satisfaction reached an average of 8.2, and the men rating was 9.2. This slight difference suggests that men welcome more female colleagues in the business. However, the true reasons for this rating were not further explored during the survey.

The authors hope that the participants' opinions expressed during the survey and presented in this paper, provide some light about the need to devote more efforts in changing the current male-dominated culture and may serve to promote and increase the participation of women in the maritime industry.

Acknowledgements The authors would like to express their gratitude to the persons that voluntarily participated in the questionnaire survey. Some of the information presented in this paper about the SAFEPEC project is based in the proposal submitted by the respective consortium to the European Commission (www.safepec.eu).

Disclaimer
The views and opinions expressed in this paper are those of the authors and do not necessarily reflect the position of their affiliated companies.

References

Borg, B. (2002). Predictive safety from near-miss and hazard reporting. Resource document. Signal Safety & Training Ltd. http://signalsafety.ca/files/Predictive-Safety-Near-Miss-Hazard-Reporting.pdf. Accessed 1 Apr 2014.

Cariou, P., Mejia, M., & Wolff, C. H. (2008). On the effectiveness of port state control inspections. *Transportation Research Part E: Logistics and Transportation Review, 44*(3), 491–503.

Heij, C., & Knapp, S. (2011). Risk evaluation methods at individual ship and company level. Resource document. Erasmus University Rotterdam. http://repub.eur.nl/pub/25603. Accessed 1 Apr 2014.

Knapp, S., & Frances, P. H. (2010). Comprehensive review of the maritime safety regimes: Present status and recommendations for improvements. *Transport Reviews: A Transnational Transdisciplinary Journal, 30*(2), 241–270.

Knapp, S., & van de Velden, M. (2009). Visualisation of differences in treatment of safety inspections across port state control regimes: A case for increased harmonisation efforts. *Transport Reviews: A Transnational Transdisciplinary Journal, 29*(4), 499–514.

Mascaro, S., Korb, K., & Nicholson, A. (2010). Learning abnormal vessel behaviour from AIS data with Bayesian networks at two time scales. Resource document. Bayesian Intelligence. http://www.bayesian-intelligence.com/publications/TR2010_4_AbnormalVesselBehaviour.pdf. Accessed 1 Apr 2014.

Norris, A. J. (2011). The 'other' law of the sea. *Naval War College Review, 64*(3), 78–97.

Özçayir, Z. O. (2001). The role of port state control. *International Maritime Law, 8*(5), 147–159.

Poulsen, C. (2003). Women in European universities: Statistical profile of women in the Austrian higher education system. Resource document. Projektübersicht von Prof. Dr. Annette Zimmer. http://csn.uni-muenster.de/women-eu/download/PoulsenTP02_05.pdf. Accessed 1 Apr 2014.

Taeb, M. (Ed.). (2005). Revisiting women's participation in science and technology: Emerging challenges and agenda to reform. Resource document. United Nations University. http://i.unu.edu/media/unu.edu/publication/28002/WomenST_final.pdf. Accessed 1 Apr 2014.

Tansey, P. (2000). Women on board, ten years of the IMO women in development programme. Resource document. IMO. http://www.imo.org/blast/mainframe.asp?topic_id=406&doc_id=1082. Accessed 1 Apr 2014.

Zhao, M. (2001a). Globalisation and women's employment on cruise ships. *Maritime Review, 2001*, 77–82.

Zhao, M. (2001b). Women seafarers onboard cruise ships. In *Proceedings of SIRC Symposium 2001* (pp. 145–163). Cardiff: Cardiff University.

Conclusion

Momoko Kitada, Lisa Loloma Froholdt, and Erin Williams

The 19 papers in this volume exemplify well the breadth of presentations at MWGL 2014. The papers concern diverse topics of policy, career, education, leadership and sustainability, which women in the maritime sector commonly confront during their careers. Overall, the lack of gender policies was identified in the shipping industry, as there is no effective implementation and monitoring mechanism for them. One of the keys to reflect women's voice at policy levels, appeared to be "leadership"; promoting women's leadership in public and corporate economic decision-making is a crucial agenda around the world.[1] Women's career development in male-dominated industries, such as shipping, tends to be hindered by various factors. For example, the idea of work-life balance is neither institutionalized nor practiced in the shipping industry. There is a tendency to pre-assume that the STEM field is not suitable for women, resulting in unequal access to employment. In order to change such assumptions, "education" and "research" should be key areas of focus, but also necessary, are efforts to increase the visibility of maritime women by highlighting best practices in the maritime sector. However, policy handles may be necessary in order to enhance educational and employment opportunities for women. Last, but not least, this volume also draws out that women's contribution to the shipping industry will serve the International Maritime Organization (IMO)'s concept of a sustainable maritime transportation system.[2]

---

[1] See also UN Women document "Policy brief, decent work and women's economic empowerment: Good policy and practice" (2012).

[2] See also the IMO document "World Maritime Day: A Concept of Sustainable Maritime Transportation System" (2013).

M. Kitada (✉) • L.L. Froholdt
World Maritime University, Malmö, Sweden
e-mail: mk@wmu.se

E. Williams
Brunssum, The Netherlands

© Springer-Verlag Berlin Heidelberg 2015

M. Kitada et al. (eds.), *Maritime Women: Global Leadership*, WMU Studies in Maritime Affairs 3, DOI 10.1007/978-3-662-45385-8_21

Based on scientific findings of research presented at MWLG 2014, it is apparent that all of these evidence-based papers in this volume help us to construct the notions of gender-related issues observed over various maritime sectors, including seafaring, ports, administration, law and education. It is apparent that we need more women leaders to make positive changes in the industry. Bearing this in mind, how can we increase the number of professional women, as well as the number of women leaders in the maritime sector?

The conference debates at MWGL 2014 were vibrant among the 265 participants from 74 countries across Asia, Pacific, Africa, Middle-East, Europe, North and South America that took part in this international 2-day event. Indeed, the participants appeared happy and excited to be there, and to meet interesting people at the conference. The energized and positive atmosphere directly contributed to partisans forging enduring connections to address the common issues specific to women in the maritime sector. They confirmed the importance of networking and mentoring as an effective strategy for the integration of women in the maritime sector. Karin Orsel, President of the Women's International Shipping and Trading Association (WISTA), encouraged young peers to be role-models and use mentorship to support each other by saying 'Identify role models within the industry and support and promote them. If you can't find a good role model, be one!'[3] Mentoring projects are also regarded as an effective tool for increasing leadership capacity in trade unions, according to Alison McGarry, Coordinator of the Women Transport Workers' Department of the International Transport Workers' Federation (ITF). Successes of maritime women were highlighted during MWGL 2014 and boosted networking opportunities among the participants. A new maritime women's network, the World Maritime University Women's Association (WMUWA), was born through the process of organizing MWGL 2014. Even existing networks for maritime women, including the IMO regional support networks and WISTA networks, seemed to have gained additional momentum to address some of the organizational issues. For example, the Women In Maritime Association – Asia (WIMA-ASIA) started to prepare for setting up several new Asian national chapters within the organizational framework; the Papua New Guinea Women in Maritime Association (PNGWiMA) also began to discuss organizing a conference on maritime women in Pacific regions in a few years' time; Naa Densua Aryeetey, President of WISTA Ghana, advocated the need of targeting maritime women in the West African region to increase their visibility during the conference; and similarly, one of the founding members of WISTA South Africa, started the discussion of sustaining the organization. These are only a few examples of the many outcomes of MWGL 2014.

From the experiences of hosting two international conferences on Maritime Women, in 2008 and 2014, the World Maritime University (WMU) recognizes the importance of creating an opportunity of face-to-face gatherings to encourage and empower women in the maritime sector. This also echoes the WMU's mission

[3] Quoted from Karin Orsel's presentation titled 'WISTA – 40 years of female Global Leadership' at MWGL 2014.

to provide a forum for international collaboration on maritime transportation.[4] In the past 30 years, WMU has produced 3,663 graduates from 165 countries around the world, including 421 female graduates in 78 countries. While studying in Malmö, they were exposed to a great diversity of people from around the globe and shared a number of multi-cultural opportunities at WMU. This process of understanding and sharing helped to build a useful global network to support their work back home. The accumulation of this maritime professional network at the global level is a powerful tool that can be a genuine contribution to the further development of promoting diversity issues in the maritime sector, thereby serving a sustainable maritime transportation system.

To support the IMO's regional initiatives through the "Strategy on the Integration of Women in the Maritime Sector (IWMS)" programme, WMU brought this effort together in the global arena under the theme of 'Maritime Women: Global Leadership'. MWGL 2014 aimed at providing a forum for women and men, both in public and private sectors across all regions, to openly discuss gender-related challenges in the maritime industry and share any coping strategies, which might be applicable and useful for other women in different sectors. During the conference, Julia Lear of the International Labour Organization (ILO), proposed the use of social dialogue by governments, employers, workers, and other concerned stakeholders, to promote all forms of cooperation.[5] WMU will continue to promote social dialogues among maritime professionals and follow up the progress of IWMS by calling for the third International Conference on Maritime Women, in the future.

In the meantime, what do we want to see from now until the next conference? MWGL 2014 concluded with the adoption of the Maritime Women: Global Leadership Declaration, which is included at the end of this volume. The Declaration invites all stakeholders in the maritime sector to actively support the career and mentoring opportunities for women, to lead and achieve sustainable development in shipping, while recognizing the importance of education and research to enhance such opportunities. The MWGL Declaration was reported at the IMO Technical Co-operation Committee's 64th session as an information paper.[6] The Declaration is indeed the most significant outcome from the conference, however all of us, including the conference delegates and other maritime professionals, are expected to be proactive in supporting the Declaration. Based on the MWGL Declaration, the third International Conference will report the progress of IWMS and focus on the linkages among various maritime women networks, including the newly-born association, WMUWA.

[4] See also the website of WMU, http://wmu.se/about-us/mission-statement.

[5] See also ILO document 'Transport policy brief 2013 – Women in the transport sector' (2013).

[6] IMO document TC 64/INF.7.

1 World Maritime University Women's Association (WMUWA)

During the organization of MWGL 2014, it is noteworthy that WMU students started an initiative to create a network for the WMU female students, both current and alumni. This initiative was greatly welcomed and quickly spread among all students, as the preparation of MWGL 2014 proceeded. The fundamental organizational structure of the association was formed by the time of the conference, and it was named the 'World Maritime University Women's Association (WMUWA)'.

WMUWA adopted the UN Millennium Development Goal 3 of 'Promote gender equality and empower women', as well as serving the IMO's capacity building activity in the integration of women in the maritime sector. WMUWA aims to sponsor at least one female student to WMU each year and, with the tremendous support of IMO, has already accomplished this goal for the WMU's class of 2015; Qyunh Thang Nguyen from Vietnam is the first-sponsored female student, serving as an executive member in the WMUWA committee. WMUWA will function not only to connect current female students and alumni members, but also to work closely with the IMO regional support networks, acting as the link across the various regions. For example, WMUWA wishes to organize regular seminars and workshops, where it will invite speakers from both the IMO regional support networks and WMU alumni, to discuss topics such as leadership and management skills. The first WMUWA workshop will be held in March 2015 for the International Women's Day event by inviting the speakers from the IMO regional support networks, such as Meenaksi Bhirugnath Bhookhun, President, WOMESA, and Layla El Saeed, Chair, International Women's maritime Forum for MENA and Africa.

It was fortunate that the conference was supported by a number of WMU student volunteers, mostly WMUWA members. Deniece Melissa Aiken from Jamaica was appointed to be the first President of WMUWA, and honorably presented the Declaration at the closing of MWGL 2014. The launch of WMUWA was officially announced on the WMU International Day, 9 August 2014, and the first handover of WMUWA to the next class was completed in October 2014. The new president is Janelle Teresita Meloney from Trinidad and Tobago, second officer on LPG tankers.

The launch of WMUWA was also reported at the IMO Technical Co-operation Committee's 64th session as an information paper.[7] A request to recognize WMUWA as an association, with the same status, rights and obligations as other IMO regional support networks, was noted by the Committee.[8]

---

[7] IMO document TC 64/INF.6.

[8] IMO document TC/64/14 states in Article 8.8 that 'the Committee also noted the information provided in documents TC 64/INF.6 (Secretariat), on the establishment of the World Maritime University Women's Association, and TC 64/INF.7 (Secretariat), on the Second International Conference on Maritime Women: Global Leadership, held under the auspices of WMU in Malmö, Sweden, from 30 March to 1 April 2014'.

2 MWGL Evaluation Study

An online survey was conducted with participants outside of WMU, by using e-mail invitations from 3 to 15 April 2014, resulting in 61 non-WMU responses, a response rate of 51 %. According to the survey, a high percentage of respondents agreed with the following:

1. the MWGL 2014 provided clear information about the progress of the Integration of Women in the Maritime Sector (IWMS) across the different sectors as well as in different regions;
2. the Conference provided an effective platform to promote women's leadership in the maritime sector;
3. there was value in WMU offering future conferences focused on maritime women;
4. the MWGL 2014 demonstrated WMU's role as a global centre for advanced education and research in the maritime field; and
5. through the MWGL 2014, WMU is contributing to maritime capacity building and the development of effective policies for the global maritime community.

The complete results of the MWGL 2014 Evaluation Study were submitted as an Annex to the information paper to the IMO Technical Co-operation Committee's 64th session, under the name of the Secretariat.[9]

3 Post-MWGL 2014: The Impact of Capacity Building

MWGL 2014 was received as informational and inspiring to many participants around the globe. The impact of capacity building through MWGL 2014 included various positive elements, from the individual to the organizational level. After the conference, the participants brought their experience back to their home countries and disseminated the outcome of MWGL 2014 to their local maritime communities.

For instance, Chen Qi, Professor of the Massachusetts Maritime Academy (MMA), on her return, had several talks with the Dean and the President of MMA, about how to help the female cadets in their academy gain a world vision, build self-confidence and access opportunities in the male-dominated environment. As a result, MMA invited one of the keynote speakers at the MWGL conference—Rear Admiral, Sandra Stosz—Superintendent, U.S. Coast Guard Academy, to give a talk to their female cadets and she immediately agreed. Furthermore, one of her female colleagues established the "Women at MMA" at their campus, to hold regular meetings and talk about the issues of common interest to women in the

[9] IMO document TC 64/INF.7.

maritime sector. The most recent meeting showcased two female cadets, who discussed their experiences with a rescue mission in Haiti.

Ayse Asli Başak presented the research paper on Turkish women seafarers and had a great deal of exposure to the Turkish media when she returned to Turkey. One of the biggest online news websites, "Vatan Gazete", published her photograph and extracts from her paper in Turkish translation, which achieved 193,000 accesses. Similarly, other Turkish national maritime magazines such as "Denizcilik", "Neta Deniz", and "7deniz", as well as the "World Trade Newspaper" Turkish version, highlighted her paper at the MWGL 2014 and also mentioned her work at Çebi Denizcilik Ve Ticaret A.Ş. Başak's success, and her representation of her company, were widely reported across the Turkish maritime industry, which influenced her company's decision to employ one more female seafarer. This story highlights the importance of women's visibility in the maritime sector and she expressed her whole experience in her message, 'Thanks to World Maritime University and MWGL Conference!'

A French Professor, Bernard Dujardin, presented his paper on how a Shore-Controlled and Monitored Vessel (SCMV) can assist women's participation in the maritime sector, at the workshop D: "Sustainable Issues in Shipping". He made a report on his MWGL presentation at another conference, called the "24th Global Summit of Women 2014" in Paris, June 2014. His article describing his participation in the MWGL 2014, was published via the Summit.[10]

Maria Boström Cars and Cecilia Österman from Kalmar Maritime Academy, Linnaeus University, Sweden also reported that when the abstract of their study was accepted, the Head of their Academy asked them to give a presentation to the entire academic staff. Their presentation was then followed by discussions on how the Kalmar Maritime Academy compares to their findings regarding gender diversity, and how the Academy can improve in this particular area. The senior leadership at the Academy decided to continuously review and update their steering documents for education to increase gender sensitivity. Giving further attention to the conference, their study was published in the Swedish shipping magazine, "Sjöfartstidningen",[11] and has also inspired one of their students in the Nautical Science programme to work on a student thesis on the topic of maritime women. Last, but not least, on a less formal note, and since our language represents our image of reality, they observed that their colleagues now started to realize the importance of using gender-neutral terms, instead of saying "he" when referring to a student, or a seafarer in general.

These examples of the immediate post-MWGL months are only a few of the many positive outcomes of this conference. MWGL 2014 has provided a platform for maritime professionals to openly discuss gender and leadership, and such a

---

[10] See also Dujardin, B. (2014). Femmes et politiques publiques: L'accès de la mere à la mer est-il possible? *l'ENA hors les murs, 441*, 36–37.

[11] See also Lundberg, A. (2014). Genusperspektiv saknas: Sjöfartshögskolor missar genusperspektivet – kritiseras på Maritime Women: Global Leadership. *Sjöfartstidningen, 4*, 24.

small investment seems to have created a circle of good will across the globe. WMU, as a world-leading maritime education and research institution, is committed to serve the global maritime community through the capacity-building activities with our global partners, such as the IMO, ILO, ITF, WISTA and others.

4 Women at the Helm of Future

MWGL 2014 dropped an anchor in the effort to strengthen women as maritime leaders. This figurative dropping of the anchor has initiated a ripple effect, in that the impact of the conference has already made waves around the globe. Through the creation of this book via the Scientific Committee of MWGL 2014, the successes and challenges of women in the maritime sector are presented in a way that emphasizes the significant role of women leaders, and focuses on how organizations can improve their support in this area.

Approaching the gender issue from various aspects will bring the greatest success. The perspective must not only be through the key themes of policy, education, leadership and sustainability, but also from the private and public sector, through the MWGL Declaration to IMO, or by enhancing the networking opportunities through associations such as WMUWA and the IMO regional networks. Through these methods, policy, attitudinal and cultural changes will take effect, positively impacting the global maritime industry to make as our common goal, the achievement of a sustainable maritime transportation system. Because our greatest asset is people - men and women alike, the value in the global impact of maritime women should be emphasized.

Maritime Women: Global Leadership Declaration

We, the participants of the "Maritime Women: Global Leadership Conference", held in Malmö, Sweden, from 31 March to 1 April 2014, having deliberated on the leadership role that women play in the sustainable development of the maritime sector,

RECALLING articles 2(e) and 15(k) of the Convention on the International Maritime Organization (IMO) concerning the functions of the Organization and the Assembly in relation to the facilitation and promotion of technical co-operation,

RECALLING ALSO that the World Maritime University (WMU) was established to serve the global maritime community as IMO's apex institution for capacity-building and educating maritime administrators, in furtherance of IMO´s purposes and objectives,

RECALLING FURTHER in particular IMO resolutions A.900(21), on Objectives of the IMO in the 2000s and A.1031(26) concerning Sustainable Financial Support for the WMU, through which the Assembly, respectively, acknowledged the special contribution of WMU to the attainment of the objectives of IMO, and recognized the high esteem in which WMU is held throughout the maritime world and its significant contribution to enhanced safety, security and environmental protection,

RECALLING IN PARTICULAR resolution A.1060 (28) on the Strategic Plan for the Organization concerning the contribution made by the Integrated Technical Cooperation Programme (ITCP) to assist developing countries to achieve relevant Millennium Development Goals (MDGs), and resolution A.1061 (28) on the High Level Action Plan of the Organization and priorities for the 2014–2015 Biennium and the High Level Action of strengthening the role of women in the maritime sector,

© Springer-Verlag Berlin Heidelberg 2015

M. Kitada et al. (eds.), *Maritime Women: Global Leadership*, WMU Studies in Maritime Affairs 3, DOI 10.1007/978-3-662-45385-8

RECOGNIZING IMO's efforts to promote the advancement of women in maritime activities through its capacity-building programme, MDG 3: Strengthening Maritime Resource Development, previously known as the Integration of Women in the Maritime Sector (IWMS),

UNDERSCORING the adoption by the Technical Co-operation Committee (18 June 1998), resolution TC.3 (45) on the "Promotion of the participation of women in the maritime industry",

APPRECIATING the initiative taken by WMU to host a First International Conference on the Empowerment of Professional Women in the Maritime World in 2008 and the Second International Conference on Maritime Women: Global Leadership in 2014.

WELCOMING WMU's policy aim of increasing the opportunities for professional women by aiming to sustain the level of intake of qualified women graduates at least to a level of 30%,

CONGRATULATING the University on the significant increase in the recruitment of professional women in the WMU faculty,

APPRECIATING WARMLY the generosity of all donors to, and sponsors of the Conference and thanking in particular the principal donor: the IMO,

WELCOMING the wide geographical representation of the speakers and participants at the Conference, covering all IMO's regional networks,

NOTING the diverse experience and broad perspectives of all the speakers and poster presenters and appreciating their insights into the increasing contribution of women's leadership in the maritime sector and the economic and social benefits from improved gender balance in the workplace,

APPRECIATING the thoughtful contributions of the Scientific Committee members, who assured the quality of academic and scientific levels of papers presented at the Conference,

WELCOMING the WMU's plans to publish the Conference papers in cooperation with the IMO,

COMMENDING the spirit of co-operation and determination amongst all participants to make an effective and durable contribution furthering the leadership opportunities for professional women in the maritime industry in the public and private sectors,

RECOGNIZING the importance of education and research as a building block in achieving the increased participation of women in economic life,

DESIRING to encourage WMU to build further on its contributions to capacity-building and promote increased opportunities for professional women, and to promulgate new research-based knowledge on the economic benefits from increased women´s leadership,

RECOGNIZING AND WELCOMING the varying regional perspectives presented at the Conference;

INVITE the IMO Member States, the IMO governing bodies, the shipping industry and the donor community to:

- EMPLOYMENT POLICY AND PRACTICE
  - Acknowledge that women are endowed with unique qualities and talents, which if nurtured and incorporated in the maritime sector, can serve to strengthen the industry;
  - Make concerted efforts to provide mentoring, sponsorship and networking opportunities so as to build a critical mass of women in the maritime sector;
  - Make efforts to enable women to incorporate their traditional roles with the careers in the maritime sector, for example maternity leave, flexible hours of work, child-care amenities at the workplace;
  - Develop and implement uniformed evaluation and reward systems to attract the critical mass of women to the maritime industry.

- EDUCATION FOR CAREER BUILDING
  - Encourage all stakeholders in the maritime sector to recognize that education is the key to promote the integration of women in the maritime sector;
  - Encourage the international exchange of students towards improving cultural awareness, tolerance and understanding and towards improved job opportunities for women;
  - Support leadership and mentoring alongside male sensitivity training to facilitate career development for female professionals.

- LEADERSHIP, MENTORING AND NETWORKING
  - Identify existing female networks in shipping in order to make women in shipping more visible as role models, paving the way for the next generation of women in shipping;
  - Support and encourage the development of mentoring, sponsoring and networking schemes for women as maritime leaders for today and tomorrow;
  - Encourage the maritime industry to take active steps to attract talented young people to the industry.

- SUSTAINABLE DEVELOPMENT ISSUES IN SHIPPING
  - Encourage all maritime stakeholders to create an enabling environment for women allowing them to understand career opportunities, and providing advocacy and mentoring opportunities;
  - Encourage more women to enter engineering and technical fields of maritime professions;

- Encourage all stakeholders to adopt consequence analysis and values-based evaluation methodologies when exploring and addressing sustainable development of the industry.

Annex - Maritime Women: Global Leadership 2014 Conference Programme

31 March–1 April

Orkanen, Malmö Högskola, Malmö, Sweden

Monday, 31 March

09:00–10:00 Welcome session

Welcome remarks, María Carolina Romero Lares, MWGL 2014 Conference Chair; Associate Professor, World Maritime University

Welcome address, Björn Kjerfve, President, World Maritime University

Opening address, H.E. Lina Shbeeb, Minister of Transport, Jordan

Opening address, Wendy Watson-Wright, Assistant Director General and Executive Secretary, UNESCO-IOC

10:00–10:45 Plenary session 1: Global Maritime Impact of Women (Session chair: Pamela Tansey, Senior Deputy Director, Technical Co-operation Division, International Maritime Organization)

Keynote address: IMO and Women at the Helm, Pamela Tansey, Senior Deputy Director, Technical Cooperation Division, International Maritime Organization

Keynote address: *Maritime Women: Leading at all Levels,* Sandra Stosz, Rear Admiral, Superintendent, U.S. Coast Guard Academy

Keynote address: *Women's Leadership: A Challenge?,* Judith Melin, Director General, Swedish Coast Guard

11:15–12:00 Plenary session 2: Global Maritime Impact of Women (Session chair: Şadan Kaptanoğlu, Vice President, BIMCO; Managing Director of H.İ Kaptanoglu Ship Management Company)

Keynote address: *Challenges Facing the Maritime Businesses - Role of Women and a Way Forward,* Şadan Kaptanoğlu, Vice President, BIMCO; and Managing Director of H.İ Kaptanoglu Ship Management Company

© Springer-Verlag Berlin Heidelberg 2015

M. Kitada et al. (eds.), *Maritime Women: Global Leadership*, WMU Studies in Maritime Affairs 3, DOI 10.1007/978-3-662-45385-8

Keynote address: *Panama: developing policies to support the role of women in the maritime sector,* H.E. Ana Irene Delgado, Ambassador Extraordinary and Plenipotentiary and General Consul of the Republic of Panama to the United Kingdom of Great Britain and Northern Ireland and Ambassador of the Republic of Panama to the Republic of Iceland

Keynote address: *40 years of Female Global Leadership,* Karin Orsel, President, WISTA International; Vice Chairman, International Chamber of Shipping

12:00–13:30 Poster session

PMSC: Piracy and Women, Helen Tung, Ph.D. Candidate, University of Greenwich

Indicators for health, safety and environmental performance in European ports: the role of women in this sector, Marlene Calderón, Scientific Coordinator, Glintt Inov, Global Intelligent Technologies; Rosa Mari Darbra and Martí Puig, Center for Technological Risk Studies (CERTEC), Polytechnic University of Catalonia (UPC); Chris Wooldridge, School of Earth and Ocean Sciences, Cardiff University; and Pedro Antão, Glintt Inov, Global Intelligent Technologies

Pedagogical support of professional development of women for work in the shipping industry, Irina Makashina, Professor, Admiral Ushakov Maritime State University

Unfolding the question of female leadership in the maritime sector, Chrysanthe Kolia, Post graduate research applicant

Employment and career situations of women seafarers at Turkish fleet, Hatice Yilmaz, Research Assistant, and Ersan Başar, Associate Professor, Karadeniz Technical University

Education for Career-Building: How women in the maritime industry can use education to improve knowledge, skills, organizational learning and development, and knowledge transfer, Wilson Thoya Baya, Managing Director of Bacha Maritime Movers

Female and male students' perceptions on sustainable maritime development concept: A case study from Turkey, Cemile Solak, Research Assistant, and Durmuş Ali Deveci, Associate Professor, Dokuz Eylul University

Gender equality in sustainable development - nowadays challenges for women in maritime sector, Ljubov Tiberti, Ph.D. Candidate, University of Warsaw

Female students' point of view on the maritime career, Patrycja Mordas, and Lidia Sobota, Maritime University of Szczecin

Integrating women into Ghana's maritime industry through strategic recruitment and employment, Naa Densua Aryeetey, Head of Shipper Services, Ghana Shippers' Authority

The integration of women into the Ecuadorian maritime community, Javier Acuña, Professor, University of the Pacific

Maritime Women: Case study in Latvian Maritime Academy, Inese Barbare, Ph.D. Candidate, University of Latvia

MONALISA 2.0 contributes to empower women in the maritime breaking barriers through training in leadership, Olga Delgado Ortega, Department of Nautical Sciences and Engineering, Polytechnic University of Catalonia; Ulf Siwe,

Communication Officer, Sjöfartsverket; and Kjell Ivar Øvergård, Department of Maritime Technology and Innovation, Vestfold University College

13:30–15:00 Parallel session, Workshop A: Employment, Policy & Practice (EPP) (Session chair: Nancy Karigithu, Director General, Kenya Maritime Authority)

Women sustaining a maritime industry career: Identifying attitudinal and structural impediments, Ana M. Albert, MBA Candidate, Florida Atlantic University; Joan Mileski, Associate Professor, Texas A & M University; and Wyndylyn von Zharen, Regents Professor, Texas A & M University

Women leadership in maritime law firms: the Antwerp case, Anniek Wouters, Maritime Law NUS Singapore, Roosendaal - Keyzer Lawyers

The evolution of the condition and role of women in fishing activities, Gwenaele Proutière- Maulion, Vice President European Affairs and International Relations, Maritime and Oceanic Law Centre, University of Nantes

Advancing women participation in the maritime sector - The South African Experience, Sindiswa Nhlumayo, Executive Head, Centre for Maritime Excellence, South African Maritime Safety Authority

13:30–15:00 Parallel session, Workshop B: Education for Career Building (ECB) (Session chair: Neil Bellefontaine, Vice President (Academic), World Maritime University)

Full ahead - Why we have too few women in maritime industry, Sohyun Jo, Assistant Professor, Korea Institute of Maritime and Fisheries Technology

The road to the helm - female students' perspective, Dominika Czyżowicz; Elwira Kałkowska; Pola Raciborska; Julia Raczkowska; Monika Skowronek; and Zbigniew Szozda, Assistant Professor, Maritime University of Szczecin

Let numbers speak: Job opportunities and international exchange programs for female cadets, Chen Qi, Professor, Massachusetts Maritime Academy

Mind the gap! Maritime education for gender-equal career advancement, Maria Boström Cars and Cecilia Österman, Kalmar Maritime Academy

Stalwart in sailing global maritime women leadership, Balakrishnan Rajagopal, Member of the Institute of Chartered Ship-brokers and Malaysian Maritime Institute

15:30–17:00 Parallel session, Workshop C: Leadership, Mentoring & Networking (LMN) (Session chair: Lena Göthberg, Secretary General, Institute of Shipping Analysis)

My journey as a seafarer, Anuradha Jha, Captain, Shipping Corporation of India

Women are better leaders than they think: Gender differences in the self-assessment of leadership skills in the maritime industry, Olga Delgado Ortega, Department of Nautical Sciences and Engineering, Polytechnic University of Catalonia; Kjell Ivar Øvergård; and Veronica Henden, Department of Maritime Technology and Innovation, Vestfold University College

Board characteristics and the presence of women in the Board of Directors: The case of Greek shipping sector, Aspasia S. Pastra, Gnosis Management Consultants; Dimitrios N. Koufopoulos, Senior Lecturer; and Ioannis P. Gkliatis, Brunel University, Brunel Business School

How to cope with second generation gender bias in male-dominated occupations, Pınar Özdemir, Lecturer, and Taner Albayrak, Assistant Professor, Piri Reis University

Global seafarers and leadership from the perspective of diversity in CSR, Momoko Kitada, Lecturer, World Maritime University

15:30–17:00 Parallel session, Workshop D: Sustainable Development in Shipping (SDIS) (Session chair: Katharina Stanzel, Managing Director, INTERTANKO)

MoU on Port State Control for West and Central African Region, Sustainable maritime safety and marine environment management through effective and efficient Port State Control, Mfon Ekong Usoro, Secretary General, MoU on Port State Control for West and Central African Region

Sustainability or CSR - the next challenge, Anne-Marie Warris, Principal, ecoreflect Ltd.

Improving the current regime for ship safety inspections - Opportunities for technology research and women employment?, Marlene Calderón, Scientific Coordinator, Glintt Inov, Global Intelligent Technologies; Diana Illing, IHS Global SAS; Ingrid Schipperen, TNO – Nederlandse Organisatie Voor Toegepast Natuurwetenschappelijk Onderzoek; and Pedro Antão, Glintt Inov, Global Intelligent Technologies

Towards an equality between women and men in ocean navigation working conditions, Bernard Dujardin, Professor, National School of Advanced Technology (ParisTech)

Tuesday, 1 April

09:00–10:00 Plenary session 3: Promoting Diversity (Session chair: Ken Peters, Reverend, Director of Justice and Welfare of Seafarers, Mission to Seafarers)

Keynote address: The 21st century view of a seaport...or why the world needs more women port directors, Geraldine Knatz, Board Member, International Association of Ports and Harbours

Keynote address: Promoting the employment of women in the transport sector: obstacles and policy options - The case of preventing violence against women in the maritime sector, Julia Lear, Transport & Maritime Specialist, International Labour Organization

Keynote address: Leading Change – developing women maritime trade union leaders, Alison McGarry, Coordinator of Women Transport Workers' Department, International Transport Workers' Federation

10:30–12:30 Parallel session, Regional perspectives A: The Americas & Europe (Session chair: Minghua Zhao, Assistant Director, Greenwich Maritime Institute, University of Greenwich)

Report of the Regional Conferences "Role of women in management positions within the maritime sector, Latin America (2012–2014)", Tanya Tamara Carlucci Sucre, Head of Compliance and Enforcement Department, Merchant Marine Directorate, Panama Maritime Authority, and Noelia Mabel López, International Affairs Office, Argentine Coast Guard, Panamá & Argentina

The "Leaky Pipeline" - examining and addressing the loss of women at consecutive career stages in marine engineering, science and technology, Sarah Cornell, IMarEST - London, United Kingdom

Central American Model for the integration of women in the maritime port sector, Darling E. Rojas Mendoza, Consultation on Gender Equality and Women's Empowerment and Training Programs Maritime Port, Nicaragua

Women's role in Turkish maritime sector and global maritime, Ayşe Aslı Başak, Deputy D.P.A., CEBI Maritime & Trading SA, Turkey

Women in the Maritime Sector: Surviving and thriving in a man's world - A Caribbean perspective, Claudia Grant, Deputy Director General, Maritime Authority of Jamaica, and Vivette Grant, Deputy Executive Director, Caribbean Maritime Institute, Jamaica

Participation of Ecuadorian women in the oil marine transportation sector, Margarita Dávila Cevallos, Consultant, Oil Trading & Shipping, Ecuador

Is there a helm for women in maritime sector? Case study from Ukraine, Victoria Radchenko, Operational Centre of the International Ocean Institute, Ukraine

10:30–12:30 Parallel session, Regional perspectives B: Asia, Arab States & Africa (Session chair: Carla S. Limcaoco, President, Women in Maritime Philippines; Director, PTC Management Corporation)

Women Seafarers Career, Christiana Yustita, Captain, Chief of Marine Pollution Prevention and Ship Safety Management, Ministry of Transportation, Indonesia

Arab Maritime Women: An Egyptian Leadership Perspective, Layla El Saeed, Assistant Academy President, MENA and Africa Arab International Women's Maritime Forum, Egypt

The development environment and challenge of Chinese female crew, Bao Junzhong; Wang Xizhao; Lin Yihui; Huang Lin; Wang Jing; and Chu Yunyun, Dalian Maritime University, China

Maritime Women: Global Leadership and Networking - "WOMESA - A dream comes true", Meenaksi Bhirugnath Bhookhun, Maritime Officer, the Ministry of Public Infrastructure, National Development Unit, Land Transport & Shipping, Mauritius

Young Bangladeshi Women embarking on blue highways!, Sajid Hussain, Commandant, Bangladesh Marine Academy, Bangladesh

Iranian women's role in the sustainable development of maritime industry, Mehdi Amooahmadi; Nasrin Atabak; and Bahman Nakisa, BPMO, Iran

14:00–15:00 Chair Reports

Moderator: María Carolina Romero Lares, MWGL 2014 Conference Chair; Associate Professor, World Maritime University

Global Maritime Impact of Women; Employment, Policy and Practice; Leadership, Mentoring and Networking; Education for Career Building; Sustainable Development in Shipping; Promoting Diversity; Regional Perspectives A: The Americas & Europe, and B: Asia, Arab States & Africa

Adoption of the Maritime Women: Global Leadership Declaration

15:00–15:30 Closing Ceremony

MIX
Papier aus verantwortungsvollen Quellen
Paper from responsible sources
FSC® C105338

If you have any concerns about our products,
you can contact us on
ProductSafety@springernature.com

In case Publisher is established outside the EU,
the EU authorized representative is:
Springer Nature Customer Service Center GmbH
Europaplatz 3, 69115 Heidelberg, Germany

Printed by Libri Plureos GmbH
in Hamburg, Germany